Christ With Us

Instruction and Encouragement from the Sanctuary

Warren Shipton

TEACH Services, Inc.
P U B L I S H I N G
www.TEACHServices.com • (800) 367-1844

World rights reserved. This book or any portion thereof may not be copied or reproduced in any form or manner whatever, except as provided by law, without the written permission of the publisher, except by a reviewer who may quote brief passages in a review.

The author assumes full responsibility for the accuracy of all facts and quotations as cited in this book. The opinions expressed in this book are the author's personal views and interpretations, and do not necessarily reflect those of the publisher.

This book is provided with the understanding that the publisher is not engaged in giving spiritual, legal, medical, or other professional advice. If authoritative advice is needed, the reader should seek the counsel of a competent professional.

Copyright © 2017 Warren Shipton

Copyright © 2017 TEACH Services, Inc.

ISBN-13: 978-1-4796-0338-1 (Paperback)

ISBN-13: 978-1-4796-0339-8 (ePub)

ISBN-13: 978-1-4796-0340-4 (Mobi)

Library of Congress Control Number: 2016919756

Book cover: Frank Rohde at 123RF.com

Unless otherwise indicated, all Scripture quotations are from the *New King James Version®* (NKJV), copyright © 1982 by Thomas Nelson. Used by permission. All rights reserved. Italics indicate words added in the translation that are not in the original text.

Other Scriptures are taken from *Brenton's English Septuagint* by Sir Lancelot Charles Lee Brenton (1851); the *Douay-Rheims Bible* (1899); the *King James Version* (KJV); the English *Revised Version* (RV), 1881–85; Scrivener's Greek Interlinear, based on the Textus Receptus (1894), and *Young's Literal Translation* (YLT), all public domain.

Other versions used are: *Amplified Bible, Classic Edition* (AMPC) copyright © 1954, 1958, 1962, 1964, 1965, 1987 by The Lockman Foundation. The *Common English Bible* (CEB). All rights reserved. *Contemporary English Version* (CEV), copyright © 1995 by American Bible Society. *Good News Translation®* (GNT). Copyright © 1992 American Bible Society. All rights reserved. *The Interlinear Hebrew-Greek-English Bible* (Green's Interlinear Bible), Jay P. Green, Sr., translator. Copyright © 1976, 1978, 1980, 1981, 1984. *The Lexham English Bible* (LEB), copyright © 2012 by Logos Bible Software. Lexham is a registered trademark of Logos Bible Software. *The Holy Bible, Modern English Version* (MEV), Copyright © 2014 by Military Bible Association. Published and distributed by Charisma House. All rights reserved. *The New American Standard Bible* (NASB), copyright © 1960, 1962, 1963, 1968, 1971, 1972, 1973, 1975, 1977, 1995, by The Lockman Foundation. *The New English Bible* (NEB). Copyright © 1970 by Oxford University Press and Cambridge University Press, printed in The United States of America. *The Holy Bible New International Version®.* (NIV). Copyright © 1973, 1978, 1984 by International Bible Society. All rights reserved. *The Peshitta Aramaic-English New Testament: An Interlinear Translation*, translated by Glenn David Bauscher. Copyright © 2006 by Lulu Publishing. *The Revised Standard Version of the Bible* (RSV), copyright © 1946, 1952, and 1971, the Division of Christian Education of the National Council of the Churches of Christ in the United States of America. Used by permission. All rights reserved. *The Holy Scriptures According to the Masoretic Text. A new translation* (*The Tanakh*). Copyright © 1917. The Jewish Publication Society of America. *The Living Bible* (TLB). Copyright ©1971 by Tyndale House Publishers, Wheaton, Illinois 60187. All rights reserved.

"We should not rest until we become intelligent in regard to the subject of the sanctuary, which is brought out in the visions of Daniel and John. This subject sheds great light on our present position and work, and gives us unmistakable proof that God has led us in our past experience." (Ellen G. White, *Evangelism*, pp. 222, 223)

FOREWORD

Glancing across at my bookshelf as I write this foreword, I see at least twenty-seven books on the Biblical doctrine of the sanctuary. No doubt there are many more. That, of course, raises the question of why? Why another book on the sanctuary? Clearly, the author thinks that everything that could be said on this important subject has not been communicated, hence the book you now hold in your hand.

I have had the pleasure of knowing Warren Shipton now for over twelve years since originally becoming acquainted with him up in Northern Queensland, Australia, where I was assigned my first pastorate straight out of Bible college. I initially became aware of his work through an informative set of Bible studies that he produced, which analyzed the sanctuary teaching with its function, services, and furnishings. Since becoming a Seventh-day Adventist Christian, I have always had a keen interest in this uniquely Adventist teaching and have been drawn like a moth to a flame to anything within Christian literature that remotely resembles a tent like structure with obscure rites and rituals. Since discovering that little gem and meeting the man, I have since had many an occasion to sit down with the author and discuss sanctuary history and theology. I have also taken advantage of our friendship and invited him to speak on this topic in my local church.

So what makes this book different from any other book on the sanctuary? In the devotional, *Our High Calling*, page 16, Ellen G.

White wrote: "Christ, His character and work, is the center and circumference of all truth. He is the chain upon which the jewels of doctrine are linked. In Him is found the complete system of truth."[1] This statement fittingly summarizes the purpose of this book. Unlike authors of previous works, the author isn't so much interested in the intricacies of every article of furniture and ceremony. Other books on the market have done a great job of dissecting the meaning and significance behind every piece of metal, fabric, symbol, color, and sacrifice. The author is more interested in seeing Jesus—especially Jesus—in the sanctuary. As the title suggests, *Christ With Us, Instruction and Encouragement from the Sanctuary* sets out to explore the major themes associated with sanctuary worship and how those themes find their ultimate fulfillment in the life and death of Jesus. Many of the theological teachings that arise from a study of the sanctuary lay at the theological foundation of Seventh-day Adventism today. This book rightly places Jesus at the heart of every Biblical doctrine. The author also shows the reader that the sanctuary doctrine has at its center the covenant of grace. Throughout both Testaments, we find a God who progressively reveals His plan to save fallen humanity by constantly drawing near to them. Whether it be in the garden, Mt. Sinai, the earthly tabernacle, Solomon's Temple, or through the incarnation of His Son, God desires to reconnect with those who have been separated by sin. Thus, the sanctuary is all about relationships. This important emphasis is found throughout the entire book.

On a practical level, the reader will appreciate the simple layout of the book. The book covers seven areas of study that draw significance from various aspects of the sanctuary. These include: (1) Creation and Covenant, (2) Christ and Ministry, (3) The Nature of Humanity, (4) Salvation, Atonement, and Reconciliation, (5) Christian Life and Worship, (6) Last Events, and (7) Lasting Assurances. As can be seen from the carefully selected titles, the author clearly has the great controversy narrative in mind. I for one especially appreciate the helpful *"Chapter Emphasis"* and *"Spiritual Link"* located at the beginning of every chapter. These thought statements not only show where the chapter is heading but also get readers thinking about how Christ and a particular element of the sanctuary are connected. The author's use of summary charts, diagrams and the *"In this section, I will ..."* introductions add clarity, conciseness, and interest.

For anyone interested in learning about the biblical sanctuary, this book will become an invaluable addition to your library. The sheer amount of research and detail—not to mention supporting biblical references—that has gone into producing this book will be especially appreciated not only by the seasoned Bible student but will also appeal to the first time reader or novice of Old Testament cultic practices. This work is also an excellent resource for the person wanting to dig deeper into the Word of God, especially as it pertains to how God is dealing with the problem of sin. The connections the author makes between the sanctuary services and the redemptive work of Christ on behalf of sinful humanity make for an inspirational read.

Finally, and most importantly, this book is about Jesus Christ and His character, ministry, and teaching as illustrated through the sanctuary service. I highly recommend this book to anyone wanting to know more about Jesus and how the Old Testament sanctuary not only points forward to what He did for humankind in coming to this world to die on the cross, but also on the work He continues to do today as our High Priest in the heavenly sanctuary above. Enjoy!

Pastor Ernst William, B.A. Theology
Ormeau, Queensland
Australia
June 2016

PREFACE

The sanctuary constructed by Moses during the wilderness wanderings of the children of Israel was divinely appointed to teach important lessons regarding the plan of salvation. This plan did not cease at Calvary; rather, it extended forward in time, and it will culminate when Satan and every reminder of sin are forever swept away and this sin-ravaged earth is made anew.

In the sanctuary, God symbolized the redemptive work of Christ in a manner that the people could understand. The enormity of sin and the magnanimity of God were symbolized in the ceremonies associated with it. God's presence, evidenced by the cloud of glory, assured all of His people of His desire to be their Shepherd. Today, we are directed to the sanctuary in heaven where Christ ministers on behalf of sinners in the last phase of His ministry. In this antitypical day of atonement, all are urged to "make your call and election sure" (2 Peter 1:10).[2] A study of the truths of the sanctuary is valuable because: "The belief that Christ is our High Priest in the heavenly sanctuary ... illuminates all other doctrines; it brings God and His salvation near us in a way that gives us 'full assurance' (Heb. 10:22); it shows us that God is on our side."[3] We look forward with keen anticipation to the time when God is the "temple" in the earth made new (Rev. 21:22). Then, the glorious communion with God, experienced by the holy pair in Eden, will be re-established.

The purpose of this book is to explore the major themes presented through the sanctuary worship instructions outlined in the Old Testament and the meaning of the sanctuary symbolism used in the New Testament. The character of Jesus Christ will become clearer to us as we do this. We also wish to discover the roots of our belief in some major biblical doctrines, as these find strong support in the teachings of the sanctuary. The sanctuary typologies lead to understanding the Bible as a complete and harmonious body of writing, which has great significance for the church till the end of time. Professor Fernando Canale has observed that appreciating the sanctuary leads to an understanding of "the moral law, Sabbath, sacrificial atonement, High-Priestly Mediation, Judgment, Justification and Sanctification, Righteousness by Faith, final rewards and punishments, Second Advent, and total destructions of the incorrigible wicked."[4] Furthermore, "the Sanctuary Doctrine provide[s] the inner theological framework for the theological interpretation of Salvation History as the Great Controversy."[5] All readers should understand clearly that "the foundation and central pillar of the advent faith was the declaration: 'Unto two thousand and three hundred days; then shall the sanctuary be cleansed.' Daniel 8:14."[6] I pay special attention to this prophecy, for it has become the point of vigorous attack by individuals both inside and outside the church. This should not surprise us, as fidelity to the grammatical-historical method of biblical interpretation has been under siege for well over a hundred years in the world of biblical scholarship. Understanding this interpretive method is vital to exposure of those forces bent on obscuring God's last-day message of mercy to the world.

The book does not intend to look at the sanctuary furnishings and ceremonies in minute detail, although some knowledge is necessary to develop various themes. The book was prepared as a supplementary text for a workshop run at Witness Conference 2015 in Brisbane, Australia (Jan. 21–25). Texts are quoted from the New King James Version of the Bible unless otherwise stated.

ACKNOWLEDGMENTS

The author gives sincere thanks to those who have made constructive comments and suggestions concerning the original manuscript published in 1999. Special mention is made of those who spent time assessing the material and giving encouragement. Dr. Gerhard Pfandl, Field Secretary and Spirit of Prophecy Coordinator, South Pacific Division (now retired Associate Director, Biblical Research Institute), encouraged the submission of the material to the Biblical Research Committee and gave many valuable suggestions dealing with issues of accuracy and acceptability. His gentle yet entirely constructive criticism did much to make the redrafting of sections of the manuscript pleasurable. The Biblical Research Committee deemed the original manuscript mainstream in perspective.

Now it has come time to revise the manuscript so as to emphasize the foundational significance of sanctuary understandings to various beliefs held in the Seventh-day Adventist Church. This has involved a thorough reorganizing of the material, eliminating repetitious elements, adding new material, and changing and simplifying the format. Despite these changes, the principal thrust of the text remains unaltered. Signs Publishing Company, Warburton, Victoria, published the original version under the title, "The Pattern of Salvation."[7]

I am thankful for the kindly forbearance of my wife, Jan, during the production of the present document.

Acknowledgments of specific sources of information are made in the endnotes. Other sources used more generally are noted below, and these are recommended to the reader:

Roy Gane, *Altar Call*. Berrien Springs, MI: Diadem, 1999.

Clifford Goldstein, *False Balances*. Boise, ID: Pacific Press Publishing Association, 1992.

Clifford Goldstein, *Between the Lamb and the Lion*. Boise, ID: Pacific Press Publishing Association, 1995.

Paul A. Gordon, *The Sanctuary, 1844, and the Pioneers*. Washington, DC: Review and Herald Publishing Association, 1983.

Leslie Hardinge, *With Jesus in His Sanctuary*. Harrisburg, PA: American Cassette Ministries Book Division, 1991.

Stephen N. Haskell, *The Cross and Its Shadow*, facsimile reproduction of 1914 printing. Washington, DC: Review and Herald Publishing Association, 1970.

Frank B. Holbrook, ed., *The Seventy Weeks, Leviticus, and the Nature of Prophecy*. Washington, DC: Biblical Research Institute, 1986.

Frank B. Holbrook, ed., *Doctrine of the Sanctuary: A Historical Survey (1845–1863)*. Silver Springs, MD: Biblical Research Institute, 1989.

Frank B. Holbrook, ed., *Issues in the Book of Hebrews*. Silver Springs, MD: Biblical Research Institute, 1989.

Ministerial Association, General Conference of Seventh-day Adventists, *Seventh-day Adventists Believe*. Hagerstown, MD: Review and Herald Publishing Association, 1988.

Francis D. Nichol, Raymond F. Cottrell, et al., eds., *The Seventh-day Adventist Bible Commentary*. Washington, DC: Review and Herald Publishing Association, 1953–1957), vols. 1–7.

Charles H. Watson, *The Atoning Work of Christ, His Sacrifice and Priestly Ministry*. Washington, DC: Review and Herald Publishing Association, 1934.

Ellen G. White, *Christ in His Sanctuary*. Mountain View, CA: Pacific Press Publishing Association, 1969.

Table of Contents

CREATION AND COVENANT 17

Chapter 1. Covenant, Salvation, and Sanctuary 19
The sanctuary and Christ as the central figure in the Creation and in the work of salvation

CHRIST AND HIS MINISTRY 47

Chapter 2. Dwelling Among His People 49
Christ's plan to dwell with humanity as both promise and fulfillment

Chapter 3. The Mystery of "God with Us" 57
The nature of Christ, the God-man

Chapter 4. Symbols of Restoration 67
What the sanctuary services convey about our faith journey

Chapter 5. CHRIST'S THREE-FOLD MINISTRY 84
Christ's ministry as prophet, priest, and king

Chapter 6. Thine Is the Power and the Glory 93
The beauty of Christ's character and His creative and re-creative abilities

Chapter 7. Christ Will Build His Temple 103
Understanding the foundation, message, and mission of Christ's church since Eden

THE NATURE OF HUMANITY 121

Chapter 8. The Life Is in the Blood 123
Human nature and mortality

SALVATION, ATONEMENT, AND RECONCILIATION 137

Chapter 9. The Way of Salvation in the Sanctuary 139
The gospel, or way of faith, as taught in the sanctuary

Chapter 10. The Law and the Gospel 149
The unity of the gospel and the moral law and the law's function in the Christian life

Chapter 11. The Veil of the Temple Was Torn 160
Christ's salvation activities after the cross in the context of the sanctuary and the great controversy theme

Chapter 12. Examine Your Relationship with God 175
The necessity of a genuine and dynamic relationship with God

CHRISTIAN LIFE AND WORSHIP 191

Chapter 13. The Creator Is in His Temple 193
Christ's creative ability as revealed in the sanctuary

Chapter 14. Measure the Temple 204
The memorial of Creation and redemption revealed through the heavenly sanctuary

Chapter 15. Worship 215
The type of worship that God accepts

Chapter 16. Cleansed by Water and the Blood 231
Symbols of cleansing carried over into the Christian church—communion and baptism

Chapter 17. The Body Temple 241
Caring for our bodies as the temple of God

LAST EVENTS

Chapter 18. The Lord Will Come Suddenly to His Temple ... 253
Christ's closing activities in heaven and on earth among His people

Chapter 19. The 2300-Day Prophecy 269
The significance of the time prophecy of 2300 years in Daniel

Chapter 20. The Sanctuary and the Judgment 290
The central theme of the pre-advent judgment gives assurance

Chapter 21. When Smoke Fills the Temple 305
Events in earth's history surrounding the close of probation

Chapter 22. God Is the Temple in the New Earth 317
Reminders of the sanctuary in heaven and the commemorative activities there

LASTING ASSURANCES 329

Chapter 23. Fiery Coals, Living Stones 331
The involvement of the Godhead and other celestial beings in the salvation of even the weakest believer

ENDNOTES 343

Creation and Covenant

Chapter 1.
Covenant, Salvation, and Sanctuary

Chapter Emphasis: *Jesus Christ is the central figure in the Bible. The earthly sanctuary was patterned after the heavenly one. Christ's activities in both places are connected with the salvation of humanity. The covenant of rest established at Creation and the privilege of interacting personally with God was lost upon the entrance of sin. The covenant of grace announced in Eden was illustrated in the earthly sanctuary and provided the possibility of entering God's rest and being fit candidates for the world made new. The gospel invitation still offers hearers the invitation to enter God's rest and experience peace in the new earth in the absence of sin and death. There the redeemed will dwell with God continually.*

Spiritual Link: *Salvation cannot be separated from the concept of judgment, for the former implies that the reign of sin will be brought to an end.*

When sin entered this world, God announced His agreement, or covenant, to provide a way to save humanity from eternal death

(Gen. 3:15). The details of this plan were progressively revealed. There is only one plan of salvation, which means that the covenant is everlasting in nature (Gen. 17:13; Heb. 13:20). This follows, too, from the concepts that God is love and is unchangeable (James 1:17; 1 John 4:7, 16). In reality, accepting the covenant provisions represents the development of a relationship with God.

Even though the nation of Israel rejected the covenant relationship with tragic results (see Jer. 11:1–17; 18:9, 10; Matt. 21:43; Heb. 8:9), spiritual Israel has an open invitation to accept God's rest in salvation. The apostles Paul and John make this exceedingly clear (Gal. 3:29; Rev. 22:17). Now, through the new covenant, God makes His offer to individuals rather than to a nation as He did in the old covenant (Gal. 4:22–31; Rom. 2:29).

Details of the covenant arrangement and preliminary indications of how God planned to accomplish it through history were outlined to Moses at Mount Sinai when He delivered to him both the Decalogue and the plans for the earthly sanctuary. The primary focus of the covenant outlined at Sinai—the old covenant—was the coming of Christ, the Lamb, and His sacrifice, hence fulfilling the promise made to Adam and Eve. Once the sacrifice was made, the focus shifted to the heavenly sanctuary and the remaining provisions of the new covenant. The focus is now on heralding the achievements of the cross and the administration of justice, which means ultimately the elimination of Satan and the return of the universe to a state of harmony. Thus, the study of the sanctuary reveals to us the necessary aspects of a saving relationship with God and allows the interpretation of past and future events. The prophecies of Daniel and Revelation become clearer, as the whole package fits into a cohesive great controversy meta-narrative.[8]

The instructions given to Moses concerning the construction of a tabernacle in the wilderness is intensely interesting. God instructed him regarding the exact details of both the building and the services associated with it. The articles of furniture, the coverings, the layout of the tabernacle, and the nature and order of the services all have deep spiritual meaning. We find that God, in outlining the plan of salvation more fully to the human race, chose to reveal His will and way through a system of animal sacrifices and ceremonies associated first with a moveable tabernacle and later with a permanent temple. Although animal sacrifices were introduced at the Fall, to represent the necessity of the Savior's death, it was not until the children of

Israel were delivered by God from Egyptian bondage, paralleling the slavery of sin, that a more complete system of worship was introduced in the tabernacle services and associated ceremonies, which were to prepare the Israelites and the world for the coming of the Lord Jesus Christ as a babe in the manger.

The encounter with God, the giving of the Decalogue, and the sanctuary plans represent a high point in human history. They provide the clearest evidence since the Creation of God's determination to establish a relationship with the human race by appearing in time and space. The symbols introduced in the sanctuary ceremonies have deep meaning relevant to our Christian living right to the end of human history. The central figure in the sanctuary was Christ, and the central concept conveyed by the services was how God intended that people relate to His covenant of grace. The location of the tables of the covenant—the Decalogue—in the ark in the Most Holy Place indicated their sacred nature and their function in directing the worshiper to Jesus Christ, represented by the mercy seat. Through a faith relationship with Him, the moral principles engraved in the Decalogue can be honored.

In this chapter, I will look briefly at the features of the covenant of grace and illustrate how this covenant intersects with the covenant established at Creation.

Features of the Covenant of Grace

In this section, I will

- *outline the essential features of God's agreement to save humanity;*

- *emphasize that the agreement of the covenant of grace stretched from the entrance of sin and will continue until harmony is re-established following Christ's second coming.*

When we use the term "covenant" to describe God's plan of salvation, it represents a scheme that God introduced to sinful humanity for them to accept or reject. It does not represent a plan in which humanity negotiated the terms. The covenant is an expression of God's loving nature. A preliminary form of God's plan to save humanity was delivered to Adam and Eve in the brief statement given in Genesis 3:15—"And I will put enmity between you and the woman, and between your seed and her Seed; He shall bruise your head, and you shall bruise His heel." Satan had deceived Eve, and death was introduced into the human experience. However, the text indicates that the "Seed," which is Christ, would come and gain victory over the enemy, thereby overturning the sad outcome of yielding to him. In the grand struggle that followed, Satan was to be mortally wounded. The essential features of the covenant of grace are illustrated in Table 1.1.

This Edenic covenant of grace was expanded and repeated to successive generations, most notably to Abraham. It was more fully outlined for Moses at Sinai. A still clearer understanding of it became evident to the generation of Christ who saw a multitude of connections with the sanctuary symbols and ceremonies fulfilled in the life, death, and resurrection of Christ. Today, our focus must shift to the heavenly sanctuary where Christ ministers on our behalf.

The covenant introduced at Mount Sinai was an arrangement with the children of Israel whom Christ had just delivered from physical bondage in Egypt. (See Table 1.1.) He wished to add to this achievement deliverance from spiritual bondage through their entrance into a faith relationship with Him. He also wished to emphasize the significance of relationship building through the covenant and sanctuary symbols and ceremonies. The Sinai covenant is termed the first, or old, covenant and was inextricably connected with the earthly sanctuary services (Heb. 8:7, 13). The people promised to obey the provisions of the covenant, and Moses ratified the covenant with a blood offering (Exod. 24:3–8). These provisions were outlined in summary form in the Decalogue. The covenant was superseded in meaning after Jesus' death and rejection by the Jewish nation (Matt. 21:43). Few among the nation accepted the proposition that keeping the covenant involved the creation of new attitudes and the acceptance of holy objectives through the development of a faith relationship (Heb. 3:7–11; 4:2).

Christ's spilled blood (Heb. 13:20) ratified the new arrangement He announced on the eve of the crucifixion (Matt. 26:28). The system of animal sacrifices passed away, and the earthly sanctuary ceased to be a sacred place (Matt. 27:51). This new covenant was not made with a single people group but encompassed all who would accept the provisions of the gospel. It focuses on what Christ has done for us and what He wishes to do in us. It also focuses on the remaining aspects of the atonement necessary to enable universal harmony to be re-established. The new covenant activities center on the heavenly sanctuary, rather than on the earthly, for the agenda has its focus on both mercy

Chapter 1. Covenant, Salvation, and Sanctuary

and universal justice. The promises surrounding this covenant have to do with possession of the heavenly Canaan and the ultimate goal of terminating the reign of sin under its instigator Satan. This will bring in the reign of peace under Christ the King.

The provisions of grace have not changed since Eden, so we can speak confidently of God's covenant with humankind being an everlasting covenant. The history of human responses has been either after the fashion of Israel's relationship to the old covenant provisions, which was salvation by works, or Abraham's relationship under the new covenant, which is salvation by faith (Gal. 4:21–26; cf. Heb. 8:7–13). In the epistle to the Hebrews, the apostle Paul emphasized the truth that salvation has always been through faith (Heb. 4:2, 11).[9] Under these conditions, hearers acknowledge the Holy Spirit and respond to the love that God has shown, they give willing obedience, and they offer genuine worship to God their Savior. They also accept the Sabbath as the legitimate sign of the everlasting covenant made by Christ, signifying their acceptance of the sanctifying work of God in their lives. Thus, the Sabbath is the sign of their possession of a beautiful, transforming human-divine relationship.

Table 1.1. Essential features of the covenant agreement announced by God through His prophets, apostles, and spokespersons.

Feature	Detail	Text
Parties involved	• Israel and God under the old covenant* • Spiritual Israel and God under the new, or everlasting, covenant	• Gal. 4:24, 25 • Rom. 9:30–33; Gal. 3:26–29
The Initiator	God	Gen. 3:15; Exod. 19:5; Jer. 31:31–33; John 3:16
Provisions	• Salvation from physical slavery under the old covenant • Spiritual freedom under the everlasting covenant	Exod. 19:4; 20:2; Rom. 6:1–7

Feature	Detail	Text
Means	• Substitutionary sacrifices using animals under the old covenant • Pointing to the offering of Christ under the everlasting covenant	Lev. 9:7–21; Heb. 9:9–15; 10:5–10
Ideal relationship with God	• Separateness from the world • National and personal sanctity	• Exod. 19:5; Ps. 135:4 • Exod. 19:6; 1 Pet. 2:4, 5
Sign of the relationship	Sabbath	Exod. 31:16; Heb. 4:1, 4–7
Experience needed for attitude change	New birth with mind transformation and a "clean heart" and a right spirit	Deut. 6:5; Ps. 51:10; John 3:3, 5–8; Rom. 12:2
Response flowing from relationship change	Love to God and one's neighbors	Deut. 10:12, 18, 19; Matt. 22:36–40
Goals of the relationship	Described by the Decalogue	Exod. 20:1–17; Matt. 22:36–40; Rev. 14:12
Means of attaining holiness	Faith not works	Rom. 9:30–33; Heb. 11:23–29, 39, 40
Primary agent facilitating the harmonious relationship	The Holy Spirit	Rom. 8:13–17; Heb. 3:7–11
Fruitage of the relationship	Fruit of the Spirit	Gal. 5:22–25

Feature	Detail	Text
Blessing promised	• The new birth, the experience of re-creation • Arrival in the promised land and associated blessings under the old covenant • Inheritance of the New Earth with attendant blessings under the everlasting covenant	• Ps. 51:10; Rom. 12:2; 2 Cor. 5:17 • Deut. 28:1–14; Ps. 78:54, 55 • Matt. 5:5; Gal. 4:24–26; Heb. 11:13–16, 39, 40
Response to the agreement	• Worship through entering rest • Praise • Obedience	• Exod. 20:11; 31:12, 13; Heb. 4:1–4 • Deut. 26:3–5, 10, 11 • Deut. 10:12, 13, 20

* Non-Jews were also invited to accept the invitation (Deut. 29:10–15; Isa. 56:1–8).

Creation and Covenant

In this section, I will

- *introduce the idea that God also established a covenant at Creation in humanity's resting with Him;*

- *show that the Creation covenant is consistent with the covenant of grace. The redeemed will rest in God in the New Earth just as Adam and Eve rested with Him in Eden.*

God established an agreement with the human race at Creation, which has features that are reflected in His everlasting covenant (Table 1.2). In the earth made new, the covenant established at Creation will be re-established in its essential details. If we view the idea of the covenant in this manner, it enables easy integration with the great controversy worldview. The apostle Paul introduces us to this line of argument in the initial chapters of Hebrews. He refers to the arrangement—the covenant—established at Creation and mentions the lordship of the Creator God (Heb. 4:3, 4). Here we remember that on the first Sabbath day the members of the human race, who were created in the image of God, participated with Him in a worshipful relationship

(Gen. 1:27; 2:2, 3).[10] This represented none other than the race "tabernacling" with God in the set apart place, or "divine sanctuary," called the Garden of Eden.[11] While the progenitors of the human race rested with God in this fashion, they were safe. They enjoyed harmonious relationships and experienced regular interaction with God. The Sabbath was a sign of this relationship.

After sin entered the world, Adam lost his dominion, and the image of God was marred. It was then necessary for individuals to choose to find rest with God by faith so that the marred image might continue to be restored. The apostle Paul says of this experience: "Therefore, if anyone *is* in Christ, *he* is a new creation; old things have passed away; behold, all things have become new" (2 Cor. 5:17). Those experiencing this transformation will be among the redeemed. Such individuals will populate the earth made new. There God again will "tabernacle," or dwell, with redeemed humanity (Rev. 21:1–3), in an environment with items featured in the original Garden of Eden (Rev. 22:1, 2). There the redeemed will be able to rest in peace because their natures will have been transformed (Rev. 22:3, 4; cf. Rev. 14:1, 4, 5).

Adam lost his dominion to Satan in Eden (cf. John 14:30; 2 Peter 2:19). The lost dominion will be handed back to Adam in the earth made new. (See Table 1.2.) Of Adam's experience it is said: "Faithfully did he repent of his sin and trust in the merits of the promised Saviour, and he died in the hope of a resurrection. The Son of God redeemed man's failure and fall; and now, through the work of the atonement, Adam is reinstated in his first dominion."[12]

The concept of entering into God's rest was outlined rather well at Mount Sinai. In the sanctuary services, when sins were confessed, suppliants were forgiven, and the priest took the record of the sacrifices into God's presence (Lev. 4:1–7). Sinners were hence assured that they were safe in God's care. The continual offerings spanned the entire year (Exod. 29:38–42), thereby assuring worshipers that there was continual access to forgiveness and divine help. At the same time, a sequential outline was given on a repetitive basis of the progression of God's plan toward its conclusion—the establishment of a joyful environment in which rest with God again would be possible on a personal basis (Lev. 23:1–44). This means that the covenant of grace, as taught through the sanctuary model, was inextricably linked to an understanding of a developing great controversy worldview that represents mercy and justice as foundational aspects of God's kingdom (Ps. 89:14). Under the provisions of the new covenant, the basic features essential to a meaningful relationship with God were outlined clearly.

The prophets Daniel and John, in particular, recognized the features of the covenant of grace existing from Creation. Their prophecies give historical witness, assuring readers, that God interacts with humanity in space and time and that He will once again establish an Edenic home for the redeemed. (See Table 1.2.)

Covenant and Controversy Illustrated

In this section, I will

- *remind readers that the wilderness sanctuary was patterned after the heavenly one;*
- *highlight the fact that the services and symbols of the earthly sanctuary pointed to Christ;*
- *emphasize that Jesus Christ is the central figure in the heavenly sanctuary.*

God's plan of salvation was shown to Adam and Eve as soon as they recognized their lostness and their need of a covering for their nakedness (Gen. 3:7–15). God provided them a way of escape from eternal death and a plan to remind them continually of His promised sacrifice (Gen. 4:1–5). Thus, we find that, during the time of the patriarchs and prophets, those loyal to God faithfully erected altars and sacrificed perfect animals as an expression of their faith in the deliverance promised through Christ (e.g., Gen. 12:7; 35:1; Exod. 20:24).

Table 1.2. Fundamental features found in the covenant at Creation and the corresponding repetition of the theme in the covenant of grace and in the writings of specific witnesses.

Feature	Covenant at Creation	Old covenant	New covenant
Lordship of the Creator	Gen. 1:26	Exod. 19:18–21; 20:18–20	Col. 1:13–18
Call to worship and to enter God's rest	Gen. 2:2, 3	Exod. 31:13, 16	Rom. 15:9–13

Feature	Covenant at Creation	Old covenant	New covenant
The covenant sign of the Sabbath	Gen. 2:2	Exod. 31:16, 17; Ezek. 20:13, 20	Heb. 4:4, 11–13
Image of God possessed	Gen. 1:26, 27		
Image being restored		Exod. 32:32–34; 33:13, 14, 17–19	Rom. 6:4–6, 17, 18; 12:2; Gal. 5:22, 23
Dominion	Gen. 1:28		
No dominion		Job 1:6–9; 2:1–3	Eph. 2:2; 6:12
Obedience through faith	Gen. 2:16–19 (implied)	Exod. 19:5; Deut. 10:12, 13, 20	Rom. 2:13; 1 John 5:2, 3
Goal of peace and harmony	Gen. 2:19, 20, 24	Exod. 19:8; 24:3	Rom. 5:1, 10, 11; Col. 3:15
Regular personal divine-human interaction	Present at Creation, Gen. 3:8, 9	Absent after the Fall	Ultimate goal, 1 Thess. 4:14–17
Feature— Covenant at Creation	Daniel	John	Christ
The Lordship of the Creator	Dan. 3:24–28; 5:23	Eph. 2:2; Rev. 21:1; 22:2, 3	Mark 10:6–8; John 5:21; 11:25
Call to worship the Creator and enter God's rest	Dan. 6:7, 10, 11	Rev. 14:7	Matt. 4:10; 11:28; 12:6–8
The Covenant sign of the Sabbath	Dan. 7:25, 28; cf. Isa. 56:6; 2 Kings 23:25[13]	Rev. 11:9; 14:7	Matt. 12:5, 6, 8: cf. Num. 28:9, 10; Luke 4:16

Feature—Covenant at Creation	Daniel	John	Christ
Image of God possessed		In heaven, Rev. 14:1–5	
Image being restored	Dan. 10:11, 12; 12:13		John 3:3, 5–8, 21
Dominion		In heaven, Rev. 1:6; 5:10	
No dominion	Dan. 1:3–5	Rev. 1:9	Matt. 19:28
Obedience through faith	Dan. 1:8; cf. Dan. 7:25	Rev. 14:12	Matt. 5:17–19; 22:26–40; 23:23; John 14:21, 23
Goal of peace and harmony	Dan. 12:13; cf. Dan. 2:44; 7:26, 27	Rev. 21:1–5	John 15:9–12; 17:11, 20, 21
Regular divine-human interaction		At the new creation, Rev. 21:3; 22:4; cf. Rev. 2:17; 3:12, 21	Goal toward which all is progressing, John 14:1–3; 17:2, 24

The line of patriarchs stretching back to Abraham ultimately gave rise to the nation of Israel with its most famous king, David, and the succeeding generations that constituted the line through which Christ was to be born (Matt. 1:1–17). In His wisdom, God gave the nation of Israel a more substantial and far-reaching system of ceremonies and worship plans to illustrate His covenant of grace and to demonstrate that this plan would end in the elimination of sin and sinners. This system consisted of the earthy sanctuary, which was *patterned* after the heavenly sanctuary (Exod. 25:8, 9, 40; Heb. 8:1, 2, 5).[14] Of all the lessons taught through the sanctuary, the idea of the restoration of broken relationships was central.[15]

Significantly, the basic events associated with God's plan to rescue humanity were outlined in the sanctuary festivals and services. These provided constant reminders of the covenant at Creation. Other features of the festivals provided a preliminary outline of the great controversy meta-narrative, filling them with great meaning for believers in all ages. In Chapter 11, I will take up the controversy theme in more detail. Suffice it to say here, the religious year commenced in the Passover, Feast of Unleavened Bread, firstfruits, and Pentecost with emblems of Christ's sacrifice and its acceptance in heaven. The religious year ended with emblems of judgment, rejoicing and the rest in the Feast of Tabernacles (Leviticus 23).

The covenant at Creation and the covenant of grace revealed after sin were linked by the Sabbath. As a set apart day, the Sabbath is a memorial of Creation and a reminder of liberation from slavery (Exod. 31:13; Lev. 23:3; Deut. 5:12–15).[16] In the set apart place of the sanctuary in the ark of the covenant, a copy of the fourth statute of the agreement was preserved. On the Sabbath described in that statute, two extra lambs were sacrificed besides those sacrificed in the continual burnt offering (Num. 28:9, 10). This additional sacrifice made tangible the connection between the Sabbath and the re-creation of redemption. As time went on, Israel came to sing the Sabbath hymn of Psalm 92, commemorating both Creation and salvation. The Sabbath is most certainly a day pregnant with meaning.

The Earthly Sanctuary and Temples. The pre-incarnate Son of God gave Moses details concerning the building of the sanctuary during the same period of forty days on Mount Sinai that He wrote the Ten Commandments with His own finger on tables of stone (Exod. 25:8, 9; 31:18). Lest we be tempted to think that the earthly sanctuary was a precise copy of the one in heaven, the author of the epistle to the Hebrews sets our thinking right. He confirms that the "basic contours" of the heavenly sanctuary—the genuine, or "true sanctuary" (Heb. 8:2, 5)—were reflected in the sanctuary on earth.[17] This becomes evident when we compare the details of the first sanctuary with those of Solomon's temple (cf. 1 Kings 6).

The services and symbols used in the sanctuary on earth pointed to Christ, to the beauty of His character, and to His love and justice (Heb. 8:4, 5; 9:21–24). To reinforce this thought when Jesus yielded up His life, the veil of the temple was torn in two "from top to bottom" (Matt. 27:50, 51; Mark 15:37, 38). The manner of the rending of the veil made known that no human hand was responsible for the act. The veil represented Christ's flesh (Heb. 10:20). Exposing the Most Holy Place to the common priest was against the most explicit instructions of God, and it signified that the relevance of the temple's services were at an end as Christ the Lamb of God had given His life for the human race. The tearing of the veil also signified that Christ, as High Priest, was about to become humanity's Advocate in the sanctuary of heaven. Through Christ, believers would have unhindered access to God.

The Jews repaired the damage to the veil, and the temple services continued until AD 70 when the whole temple complex was destroyed by the invading Roman army. After this, the temple was never rebuilt. A chief reason for this was that the thorough destruction of the temple by the Romans made it impossible to determine the exact site of the temple precincts and the location of the altar of burnt offering. Then too, the Jews had no ashes of the red heifer, which were considered essential for the reconsecration of the temple and people. The debate over the possible rebuilding of the temple continues to the present with additional problems for the renewal of the sacrificial system, such as who is entitled to minister as a priest and the exact details of the priestly garments.[18]

The Heavenly Temple. No adequate human words exist to describe the temple in heaven. This is immediately made evident in the prophets' descriptions of the edifice. It is not surprising that the temple's central feature is the space containing the throne of God (Rev. 4:1–11). In the Revelation, John described the throne room of heaven as a place of awesome glory. He also portrayed it as a hub of communication and action, where all intelligent beings worship God for His righteousness and power. The scenes He described convey the relational details central to God's salvation enterprise.

John also pictures in Revelation an angel ministering before God in the temple (Rev. 8:3). The items of furniture used in this ministry correspond to the ones constructed by Moses for the sanctuary in the wilderness. In the earthly sanctuary, the ark in the Most Holy Place represented God's throne (Exod. 26:34). This piece of furniture was a rectangular gilded box containing the Decalogue. Martin Luther is responsible for giving the elaborate lid of the ark its English designation—"the mercy seat" (Exod. 25:16–22).[19] These features of the ark conveyed the foundational concepts of justice and mercy underpinning God's government, or throne (cf. Ps. 89:14).

Isaiah was also given a glimpse of God's throne room (Isa. 6:1–4). The glory of God, representing the magnificence of His character, filled the sacred pavilion. The angels veiled their faces in the presence of the heavenly King. With notes of deep and sincere adoration, they sang Him their praises. The very posts of the temple trembled at His voice (verse 4). From the vision of God's greatness and purity, Isaiah gained a startling realization of his own unworthiness (verse 5). The prophet Daniel saw in vision (Dan. 7:9, 10, 13, 14) the heavenly temple when God calls the tribunal of judgment before the second advent of Christ. The audience chamber was vast enough to accommodate large numbers of heavenly beings, ministering around God's throne. From Isaiah's description of the temple in heaven and God's throne room, it is evident that the tabernacle on earth was a faint image of the vast and more glorious tabernacle in heaven.[20]

As we will indicate shortly, various activities are carried out in the heavenly sanctuary. Yet, the day is hastening when the proceedings in the heavenly temple will cease. When Christ's work on behalf of the human family in the heavenly temple is complete, the seven last plagues will be poured out (Rev. 11:19; 16:1, 17–21). As the temple services on earth reached their fulfillment, Christ cried out, "It is finished!" (John 19:30). When the temple in heaven is opened to full view, revealing its final proceedings, Christ will declare, "It is done!" (Rev. 16:17). These words signal that the plan of salvation has come to an end and the mystery of iniquity has been fully exposed. The judgment scene portrayed in Daniel 7 (verses 9, 10, 13) takes place just before Christ delivers that signal. To convey this idea, Daniel the prophet pictures Michael (who is Christ) standing up, thereby signaling that the door to mercy has been forever closed.[21] What follows on the earth will be such a time of trouble, destruction, and war as has never been witnessed before (Dan. 12:1). Jesus will then appear in the clouds of glory to deliver His people (verses 2, 3).

It is fitting to note that, in the earth made new, there will be no temple to facilitate the worship of the redeemed. This is because the work of salvation has ceased. In paradise, the Lord God Almighty and the Lamb are the temple (Rev. 21:22). When sin entered our world through the disobedience of our first parents, direct and daily fellowship with God was cut off. The Bible makes it abundantly clear that our sins have brought separation from God (Isa. 59:2). However, when sin is finally eradicated from the universe, God will once again be found in the presence of His people. There will be no more need of a tabernacle or a temple, for the close relationship that God established with His creatures at the Creation will be restored and enjoyed throughout eternity.

The Tabernacle Made with Hands

In this section, I will

- briefly describe the earthly sanctuary.

The Israelites had been delivered from Egyptian bondage and were camped about Mount Sinai when God called Moses to the mount. There, Moses was shown the heavenly sanctuary and was given minute instruction on the sanctuary building he was to have constructed at Sinai. Around this structure the entire life of the encampment was to be organized. Once built, the sanctuary was to be situated in a hollow square in the midst of the assembled tribes (Num. 2:2, 3, 10, 18, 25). It is interesting to consider that the tents of the twelve tribes are thought to have been pitched the same distance from the sanctuary as the Israelites maintained from it when they moved from place to place (Josh. 3:3, 4). This would place the sanctuary about half a kilometer from the nearest tents. This arrangement undoubtedly pointed forward to the time when the twelve tribes of the redeemed will stand on the sea of glass waving palm branches and singing praises to God who is seated on a throne in their midst (Rev. 7:5–10).

Earthly Sanctuary Layout. Not all our knowledge of the aspects of the first tabernacle comes from Scripture. Some of it is from historical records and other sources. For example, the Bible does not give the exact dimensions of the tabernacle. Nonetheless, we can calculate what they were by comparing the tabernacle with Solomon's temple (1 Kings 6). The initial earthly sanctuary is believed to have been 30 cubits (15.6 meters) long by 10 cubits (5.2 meters) wide by 10 cubits (5.2 meters) high (cf. Exod. 26:16, 18).[22] The sanctuary tent was divided into two apartments. The most sacred of these, the Most Holy Place, contained the ark of the testament as its only piece of furniture (Exod. 26:34). This apartment was a perfect cube. The other apartment, the Holy Place, was separated from the Most Holy Place by a veil (Exod. 26:33). The Holy Place was twice as long as the Most Holy Place and contained three items of furniture. The candlestick was located on the south side of the tent, and the table of shewbread was located on the north side, directly opposite the candlestick (Exod. 26:35; Figure 1.1). The altar of incense was set before the ark of the testimony, in line with the entrance to the tabernacle (Exod. 40:5). A veil, or curtain, was hung at the door to the tabernacle, and another was hung between the Holy Place and the Most Holy Place, separating the ark and the altar of incense (Exod. 26:33, 36).

A rectangular courtyard fence, measuring 100 cubits (52 meters) long by 50 cubits (26 meters) wide and five cubits (2.6 meters) high, surrounded the tabernacle (Exod. 27:18). An opening in the east side gave entrance to the courtyard (Exod. 27:12–16; Figure 1.1). Inside the courtyard was an altar of burnt offering, located just inside the entrance (Exod. 27:1, 2; 40:6). The opening was covered by a hanging (Exod. 40:33). Thus, there were three veils, curtains or hangings, associated with the building complex. Also located in the courtyard, between the altar of burnt offering and the tabernacle, was a laver for cleansing (Exod. 40:7). The sacrificial victim was offered on the north side of the altar of burnt offering (Lev. 1:11), which means that the laver was offset to the south.

Figure 1.1. Generalized layout of the earthly sanctuary. The basic outline of the Most Holy Place was a square, and the Holy Place was the equivalent of two such squares. Each side of the square measured 10 cubits, or 5.2 meters (Exod. 26:6, 18).

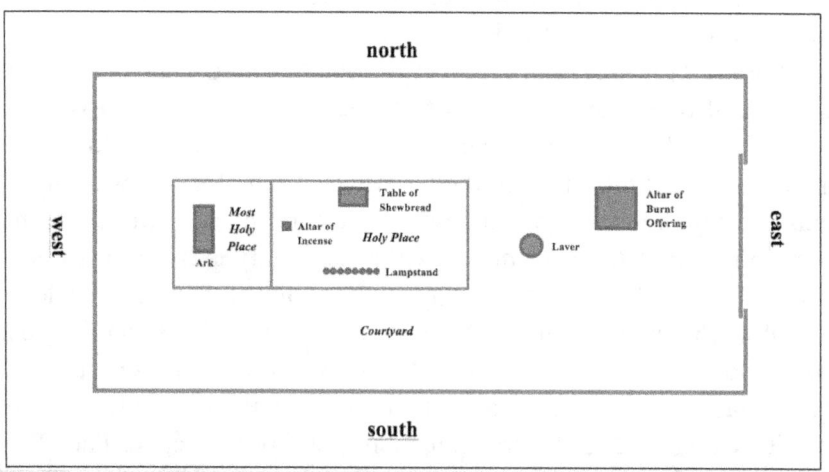

The Shedding of Blood

In this section, I will

- *emphasize that the blood sacrifices associated with the earthly sanctuary pointed to the death of Jesus;*

- *establish that the first phase of ministry in the earthly sanctuary was performed on a daily basis and pointed to Jesus' continual ministry in the heavenly sanctuary;*

- *indicate that the second phase of ministry in the earthly sanctuary involved judgment-related activities having their counterpart in the heavenly sanctuary.*

As soon as sin entered the world, God instituted a system of animal sacrifices to indicate symbolically that the penalty for sins would be paid for by a perfect substitute and Savior (Gen. 3:21; 4:3, 4). The death of the innocent victim reminded the supplicant that "the wages of sin is death" (Rom. 6:23). Until Sinai, the head of the household acted as the priest for each family. However, at Sinai, God established a special priesthood (Exod. 29:9).

The blood sacrifices of the earthly sanctuary service were to point forgetful humanity to the promised sacrifice of the Lamb of God (Isa. 53:5-7; John 1:29, 36). The yearly religious activities were organized around the feasts, beginning with the Passover to highlight the central figure involved in salvation—Jesus Christ (Lev. 23:4-8; 1 Cor. 5:7). The blood sacrifices could only point the supplicant in faith to the sacrifice that Jesus would one day make on the sinner's behalf (Heb. 9:9, 12). The apostle Paul reminds us in Hebrews that the sacrifices could "never take away sins" and that we "have been sanctified through the offering of the body of Jesus Christ once for all" (Heb. 10:11, 10). Through the offering of Christ's body, the perfect sacrifice, the way of redemption is assured to all who sincerely repent. We now look back by faith to Christ's sacrifice and claim God's promises.

Continual Activities. There was one sacrifice that was offered continually in the earthly sanctuary. A lamb was offered as a burnt offering in the morning and another in the evening on a daily basis (Exod. 29:39, 41; Num. 28:3, 4). This ceremony symbolized the giving of Christ for lost humanity. It invited each member of the congregation to reconsecrate his or her life to God.[23] Irrespective of the member's location or situation, the assurance of God's care was continual. The word "daily," or "regular," which is sometimes translated "continual," is frequently used in the Bible when speaking of the sanctuary services. We notice with interest that, besides the continual animal sacrifices, the bread was always kept on the table of shewbread (Lev. 24:8), the lamps in the Holy Place and the fire on the altar were kept burning (Exod. 27:20; Lev. 6:13), and incense was offered every morning and evening (Exod. 29:39; 30:7, 8; Num. 28:3, 4, 6). The term "continual" (Hebrew *tamid*) points forward to the continual priestly ministry of Christ. His ministry is to continue without interruption until the close of human probation (Dan. 12:1). He is always available to plead on our behalf, and we have no need of a human intermediary. What assurance that gives!

The continual evening and morning offerings expressed faith and gratitude in the provisions of God for the salvation of the human race. These offerings also pointed forward to Christ as the invisible head of the redeemed church—ever available to represent the penitent sinner. The apostle Paul assures us that Christ "ever lives to make intercession" in the heavenly sanctuary today (Heb. 7:25). The obvious invitation is to commit our life to God each morning and evening.

Sacrifices for Intentional and Unintentional Sin. Besides the continual morning and evening sacrifices, individuals could also make offerings for specific sins. Those who sinned unintentionally and brought a sacrificial victim as an offering for their sin were continually reminded of the necessity of faith. The procedure for the sacrifice was as follows: The repentant sinner laid hands on the head of the victim and personally slew the animal. The laying on of hands indicated that the guilt of sin was symbolically transferred to the sinner's substitute. By this act, the sinner was justified and the sin was forgiven. In all instances, the officiating priest, who carried out the remainder of the ceremony, caught the blood of the innocent victim and applied it in the sanctuary. By this ceremony, the repentant sinner acknowledged that forgiveness was wholly dependent upon God's mercies. It was a faith transaction, and the spilled blood needed to be applied. All blood that was sprinkled in this manner in the sanctuary throughout the year was in the Holy Place (see Lev. 4:2–7, 13–18). In this way, the sins of the repentant sinner were transferred symbolically to the Holy Place and accumulated there.

Sometimes, the priest ate a portion of the flesh of the sacrifice in a holy place in the court, indicating that he identified completely with the sinner and bore the sinner's guilt. By this act, he made atonement for the particular sin (Lev. 10:17–19). The ceremony was to point to Christ who "bore our sins in His own body on the tree" (1 Peter 2:24) and then ascended to heaven to minister in the heavenly sanctuary for us.

These symbols offer great assurances for the penitent. Whether sins are intentional or unintentional, the benefits of Christ's sacrifice are available to all who sincerely repent and confess their sins (cf. 2 Samuel 12:12–14; Luke 23:39–45). Christ has borne the guilt of the sinner into the place where God dwells. In other words, our confessed sins are safe in God's care, beyond the concern of those who repent. This is one of Christ's functions today in the heavenly sanctuary—ministering there the benefits of His sacrifice. He also promises to transform lives, giving everyone a clear reason to rejoice.

Judgment Symbolism. One sanctuary ceremony occurred only on the Day of Atonement, near the end of the yearly round of religious activities. This ceremony was connected with the Most Holy Place, placing it "inside the veil" (Lev. 16:12; see also Lev. 16:13–16; 23:27–32). During the yearly round of services, sin was symbolically transferred to the sanctuary by the ministration of the priests. Before and on the Day of Atonement, every individual was to examine his or her relationship with God or be cut off from the congregation of Israel (Lev. 23:27–29). This conveyed the important lesson that, unless sinners maintain a right relationship with God, their previously confessed sins will return to their account (Ezek. 18:24; 33:13; Matt. 18:23–35). To the Israelites, the Day of Atonement was a day of judgment and a day of "purging the people," an emphasis which is well recognized in Jewish writings.[24] It is important to note that the Day of Atonement was followed five days later by the Feast of Tabernacles, or Ingathering, (Lev. 23:34–43), which was a day of gladness and rejoicing. It represented, in its antitypical application, the rejoicing of the redeemed after Christ's second coming (Rev. 21:3). Because the earthly tabernacle served as a "copy and shadow of the heavenly things" (Heb. 8:5, NASB), we should expect a judgment scene as in Daniel 7 to have commenced before Christ returns in glory. (The heavenly judgment will be covered in Chapter 20.)

Christ's Ministry in Heaven

Christ is now our High Priest in the heavenly sanctuary (Heb. 8:1, 2, 6; 9:11–15). In the epistle to the Hebrews, Paul urged readers to consider the ceremonies in the earthly sanctuary as "patterns" (Heb. 9:23, KJV), or "shadow" (Heb. 8:5), of the heavenly sanctuary. They were to study the lessons that the earthly sanctuary teaches about the plan of salvation (Heb. 4:1, 2; 9:1–15). It is not the explicit purpose of the epistle to the Hebrews to elaborate on the two types of ministry—mediatorial and judicial—highlighted in the earthly sanctuary, though the language of Hebrews does point to "holy places." Rather, its main purpose is to aid the reader in focusing on Christ, His all-sufficient sacrifice, His continuing saving ministry, and the ineffectiveness of temple-associated rituals to save. It was aimed initially at helping the Hebrew Christians, who were experiencing difficulties in laying aside Mosaic rituals, to accept Christ's ministry fully.[25]

The message of Hebrews regarding Christ's ministry is obscured in some Bible translations by their rendering of the term for the sanctuary—*ta hagia*. Their translating it as "the holiest of all" has supported the claim that the first apartment in the earthly sanctuary represented the Mosaic era and the second apartment applies to heaven itself under the Christian era.[26] The contrast in understanding can be illustrated by just two translations of Hebrews 9:12. (Note the added emphasis.) The *New King James Version* renders it: "Not with the blood of goats and calves, but with His own blood He entered *the Most Holy Place* once for all, having obtained eternal redemption." The *New English Bible* has: "The blood of his sacrifice is his own blood, not the blood of goats and calves; and thus he has entered *the sanctuary* once and for all and secured an eternal deliverance." The Greek term translated "the Most Holy Place" in the one and "the sanctuary" in the other is the plural "*ta hagia*."[27] The singular form, "*to hagion*," means "the holy." Other forms of the term in the epistle to the Hebrews are listed in Table 1.3.

The plural form of the term is used consistently in the epistle to the Hebrews (the only exception occurs in Heb. 9:1). Reference to the Septuagint version of the Scriptures indicates that *ta hagia* refers primarily to the sanctuary as a whole. One authority notes that it "is best understood as a general term for the entire heavenly sanctuary rather than the Most Holy Place alone, unless it is definitely qualified, as it is in Hebrews 9:2–5."[28] This applies to Hebrews 9:12 as well, for the priest passed through the outer sanctuary to reach the inner sanctuary.

Some critics have asserted that the apostle Paul sided with those who argue that the distinction between the Holy Place and the Most Holy Place does not matter any longer. This is as a result of their understanding of Hebrews 9:3, 4, which appears to locate the golden censer (NKJV, YLT), taken by some to refer to the altar of incense (CEB, NIV), in the holiest. These critics assert that this did not represent reality. However, the apostle Paul was much wiser than the critics, for he was simply expressing the thought that the altar of incense belonged *functionally* to the Most Holy Place (1 Kings 6:22) while a golden censer was *physically* taken into the Most Holy Place on the Day of Atonement offering incense from the altar there.[29]

Table 1.3. Forms of the Greek noun for "sanctuary" and the literal translation of each form.

Form of Greek noun	Literal translation[30]	Reference in Hebrews
Hagia	"holies," "holy places"	9:2, 24
hagia hagiōn	"holy of holies"	9:3
ta hagia	"the holies," "the holy places"	9:12, 25; 13:11
to (te) hagion ["te" interrupts the article and noun]	"the (and) holy place," "(and) the sanctuary"	9:1
tōn hagiōn	"of the holies," "of the holy things," "of the holy places"	8:2; 9:8; 10:19

The principles of literal translation outlined above, when applied consistently with due consideration for the context, present a picture of activities in the heavenly sanctuary by our High Priest in perfect agreement with the pattern outlined by the order of the priestly services performed in the earthly sanctuary. The earthly priests functioned regularly in a mediatorial role in the Holy Place ministry, and the high priest functioned in a judicial role once a year in the Most Holy Place ministry. These two phases of ministry are evident in Hebrews (e.g., Heb. 4:14–16; 7:25; 8:6; 9:6, 7, 24, 25, 27, 28; cf. "judgment seat" of 2 Cor. 5:10).

Christ died on the cross to bear our sins. We are justified, or declared righteous, when by faith we accept Him as our perfect substitute. In heaven, Christ administers the merits of His blood. That is justification. Christ desires not only to forgive our sins but also to empower us to live a victorious life. That is sanctification. The apostle Paul expressed it thus: "... having been reconciled, we shall be saved by His life" (Rom. 5:10). Both aspects of Christ's ministry are essential for salvation.

The Sanctuary/Great Controversy Worldview

At the beginning of this chapter, I referred to the concept of the great controversy. Now that we have presented an overview of the sanctuary services, we can consider how the sanctuary services fit together with the great controversy in forming one consistent worldview. We will see that the pattern of ceremonies conducted throughout the religious year—Passover to the Feast of Ingathering—parallel many of the events in the great controversy as highlighted by Bible writers.

There is indeed a cosmic battle between good and evil. The triumph of Christ, the hero in the drama, permeates the pages of the Bible. The text, "Surely the Lord GOD does nothing, unless He reveals His secret to His servants the prophets" (Amos 3:7), emphasizes the central place of Christ in communicating with His servants and encouraging them concerning the righteousness of His principles (see John 5:39).

The conflict with God began in heaven when Lucifer, a created being and the principal angel in heaven, became dissatisfied with the position and duties allocated him (Isa. 14:12, 13; Ezek. 28:14, 15; Rev. 12:7–9). He wished to be like God (Isa. 14:12–14) and, particularly, to be included in the counsels of heaven. Pride dominated his thinking, and he began a campaign for God to promote him above Christ. This movement, which began in secrecy, ended in public with the deception of a great host of his fellow angels (Rev. 12:4). The transition from innocence to corruption was a long and gradual process. Yet, there was no excuse for the existence of sin. In the end, God expelled from heaven all who were unhappy with the principles of His kingdom. Cast to the earth, the light bearer Lucifer became Satan, the devil and "adversary" (Rev. 12:7–10; 1 Peter 5:8).

God's creative activities did not cease because of the controversy with Satan over his insistence that he be involved in planning this world. Neither did God cease His creative activities even though He knew that the emergence of evil would involve an incredible sacrifice to allow the principle of *agapē* love to ensure the perpetuity of His kingdom throughout eternity. The creation of the human race was a judgment on Satan and, actually, proclaimed that good would triumph over evil. However, before this outcome could be secured, a trail of suffering and misery, punctuated by faith and hope, would burst upon the human race. The first step down this trail commenced

Chapter 1. Covenant, Salvation, and Sanctuary

soon after the creation and fall of the progenitors of the human race. Eve was deceived and believed the devil's lies. Furthermore, she questioned God's integrity and chose to disobey His direct instructions. Adam, unable to see a future without his companion, began to doubt God's abilities (Gen. 3:1–7). Through this act of deception in the Garden of Eden, Satan became known as "the prince of this world" (John 14:30, KJV).

In the process of time, Satan succeeded in bringing so much wickedness into the world that God destroyed all but a remnant in the great Flood (Gen. 7:17–23). Despite this judgment, many of the descendants of this handful of survivors turned from God in rebellion. The construction of the tower of Babel was an act of disbelief, defiance, and an expression of resentment concerning the Flood (Gen. 11:1–4). The rebellion continued through the long ages to follow and climaxed in the crucifixion of Christ who was sent to save the race (Matt. 21:33–44).

The Bible presents Satan's rebellion as turning this earth into the one blighted spot in the universe. It also presents this earth as a testing place where God's servants demonstrate their loyalty to Him (Job 1:6–2:7). All heaven is interested in the outcome of the rebellion (1 Cor. 4:9).

Issues in the Controversy. The foundation of God's kingdom is *agapē* love. God gave this principle central place in the Decalogue (Matt. 22:36–40). Love speaks of a relationship, and when this relationship is broken, men and women feel free to disobey God's will as expressed in His law (John 14:15). The lawless state of this world is the result of the transgression of God's code of love (1 John 3:4).

God's throne—his authority and rulership—is established upon mercy and justice (Ps. 85:10; 89:14), which are simply expressions of the *agap* principle. These concepts took center stage in the earthly sanctuary services. Mercy was shown daily in the round of ceremonies pointing to Christ's coming sacrifice. Then, once a year, on the Day of Judgment, justice was shown in its proper perspective as the companion to mercy. This indicates that there will be a day of reckoning. The ceremonies of that day pointed to the final scenes of the great controversy, which end with the close of the plan of salvation, an event yet to transpire.

Satan alleged from the beginning that God's character was faulty and that such faultiness is evident in His Law. He also claimed that it was not possible for the human race to keep God's law. These claims he has consistently made in an attempt to both discredit and overthrow God's government. Christ, while on earth, held firm to the Word of God. He trusted the righteousness of His Father's character and obeyed His will through faith (Matt. 4:4). Furthermore, He depended on the exercise of faith to deliver a singular victory at Calvary. There He declared triumphantly: "Now the prince of this world will be driven out" (John 16:11, NIV).

Even though victory was gained at the cross, the controversy continues. The Bible, the Decalogue, and Christ's provisions of salvation are all under attack. This controversy impacts each individual as he or she answers the question: "But who do you say that I am?" (Matt. 16:15).

Strategies Pursued. Questions about philosophical issues dealing with human existence, purpose, and appropriate ways of acting are generally answered in today's world without reference to the principles outlined by God in the Bible. Satan has steadfastly attacked the credibility of God's Word and has promoted the superiority of human reason. Doubts about the Scriptures arise through pride of intellect, the commencing point for Satan's rebellion in heaven (Isa. 14:12–14). Such thinking has led to a steady decline in the appreciation of the character of God, an increase in human arrogance, and other shameful results based on the rejection of God's principles of ethics. Today, another avenue of attack is when people doubt the relevance of Christ's ministry in the heavenly sanctuary (cf. Dan. 8:11, 12), which undermines the great controversy theme, as we will discover later.

In opposition to God's absolute truths, many seek relative truth through appeals to human wisdom (Prov. 14:12; 16:25), nature or the universe (see Acts 17:18, 23), religious authorities and critical scholars (cf. Dan. 7:25; Mark 7:9, 13; 2 Peter 3:16), or the occult (Isa. 8:19). While limited truth may be associated with some of these sources, divine principles cannot be established apart from God's Word (John 17:17).

The magnitude of Satan's influence is well expressed by the apostle Paul: "For we do not wrestle against flesh and blood, but against principalities, against powers, against the rulers of the darkness of this age, against spiritual *hosts* of wickedness in the heavenly *places*" (Eph. 6:12). Satan's chosen agencies are revealed more explicitly in Bible prophecy. God has promised to stand by those who are faithful to His cause, giving them a sure reward (Rev. 14:1–4).

The history of the struggle between good and evil from the Fall in Eden until the captivity of Judah is related in the Old Testament. The history of the church and the major influences that impacted it well after the Jewish nation was rejected by God are related more explicitly in Daniel's prophecies. John the Revelator also fills in some vital details regarding the long ages after the ascension of Christ. His account serves to warn and encourage the church to be faithful. John's advice is that all believers be watchful and lean continually on the Holy Spirit for help (Eph. 6:13–18), and God's assurance is that, if we exercise faith in Christ, we can be "more than conquerors" (Rom. 8:37).

The Cross Highlighted. Satan was cast down when mercy and justice met at the cross (Ps. 85:10; 89:14). On the basis of the victory following the resurrection, Christ is carrying out the last phases of the atonement in the heavenly sanctuary, and He will soon return to execute judgment. At the end of the millennium, Satan will finally be consigned to oblivion (Rev. 20:10), for it will be evident to all that the principles of his kingdom are utterly untenable. He will be recognized for who he is—the author of sin and suffering, and he will have given ample demonstration that the principles of his government are flawed and antagonistic to the development of peaceful and harmonious relationships. He and his followers will be destroyed forever. Sin and suffering will not arise a second time (Nah. 1:9). This is how the reality of the ceremonies conducted on the Day of Atonement in the ancient earthly sanctuary will be acted out.

The Remnant. The great controversy theme has embedded in it the concept of "the remnant." This concept carries with it a note of certainty that God will be victorious and save those people who value His friendship and the principles of His kingdom. Throughout the history of the controversy, God has always had a remnant of people to preserve His name and righteous principles. In the period of the patriarchs, Abraham was called to stand apart from his idolatrous peers and enter covenant relationship with God (Gen. 17:1, 2). He worshiped the living Creator God rather than idols. His faith was proverbial, and he kept God's ways faithfully (Heb. 11:8–10; 17–19; Gen. 18:19). In the experience of the Israelites during the Exodus, there were individuals who exercised faith in God (Num. 14:30; Heb. 3:5). During the Dark Ages, God condemned the church of the Thyatira period (AD 538 to the Reformation) for its apostasy. Yet, even then there remained a faithful remnant (Rev. 2:24, 25). Those who are part of God's remnant are sanctified through the truth (John 17:17). The remnant know that it is only through the life, death, resurrection, and ministry of Christ that they have the assurance of an eternal future. Christ defeated the cosmic forces of evil at the cross, and He will soon come as the victorious King.

Satan has been active throughout history, seeking to frustrate God's plans and destroy those trust in Him. Revelation 12 pictures a time in history that religious forces cooperate with the civil powers of earth to impose religious views upon the people of the earth. This will lead to great difficulty and suffering. In spite of the pressure, a remnant will stand firm. Immediately before the close of earth's history, God will have a visible remnant on earth who uphold the truths of God's Word. Seventh-day Adventists believe that their church champions the characteristics of the remnant portrayed in Revelation 12:17 and 14:6–12. These characteristics include holding fast to the Commandments of God through faith, honoring the Creator on the Sabbath, accepting the prophetic word and the last ministrations of Christ in the heavenly sanctuary, valuing the gifts of the Spirit, including prophecy, giving centrality to the life and teachings of Jesus, and rejecting human systems of worship. Individuals in this and other communions of believers who worship God in sincerity and hold a vital relationship with Christ are counted as God's remnant as they patiently wait for Jesus' return.

The remnant people are characterized by their clear view of God's world-encompassing mission of salvation. This includes giving widespread voice to the everlasting gospel within the context of God's judgment of this world and believing firmly in the Creator God, who fashioned the world in seven days and left a memorial day in the Sabbath upon which humans are to worship Him. This group also holds fast to the ethical and moral principles of Scripture in the midst of widespread apostasy in the world. They not only identify the elements of human departure from God's ideal, but they give a certain and clear call to come back to the truths of His Word and be saved. This is the gist of the three angels' messages. Many will respond to these appeals and come out of spiritual Babylon to be part of the final remnant people.

Every member of God's remnant will have a vibrant, personal relationship with Christ. They will all have experienced the truth of what Jesus declared, "And this is eternal life, that they may know You, the only true God, and Jesus Christ whom You have sent" (John 17:3).

Chapter 1. Covenant, Salvation, and Sanctuary

Without question, Adventists understand that "the universal church is composed of all who truly believe in Christ."[31] This means, in the context of our discourse, that God has many earnest, faithful, and sincere followers in other Christian groups. These He is calling out of confusion to take their stand with His faithful people in preparation for the soon coming of Christ. In this way the principles outlined in Isaiah 58 will be fulfilled before the world.

> "*Is* not this the fast that I have chosen? to loose the bonds of wickedness, to undo the heavy burdens, to let the oppressed go free, and that ye break every yoke? *Is it* not to share your bread with the hungry, and that you bring to your house the poor who are cast out; when you see the naked, that you cover him, and not hide yourself from your own flesh? Then your light shall break forth like the morning, your healing shall spring forth speedily, and your righteousness shall go before you; the glory of the Lord shall be your rear guard." (Isa. 58:6–8)

Christ and His Ministry

Chapter 2.
Dwelling among His People

Chapter Emphasis: *Though Christ's desire to dwell with humanity was frustrated in Eden through the entrance of sin, His goal was partially realized in the sanctuary of the ancient Israelites and more fully realized in the coming of Jesus Christ to this earth some two thousand years ago. Its full realization will occur in the new earth. God's actions portray Him as social and loving.*

Spiritual Link: *The ministry of the Holy Spirit has always been essential to humankind.*

The entry of sin into the world, when Adam and Eve exchanged their innocence for the knowledge of evil, meant that Satan became the Prince of this world. Face-to-face communication between the human pair and their Maker was no longer possible. Such separation was not God's plan. Therefore, God sought to identify with the lost race and place constant reminders before them of His plan of salvation. Immediately after the Fall, He introduced animal sacrifices to impress upon sinners the enormity of sin and its great cost. These sacrifices were also to point them to the promised Savior (Gen. 3:15; 3:21; 4:3, 4). He more fully revealed the details of the plan to succeeding generations. The most fundamental aspects of the plan were taught through the sanctuary system in the period before Christ's sojourn on earth. Today, the lessons given are for our instruction.

In our present world, the desire of exiled monarchs to again dwell among their people is often motivated by a desire for power, wealth, and adulation. God, on the other hand, has nothing to gain along these lines. He offered, and still offers, a sacrifice of love in return for grateful and undiminished love from His subjects. God's objective is to dwell among His loyal subjects in a universe made forever secure from sin and operating under the principles of His government.

In the Presence of the Lord

In this section, I will

- *highlight the close communion that existed between humanity and God at Creation;*

- *establish that sin broke the close bond between God and humanity.*

After creating Adam and Eve, the LORD God walked in the Garden with the newly created pair on a regular basis (Gen. 3:8, 9, implied). The personal interest and care that God showed toward the human family are indicated further by the cooperative bond that God established with Adam in the confidence He showed in Adam's judgment as He brought the animals to him for naming (Gen. 2:19, 20). All of God's created intelligences have the powers of reason and choice. These were essential for the development of the strongest personal bonds. Adam and Eve subsequently chose to disobey God and break their relationship with Him. As a consequence of their disobedience, they became afraid of God and hid from Him (Gen. 3:10). The scriptural account appears to indicate that, as soon as the conversation between God and the frightened pair was concluded, He banished them from the Garden, guarding their Eden home by an angel with a flaming sword. Nonetheless, God did not banish them from Eden without first introducing them to His plan to save them (Gen. 3:15). How merciful is our God!

As a consequence of yielding to sin, humanity has in its "nature a bent to evil, a force which, unaided," they "cannot resist."[32] All subsequent generations of men and women have faced temptations and have at some time failed to claim God's promise of power to overcome (Rom. 6:14; 1 Cor. 10:13; James 1:14; 1 John 2:1). Today, God desires our cooperation with Him. The challenge comes to us, "Choose for yourselves this day whom you will serve" (Josh. 24:15). Those who are eternally lost will not be able to blame Adam for their failure; eternal death will be due to their own choice.

By obeying Satan, by succumbing to his influence, Eve became his servant (John 8:34; Rom. 6:16). Eve then followed her new master in influencing her husband to join her in the discovery of new knowledge. When they realized that the principles of behavior they had chosen were diametrically opposed to the principles of heaven, they became afraid and hid themselves. There can be no effective communication when individuals subscribe to different principles of action (2 Cor. 6:15).

Satan uses the same methods of mind control today that he used in Eden. He "beguiled," "charmed," or "deluded" Eve through the fascinating charm and hypnotic movements of the serpent.[33] He then made appealing suggestions when she was in this altered mental state (Gen. 3:13). Today, the world is in the grip of powerful mind control devices, such as the hypnotic beat of rock music, various systems of meditation like "centering prayer" and entering "the silence," and the pleasing and disarming ways of neuro-linguistic programming.[34] These devices induce an altered state of consciousness, allowing the person's belief system to be bypassed. The founders of neuro-linguistic programming have stated openly: "The major positive attribute of an altered state of consciousness is that you don't have to fight with a person's belief system. The unconscious mind is willing to try anything."[35] Is this not a time that we should seek our God rather than new knowledge from the tree of knowledge of good and evil? (See Isa. 8:19; Gen. 2:9.)

Yahweh of the Old Testament

In this section, I will

- *explore God's interest in human affairs after the Fall;*
- *establish how that Christ was the chosen member of the Godhead to communicate with humanity.*

Strictly speaking, the only true name of God is "Yahweh," which was mistakenly transliterated "Jehovah." The name represents God as a person and conveys His interest in interacting with others. Indeed, God spoke "to the Patriarchs as one friend to another."[36] Yahweh means the "self-Existing one," and it is the personal name of God in contrast with "Elohim," which is the generic, plural name of God. As we examine the Bible record, it reveals God's continual desire to communicate with humanity.

The experiences of the patriarch Abraham illustrate the Lord's intense interest in human affairs. For example, the Lord showed Abraham the fate of the cities of Sodom and Gomorrah (Gen. 18:20–23, 33). In this instance, He came down to communicate directly with Abraham. It is evident from the biblical account that the three heavenly visitors physically spoke and walked with Abraham and that, subsequent to the departure of the two angels who went to Sodom, Abraham spoke with the Lord (Gen. 18:2, 4, 9, 13, 16, 22–33). God knew about the wickedness in the cities of the plain, yet He came to speak with faithful Abraham so that there would be no misunderstanding about divine justice. Actually, it is the pre-incarnate Jesus who is revealed in this instance, for John declares that no one has seen God the Father at any time (John 1:18). Yet, Abraham both saw and spoke with the Lord on this occasion. Thus, it could not have been the Father who was present to speak with him.

Other great personalities of the Old Testament communed with Jesus face to face. We think of Jacob who wrestled with "a man" whose identity was later shown to be that of the Son of God (Gen. 32:24, 28–30; Hosea 12:3–5). The great leader Moses encountered God at the burning bush and received divine instructions from Him there (Exod. 3:2–4). Later, he communed with God on Mount Sinai over a period of forty days (Exod. 24:12–18). Centuries later, the three worthies thrown into Nebuchadnezzar's fiery furnace were accompanied in the fire by the Son of God (Dan. 3:25). These examples serve to illustrate that God has a deep, yearning interest in the welfare of the fallen race. He is a personal and loving God. So, even in the Old Testament, Jesus was *Immanuel*—"God with us."

We have noticed in a number of texts that Yahweh of the Old Testament is called by other names. He is "a Man" (Gen. 32:24), "the Angel" (Exod. 3:2; 14:19; Hosea 12:2–4), and "I AM WHO I AM" (Exod. 3:14). The Bible unequivocally indicates that the Person of the Godhead who has been intimately associated with fallen humanity from the commencement of the biblical record is Jesus Christ. The apostle Paul clearly said that "the Lord" who followed the Israelites was Christ "the Rock" (1 Cor. 10:4). "Yahweh" of the Old Testament (generally rendered "Lord") was indeed the Lord Jesus Christ. In fact, Jesus made this claim directly when He told the Jews, "Most assuredly,

I say to you, before Abraham was, I AM" (John 8:58). Immediately, the Jews took up stones to kill Him for they recognized His claim to be the "I AM" of the Old Testament (John 8:58), while they only saw Him as a man (John 10:33).

I have emphasized the reality of God's presence with His people in space and time. In their understanding of this subject, Seventh-day Adventists differ from many other Christian groups. Their understanding represents the acceptance of biblical principles rather than Greek philosophical thinking.[37]

Christ in His Sanctuary

In this section, I will

- *emphasize that the earthly sanctuary constructed by Moses was built as a symbol of God's abiding presence among His people;*

- *remind readers that God's continual interest in the human race is shown by Christ's coming to this earth and hallowing the earthly temple with His physical presence.*

God's primary purpose in instructing Moses to build a sanctuary was that He might dwell among His people (Exod. 25:8). This was for the express purpose of teaching them about His character and plan of salvation. The system of worship based in the earthly sanctuary pointed forward to Christ's sacrifice on earth and His subsequent ministry in the heavenly sanctuary. More importantly, it indicated continually that God was seeking after the sinner and providing every opportunity to restore the fallen race to a rightful relationship with Him. God desires an intimate relationship with His people. He wishes to transform the life of every individual believer to conform to His will. It is informative to notice that the Hebrew word *shakan*, translated "dwell," has the meaning of being a "permanent resident in a community."[38] The word can also be translated "tabernacled among us." Moses had the tabernacle placed in the midst of the congregation (Num. 2:2, 3, 10, 18, 25). This was to convey the idea that God desired to dwell among the people (Exod. 25:8; John 1:14) and become the sinner's friend (Matt. 11:19; Luke 7:34). Thus did God seek to impress His divine character and life upon the people and help them to recognize His desire to sanctify them by His presence.

The imagery of the sanctuary and description of His goal of dwelling among them is in no way intended to convey the idea that the God of the universe can be confined to a building made with human hands. The Scriptures clearly indicate that heaven and earth cannot contain Him (1 Kings 8:27; 2 Chron. 2:6; Isa. 66:1). From this apparent contradiction arises an imponderable thought: How can God who is eternal, all knowing, and all powerful dwell in a habitation made by human hands? The idea that God interacts with humanity in time and space is biblical but not widely acknowledged in the Christian world.[39] Yet, God promises that He is always near at hand to hear, help, and encourage every true believer, and He has expressed His desire to be a companion of every believer through the Holy Spirit (Rom. 8:9; 1 Cor. 6:19). This will be a source of praise and wonder throughout eternity.

After the wilderness wanderings and Israel was established in the Promised Land, Solomon built the temple for God in Jerusalem, a city also known as Zion (2 Chron. 3:1). Solomon built the temple on the site of Ornan's (or Araunah's) threshing floor (1 Chron. 21:28–22:6; 2 Chron. 3:1; 2 Samuel 24:16), which was on Mount Moriah, the place where Abraham was willing to offer his son Isaac (Gen. 22:1–14). By placing the sanctuary on Mount Moriah, God reminded the Israelites of Abraham's experience and called attention to the central quality required of true worshipers—faith.

God honored Solomon's temple with His presence (2 Chron. 5:13, 14; 6:1, 2). The temple was a magnificent structure. During its dedication, when the ark of the covenant containing the tables of the law was brought into the Holy Place, the glory of the Lord filled the Holy Place (1 Kings 8:6, 9–11). Sadly, the temple was destroyed by Nebuchadnezzar's army in 586 BC. After the Jews returned home from their exile in Babylon, Zerubbabel the governor, with the permission of Cyrus, rebuilt the temple at Jerusalem, though the structure was greatly diminished in grandeur. Not many years before Jesus was born, the temple built by Zerubbabel was remodeled and refurbished by Herod the Great.

The reason that God's glory was not present in the post-exilic temple is that the ark of the covenant, which was the focal point of the temple services, was not present. There is some indication that Jeremiah hid the ark in a cave in the mountain that Moses climbed before he lay down in the sleep of death and then blocked the entrance to the ark's hiding place. Some of his companions tried to find the location and mark the spot but were unable to do so. To this day, the location has not been found (2 Mac. 2:4–6, Apocrypha).[40] Indeed, the historian Josephus confirmed the idea that the ark was not in the second temple in 63 BC.[41] The temple was finally destroyed in AD 70. The treasures taken from this temple are illustrated in stone relief in the victory arch of Titus found in present-day Rome. The ark is notably absent from the relief.[42]

Even though the presence of the Lord was no longer reflected in the second temple, God had a better purpose in mind for it. The member of the Godhead who delivered the plans of the earthly sanctuary to Moses and proclaimed the Decalogue amid awful glory on Mount Sinai now hallowed the earthly sanctuary with His presence (Acts 7:38; Isa. 63:9; Matt. 12:1, 6; Mark 11:9–11). What more telling way could God have chosen to convey to humanity the concepts of His great love and abiding interest in the salvation of the human race? The prophet Haggai declared: "The glory of the latter temple shall be greater than the former" (Hag. 2:9). This greater glory was due to Christ's presence in the last temple in His incarnate form.

King of Kings

In this section, I will

- *outline God's purpose to fully re-establish, in the earth made new, the relationships broken by sin;*
- *establish that Jesus has given Himself to the human race for all eternity.*

From the time of the Creation, Christ has been the primary agent of communication with earth's inhabitants. When He returned to heaven, triumphant after the resurrection, He sent the Spirit of truth—the Holy Spirit—to guide His people (John 14:16, 17, 26).

The Holy Spirit, who is the third Person of the Godhead, became active on earth in a remarkable manner from Pentecost onward. The Holy Spirit has always wrestled with humanity as the voice of conscience communicating warning, counsel, reproof, and invitation and impressing truth on hearers and readers (Gen. 6:3; Ps. 51:11; Zech. 4:6; John 15:26; 16:13; Rev. 22:17). We should never doubt that all the members of the Godhead are devoted to the salvation of humanity (John 3:16).[43]

When the message of truth is preached, the word is accompanied with power. The Holy Spirit quickens the conscience of hearers.

Through His Spirit, God desires that He be each believer's companion. This is made possible as concepts and erroneous practices are put away and hearers respond to the sanctified call of conscience (1 Cor. 6:19; Gen. 6:3; Ps. 95:7, 8). If permitted, the Holy Spirit will change people's thinking and behavior and empower them to witness (Acts 1:8; Rom. 12:2). If Christ is our companion today through the ministry of the Spirit, then we will have the assurance of dwelling with Christ in His glorified kingdom (Col. 1:27). Every day we can come in contact with the Infinite One through sincere prayer and the study of God's Word.

God intends to make His dwelling place forever among the redeemed when the great controversy has ended. At the end of the one thousand years spent in heaven, the Lord will return to this earth in the New Jerusalem—the new Zion—with all the saints. Zion then will be His resting place forever (Ps. 132:13, 14; Rev. 21:2, 3). The prophet Zechariah used the phrase "in that day" to refer to the time when "the LORD shall be King over all the earth" and again stand on the Mount of Olives (Zech. 14:4, 9). "That day" is still future. "That day" God will again dwell among His people and commune with them face to face. God's great purpose, revealed at the Creation, will "that day" be fulfilled in the redeemed and recreated ones in the earth made new. The Scriptures triumphantly declare that God "will dwell with them, and they shall be His people, and God Himself will be with them *and be* their God" (Rev. 21:3).

The saints will praise and adore "THE KING OF KINGS AND LORD OF LORDS" in the new earth (Rev. 19:16). This phrase is the superlative title of the triumphant Jesus (Rev. 19:13; cf. John 1:14). His triumph will be expressed as He returns to the earth the second time to claim His people and His dominion as the Son of Man (Rev. 14:14–16). The title expresses the idea that our Savior has given Himself to the human race for all eternity. He ever bears in His body the marks of His suffering on our behalf (John 20:27). What a glorious Savior we have! Let us plan to be among that glad number in the earth made new. We *must* be there so that we can participate in the glorious praise to our Redeemer recorded in Revelation 19:6, 7:

"Alleluia! For the Lord God Omnipotent reigns!
Let us be glad and rejoice and give Him glory,
For the marriage of the Lamb has come,
And his wife has made herself ready."

Chapter 3.
The Mystery of "God with Us"

Chapter Emphasis: *Jesus Christ is truly God, uncreated, and immortal. He also became truly human when He was born of the virgin Mary. His earthly life enabled Him to experience temptation, the privations common to humanity, and death. He chose to die on the cross on behalf of the human race in order to pay the ransom price for sin. He lived a life without sin, and He now ministers in the heavenly sanctuary on our behalf, providing power to His followers to enable them to live a life pleasing to Him.*

Spiritual Link: *Since the Fall, Christ has functioned as the Communicator between God and humanity; since the cross, Christ has acted as our Mediator in heaven.*

God's plan to save humanity through sending the Son to pay the just penalty of sin is a mystery. It began as He came as a baby, born of a human mother, and then grew up in a peasant household. His youth and early manhood were spent in useful labor as a carpenter.

The concept of one equal with God the Father coming to earth in human form to live, suffer, and die as a man to save humanity cannot be adequately explained. This mystery is deepened by Jesus' statement to His disciples at the time of the first cleansing of the earthly temple,

"Destroy this temple, and in three days I will raise it up" (John 2:19). On that occasion, He spoke of the loss of His life on the cross and His subsequent resurrection from the dead by the life contained within Himself (verses 21, 22). In this chapter, I will seek to expand the reader's understanding of the nature of Christ, although I hasten to add that one's relationship with Christ is more important than theological understanding. The topic of Christ's nature can be addressed legitimately within this series because of the temple imagery that He used in presenting the truth about His immortality. (In Chapter 17, I will discuss the implications of the human body also being the temple of the Holy Spirit.)

Jesus Christ, Truly God

In this section, I will

- *indicate that Jesus Christ possesses the attributes of divinity.*

The uniqueness of Christianity is that it holds two propositions: the first is that Christ possessed divine attributes while on earth; the second is that salvation cannot be attained through the sacrifice of a person who is not divine. These propositions can best be understood in terms of the great controversy worldview. The dispute between God and Satan has always been about the principles of God's government. No one other than God could demonstrate their soundness. Making this demonstration involved Christ's making the ultimate sacrifice for the human family that He created. In so doing, He demonstrated that mercy and justice are compatible with the principle of *agapē* or divine love. No one other than a divine, non-created being could reveal the true nature of God's love and provide the means to restore humanity.

New Testament Witness. Jesus Christ claimed omniscience, omnipotence, and omnipresence through His Spirit (Matt. 28:18, 20; John 1:1, 14; Col. 2:3; Jer. 23:34; Zech. 4:10; cf. 1 Cor. 10:4; John 8:58).[44] Words commencing with the prefix "omni" mean "all" or "everywhere." This means that, in His divinity, Christ has all knowledge (*omniscience*), and that He is all-powerful (*omnipotence*). Such a conclusion follows logically from the knowledge that Jesus was the Creator of the worlds. On this point, the apostle John is clear: "Without Him nothing was made that was made" (John 1:3). John prefaces this statement by telling us that the "Word was God," and then He goes on to identify who the "Word" is—the One who "became flesh and dwelt among us"

Chapter 3. The Mystery of "God with Us"

(John 1:1, 14). The apostle Paul is equally emphatic on this point in the epistle to the Hebrews, asserting that the Son "made the worlds" (Heb. 1:2) and that He is the "express image of" the "person" of God the Father (verse 3). As God, Christ would also have possessed *omnipresence*. Since the incarnation, He has chosen to operate through the ministry of the Holy Spirit. He told His disciples: "And I will pray the Father, and He will give you another Helper, that He may abide with you forever, *even* the Spirit of truth, whom the world cannot receive, because it neither sees Him nor knows Him; but you know Him for He dwells with you and will be in you" (John 14:16, 17). He ended with the promise: "I will not leave you orphans; I will come to you" (John 14:18). By this, He meant that *He* would come to His followers through the Person of the Holy Spirit.

Besides these, Christ possessed other divine attributes. He was not created (Mic. 5:2); He is holy by nature (Luke 1:35); He is love (1 John 3:16; 4:8, 9); He has life in Himself (John 1:4; 10:17, 18; 11:25). In case we might puzzle over the identity of "the One to be Ruler" mentioned in Micah 5:2, the apostle Matthew has interpreted the expression for us, applying it to Christ (Matt. 2:4–6). The apostle Paul confirmed the significant thought that Jesus was not created when he declared that He was "before all things" (Col. 1:17). Other Bible writers and fallen and unfallen angels as witnesses have further amplified Christ's divine attributes.

The angel who announced Jesus' birth to Mary said that the baby who would be born to her would be called "Immanuel." This means quite literally "God with us" (Matt. 1:23). The demons that Jesus cast out of a man confirmed Jesus' identity, saying, "What have we to do with You, Jesus of Nazareth? ... I know who You are—the Holy One of God!" (Mark 1:24; cf. Isa. 17:7).

The apostle John, in his much-loved Gospel, gives a discourse on love in which he identified Christ as the One who demonstrated divine *agapē* love as He lay down His life for us (see especially John 15). He later wrote in his epistle: "God is love" (1 John 4:8, 16)—indeed, He is the source of love (verse 7). Such love is beyond measure; it is spontaneous; it is God's way to humanity (John 3:16). No other quality can compare with it.

Christ's announcement that He was the source of life supports His claim to this divine attribute (cf. Gen. 1:1). His possessing the ability to create enables us to understand His claim that, if His body were destroyed, He would raise it up again in three days (John 2:19). Jesus rose by the creative power resident in Himself at the call of the Father and the quickening of the Spirit (John 10:18; Rom. 6:4; Gal. 1:1; 1 Peter 3:18). At the cross, Christ's humanity died, but not His divinity. It could not do so.

Christ accepted His disciples' addressing Him as God and their worshiping Him as God (Matt. 28:9, 17; John 20:28).[45] The apostle Paul specifically noted that name of Jesus is above all other names because of His humiliation and death for humanity. The only appropriate response for humans is that "every knee should bow" in worship (Phil. 2:10).

Old Testament Witness. Jesus' divine nature is indicated in the Old Testament where He is frequently called the "Lord." John the Baptist made this connection when he quoted from Isaiah 40:3, applying the term "Lord" to Jesus (Matt. 3:3). The apostle John provided a similar application to Jesus of other of Isaiah's pronouncements regarding the Lord (John 12:38–41). It is significant that the word translated "Lord" in Isaiah is "Yahweh" when the original language is transliterated. By making this connection, Christ is identified as the God of the Old Testament who communicated with humanity. In fact, Jesus made this very claim when He identified Himself as "I AM" (John 8:58) and then claimed oneness with God the Father (John 10:30).

We might imagine that some of the divine attributes of the Lord would have been revealed specifically through experiences leading up to and connected with the Exodus and the installation of the earthly sanctuary. The Lord's control over nature and His assumption of the title "I AM" in His encounter with Moses at the burning bush were early evidences of His divinity (Exod. 3:14). The Lord's foreknowledge, power, and creative ability were also revealed during the Exodus (see Exod. 6:1; 8:16–19; 16:2–4). On Mount Sinai, in giving the law and the instructions for the construction of the earthly sanctuary, He illustrated His knowledge, skill, and power in spectacular fashion (see Exod. 19:16; 20:18–21; 32:7–9). Then, in the sanctuary itself, He revealed the glory of His presence, judgment, and creative power (see Exod. 40:34; Lev. 10:1, 2; Num. 17:8). The New Testament writers would have been fully prepared by statements the prophet Isaiah made concerning the divinity of the Lord Jesus. Isaiah described Christ as the Maker and Redeemer and as the righteous Child (e.g., Isa. 9:6; 17:7; 40:25–28; 47:4; 54:5). Other Bible writers make similar identifications.

Christ, Truly Human

In this section, I will

- *indicate that Jesus Christ possessed the attributes of humanity, dwelt in this sinful world, and overcame where the first Adam failed.*

From our human standpoint, it is important to understand that Christ assumed human characteristics when He came to earth. He identified fully with the human race. There are many indicators of this fact. Even before Jesus' birth, a ceremony in the earthly sanctuary conveyed the truth that the Son of God would put off the exalted state He had in heaven. The high priest, who represented Christ, officiated on the Day of Atonement. His robes were magnificent (Exod. 28:3–43). However, after the ceremonies of the daily services were complete, the high priest put off his gorgeous high priestly robe and put on a white linen robe (Lev. 16:4). This foreshadowed Christ's emptying Himself of His divine attributes and identifying with humanity in the role of a servant (Phil. 2:5–9).[46] Presbyterian minister Charles Beecher succinctly expressed this thought: "As the high-priest laid aside his gorgeous pontifical robes, and officiated in the white linen dress of a common priest, so Christ emptied himself, and took the form of a servant, and offered sacrifice, himself the priest, himself the victim."[47]

The fact that Jesus was born of Mary, a human mother who conceived Jesus as a virgin through the agency of the Holy Spirit (Matt. 1:20–23; Gal. 4:4), indicates the reality of His humanity. He progressed through the stages of human development and was obedient to His parents (Luke 2:21, 42, 51). He referred to Himself as the "Son of Man," and others referred to Him as the "Man" (Matt. 8:20; Matt. 26:72, 74; John 1:30; Rom. 5:15). We note with interest that the apostle John used the term "Son of Man" in referring to Christ's care of the churches while He ministers in heaven (Rev. 1:13). His eternal identification with the human race is further indicated by the apostle Paul who declared that there is "one Mediator between God and men, *the* Man Christ Jesus" (1 Tim. 2:5). "Doubting Thomas" saw the wounds inflicted by the crucifixion in His glorious body after the resurrection (John 20:27).

Jesus demonstrated the mental and physical characteristics of humanity (see Matt. 4:2; John 4:6, 7; 19:28). In fact, there was nothing especially remarkable about Jesus' physical appearance "that we should desire Him" (Isa. 53:2). The apostles went on record to assure us that Christ experienced hunger, thirst, and weariness. Besides this, Christ showed human emotions such as grief, sorrow, compassion, and righteous anger (Matt. 9:36; Mark 3:5; John 11:35). In a final demonstration of His humanity, He suffered death, though His divinity did not perish, and neither did His body decay (John 19:30, 40; Acts 2:24, 31). Only His human life ceased at the cross.

In identifying with humanity, Jesus made an incredible sacrifice. The apostle Paul tells us that He "made Himself of no reputation" (Phil. 2:7). This means that Jesus chose not to exercise the attributes of deity (omnipotence, omniscience, and omnipresence) in His struggle against Satan while on earth. He was born of the line of David "in the likeness of sinful flesh" (Rom. 1:3; 8:3). The earthly sanctuary symbolized this truth through the provision of the veils associated with it. These, the apostle Paul informs us, represent Christ's flesh (Heb. 10:20).

The expression "in the likeness of human flesh" (Rom. 8:3) requires some explanation. We have noted already that Jesus possessed a human mother, Mary. There is no evidence in Scripture that Mary was born free from fault or that she was "immaculate." In fact, the opposite is affirmed in Scripture (Luke 1:47; Rom. 3:23; Gal. 3:22). Jesus identified Himself with the human race and took on the role of a servant (Acts 3:22; Heb. 2:11; Phil. 2:7). His divinity took on humanity that it could be said that He was like us. This is not to infer that Christ was sinful. Anglican minister Henry Melvill has encapsulated one widely recognized and helpful explanation of Christ's nature: "Christ's humanity was not the Adamic humanity, that is, the humanity of Adam before the fall; nor fallen humanity, that is, in every respect the humanity of Adam after the fall. It was not the Adamic, because it had the innocent infirmities [hunger, pain, sorrow, etc.] of the fallen. It was not the fallen because it had never descended into moral impurity. It was, therefore most literally our humanity, but without sin."[48] In the simplest terms, Jesus' moral nature was like that possessed by Adam *before* the Fall. that is, He had no sinful inclinations. His physical nature, conversely, was that of Adam *after* the Fall, having "innocent infirmities"—"hunger, pain, weakness, sorrow, and death."[49] This means, in effect, that His task was infinitely greater than that faced by the first Adam.

Jesus was made like His brethren (Heb. 2:16, 17). He did not come to minister to angels but to suffering humanity. If Jesus had failed to reach us where we are, we would have been lost without hope

(Gen. 28:12; Heb. 2:14, 15). "But Christ reaches us where we are. He took our nature and overcame, that we through taking His nature might overcome" (2 Cor. 5:21).[50] At the same time, Jesus was still truly God (John 1:1, 14; Phil. 2:6; Heb. 2:16, 17).

The Reasons Jesus Assumed Human Nature

In this section, I will

- *indicate that Jesus Christ took on human nature in order to pay the just penalty for sin and to act as an effective Mediator and Helper of sinful humanity.*

The apostle Paul is very clear about the penalty for sin: "For the wages of sin is death, but the gift of God is eternal life in Christ Jesus our Lord" (Rom. 6:23, NIV). The question may appropriately be asked whether Christ could have paid the penalty for sin or have been an effective Mediator for sinners without having taken on human nature. Perhaps the simplest response is that, as a divine individual with immortality (1 Tim. 6:15, 16), it would have been impossible for Him to suffer death in any form without taking on humanity. Jesus felt the pain and misery of the event to a much larger degree than other humans, for compounding the experience of death was the tangible sense of separation from His Father (Matt. 27:46). From our perspective, the experience of Christ's living a human existence, with human attributes, effectively convicts all honest people that He understands our difficulties and temptations (Heb. 2:18; 4:15). We all understand the benefits of experience when it comes to helping others. Although Christ's ability to know all things could have been called into operation, His having passed through the experiences, temptations, and trials of the human race ideally fit Him to be a treasured Helper and Mediator. His example to us is impeccable (Phil. 2:5; 1 Peter 2:21–24).

Just because Christ took on human nature does not imply that He or other descendants of Adam inherited part of Adam's guilt. This is made clear by the prophet Ezekiel when he said: "The son shall not bear the guilt of the father" (Ezek. 18:20). This text informs us that Adam's guilt is not imputed to us or to Christ. We do inherit desires and dispositions to sin on account of Adam's fall, and without divine help, we cannot overcome and be saved (Rom. 5:12; 8:7, 8). If we choose to sin—to work independently of God—and remain unrepentant, we will be eternally lost. The concept of choice and destiny is certain in

Scripture (Rom. 6:12, 13; James 4:17). Joseph chose not to respond to the seductive advances of Potiphar's wife (Gen. 39:9). Moses chose to suffer affliction with God's people rather "than to enjoy the passing pleasures of sin" (Heb. 11:25). Daniel chose, or "purposed," not to "defile himself with the portion of the king's delicacies" (Dan. 1:8). Jesus chose to maintain His faith connection with His Father, and He "resisted to bloodshed" (Heb. 12:4). What an example this presents for us to follow by faith! (See 1 Peter 2:21–25.) The promise comes to us that we "may be partakers of the divine nature, having escaped the corruption *that is* in the world through lust" (2 Peter 1:4).

Even though Christ was the Son of Man, He lived a sinless life on earth. The Scriptures are very emphatic on this point (2 Cor. 5:21; Heb. 4:15; 1 Peter 2:22). These texts are in absolute agreement with the message given in the sanctuary services. The lambs chosen for the morning and evening sacrifice at the sanctuary were to be without spot or blemish (Num. 28:3, 4). These symbolized Christ who also was without blemish. The shed blood of the perfect lamb represented Christ's death for us. The Scriptures declare that the "blood of Jesus Christ His Son cleanses us from all sin" (1 John 1:7). Satan's intense efforts to lead Christ to yield to temptation were ineffective (John 14:30). It is significant to note that temptation is not sin. At critical points throughout the life of Christ, the Father declared that He was well pleased with Christ's example in word and deed. These affirmations occurred after His baptism (Matt. 3:16, 17; Mark 1:11; Luke 3:22), on the mount of transfiguration (Matt. 17:1–5; Mark 9:7; Luke 9:35), as He was facing death (John 12:27, 28), and after He returned to heaven (John 14:26; cf. Acts 2:1–4; Eph. 1:6).

Jesus was born of the Holy Spirit (Luke 1:35), and He continually relied on His Father's power (John 5:30). His life here on earth was sinless. Through Christ's life, God showed that the principles of His government are just and reasonable and that Satan's claims about Him are false (John 8:44). He also showed by Christ's life that He is able to empower all to live by the principles of His kingdom. The concept that Jesus "was in all *points* tempted as *we are, yet* without sin" (Heb. 4:15; cf. 1 Cor. 10:13) implies that God is able to offer salvation to those who establish a relationship with Him in faith. This concept was taught through the sanctuary services. God wishes us to die to self and sin and to live a new life of faith in which we can continually walk according to His will (Ezek. 36:26, 27).

We are redeemed through Jesus' blood (Rev. 5:9). In other words, we are redeemed not only because Christ forgives us our sins when we confess and forsake them, but we are delivered from the power of sin through the strength that we may daily gain from Christ. Victory over sin is assured through Christ. The individual claims no part except to show a deep willingness and commitment to follow Jesus.

Symbols of Christ's Dual Nature

In this section, I will

- *indicate that the concept of Jesus Christ's dual nature was represented in symbolic form in the Old Testament and in the sanctuary;*

- *establish that Christ's example of living on earth as the God-man enabled Him to reconcile the believer to God.*

The question over the nature of Christ has stirred the Christian church for millennia, and it will no doubt continue to do so. From the beginning, the Scriptures have provided sensible answers. Two symbols used in the Old Testament can reasonably be interpreted to indicate that Christ would take on human nature when He came to earth. The first involves the vision of the ladder stretching from heaven to earth, which Jacob saw when fleeing from his brother (Gen. 28:12). A second involves the cherubim overshadowing the mercy seat in the Most Holy Place. They are represented as having four faces, including the face of a man (Rev. 4:7).

Jacob's vision of a ladder stretching from heaven to earth represented Christ's reaching down to perishing humanity. With one hand He grasps the throne of God and with the other the human race—"Christ connects man in his weakness and helplessness with the source of infinite power."[51] Christ explained this vision to Nathanael in the words, "… hereafter you shall see heaven open, and the angels of God ascending and descending upon the Son of Man" (John 1:51). The angels are protectors and communicators of Christ's will to the human race. The same symbolism of angels is used in Revelation 14, where three angels are pictured as cooperating with God's servants to herald His soon coming and impart power to God's servants for witnessing.

There are no explicit descriptions in Scripture of the faces of the cherubim for either the sanctuary built by Moses or by Solomon. The description John gave in the book of Revelation is the only indication we have of the cherubim's nature. The four faces of the cherubim presented in Revelation are thought to represent the four divisions of the tribes of Israel that camped about the sanctuary, each with its own standard, or ensign (Num. 2:2). The symbols used on the ensigns of Israel were a lion, a man, an eagle, and an ox. In these symbols, the characteristics of Christ may be seen. The Lion of the tribe of Judah (Rev. 5:5) and the Son of Man (Rev. 1:13; 14:14) are apt illustrations of the dual nature of Christ while on earth, as are the King of Israel (John 19:14) and the Sacrificial Servant (John 13:3–8), which are well represented by eagle and the ox.[52]

Only in taking humanity could God demonstrate that the requirement that He placed on Adam and Eve when their moral nature had not been compromised, was not unreasonable (cf. 2 Peter 1:1–4). The instruction that He gave them was based on the law of love and, specifically, on its first provision to honor and obey Him (Matt. 22:37, 38). Through Christ's victory, it is possible for humanity to "be partakers of the divine nature" by exercising faith in Christ's enabling power and escape the "corruption *that is* in the world" (2 Peter 1:4). Furthermore, the Christian life is one of growth, fruitfulness, and attractiveness (verses 5–8). The apostle is at pains to tell readers that, if the believer utilizes the enabling power of the Son of God, then "Jesus Christ will give you a glorious welcome into his kingdom that will last forever" (2 Peter 1:11, CEV).

Chapter 4.
Symbols of Restoration

Chapter Emphasis: *The necessity of a faith experience in Christ's role as the sacrifice is foundational to understanding the ceremonies in the sanctuary. The activities of the sanctuary have continuing significance in helping us understand God's plan of salvation. After Christ's resurrection, He commenced mediatorial activities in the first apartment of the heavenly sanctuary in order to fulfill the undertakings of the new covenant promises. Finally, at the time specified, Christ commenced His second-apartment ministry, which involves a judicial role. Both roles are essential to bring the plan of salvation to a just conclusion.*

Spiritual Link: *Christ's intercessory ministry is remembered in the Communion service.*

The priests who officiated in the earthly sanctuary were instructed were instructed regarding the ceremonial particulars through Moses. They knew the procedures that God had stipulated for the rites of the sanctuary—rites that had no merit in themselves, but rather pointed forward to the life, death, and ultimate victory of the Lord Jesus Christ over sin and Satan. Their meticulous attention to "performing the divine worship" (Heb. 9:6, NASB), according to the details revealed on the mount, was of utmost significance as each part of the service conveyed deep meanings concerning the character of God and the great plan of redemption.

Each individual born into this world is invited to respond to God's offer of salvation and, in like manner, to enter His service. Relatively few respond wholeheartedly to this call. Many have an unusual relationship with God in that they wish to respond to His invitation in their own will and ways and not according to His stipulations. Of such, Jesus said while on earth, *"And in vain they worship Me, teaching as doctrines the commandments of men"* (Matt. 15:9).

In this chapter, I will briefly examine the services in the earthly sanctuary and the deep meaning for the faith journey of believers. Then I will focus on Jesus' ministry today in the heavenly sanctuary in light of the pattern revealed to us.

Apartment Ministry—Following Christ by Faith

In this section, I will

- *briefly outline the principal activities of the priests in the apartments of the earthly sanctuary.*

The daily services of the sanctuary were inextricably associated with the Holy Place. The second apartment, or Most Holy Place, was entered but once a year, and it was only the high priest who was permitted to enter this apartment. The regular priests could only minister daily in the Holy Place.

Daily Services. There were a number of significant duties the priests performed daily in the Holy Place. The most common of these was performed when worshipers fell short of God's standard in ignorance. Though they had not premeditated committing the unwholesome act, the worshipers learned, subsequent to committing the act, that they had failed to meet God's requirements. It was then that they brought an animal without blemish as a sacrifice. This offering was termed a "sin offering." The priest commonly entered the Holy Place to minister the blood before God, or, alternately, to eat a portion of the flesh of the sacrifice in the court of the sanctuary (Lev. 4:2–7, 13–18; 6:25, 26; 10:17).

The ceremony associated with the sin offering involved the sinner entering through the outermost veil of the outer court at the priest's invitation, confessing his sin over the head of the animal and then slaying it. This represented an act of faith in the sacrifice of the coming Savior, who was represented by the perfect animal. It was a fitting representation that justification had taken place. The sinner was declared to be without guilt. The priest, representing Christ, now entered through the veil into the Holy Place and sprinkled some of the blood before the inner veil of the sanctuary, which separated the Holy Place and the Most Holy Place, and placed some of the blood on the horns of the altar of sweet incense (Lev. 4:6, 7, 17, 18; cf. Lev. 4:27–30). The suppliant could conceptualize the significance of these acts by considering the items of furniture in the Holy Place and the commitment required of the repentant sinner in following Christ by faith in sanctification. The steps in this journey of faith recognize Christ's intercessory ministry by forming a relationship with Him through prayer, represented by the altar of incense, walking in the light, represented by the candlestick, and treasuring and studying God's revealed will, represented by the bread on the table of shewbread.[53]

On other occasions, the priest ate a portion of the flesh of the sacrifice in a holy place (Lev. 10:17). Eating a portion of the flesh symbolized the priest's identifying fully with the sinner. Moses was, on one occasion, upset with Aaron's sons when they did not follow God's directions to eat the flesh of the sin offering in making atonement. Neglecting this part of the service meant that they had failed to make mediatorial atonement for sin (Lev. 10:16–20). They failed to point the believer to a central aspect of Christ's ministry in the plan of salvation.

We note that the sinner was justified immediately after the animal's life was taken. In the act of applying the animal's blood, sin was symbolically transferred from the sinner to the sanctuary. Sins confessed were now in God's care. The sinner was assured of salvation. Through the ministration of the priest in the Holy Place, the repentant one would have seen the fulfillment of Jesus' instructions: "… unless you eat the flesh of the Son of Man and drink His blood, you have no life in you" (John 6:53). In performing these services with their whole mind, the priests identified fully with Christ.

The priests officiated in other offerings besides the sin offering mentioned above. In fact, there were many burnt, sin, trespass, and peace offerings specified. Of these, the daily, or continual, morning and evening burnt offering is especially worthy of mention (Exod. 29:38–42; Num. 28:3–8). This offering involved the sacrifice of a year-old lamb each morning and evening on the altar of burnt offering in the courtyard of the sanctuary. The offering was not made for a particular individual, but for all the people of Israel. The shedding of the blood of the animals pointed to the Lamb of God whose death on Calvary would be a sacrifice for all and would be "continually" effective (Heb. 10:12, 14). The atonement purchased by the shedding of Christ's blood was a fully adequate sacrifice.

The Once-Yearly Service. The high priest performed a cleansing service once a year that involved the people, the priests, and the sanctuary. The ceremony could be performed only by the high priest, for only he could perform the necessary rites in the Most Holy Place. The ceremony functioned to remove the burden of confessed sins from the sanctuary in a ceremony of cleansing (Lev. 16:2, 17, 29–34). It involved atonement, which means putting things right. Symbolically, the record of confessed sins held in the sanctuary was taken from the sanctuary, and the responsibility for causing the people to sin was put back upon its original source, the angel adversary of God, symbolized by "Azazel," the scapegoat.[54] Every account had been settled during the services leading up to this day. Hence, at the close of the Day of Atonement, the congregation of believers was at peace with God.

Besides these features, the concept of glorification was highlighted in the Most Holy Place. Aaron's rod held in the ark of the covenant pointed forward to the resurrection, the law of codified love held within it foreshadowed the entrance into an abiding relationship with Christ, and the mercy seat assured worshipers of the promise of being able to sit on Christ's throne with Him. The manna pointed forward to the continuing journey of faith sustained by the ministry of the Holy Spirit.[55] The ceremonies of the Day of Atonement were forward-looking as they prepared worshipers for the Feast of Tabernacles, a time of rejoicing that came shortly after the Day of Atonement (Lev. 23:27, 34).

Holy Place Symbols

In this section, I will

- *establish the identity of the items of furniture located in the first apartment of the earthly sanctuary;*
- *highlight the aspects of salvation pointed out by these items of furniture.*

Chapter 4. Symbols of Restoration

Much has been written about the symbolism of the sanctuary furnishings, furniture, and ceremonies. I wish to highlight understandings of the more obvious aspects of God's ministry indicated by the items contained in it.

Furniture, Contents, and Meaning. The various items of furniture in the Holy Place, as those elsewhere in the sanctuary, conveyed important truths through symbolism. First, on the right-hand side of the room stood the table of shewbread bearing the twelve loaves of unleavened bread (Lev. 24:5–9). The term "table of shewbread" meant the "table of the bread of the Presence" (Num. 4:7).[56] The bread was unleavened, as leavening is a symbol of sin in the Bible (Matt. 16:6; 1 Cor. 5:6, 7). The unleavened bread represented the life of Christ untainted by sin (1 Cor. 5:18; Heb. 4:15; 1 Peter 2:22; 1 John 3:5). This is the meaning of the term "bread of life," which is applied to Christ (John 6:35, 48).

In the sanctuary, there were twelve loaves of bread, one for each tribe, thus signifying that God had made ample provision for everyone to gain salvation. The bread also signified that the people of the tribes were dependent on Christ to supply not only their physical needs but also their spiritual ones. The needs of believers can be satisfied today through prayer and the study of God's Word. The shewbread was kept continually before the Lord. These loaves were changed once a week (Lev. 24:5–8). The "bread of the Presence" was made of fine flour (Lev. 24:5). To produce the flour, the grain was ground between millstones. For Jesus to qualify as the eternal source of sustenance, the Bible portrays Him as "bruised" and "wounded" for us (Isa. 53:5, 10) just as grain must be "bruised" by grinding to produce flour and as loaves of bread must be broken to enable their consumption.

On the left, or south, side of the Holy Place stood the seven-branched candlestick (Exod. 25:31–39). It consisted of a central pillar with three branches on each side. Each branch ended in a head (Zech. 4:2), all reaching the same height. This article was made of solid gold and contained decorations consisting of almonds and flowers. Josephus records that there were seventy decorations on the candlesticks.[57] The light of the candlesticks was to be kept continually burning through the provision of olive oil, a symbol of the ministry of the Holy Spirit (Exod. 27:20, 21; Lev. 24:2; Zech. 4:2–6). This was partly to enable the priests to see clearly in the windowless building, it was also to point forward to Christ, "the light of the world" (John 8:12; 9:5).

Light is used consistently in the Scriptures as a symbol of purity and righteousness. The good news of salvation through the knowledge that Jesus brings is termed the "light of the gospel" (2 Cor. 4:4). The Word of God is itself termed a "light" (Ps. 119:105; Prov. 6:23) as it gives instruction to lead all who choose eternal life. Hence, it is evident that light, in a primary sense, pointed to Christ. In a secondary sense, it pointed to God's Word, the Bible, which directs us to Christ. The light also taught the priests and worshipers that God wished them to share the good news of salvation with others. Jesus instructed His disciples: "Let your light so shine before men, that they may see your good works and glorify your Father in heaven" (Matt. 5:16).

Closer attention to the details regarding the candlesticks reveals other fascinating points. The priests' garments consisted of fine, white linen. The wicks placed in the lamps were made from the used articles of clothing of the priests (Sukkah 5:3).[58] The fine linen represents none other than the righteousness of Christ. Such a garment the Lord offers to give all in order to qualify them to enter heaven (Matt. 22:11–13). In Zechariah 3, Joshua, the high priest, is portrayed as standing before the Lord. His own righteousness was as filthy rags. Yet, Jesus exchanged Joshua's garments for ones that were glorious (Zech. 3:1–5). The prophet John portrays all who are fit for heaven as wearing the robe of Christ's righteousness, which is obtained only through faith (Rev. 6:11; 7:9, 14).

The remaining item of furniture in the Holy Place was the golden altar of incense (Exod. 30:1–10). This altar was located nearest the ark. The priests carried glowing embers from the altar of burnt offering in a golden censer, placing them on the altar of incense and sprinkling incense on top. This they did every morning and evening. The altar of incense and the altar of burnt offering had the coordinated aspects of both having horns at the corners (Exod. 27:2; 30:3), which symbolically denoted power (Dan. 8:7; Hab. 3:4; Zech. 1:18, 19). This meant that the altar of burnt offering represented the place where *perpetual atonement* was available (Neh. 10:33), while the altar of incense was the place where *perpetual help* through intercessory prayer was available (Ps. 141:2; Rev. 5:8). In symbolism, God thereby indicated that deliverance from the penalty and power of sin was available as the sinner approached Him through faith. The priests went into the first apartment every morning and evening to tend the lamps and to offer incense on the altar before the innermost veil (Exod. 30:7, 8).

The incense was offered at the time of the morning and evening sacrifices and fittingly represented the merits of Christ ascending with the prayers of the people (Ps. 141:2; Rev. 8:3). Our prayers are presented to God by the Holy Spirit (Rom. 8:26).

Other Symbolic Applications. There were two veils associated with the Holy Place. One separated it from the outer court and the other from the Most Holy Place. Both represented the flesh of Christ (Heb. 10:20). When Christ died on Calvary, the inner veil of the earthly temple was rent in two, signifying that a "new and living way" was then available for the sinner to approach God. There was no need to wait for an earthly priest to represent the sinner to God. The sinner could appeal in prayer directly to God through Jesus for mercy, forgiveness, and power to effect change in the life.

We have considered already the meaning of light, but what about the burning lamps that produced it? Revelation 4:5 uses a burning lamp symbolically to represent the Holy Spirit. In this verse, John used the phrase "seven Spirits of God." The number seven is regarded as God's perfect number, and it is frequently used in Scripture. Thus, the expression symbolizes the perfection and completeness of the Holy Spirit. Elsewhere in the book of Revelation, the Holy Spirit is referred to as the "seven eyes" of the Lamb (Rev. 5:6). In a vision recorded in Zechariah, the prophet saw a golden candlestick fed with oil via pipes from two olive trees. In answer to the prophet's question, "What *are* these, my lord?" the answer came, "Not by might, nor by power, but by My Spirit" (Zech. 4:4, 6). The burning lamp fed by the oil represents the Holy Spirit. This explains why the Holy Spirit appeared as tongues of fire when He was poured out upon the believers in Pentecostal power (Acts 2:3, 4).

The ministry of the Holy Spirit in the life is possible only as we study and respond to God's Word (John 16:13; 17:17; Acts 5:32). Jesus taught in the parable of the ten virgins that a cosmetic type of Christian living leaves participants totally unprepared for the trials of this life as well as making them unsuitable as candidates for heaven (Matt. 25:1–13). The vital proposition the vision of the candlesticks puts forth is that, without practical faith that works a reformation in the life, the Christian's journey is one of pretense without light.

Enduring Reminders of Christ's Sacrifice

In this section, I will

- indicate that the Communion service instituted by Christ on the eve of His crucifixion keeps alive the memories of the Passover ceremony that are so vital in drawing from the religious services associated with the earthly sanctuary and temple.

In the closing hours of Christ's life here on earth, He instituted the Lord's Supper to teach deep spiritual lessons. Breaking bread and taking a cup of grape juice, He instituted the Lord's Supper (Matt. 26:26–29; 1 Cor. 11:23–26). In doing this, He wove a pattern of consistent meaning into various ceremonies of the Old Testament, including those of the sanctuary and temple, and provided a link to His teachings contained in the New Testament. This means that the sanctuary services will always convey relevant meaning to Christians until the end of time.

The Lord's Supper primarily replaced the Passover, but it contained parallels to the sacrifices in the sanctuary services and even to the sacrifices instituted immediately after the Fall. In this Supper, bread and the juice of the vine were consumed. The bread represented the broken body of Christ and His "continual" involvement in the experiences of the human race. The Scriptures speak of Christ's being given for the "life of the world" (John 6:51). The apostle Paul informs us that He "ever lives to make intercession" (Heb. 7:25). His sacrifice was all-sufficient and points to the only way to eternal life (Acts 4:12).

The Passover cup and the drink offerings of wine used in the earthly sanctuary were represented in the newly instituted Lord's Supper as "the new covenant in My blood" (1 Cor. 11:25). The wine used was the pure juice of the grape for the same reason that the bread used was unleavened, with no yeast to represent the corruption of sin. The juice of the grape represented the blood of Jesus, shed to ratify, or "confirm," the everlasting covenant (Dan. 9:27). (See Chapter 1, "Covenant, Salvation, and Sanctuary.")

In the sanctuary service, symbols representing bread and wine were similarly used. Fine flour mixed with olive oil in the grain offering and the wine of the drink offering were offered in association with burnt offerings and peace offerings. The bread and oil and the wine were offered together (Num. 15:4–10). The grain offering, made of flour and oil, acknowledged the dependence of the suppliant on God for both temporal and spiritual blessings. Since the offering was produced through bruising and crushing, the flour and oil and the wine are fitting symbols of the life and death of Jesus on our behalf. It is significant to note that the word for drink offering comes from the Hebrew root word *nacak*, which means "to pour out," thus signifying that Christ "poured out" His life for the salvation of sinners. Jesus referred to Himself as "the true vine" (John 15:1). He is the true source of the pure juice of the vine.

In eating the bread and drinking the grape juice of the Lord's Supper, the believer is revived physically. Yet, the symbolism of the assimilation of the bread and juice also represents the changes that take place spiritually when the Word of God is accepted and acted on from conviction. The ceremony signifies dependence on the merits of Christ and the energizing presence of the Holy Spirit.

Christ in the Heavenly Sanctuary

In this section, I will

- *emphasize that the heavenly sanctuary was anointed after Christ ascended to heaven;*

- *indicate that He had a ministry to perform in heaven involving both mediation and judgment.*

The earthly sanctuary gives us valuable insights into the plan of salvation right down to the end of time when Christ will stand up as He finishes His ministration on humanity's behalf (see Dan. 12:1). After Christ suffered, died, and was resurrected, He became a high priest after the order of Melchizedek (Heb. 2:17; 5:8–10). In order to qualify as a high priest, Jesus needed to be "taken from among men" (Heb. 5:1). He needed to share the infirmities of humanity to be the captain and author of our salvation (Heb. 2:9, 10; 5:9). Because He took on human nature, He is able to help weak, suffering humanity in the hour of temptation.

Anointing the Heavenly Sanctuary. When the original earthly sanctuary had been completed, it and the items in it were anointed (Exod. 30:26–30; 40:9–11; Lev. 8:10, 11, 30–33). After this dedicatory service was carried out for the earthly sanctuary, the priests began their ministration in the Holy Place, or first apartment of the sanctuary (Lev. 9:1–7, 23). In like fashion, Christ participated in an anointing service when He returned to heaven after His crucifixion

(Dan. 9:24; Heb. 9:11, 12). In Daniel 9:24, the prophet Daniel informs us that, within the time period allocated to the Jewish nation, Christ would die and rise triumphant, and the heavenly sanctuary would be anointed. Indeed, the inauguration and exaltation of Christ in heaven were associated with the outpouring of the Holy Spirit on the earth at Pentecost (Acts 2:33, cf. Lev. 9:23, 24). After this outpouring, Christ commenced the first phase of His ministry in heaven.[59]

Ministering in the Heavenly Sanctuary. Following His crucifixion and ascension, Christ is sometimes pictured in Scripture as sitting on—or at—the right hand of God's throne (Heb. 1:3; 8:1; 12:1, 2). Some have argued that God's throne must always be in the Most Holy Place and that this implies that Jesus commenced ministering in the Most Holy Place in AD 31. This is a flawed argument if we consider the facts below:

> a. The verb *kathizō*, translated "sat down," signifies "a *solemn, formal* act; the assumption of a position of dignity and authority."[60] The verb can also be rendered "set up," "appoint," or "establish" (see Matt. 4:16, Luke 14:28; 2 Thess. 2:4).[61] The right hand "is used as a symbol of might and power."[62] The term for "right hand," *dexios*, can also be used metaphorically to mean "ready."[63] Hence, the phrase, "sat down on the right hand," may primarily be an expression of the readiness and right of Christ, through His sacrifice for sin, to assume the position as Mediator on humanity's behalf before God (Matt. 26:64; Heb. 9:15).[64] The primary purpose of the expression is to define His relationship and not His location. The term "right hand" is used in Matthew 20:20–22 to convey such a concept. The mother of John and James wanted Christ to place one son on the right hand and the other on the left so that no one could interfere with their close relationship with the Master. Christ, after His resurrection, was exalted to the dignified position next to the Father "by the right hand of God" (Acts 2:33, KJV; cf. Acts 5:31). The purpose of Christ's being invited into counsel with the Father is clearly presented in Scripture is that He might serve as a priest after the order of Melchizedek (Ps. 110:1, 4; cf. Zech. 6:13).
>
> b. The Scriptures give us a picture of unbroken intimacy between the Father and the Son during Christ's sojourn on

the earth (John 8:29; 14:11, 20; 17:11, 21). This intimacy is expressed in many ways, of which the following is perhaps the most succinct: "I and *My* Father are one" (John 10:30). Their oneness continued in heaven as the Father accepted Christ's sacrifice as all-sufficient and complete (Heb. 7:25, 27). Through His bruised and broken flesh, which was represented by the veil, Christ has provided effective and unhindered access to God (Heb. 10:20). The unbroken intimacy between the Father and the Son is expressed in the epistle to the Hebrews in terms of His being seated at the right hand of God.

c. The Bible does not portray God's glory as being only associated with the Most Holy Place (see Ezek. 1:26–28; 10:4, 18, 19; 11:22, 23). Hence, it is evident that the Bible does not limit God to just one location. Again, it must be remembered that, while the Scriptures often picture Christ as seated on a throne in the heavenly sanctuary (Heb. 8:1; 12:2), He is also pictured in one passage as "standing at the right hand of God" (Acts 7:55, 56). The Scriptures also record Jesus' conversing with Saul on the Damascus road (Acts 9:3–5; 22:6–8, 14; 26:14–18). He has also assured His followers that there are mansions in His Father's house and that He was going to prepare a place for them during this time that He is ministering in the heavenly sanctuary (John 14:2, 3). This would indicate that He is engaged in other activities that do not require sitting.

Knowing what Christ has been doing, it is not logical to assert that, in entering heaven in AD 31, Christ entered the Most Holy Place and remained there. He has had several functions—both mediatorial and judicial—as high priest in the heavenly sanctuary.

Mediatorial Role in the Heavenly Sanctuary

In this section, I will

- *indicate that sections of the New Testament depend for their understanding on an appreciation of the symbolism and activities carried out in the earthly sanctuary;*

- *highlight the concept that Christ commenced a mediatorial ministry in the Holy Place of the heavenly sanctuary after His resurrection.*

From the pattern of activity carried out in the earthly sanctuary, it would be expected that Christ's ministry upon His first entering heaven would involve intercession (Lev. 4:2–6; 16:2). Indeed, Jesus is shown, after His resurrection, as ministering to the churches. The symbolism of what John saw in vision pictures Him as walking in the "midst of the seven golden lampstands" (Rev. 1:13; 2:1).

It is significant that John the Revelator, writing in the last decade of the first century, portrayed Christ as caring for true believers through imagery associated with the Holy Place. Christ's ministry there involves the sprinkling of His blood on behalf of believers (1 Peter 1:2). Again, in Revelation 8:3, 4, an angel is portrayed as using a golden censer to offer incense with the prayers of the saints. Here again is portrayed powerful aspects of Jesus' mediatorial ministry (Lev. 16:12, 13; Num. 16:46). Through Christ's ministry, "His work of justification and sanctification is constantly made available to those who by faith have accepted His death."[65]

Several times the epistle to the Hebrews states, without attempting to precisely indicate the exact location, that Christ entered into the heavens (Heb. 4:14; 8:1, 2). These verses indicate the reality and necessity of Christ's ministry in heaven for us. In other places in Hebrews, Paul uses the term "holies" (derived from the plural *ta hagia*) to convey the same idea. While some translations render this Greek substantive as "most holy place," the term itself provides no such distinction. It is actually an adjective that means "separate, set apart, holy."[66] Bearing this in mind, Hebrews 9:12 reads: "Nor with the blood of goats and calves, but through His own blood, He entered once for all into the Holies, having procured everlasting redemption."[67] When the apostle Paul wished to refer unequivocally to the Most Holy Place, he used the Greek expression *hagia hagiōn*, which means "holy of holies" (Heb. 9:3, NASB). (See Table 1.3 in Chapter 1.)

Taking the earthly sanctuary as a pattern, in which the yearly cycle of activities commenced with intercession and ended with judgment, we should logically expect parallels in the heavenly sanctuary. Indeed, the prophetic Word assures us that the "daily" of the "holy place" ministry in heaven is the concept that was to be taken away by the "little horn" power, which dominated politically for 1260 years from AD 538 to AD 1798 (Dan. 8:9–11). With this in mind, let us not join God's enemies in denying the great and significant truth of the first phase of Christ's heavenly ministry.

Chapter 4. Symbols of Restoration

Focusing first on Christ's initial role in heaven, we see that He made the benefits of His sacrifice available to all believing and praying saints. The Scriptures inform us that Christ is "now to appear in the presence of God for us" (Heb. 9:24). Christ is the Mediator, providing the connecting link between the Father and the believer (1 Tim. 2:5).

Christ's Holy Place ministry represents what might be termed mediatorial atonement for believers by virtue of His all-sufficient sacrificial atonement for sin (Heb. 4:14–16). The Scriptures picture Jesus as directing the church (Rev. 1:12–20), sending forth the Holy Spirit (John 16:7), marshaling the forces of righteousness in the controversy with Satan (Rev. 19:11–16), and upholding the universe (Heb. 1:3). This is no passive, unimportant ministry.[68]

Today, Jesus gives repentance and forgiveness of sins (Acts 5:31) so that the believer can be restored to unhindered fellowship with God. Our Lord wishes us to accept the power that He can give to enable us to live victorious lives for our sanctification (Rom. 8:11; 2 Cor. 7:1; Heb. 6:1). Both the death and the ministry of Christ are important to the plan of salvation. The incense of Revelation 8, verses 3 and 4, represents the merits of Christ ascending on the believers' behalf. It is important to notice that the morning and evening sacrifices were offered every day and that the incense was burnt continually—even on the Day of Atonement. It is only on account of the merits of His continual ministry that the believer is accepted. Christ assures us that He will continue to offer guidance to His church through the Holy Spirit whom He promised to send "from the Father" (John 15:26). It is important that we do not forget the lessons taught in the earthly sanctuary.

The Final Mediation of the Final Atonement

In this section, I will

- *highlight the concept that Christ has a final judicial ministry to perform in the Most Holy Place of the heavenly sanctuary before His second coming.*

The terms "sanctuary" and "true tabernacle" include both the Holy Place and the Most Holy Place. Christ can hardly be a minister of the heavenly—or true—sanctuary and yet carry out the functions symbolized in only one apartment of the earthly sanctuary. The apostle Paul assures us that the earthly sanctuary was a copy of the true tabernacle in heaven (Heb. 9:24). It most assuredly follows, then, that the ministry of Christ in heaven was foreshadowed by the pattern of activities undertaken in the earthly sanctuary (Heb. 9:18–23). This activity commenced with the anointing of the sanctuary, which was followed by a round of activities in the Holy Place involving intercession. Once a year, on the Day of Atonement—a day of judgment—the high priest ministered in the Most Holy Place. In Revelation 14:7, the prophet introduces Christ in His second apartment ministry in the heavenly sanctuary. Indeed, we notice that, "when Christ entered the holy of holies to perform the closing work of the atonement, He ceased His ministration in the first apartment. But when the ministration in the first apartment ended, the ministration in the second apartment began. When in the typical service the high priest left the holy on the Day of Atonement, he went in before God to present the blood of the sin offering in behalf of all Israel who truly repented of their sins. So Christ had only completed one part of His work as our intercessor, to enter into another portion of the work, and He still pleaded His blood before the Father on behalf of sinners."[69]

Annual Feasts and the Great Controversy. The arrangement of the ceremonies, which were specified in the religious calendar of the Israelites and carried out in association with the earthly sanctuary, confirms for us that the second phase of Christ's ministry involves judicial activity before His second coming.

The seven annual feasts with their ceremonies in the ancient Israelite calendar were specified by the Lord. The entire system of worship, including the feasts and ceremonies, dealt with the plan of salvation and with the sequence of events that we might expect to observe historically. The first three feasts—Passover, Unleavened Bread, and Firstfruits, or Harvest (Lev. 23:1–14)—pointed to Christ's death (John 18:28; 19:14; 1 Cor. 5:7), burial (Matt. 27:59, 60), and resurrection (1 Cor. 15:20; Rom. 8:29; cf. Matt. 27:52, 53). The Feast of Weeks, or Harvest, fifty days later (Lev. 23:15–21), pointed to the outpouring of the Holy Spirit on Pentecost (Acts 2:1–4). The remainder of the feasts were as far separated from the initial four as possible. This second group of ceremonies commenced in the seventh month (Lev. 23:24) and involved (a) the memorial of the blowing of Trumpets, (b) the Day of Atonement, and (c) the Feast of Tabernacles, or Ingathering (Lev. 23:26–43). These latter feasts pointed (a) to the spiritual awakening preparatory to the antitypical day of atonement,

(b) to the heavenly day of atonement itself, which commenced in 1844 (see Dan. 7:9, 10; Joel 2:1; Rev. 14:6, 7), and (c) to the coming of the Lord in glory (1 Thess. 4:15–18; cf. Mark 14:25). The last appointment for all adult males of Israel, the Feast of Tabernacles, commemorated deliverance from Egypt and God's salvation (cf. Ps. 113–118). It involved a period of great rejoicing and came only a few days after the Day of Atonement (Lev. 23:34–43). Today we are in the antitypical day of atonement. Deliverance from the bondage of sin in this world is close at hand. Christ will come quickly after the pre-advent judgment of the antitypical day of atonement has ceased (Dan. 12:1; Rev. 22:11, 12). (The timing of the end-time sanctuary message relating to the Day of Atonement will be the subject of Chapter 19.)

Judicial Atonement. As we have indicated already, for the great controversy to be brought to a close and the universe to be returned to its perfect state, judgment must take place and sin and sinners must be removed. This represents the final phase of Christ's ministry (Lev. 16:18–20; Heb. 9:7, 13, 14).

The Most Holy Place contained just one item of furniture—the ark of the covenant, or the ark of the testimony. This was a rectangular box covered in beaten gold with a "mercy seat" (Hebrew *kappōret*, or "covering") on top. The mercy seat was overshadowed by two golden angels. Housed inside the ark was the Decalogue together with a pot of manna and Aaron's rod that had budded (Exod. 16:33, 34; 25:10–22; Heb. 9:4). The standard of justice was represented by the tables of the law. This means that any activity in this apartment of the sanctuary involved judgment. Significantly, mercy and justice were represented there as being totally compatible. In fact, they are inseparable, as both represent fundamental aspects of God's character (Ps. 89:14).

In the second phase of His ministry, Christ undertakes judicial atonement. This involves presenting the merits of His spilled blood before the Father "for all those for whom mercy still lingers, and for those who have ignorantly broken the law of God. This atonement is made for the righteous dead as well as for the righteous living."[70] Mercy must satisfy the just demands of the law. The whole plan of salvation and the stability of God's government are bound up in atonement. At the cross, both mercy and justice were satisfied (Ps. 85:10; note that the word *tsedeq*, translated "righteousness," can also be translated "justice"). Now is the time for God to seal all those who have accepted this accomplishment.

The Fulfillment of the Everlasting Covenant Promises

In this section, I will

- *emphasize the idea that there has always been only one plan of salvation;*
- *highlight the concept that the new covenant was instituted after the shedding of Christ's blood in sacrificial atonement.*

The primary meaning of the term "covenant" used in Scripture has to do with the agreement made between God and the believer concerning sin and the plan of salvation. (See Table 1.1 in Chapter 1.) The term "everlasting covenant" (cf. Gen. 9:16; Heb. 13:20) establishes firmly in the reader's mind that God has always had only one saving covenant. This covenant was first introduced in Eden (Gen. 3:15).

The everlasting covenant, which is a covenant of grace planned by God before sin entered the world (1 Peter 1:19–20), deals specifically with the details of the plan of redemption and the response of the believer. This covenant, or testament, is known generally as the "new covenant" in the New Testament because of what Jesus fulfilled in paying the penalty for sin. Now He administers the new covenant's operation in heaven (Heb. 9:15; 12:24; 13:20). The principles of righteousness that form the basis for the covenant of God's kingdom are outlined succinctly in the Ten Commandments. The psalmist has noted: "Concerning Your testimonies, I have known of old that You have founded them forever" (Ps. 119:152). Indeed, the apostle John on Patmos reaffirmed this thought when he noted the presence of the ark of the testament in heaven (Rev. 11:19; cf. Exod. 34:28, 29). This establishes the idea that the principles of God's government remain unchanged from eternity to eternity (Mal. 3:6).

The apostle Paul reminds readers that after the new revelation of the covenant made possible by Jesus' death, nothing could be altered (Gal. 3:15–17). This means that neither the goals of the relationship of the believer with God, described in the Decalogue (Matt. 22:36–40; Heb. 8:10–12; 10:16, 17), nor the sign of the relationship—the seventh-day Sabbath (Exod. 31:16)—were changed. It is no wonder, then, that the law of the Lord is proclaimed "perfect" in the New Testament (James 1:25; cf. Ps. 19:7; called "holy" in Rom. 7:12). It is our relationship to the Giver of the law that is vital. "We establish the law" through faith (Rom. 3:31). Thank God that the conditions of salvation are what they have always been—righteousness by faith in Jesus' merits, which is evidenced by our obedience (Rev. 14:12; cf. 1 John 5:4). The everlasting covenant promises are ours as we follow Christ's ministry in the heavenly sanctuary by faith.

Chapter 5.
Christ's Three-fold Ministry

Chapter Emphasis: *The successive ministry of Christ as a prophet on earth and then as a priest in the heavenly sanctuary before He returns to earth as a king is necessary for the salvation of humankind. Today, Jesus continues His high priestly ministry in heaven. When it is finalized, He will come the second time to receive the citizens of His kingdom of grace into His kingdom of glory.*

Spiritual Link: *The members of God's kingdom of grace come from all nations including Israel. His kingdom of glory will not be established on this contaminated planet.*

We often think of Jesus as the coming King. The majestic scenes of His coming are graphically described in the Bible. The hope of all Christian people since Christ's first coming has been focused on the return of the Son of Man in glory to bring an end to the reign of sin. The Bible, however, describes three roles for Christ, the Messiah. First, He came to this earth as a *prophet*. This fitted Him to act as our *high priest*. When His high priestly ministry is completed in the sanctuary in heaven, He will have made up the subjects of His kingdom and can then come as a glorious *king*.

Chapter 5. Christ's Three-fold Ministry

In this chapter, I wish to examine, in some detail, aspects of Christ's life on earth so that readers might understand how fully He identified with the fallen human race. Satan's complaint about God, which he made to Eve in the Garden of Eden, was that the principles of His government were faulty. He asserted that God was holding back from the human race ideas, abilities, and possibilities for personal development, which, if they were allowed, would lead to a universe that would be peopled by beings allowed to excel (Gen. 3:2–5). To rescue the human race from the deceptions of Satan and to enable fallen men and women to once again walk in the company of angels, God planned to demonstrate conclusively that the principles of His government are based on love. Such a foundational stone ensures that peace and happiness will be realized and maintained. Christ wishes us to respond to His love so that, when He comes in glory, we may dwell with Him.

Jesus, the Prophet

In this section, I will

- *introduce Jesus as a prophet who identified with the other humble people who performed this role;*

- *outline the work of a prophet.*

A prophet is a person "who speaks for another, most usually for God."[71] A prophet in Bible times did not simply foretell future events but preached as God's messenger. Such a person possessed the *"gift of expounding of scripture, or of speaking and preaching, under the influence of the Holy Spirit."*[72]

Office of Prophet. Christ's initial role, when He came to earth to rescue humanity, was as a prophet like Moses (Deut. 18:18, 19; John 1:45). The work of the true prophet is to reveal God's will. This Jesus did continually (John 8:28). He declared: "For I have not spoken on My own *authority;* but the Father who sent Me gave Me a command, what I should say and what I should speak" (John 12:49). Just as Moses led the children of Israel from the land of Egypt—a land of bondage and suffering—to the promised land of Canaan, so Christ came to this earth to demonstrate the way we must live that we may escape from spiritual Egypt and be fit candidates for the heavenly Canaan.

Jesus quietly claimed to be a prophet when He said, "A prophet is not without honor except in his own country" (Mark 6:4). By so doing,

He endorsed the Old Testament prophets. Some of the ordinary people recognized Jesus as a prophet, for this was a common expression used by the people during His triumphant entry into Jerusalem (Matt. 21:11). Others made similar declarations about His calling at various times during His ministry (see John 4:19; 7:40; 9:17). Some of His disciples declared that Jesus was "a Prophet mighty in deed and word before God and all the people" (Luke 24:19). However, the priests and rulers, in general, were unwilling to acknowledge Jesus as a prophet but rather claimed that He worked under the direction of Beelzebub, or Satan (Matt. 12:24).

Jesus expressed absolute faith in the surety of God's Word, as recorded by the prophets (Luke 18:31; 24:27, 44). He declared that the prophecies concerning the Messiah would be fulfilled in their smallest detail. Luke records that all the prophets did, in fact, witness concerning Jesus (Acts 10:43). The apostle Peter, one of Christ's closest associates, declared concerning prophecy, "And we have the prophetic word made more sure. You will do well to pay attention to this as to a lamp shining in a dark place, until the day dawns and the morning star rises in your hearts" (2 Peter 1:19, RSV). Jesus called special attention to the writings of the prophet Daniel (Mark 13:14). He indicated that the prophet's words, if carefully studied and obeyed, would allow the believers to escape death during the soon-coming destruction of Jerusalem. The same writer warned concerning the last-day deceptions that would appear in this world. Belief in the words of God spoken through Daniel will lead to deliverance from evil in the time of great trouble just prior to Christ's coming. In a similar vein, the Lord Himself declared, through John the Revelator, that faithful study and obedience to the words of prophecy would bring great blessing and eternal life (Rev. 1:3; 3:21, 22).

Work of Prophets and "the Prophet." The tasks performed by prophets were several besides foretelling the future. They included earnestly teaching God's ways to strengthen believers (Acts 15:32), judging in matters of dispute, and rebuking sins (1 Sam. 7:3, 15–17; 12:17–19; Dan. 4:27). The scriptural record regarding the prophet Samuel is particularly clear about the range of tasks that a prophet might be involved in. One of Samuel's outstanding contributions was the establishment of the "schools of the prophets" (see 1 Sam. 19:20).[73] Besides his contribution to education, Samuel fearlessly rebuked sin, functioned as a judge as he helped the people settle their differences, and acted in the capacity of God's messenger in outlining future events (1 Sam. 3:11–14, 17; 4:11, 16–18).

To what extent, we might ask, did Jesus undertake, in His capacity as a prophet, similar activities to those mentioned for prophets in the Old Testament? The answer is that He fully participated in similar activities. Several examples of parallel activities can be cited: teaching (Matt. 4:23; John 3:2), judging (John 8:3–11), rebuking sin (Matt. 15:7–9), and prophesying (Acts 1:4–8).

In coming as a prophet, Christ identified Himself with the humble human beings who had brought words of encouragement, rebuke, and warning to their fellow men. Like their Master, many of these prophets suffered humiliation and death. In coming as a spiritual leader, Jesus suffered the temptations that are peculiar to leaders. As a prophet, He took the most difficult spiritual role that could be assigned. By so doing, Christ, our leader, has assured us that there is no pathway we might be called to tread that He has not already trodden. He fully identified Himself with humanity.

Christ, Our High Priest

In this section, I will

- *identify that by becoming part of the human family, Christ is qualified to become our High Priest;*

- *outline the work of Christ as our High Priest.*

It has been said that Jesus "came from God to man as God's representative" and "went back to the Father from man as man's representative."[74] Jesus was qualified to be our High Priest through His life on earth as a man. The Scriptures record: "And the Word was made flesh and dwelt among us" (John 1:14, KJV; cf. Heb. 2:14, 16, 17). In coming to earth, Jesus was truly God as He also truly identified with humanity (John 1:1, 14; Mark 1:1; Phil. 2:6, 7). We notice that, notwithstanding "that the sins of a guilty world were laid upon Christ, notwithstanding the humiliation of taking upon Himself our fallen nature, the voice from heaven declared Him to be the Son of the Eternal."[75] Christ's identification with humanity was not make-believe (Rom. 5:15). He was born of Mary who was herself no different in nature from the rest of humanity (Gal. 4:4). Thus, Paul declares that Christ was not ashamed to be called our brother (Heb. 2:11). As a consequence of identifying with us, the possibility of yielding to temptation was always present. Indeed, He was tempted in "all *points* ... as *we are*" (Heb. 4:15). Yet, He did not yield to temptation (2 Cor. 5:21; 1 Peter 2:22).

Kinsman-Redeemer. The close relationship between the humanity of Christ and that of the fallen race is taught in the Old Testament through the kinsman-redeemer concept. Redemption of those who fell into bondage was reserved for the person's closest blood relative. "One of his brothers may redeem him ... or *anyone* who is near of kin" (Lev. 25:48, 49). This practice fittingly represented Christ's mission. The whole of humanity is trapped in the bondage of sin. The nearest of kin is Christ, who is the only one worthy to redeem us from such bondage.

As our Kinsman, Jesus was qualified to serve as our representative in heaven through His having "learned obedience from what he suffered" and becoming the "author" of our salvation (Heb. 5:8, 9, Green). The epistle to the Hebrews informs us that, through His sufferings, Christ was "perfected," or "completed," in the sense that He attained the goal of His mission in His humanity. He learned by personal experience what it means to struggle against temptation and through faith gain the victory. It was only through belonging in all respects to the human family that He could qualify to become our High Priest (Heb. 5:1–5). Satan had claimed that God's created beings could not keep the law of God. Therefore, to meet Satan's accusations, Christ humbled Himself, put on humanity, and fully identified with the sons and daughters of Adam (Phil. 2:6–8). He showed through His life of obedience that human beings can live righteous lives in this sinful world. This is only possible through faith in His enabling power (Rev. 14:3–5, 12).

By His sinless life, Jesus refuted Satan's accusations, proving them false (John 12:31–33). As a result, we can be "more than conquerors through Him who loved us" (Rom. 8:37). With confidence, we can follow Jesus' example through faith (cf. 1 Peter 2:21, 22), for we are assured that no temptation will ever come our way from which God is unable to deliver us. He will provide a way of escape to those who depend on Him through faith (1 Cor. 10:13). We can, therefore, come with confidence to God, knowing that we will obtain mercy and help in our time of need (Heb. 4:14–16). We believe that "Christ looks at the spirit, and when He sees us carrying our burden with faith, His perfect holiness atones for our shortcomings. When we do our best, He becomes our righteousness."[76]

Chapter 5. Christ's Three-fold Ministry

Priestly Ministry Commences. Before our discussion begins, we need to remind ourselves of a few features regarding the ministry of the earthly priests. They were anointed to their office before they ministered the blood of the sin offerings (Lev. 8:30, 33; 9:1, 2, 7). When Christ died on Calvary, God signified the termination of the Levitical priesthood in that the veil to the Most Holy Place was torn by an "unseen hand" from the top to the bottom (Matt. 27:50, 51).[77] God, in this remarkable manner, indicated to all that the heavenly priesthood of Christ was about to commence (Heb. 7:11). Jesus became sin for us and then ministered for believers the benefits of His spilled blood in the heavenly sanctuary before God (2 Cor. 5:21; Heb. 9:22–24; 1 John 1:7).

On earth, Christ was not a priest. The apostle Paul says emphatically that if Christ "were on earth, He would not be a priest" (Heb. 8:4). Christ became our High Priest after His return to heaven and after the sanctuary in heaven—"the Most Holy"—was anointed (Dan. 9:24; cf. Lev. 8:10–12). The Scriptures indicate that upon the acquisition of authority in heaven, Christ was anointed with the "oil of gladness" (Heb. 1:3, 9; cf. Lev. 8:30; Ps. 45:6, 7). The events occurring in the earthly sanctuary assure us that after its anointing and the setting aside of Aaron and his sons, God acknowledged these events by fire (Lev. 9:23, 24). In like manner, the inauguration of Christ in heaven, after the dedication of the heavenly sanctuary, was signaled on earth by tongues of fire resting on the disciples at Pentecost (Acts 2:3).[78] Recognizing how anointing preceded ministry, we conclude that Scripture does not support any claim that the first phase of Christ's priestly ministry commenced on earth.[79] The phraseology in Hebrews 6:19, 20 (KJV) about entering "within the veil" is also understood to refer to the inauguration of the sanctuary rather than to Day of Atonement imagery.[80]

Christ Is of the Order of Melchizedek. Jesus belonged to the priestly order of Melchizedek (Heb. 6:20). One unique feature of Christ's heavenly priesthood is that, once conferred, it continues without interruption (Heb. 7:16, 23, 24). Death did not intervene (Heb. 7:3). Thus, this priesthood could not have commenced before Christ's resurrection. The attributes of Melchizedek were applied to Christ (compare Heb. 7:2, 3 and Isa. 9:6), indicating that Melchizedek prefigured Christ. The superiority of the Melchizedek order of priests over that of the Levitical priesthood is a point of emphasis in the epistle to the Hebrews (Heb. 7:20–28).[81]

Work of Christ our High Priest. Christ's work in the heavenly sanctuary has a number of features. He is the believers' representative in heaven, and He forgives sins and delivers us from its guilt (1 John 1:9). Sins that are genuinely confessed are immediately forgiven, and the sinner is justified. Yet, the record of confessed sins remains in God's books of record (Eccles. 12:14), just as in the earthly sanctuary a record of blood was left in the Holy Place. Christ is ready to provide help to those who are tempted. He delivers from the power of sin (Col. 1:22; Heb. 2:18). The breaking of the dominion of sin in the life so that sin no longer has power over the believer is the great work that Christ wishes to accomplish. This process is termed *sanctification*.

Christ is also involved in a ministry of investigation, which represents judicial activity. He is putting a mark on those who love righteousness, "who sigh and cry over all the abominations" that are occurring on earth (Ezek. 9:4; cf. Rev. 7:2, 3). This means that Christ is investigating His people (cf. John 5:26, 27; 1 Peter 4:17). He notes those who grieve concerning the spiritual state of the world, who grieve for the sins of those who profess to be believers and who grieve for the lack of zeal shown by those who have been given special light to share with others. These same ones reprove sin, for they have a deep love for the truth and for the honor and glory of God. Their experience is centered in Christ (Mal. 3:16).

Christ is also erasing the record of confessed sins (Acts 3:19). Before Christ completes His ministry in the Most Holy Place, the sanctuary in heaven will forever be freed—or cleansed—from the record of the confessed sins of the faithful. When this phase of His ministry is finalized, He will then return to earth and the mystery of God will be completed (Acts 3:20). We understand the final work in the heavenly sanctuary by the pattern described in the earthly sanctuary on the Day of Atonement (Heb. 8:3–5).

Christ, the King

In this section, I will

- *introduce the concept of the kingdom of grace and the kingdom of glory;*
- *indicate the sequence of events leading to the establishment of the kingdom of glory.*

Chapter 5. Christ's Three-fold Ministry

Christ was born the Son of David, but He will not take His kingly throne until after He has finished His ministry as a priest. While Christ was on earth, the people wished to recognize Him as king, but He did not permit this to happen (John 6:15). He knew that, before the kingdom of glory could be established, He had to establish the kingdom of grace.

The Kingdom of Grace. Jesus established the kingdom of God's grace on this earth (Matt. 3:2; John 18:36, 37), and it still operates. It is Christ's desire to reign as King of our mind and life. In the future, He will establish a kingdom of glory. Jesus declared that the kingdom that He came to establish was not one dependent on the force of arms. Jesus clearly taught that He did not come to establish His kingdom of glory at the first advent (Matt. 25:31). The Jews had a misconception concerning the type of kingdom that Jesus came to establish. They imagined that the Messiah would come and cast out the hated Romans and place Himself on the throne of Israel as a temporal ruler. They thought that under His rule all other nations would be subject to the Jews. They misunderstood the truth that Christ's kingdom of grace must precede His kingdom of glory. Their confusion of the two kingdoms is evident in Luke 17:20. In responding to the Pharisees about when the kingdom of God should come, Jesus made it abundantly evident that the kingdom He came to establish was in the minds of the individual (Luke 17:21). He came to establish a "nation" of believers who obey God's ways through love arising from the innermost recesses of the mind (Matt. 21:43; Rom. 12:2; Eph. 6:6). This is the same point that He made to Pilate at His trial (Luke 23:2, 3; John 18:37).

The purpose of Christ's triumphal, kingly entry into Jerusalem was to fulfill prophecy and to draw the people's attention to His claim of being the Messiah (Isa. 12:6; Zech. 9:9). This triumphal entry, just five days before His crucifixion, made it certain that the attention of all would be focused on His claim of having established the kingdom of grace. Following His trial and burial, many would be stimulated to study the Scriptures and would realize that He was indeed the Messiah He claimed to be (Matt. 12:16–21; Acts 2:22–42).

People of all nations—including the nation of Israel—are members of Christ's kingdom of grace (Rom. 11:1, 5, 11–25). To assert that the nation of Israel will have a special place in the history of salvation after the gospel has gone to the Gentiles is a doctrine of wishful thinking and contrary to the clearest words of prophecy (Dan. 9:24–27; Jer. 18:9, 10).

The Kingdom of Glory. The kingdom of glory will be instituted at the close of Christ's ministry as a priest in the heavenly sanctuary when the heavenly court has finished examining the books of record (Dan. 7:9, 10, 13, 14). In these verses, Daniel gives us a glimpse of the great pre-advent investigation now proceeding in heaven. When Christ's ministration in the sanctuary is complete, He stands up and comes to God the Father to receive His kingdom (Dan. 12:1, 2; Luke 19:12, 15). Christ cannot receive His kingdom until the determination of who will be the subjects of His kingdom, a primary function of the judgment. Thus, His priestly role must conclude before He can be crowned king. About this time, the restraint that God has placed upon Satan and the inhabitants of the world is lifted, and a great time of trouble and destruction descends upon the impenitent world (Dan. 12:1; Rev. 15:8; 16:1).

The crowning of Christ is described in magnificent terms and is set in the context of the end of the great controversy. Jesus appears in His kingly majesty and glory accompanied by the armies of heaven to receives the citizens of His kingdom (Rev. 19:11–16). In the scene in Revelation, He is pictured as coming from heaven riding on a white horse. White symbolizes the purity of His character. His kingdom will be established forever and ever, and all earthly powers will cease to exist (Rev. 11:15).

The reception of His kingdom is likened to a marriage, and the capital of Christ's kingdom—the New Jerusalem—is likened to a bride (Rev. 19:7; 21:2). The members of Christ's kingdom are described as "those who are called to the marriage supper of the Lamb" (Rev. 19:9). They are also designated "virgins" because they have continually exercised faith in their Master (Matt. 25:1; Rev. 14:4, 5). The Holy Spirit has been active in their life to convict of sin and to lead into all righteousness as they have studied God's Word (Ps. 119:105; Zech. 4:6, 11–14; Matt. 25:4, 7, 8). How essential it is that you and I be members of Christ's kingdom! Let us accept Christ as our High Priest today so that we may be cleansed from sin and be delivered from its controlling power. In this relationship, we will be fit subjects to enter the marriage supper of the Lamb (Rev. 19:9). May we be counted worthy to sing the song of Moses and of the Lamb, saying:

"Great and marvelous *are* Your works, Lord God Almighty!
Just and true *are* Your ways, O King of the saints!
Who shall not fear You, O Lord, and glorify Your name?
For *You* alone *are* holy.
For all nations shall come and worship before You,
For Your judgments have been manifested." (Rev. 15:3, 4)

Chapter 6.
Thine Is the Power and the Glory

Chapter Emphasis: *God's glory and power are revealed in the sanctuary. God's glory primarily refers to the glorious aspects of His character, which are reflected in the Ten Commandments. His power is evident in the natural world and in His ability to forgive sins and transform lives through the ministry of the Holy Spirit.*

Spiritual Link: *When Christ comes the second time, He will reveal the full extent of His power and great glory.*

In our modern world, we speak a great deal about power. Those in the seat of authority are said to have power. They manipulate and control events and the lives of others. A surgeon is said to have the power to make the sick well again. Indeed, we daily see modern miracles, as the benefits of scientific advances are spread abroad to help humanity. Knowledge rightly used is a power, or force, for good in the world today. Again, a person may be said to be a powerful speaker, swaying the emotions and influencing the actions of individuals. The term is also used to express the degree of strength possessed by people, machines, or instruments. It is not surprising, then, that the word "power," which possesses these and other meanings, is used to express some of the notable characteristics of God. I wish to examine some aspects of the word "power" in this chapter.

Somewhat less frequently we use the word "glory." It is most commonly used to convey the idea of the splendor of a scene or to describe a blissful experience. Less frequently it is used to convey the idea of renown and fame. We may well ask: What is the most remarkable or most glorious feature of God mentioned in the Bible? Jesus must have expected His disciples to understand this, for the Lord's Prayer ends with the words, "For Yours is the kingdom and the power and the glory forever. Amen" (Matt. 6:13). In this chapter, I plan to explore some of the deep meanings of this term that are used throughout the Bible including the sanctuary.

God's Glory

In this section, I will

- *establish that "God's glory" is a term that can refer to His character;*
- *identify the Ten Commandments as a document that reveals the character of the Godhead;*
- *emphasize that Christ came to earth to reveal God's character.*

From the beginning, God has provided abundant evidence of His presence in the universe and of the principles of His kingdom. David sought to understand God more fully by contemplating His power and glory in the sanctuary (Ps. 63:2). Let us go on a journey of discovery to observe what the Bible has to say about these grand subjects and, in particular, to determine the profound meaning of God's glory as we consider Christ through faith.

When Moses asked God to show him His glory on Sinai, God made all His goodness, that is, all the gracious aspects of His character, to pass before Moses (Exod. 33:18, 19). The word "character" is not used in the text of older translations of the Bible. But, unmistakably, God here indicates the basis of the greatness of His character (Exod. 34:5–7).

The document that explains the character of God in practical terms for the human race is the Ten Commandments. These were written by the finger of God (Exod. 31:18; 34:1). We notice that God commanded Moses to cut two tables of stone on the second occasion of the writing of His law that He might inscribe the words of the law of love upon them with His own finger (Deut. 10:1, 2, 5). The Lord then passed before Moses and described in clear terms His most significant characteristics (Exod. 34:6, 7). The law He delivered is based on love (Deut. 10:12–15, 19), a fact that Jesus Himself so beautifully summarized in Matthew 22:37–40.

The term for love that Jesus used shows it to be *agapē* love (Matt. 22:36–40), which is the essence of God's nature (1 John 4:8). The distinction comes through in the Greek but not in less expressive English translations. The Scriptures mentioned above, when understood from the perspective of the original language, strengthen our understanding of the law of God being essentially a transcript, or expression, of His character, for "God is love." If we diminish the law, we have a stunted idea of God's character. Thus, declaring the Sabbath command to be without moral value is to misunderstand and misrepresent God's character and ways. Because the principles behind the Ten Commandments describe God's character, it follows logically that the principles embodied in them were in existence from eternity.

To sin is then to display characteristics that are not like God's perfect character as shown in the law (1 John 3:4). Paul expressed this thought very clearly in Romans, "For all have sinned and fall short of the glory of God" (Rom. 3:23). The human race was initially created "in the image of God" (Gen. 1:27), which included having a Christ-like character. Hence, we must conclude that love motivated humanity's every action until sin entered the world. Satan tempted Eve to selfishly desire knowledge (Gen. 3:5). She distrusted God, chose to disobey Him, and grasped the offered fruit to satisfy self-interest. Thereafter, all the descendants of Adam and Eve were weakened, and they found it easy to yield to selfish desires (Jer. 17:9). As we choose to disobey God, as we choose to yield to our selfish desires, we likewise commit acts of transgression.

Christ's Mission. Jesus' special mission on earth was to reveal God's character (John 1:14; 17:4–6). By His gracious words, deeds, and miracles, Christ showed fallen man what God is really like. He came to reveal the fullness of "grace and truth" (John 1:17). He came to sweep away the misconceptions about God's character that Satan had attempted to promote from the beginning (Gen. 3:1–6). The apostle John recorded that Jesus came and "dwelt among us," or, more meaningfully, that He "tabernacled among us" (John 1:14,

RV, margin). Thus, John clearly linked the presence of the Lord as shown above the ark of the covenant in Old Testament times with the manifestation of Christ in human flesh (cf. Exod. 25:22; Num. 7:89).[82] Jesus came to give the most spectacular display possible of the character of God so that all would be without excuse (2 Cor. 4:6). By His life, "Christ has redeemed Adam's disgraceful fall, and has perfected a character of perfect obedience, and left an example for the human family, that they may imitate the Pattern."[83]

Christ came to earth as One who possessed the "express image," or the character, of God (Heb. 1:3). Paul is here affirming that Christ perfectly—exactly—represented the character of God. The Greek word from which this phrase comes is indeed *charakter*, from which we derive our English word "character." The Revised Standard Version uses the phrase "bears the very stamp of His nature" and Moffatt's translation uses "stamped with God's own character" to convey the same idea. When Philip asked Jesus, "Show us the Father," Jesus could confidently affirm, "He who has seen Me has seen the Father" (John 14:8, 9). Truly, it may be said that Christ fully represented the character of God the Father.

The Disciples' Mission. Christ has now returned to heaven, but He has left ambassadors to work on His behalf. Through them, He intends that the world will be given a startling reminder of the nature of His glory, or character, and He appeals to earth's inhabitants: "Fear God and give glory to Him" (Rev. 14:7).

Indeed, God is "not willing that any should perish but that all should come to repentance" (2 Peter 3:9). Just before He returns to earth to give His rewards, He requests that His servants reveal to those on the earth what God is really like. "The honor of Christ must stand complete in the perfection of the character of His chosen people. He desires that they shall represent His character to the world."[84] God challenges all people to seek Him while He may be found so that the Holy Spirit may bring about the transformation of character that is necessary to enable them to meet Him in peace (Isa. 55:6, 7; 59:19; Rom. 12:2). As we experience this transformation, Christ asks us to tell the world of His transforming power!

From Glory to Glory

In this section, I will

- *remind readers that, when a believer studies God's Word and has a sincere willingness to change, the Holy Spirit acts to transform the life.*

Something marvelous happens as the believer considers Christ's beauty of character—the life is transformed under the influence of the Holy Spirit. The transformation of the Christian is progressive, as is indicated by the words "from glory to glory" (2 Cor. 3:17, 18). The believer does not effect this transformation. It occurs only through the agency of the Holy Spirit. Jesus told His disciples that the Spirit, or the Comforter, will "guide you into all truth" (John 16:13). "Through the influence of the Spirit of God, the believer is transformed in character; his taste is refined, his judgment is sanctified, and he becomes complete in Christ."[85] This is a promise that He has given to the weakest of saints.

The change brought about by the Holy Spirit means that the thought patterns and motives themselves are transformed. Every thought is to be brought "into captivity to the obedience of Christ" (2 Cor. 10:5; cf. Rom. 12:2). The apostle Paul recognized that our mind needs constantly to be under the controlling influence of God's Spirit. Mere outward conformity to the requirements of the law of God does not bring salvation (Phil. 3:6–9). The law is to be written in the mind, and our thinking patterns are to be changed. The thoughts are to be purified through considering God's ways (Heb. 9:14; 10:16; Ps. 19:7, 8). This means that the "Christian's life is not a modification or improvement of the old life, but a transformation of the nature. There is a death to sin and self, and a new life altogether."[86] If we ask for God's help, He promises to give us enabling power (1 Cor. 10:13).

Naturally, the outward acts of such individuals bear witness that they operate by the highest moral principles. Outward conformity to Christian ideals will not save. This would be salvation by works. It is only as right actions come from a pure mind, controlled by God's Spirit, that we are considered fit candidates for heaven, possessing righteousness by faith (cf. 1 Sam. 16:7). The wise man Solomon observed, "… what he thinks is what he really is" (Prov. 23:7, GNT). To be accepted before God, our thoughts must be renewed (Isa. 55:7; Matt. 5:21, 22, 27, 28). Those who are accepted into the kingdom of God are blameless through the merits of Jesus Christ (Rev. 7:14; 14:5, 12). The good news is that all can be overcomers through the power that Christ gives through the Spirit (1 John 5:4, 5; Rev. 3:21). We must ask for this gift. The psalmist, as he considered God in the sanctuary, realized this great truth. His words are immortalized in Scripture—"Create in me a clean heart, O God, and renew a steadfast spirit within me" (Ps. 51:10).

God's Presence and Power

In this section, I will

- *review the evidence of God's presence in the universe.*

The human race from the beginning has had ample evidence of the presence and power of God. This aspect of God's abilities was demonstrated remarkably in association with the earthly sanctuary and temple. We cannot fail to recognize this when we read the account of the giving of the Decalogue and the institution of the earthly sanctuary system (Exod. 19:18, 19). In the sanctuary, the mercy seat represented God's throne. From this location, God's glory appeared, His judgments were issued, and His power was revealed. This is evident in the account of Nadab and Abihu's profaning of God's name and of the 250 princes of Israel's rebellion against God (Lev. 10:1, 2; Num. 16:35). Miriam saw evidence of God's power when she saw the results of her jealous words against Moses. Israel saw God's power when they refused to enter Canaan (Num. 12:1–10; 14:10, 22–29). Many today have chosen to discount these and other evidences.

Regardless of what one chooses, there are aspects of God's power evident all about us. The creative ability of God is evident in the things that we observe in nature. These are a constant reminders of God's power, as the Bible writers so declare (1 Chron. 29:11; Ps. 66:5–7; Isa. 40:26; Rom. 1:20). God declares that His creative ability is one characteristic of His nature that separates Him from all other gods (Ps. 96:4, 5; Jer. 10:10–12). When God cares for the existence and predictable motions of the heavenly bodies, it gives evidence of His ability to maintain His creation (2 Peter 3:4–7; Isa. 40:26). Our God is not capricious, nor is He captive to natural law or the forces of nature that He established. Hence, we notice that the wind and waves were obedient to Christ's voice while He was here on earth (Mark 4:41). Other unusual events involving the use of common physical phenomena, such as the great Flood (Gen. 7) and the lengthening of the day in

Joshua's time (Josh. 10:12–14), are a tribute to God's control over the laws that He made. Our God is in control of the universe.

The Greek word *dunamis*, which is sometimes translated "miracle," can also be translated "power." Miracles are an evidence of the creative ability of God, but Satan and his agents have the power to deceive and to control natural events as far as God allows (Exod. 7:9–12; Job 2:3–7; Rev. 16:14). Every spirit must be tested against the standard of the Word of God—"To the law and to the testimony! If they do not speak according to this word, *it is* because *there* is no light in them" (Isa. 8:20). Jesus, on occasion, worked miracles of healing for the express purpose of helping those present to understand that the Son of Man has the power to forgive sins (Matt. 9:4–7).

The greatest miracle of God's power observed today is the power—the *dunamis*—of the gospel (Rom. 1:16). This power God makes available to transform the life. The same power used in the creation of the worlds is available for the recreation of the image of God in humanity. This thought is expressed in the following words: "They overcame him [that is, "that serpent of old, called the Devil and Satan"] by the blood of the Lamb and by the word of their testimony, and they did not love their lives to the death" (Rev. 12:11, 9).

God's ability to fundamentally change a person's thinking and living is evidence of the superiority of God over all other powers (Acts 4:12). Some will say that such changes are a delusion. To such, we could answer, "A redeemed drunkard, with vivid memory of past hopeless struggles and new sense of power through Christ, was replying to the charge that 'his religion was a delusion.' He said: 'Thank God for the delusion; it has put clothes on my children and shoes on their feet and bread in their mouths. It has made a man of me and it has put joy and peace in my home, which had been a hell. If this is a delusion, may God send it to the slaves of drink everywhere, for their slavery is an awful reality.'"[87]

Another unique ability of God is His capacity to predict and to control world events (Isa. 46:9, 10). God's ability to predict, with unerring accuracy, the course of world events is startling. We need only refer to the prophecy of Daniel 2, which foretold the succession of world powers from Babylon to Medo-Persia to Greece to Rome centuries in advance, to illustrate this point. However, there are many other events predicted in the Bible that history indicates have come to pass in amazing detail. The science of archaeology has confirmed that the prophecies of Scripture were, in many instances, penned well in advance of the events foretold.

You Will Receive Power

In this section, I will

- *emphasize that God promises to empower us;*
- *outline the avenues through which God commonly appeals to the believer.*

Jesus promised His disciples access to heavenly agencies through which they would receive power to become and remain the children of God (John 1:12). The primary agent He promised was His earthly representative, the Holy Spirit (Acts 1:8). Events associated with the earthly sanctuary and temple reinforced this idea. The construction of the first sanctuary was accompanied by an outpouring of God's Spirit (Exod. 31:3; 35:31). When the children of Israel believed and served God, they were given power to accomplish the task of occupying Canaan. God's presence went with them, and incredible obstacles vanished before them (Num. 21:1–3; Deut. 3:1–5; Josh. 8:1–19).

The Holy Spirit was intimately associated with the post-resurrection missionary movement, which expanded at amazing speed. Looking again to the work of the Holy Spirit in New Testament times, we find that the Greek word translated "power" in Acts 1:8 is *dunamis*. From this word our English word "dynamite" is derived. It is not altogether surprising, then, that the book of Acts is full of stories of the amazing exploits of ordinary men and women filled with the Holy Spirit. Yet, that power was not just for them. God promises the power of the Holy Spirit to all His obedient children (Acts 5:32). He is no respecter of persons, and His blessings are not dependent upon our background or educational status. In the story of Jacob's ladder, the angels are represented as communicators of Christ's power to humans (Gen. 28:12; John 1:51). This same symbolism is used in Revelation 14 where three angels are pictured as cooperating with God's servants to herald His soon coming—they impart to them power for witnessing.

Before the early disciples could experience the outpouring of the Holy Spirit in their lives, a number of issues needed to be resolved and new directions in life forged. First, they needed to recognize their spiritual blindness and their great need of unity. The Scriptures record that, after the Holy Spirit came, "these all continued with one accord"

Chapter 6. Thine Is the Power and the Glory

(Acts 1:14; contrast with Luke 22:24, 31, 32). In other words, through prayer and the study of the Old Testament Scriptures, they had discovered God's will for them (Acts 1:15–23). Not only enlightened by their study and meditation on the Word of God, they chose to obey God's revealed will through faith (Acts 1:24–26).

The marked change in the disciples was an apt illustration of Jesus' saying: "The words that I speak to you are spirit, and *they* are life" (John 6:63). As the Word of God is read, treasured, and obeyed, it becomes a source of great power and a defense against the temptations of Satan. This is evident in the record of the life of the Savior. Early in His life, the scholars were "astonished at His understanding and answers" (Luke 2:47). Later on, He repulsed Satan's temptations through the witness of the Scriptures. The people took note that "He taught them as one having authority, and not as the scribes" (Matt. 7:29). This same experience is recorded concerning the disciples. They studied the Word of God and prayed for the understanding and strength to obey through faith. As they witnessed to those present at the feast, the crowds were "amazed and perplexed" (Acts 2:12). Through reading God's Word, we are brought in contact with its Author and our life is changed. Sanctification cannot occur apart from the study of the Word, for Jesus declared, "Sanctify them by Your truth. Your word is truth" (John 17:17). Quite similar is the thought: "The word of God—the truth—is the channel through which the Lord manifests His Spirit and power."[88]

Prayer is the key that unlocks God's power. The Bible records the deeds of great men and women of prayer. It tells, for example, of Samuel, Elijah, David, Esther, and Daniel. It assures us that power over the evil one comes only in response to prayer (Matt. 17:21; Eph. 6:18; 1 Peter 4:7). This was Christ's experience (Matt. 26:36, 40–44; John 18:2). The altar of incense in the earthly sanctuary symbolized this great truth taught in Christ's life. The incense rose perpetually from the altar. The prayers of believers were to ascend to heaven with the incense. Upon Him they depended for grace in their lives.

Pentecostal power is promised to those who render loving obedience to God through faith (John 14:15; Acts 5:32; Heb. 5:9). God's Spirit is poured out in all His fullness on those who habitually respond to His promptings as they read the Word of God and pray for enlightenment.

Glory and Power to the Lamb

In this section, I will

- *identify when the redeemed, as a group, will give adoration to Jesus Christ, acknowledging His superiority in all things.*

When the plan of salvation is complete, then "every creature which is in heaven and on the earth" and elsewhere will praise Christ (Rev. 5:13; cf. Rev. 15:2–4). Then, heaven's joy will be complete as sin and sinners will have been erased from God's universe.[89] All intelligent beings will then give joyous appreciation and adoration to Jesus Christ. The redeemed and the holy angels will proclaim the greatness and perfection of God's character and acknowledge that all of Satan's charges against God are false. Heaven will be forever secure against sin's rising the second time.

The world as we know it will end with the coming of the Lord Jesus Christ in glory (Matt. 16:27). Some of the majesty of this event was seen when the cloud of God's glory filled the temple and when Jesus was transfigured on the mountain (Exod. 40:34, 35; Matt. 17:2; Mark 9:3). Those who are obedient and reflect the glory of God's character on earth will be among those who will be counted worthy to stand on the sea of glass and forever be members of God's glorious kingdom.

God assures you, dear reader, that you can be on the sea of glass. Notice: "Satan has asserted that men could not keep the commandments of God. To prove that they could, Christ became a man, and lived a life of perfect obedience, an evidence to sinful human beings, to the worlds unfallen, and to the heavenly angels, that man could keep God's law through the divine power that is abundantly provided for all that believe. In order to reveal God to the world, to demonstrate as true that which Satan has denied, Christ volunteered to take humanity, and in His power, humanity can obey God. 'As many as received Him, to them gave He power to become the sons of God.' All heaven is Christ's to give to the world."[90] May we pray for and experience this power in our life today that we may give glory to God.

Chapter 7.
Christ Will Build His Temple

Chapter Emphasis: *The bid to rescue humanity following sin's entrance was led by Jesus Christ. He is the chief cornerstone of the church, which has been likened, among other things, to a temple. This temple is composed of people from all nations, and its roots can be traced throughout the Old Testament. There has been a unity of fundamental understandings and mission in Christ's church through the ages, although the vision has sometimes faltered.*

Spiritual Links: *The Elijah message is essential to the genuine, remnant believers in the last period of church history. It is a message of rebuke and invitation.*

From the time of the entrance of sin, Christ sought to gather out those who were honest in mind and heart to worship Him. He also sought to use them to share the good news of salvation with others. Those who heard and responded to the invitation of mercy became members of His church on earth. Initially, the patriarchs themselves directed the worship of God for their households; they acted as priests and set up altars on which they sacrificed animals. In this way, they showed their faith in the promised Redeemer to come (Gen. 3:15).

The first organized church was the Old Testament Hebrew church—the "congregation in the wilderness" (Acts 7:38). I will refer to it here as "the Congregation of the People."

In this chapter, I intend to briefly trace God's church through history—the church of the God in whom is "no variation or shadow of turning" (James 1:17). Of this church, the Scriptures proclaim that Christ Himself is the "chief corner*stone*" (Eph. 2:20). The fascinating story about the builders of Solomon's temple rejecting and then finally accepting a large stone as the cornerstone is the basis for this expression (Ps. 118:22; Matt. 21:42).[91] The prophet Zechariah speaks of Christ as being the Branch and as building God's temple, which is His church (Zech. 6:12, 13). This means that Christ is both the foundation and the builder of the edifice. This He has accomplished through His sacrifice, and He is still accomplishing it through His mediation in heaven.[92] His church is composed of people of all nations. Since it is built on Christ, there is unity in belief and mission, to which all the apostles and prophets are witnesses (Eph. 2:19–22). It is my intention to look at the foundation principles on which God's church has been established.

Congregation of the People

In this section, I will

- *establish that Christ founded the church that was associated with the earthly sanctuary and identified closely with it;*

- *outline the basic principles of salvation taught in the sanctuary;*

- *introduce the concept that Satan has vigorously sought to frustrate the truths delivered by God to the human race.*

Christ was the great "I AM" of the Old Testament (Exod. 3:14), and this was His claim (John 8:58). The Jews recognized the seriousness of this claim, considered it blasphemous, and set about to stone Him (John 8:59).

Christ Established His Church. It is evident that Christ established the church of the Congregation of the People amidst an awful display of power at Sinai fifty days after the Israelites were delivered from Egypt (Lev. 23:15, 16). That event was itself connected with the keep-

Chapter 7. Christ Will Build His Temple

ing of the first Passover (Exod. 12:3–18; Lev. 23:16).[93] The Pentecostal power of the Apostolic church was thus foreshadowed as the Holy Spirit descended fifty days after "Christ our Passover" was sacrificed for us (Acts 2:1; 1 Cor. 5:7).

The Son identified closely with His chosen people. This is evident from the fact that the sanctuary was placed in the midst of the congregation and God's glory dwelt in the sanctuary (Exod. 29:43; Num. 2:17). We notice a pattern developing here. Christ the Creator walked with the sinless pair in Eden. Sin brought separation between God and humanity, but God still desired to have an abiding and constant relationship with the human race. He was not willing to abandon them to the consequences of sin. In the unfolding plan of salvation revealed by the sanctuary system, Christ purposed to identify closely with His chosen people in order to convey the important lesson that it was only through a constant and close relationship with the Creator through faith that salvation is possible.

Principles of Establishment. The Exodus-church was established on a number of fundamental principles, which are evident if we study the worship ceremonies that God instituted at Sinai. Sin was identified as the fundamental problem that the human race has to contend with. At that time, if sin remained unconfessed, the sinner's name would ultimately be removed from the book of life (Exod. 32:30–33; cf. Rev. 3:5). The joyful news of the sanctuary system was that a way of escape from eternal death was available through the death of a perfect substitute (Lev. 1:3, 10; 4:3; 9:3; 17:11). Human beings could claim the promise of salvation through faith in the substitute that represented Christ to come. This meant that eternal life could be claimed in the here and now (Lev. 1:4; 9:7; Ps. 51:16, 17; Hab. 2:4; cf. Rom. 1:17; 5:10, 11; Heb. 4:2).

These sanctuary-based ceremonies pointed forward to Christ's earthly ministry when He would reconcile humanity to God through His death. Believers before and after the cross needed to exercise faith. Before the cross, they looked forward in faith; after the cross, we look back in faith. This is the only way of escape from the *penalty*, the *power*, and, at the resurrection, the *presence* of sin.

The death of the perfect substitute for the sins of the people affirmed the eternal and unchangeable principles of God's government. The first of these principles was that God's kingdom is based on love and that His mercy is totally compatible with justice (Gen. 3:15; Ps. 89:14; cf. John 3:16). The principle of love is amplified and expressed in perfectly understandable terms in the Ten Commandments, while God's standard of justice is also revealed in them (Exod. 20:6; Deut. 7:11–13; cf. Matt. 22:36–40).

The principle of love to God and love to our fellow human beings, as found in God's commandments, encompasses the "whole duty of man" (Eccles. 12:13). The only reasonable response that humans can make to God's mercy and justice is love. The martyr Stephen and the apostle Paul termed the commandments the "oracles of God" (Acts 7:38; Rom. 3:2). An oracle can be a "divine revelation" or, as defined by the dictionary, an "infallible though mysterious guide." Hence, Paul informs us that these principles are unchangeable and that they express God's eternal characteristics. The oracles were inscribed on stone, the most durable substance available, and placed beneath the mercy seat above which the presence of God was seen. There is nothing else that God could have done to indicate the fundamental and eternal nature of His moral law.

Ministering Agencies. God placed ministering agencies in His church to encourage faith, obedience, and the sharing of the gospel, and to warn of danger. The Scriptures call these ministering agents watchmen and shepherds (Ezek. 33:7; 34:10). In more specific terms, God placed in His ancient church prophets and prophetesses, judges, priests, and pastors to guide the people spiritually. These individuals were themselves not always faithful, leading to a rapid decline in the practice of true religion. At other times, the people failed to listen to the words of warning that were given, and they persecuted and even killed God's true messengers. Irrespective of this dismal record, God continued to send His people messengers (Matt. 21:33–39; Acts 7:52).

The activities of God's ministers anciently were varied. They had a number of issues to contend with. The temptation to seek salvation by works instead of by faith was an early trend (1 Sam. 15:22; Hosea 6:6; Heb. 3:17, 18; 4:2). Sometimes obedience to God's law, especially the fourth—or Sabbath—commandment, was at a low level (Jer. 17:24, 25, 27; cf. Mark 7:9). One of the reasons for this was the people's desire to pattern their ways after the nations of the world (1 Sam. 8:5–7, 19, 20). Another reason was that the people resisted the promptings of God's Spirit (Acts 7:51). Then too, there was the idea that, since God was leading them in such a spectacular fashion, they must be better than other peoples (Ezek. 34:2–6; Matt. 3:9).

God planned that salvation should come to the human race through Christ who was born with a Jewish heritage. Prior to this time, the Jews were to be the special messengers of salvation to all nations (Isa. 42:1; 49:8–14; 56:6, 7; cf. John 4:22). In this, they were a singular failure, for they hedged about the gospel with their traditions (Matt. 23:13–16). This is not to say that all the Jews failed to clearly see God's purpose for their race. We might cite the example of Daniel who witnessed to Nebuchadnezzar in a most effective and telling manner (Dan. 4:27, 28, 37). The harlot Rahab and the Moabitess Ruth are other examples of "longing soul[s]" being satisfied (Ps. 107:9). These two women were forebears of Christ (Matt. 1:5). Ultimately, God was able to save a remnant of Israel who was faithful to Him (Joel 2:32).

The Apostolic and "Wilderness" Churches

In this section, I will

- *remind readers that Christ established the apostolic church and also led the wilderness church;*

- *review the fundamentals of salvation taught in the apostolic and wilderness churches;*

- *indicate that tragic departures from the faith were prophesied;*

- *reassure that God always has had people faithful to Him.*

Jesus chose the twelve apostles as the foundation of the Christian church (Mark 3:14; Eph. 2:20). These men were personally associated with Christ for more than three years. He had instructed them in aspects of church organization and mission. The church was formally empowered by Christ at Pentecost, fifty days after the last Passover (Acts 2:1). By this time, Matthias had filled Judas' place among the twelve (Acts 1:25, 26), and the outpouring of the Spirit promised by the Redeemer had occurred. The reception of the Spirit indicated to all that Christ's work had commenced in the sanctuary in heaven (cf. John 7:39). Henceforth, the focus of the church was on Christ's ministry in the heavenly places.

Principles of Establishment. Since Christ is the "I AM" of the Old Testament, it should be no surprise that the principles espoused by the apostolic church echoed those of the Exodus church. Believers understood that the "wages of sin *is* death" (Rom. 6:23). Faith in Christ our perfect Substitute and Example delivers humans from both the penalty of sin, which is justification (Rom. 5:1), and from the control of sin, which is sanctification (Rom. 6:2, 12, 13). Freed from sin's control, believers were advised to "walk in newness of life" by faith (Rom. 6:1–5; 1 Thess. 5:23; Heb. 9:13; 1 Peter 2:21, 22; 1 John 3:5, 6; 5:4, 5). Sanctification is an experience that was familiar to Enoch of old.

As a consequence of the change of mind that accepting Christ brings, a genuine love response occurs. This is expressed in obedience (1 John 2:4, 5; 5:3). Throughout the Scriptures, obedience to God's Ten Commandments is presented as fundamental to the Christian life (Matt. 5:17, 18; Rom. 3:31; 1 Cor. 7:19; James 2:8–12). In turn, faith and obedience give access to power through the Holy Spirit for witnessing (Acts 1:8; 5:32; John 14:15, 16). There is nothing more convincing than faith in action, which demonstrates that faith is making a practical difference in the life.

Sharing the good news of salvation with others was fundamental to the early church. Jesus' post-resurrection instruction was: "Go therefore and make disciples of all the nations" (Matt. 28:19; cf. Mark 16:15). This was always God's intention, for the fourth commandment of the Decalogue declares that the blessing of the Sabbath, which is a symbol of His re-creative power in the life, is for all people, irrespective of social or racial standing (Exod. 20:10; Isa. 56:6; Mark 2:27).

The international scope of God's appeal contrasts with the regional appeal usually associated with pagan religions. God does not recognize social, national, or racial barriers. This is well expressed by the apostle Paul: "There is neither Jew nor Greek, there is neither slave nor free, there is neither male nor female; for you are all one in Christ Jesus" (Gal. 3:28). God also sent a special vision to Peter to show him: " 'God shows no partiality. But in every nation whoever fears Him and works righteousness is accepted by Him' " (Acts 10:34, 35).

Ministering Agencies. One would imagine that with so much information and the special revelation of Jesus that nobody would depart from the faith delivered to the apostles. However, the apostles themselves warned that men would arise "to draw away the disciples after themselves" (Acts 20:30; cf. 2 Peter 2:1). Indeed, the apostles in their own day experienced the perverse teachings of former followers of Christ, some of whom drew disciples after themselves. The apostle John, for example, contended with a certain Cerinthus who taught

Chapter 7. Christ Will Build His Temple

that Jesus was a normal man who received divinity in the form of a dove at His baptism making Him the Christ, though He lost His divinity before the crucifixion. Again, in 1 John 1:1–3, the apostle argues against Docetism, which contended that Jesus was divine and only appeared to be a man. John stressed the reality of Christ's divine and human natures (1 John 4:3, 15; 5:5). He asserted that He did come in the flesh (1 John 4:2) and that this is true knowledge (1 John 5:20). John called Cerinthus "the enemy of the truth."[94] He declared that those who taught, as did Cerinthus, that Christ did not come in the flesh, are, in fact, "antichrist" (1 John 2:18, 22). Throughout the ages, the nature of Christ has been debated. Other misunderstandings entered the church, and borrowings from pagan religions were multiplied so that it became corrupt.

To encourage faithfulness, God placed other talents in the church besides apostles—prophets, pastors, elders, evangelists, and teachers (Eph. 4:11–13; Titus 1:5–9). Some of these roles have changed with time, and, to the extent that they have, the church has been weakened. However, the historian Kenneth Latourette has observed that the organization and solidarity of the church institution and the idea of service originated with Jesus, giving explanatory power to the success of Christianity over other Eastern religions that arose before and after it.[95]

Gifts were given to the disciples, who were to use the gifts to equip the saints for their God-given mission, to strengthen them spiritually, to direct them to the unifying principles of the gospel, and, above all, to point them to Christ as the center and continuing focus of their faith. The special God-given agency of the Holy Spirit continued during this period to convict people of sin and convince them to stay on the path to salvation (John 16:13; Rom. 8:1–11; James 5:7).

Such encouragement was necessary, for the apostle John observed that, under God's guidance, "the woman," which represented the church, "fled into the wilderness" (Rev. 12:6; cf. Rev. 12:14, 16). John used the well-known symbol of a righteous woman to represent God's true church. He saw the woman fleeing into the wilderness for 1260 years—from AD 538 to AD 1798—there to be protected and nourished by God. As we follow the more detailed history of the seven periods of church history recorded in Revelation, chapters 2 and 3, we observe with interest that, in every period, God has had His faithful representatives (Rev. 2:2, 9, 13, 19; 3:4, 8).

Special Testing Issues. God's prophetic Word indicates that some damaging ideas would enter the church—especially during the time that God's true believers fled to the "wilderness." I will list these ideas to encourage faith in the testimony of Scripture. (See Table 7.1.) The first damaging idea entered when Christ's pre-eminence was supplanted and His name blasphemed. The apostle Paul put it bluntly, prophesying that there would come a time when the "little horn" power would sit "as God in the temple of God, showing himself that he is God" (2 Thess. 2:4; cf. Dan. 7:25; 8:25). This would not be the only diversionary tactic that Satan would employ. Christ's daily ministration in the heavenly sanctuary and His sufficiency as the Mediator for the sinner would also be obscured (Dan. 8:11). The concept of the heavenly sanctuary and Christ's activities there would be minimized, lost sight of, or cast down (Dan. 8:11, 13). The little horn would round up its activities by changing times and law, which are proclaimed by God to be immutable (Dan. 7:25). In other words, this power would substitute Sunday worship for the sacredness of the seventh-day Sabbath and would supplant other truths of the Bible with traditions (Dan. 8:12).

The historical record is very clear that all Daniel predicted has come to pass. Religious liberty was taken away by the "little horn" power in partnership with the state in AD 538. Then, the papal leader was declared the head of all the churches.[96] The church has indicated since then that the pope is God's representative on earth and has signaled the need for intermediaries besides Christ in the pursuit of holiness.[97] It says nothing of the ministry of Christ in the heavenly sanctuary but has a full agenda of extra-biblical dogma, with teachings on purgatory, penance, hell, and the necessity of Christian unity under its leadership. Its world leadership in spiritual matters is unrivaled and, as a sign of its authority, it claims to have utilized God's authority to transfer the sanctity of the seventh-day to the first day of the week. Traditions have multiplied in the church since Constantine, as John

Henry Newman, once-Anglican-clergyman-turned-Roman-Catholic-cardinal, openly chronicled.[98]

The very principles on which Christ's church in all previous ages had been based were brought under intense attack during the Dark Ages. The saints were persecuted relentlessly for their implicit faith in God's Word (Rev. 12:13–17). By opposing this power and declaring that it would be judged unworthy and its dominion taken away (Dan. 7:26, 27), God signified to all people that the principles on which His church is based are eternal.

The Last-Day Church

In this section, I will

- *emphasize that the last-day church was established according to God's timetable. It is destined to recover lost truths and share them with the world as testing truths;*

- *identify the special agency placed in this church to confirm God's guidance.*

Without a doubt, we are in the closing period of earth's history. God's true followers who respond gladly to present truth are members of a spiritual remnant church.[99] Satan's special mission is to destroy God's credibility by destroying His church (Rev. 12:17). The last-day church arose in answer to Bible prophecy that it might proclaim the last messages of God's judgment and mercy to a perishing world (Rev. 14:6–12). The church that arose on time proclaims on time the three angels' messages of Revelation in fulfillment of Bible prophecy. It is interesting to note that all the departures of faith during the reign of the "little horn" power, the period of the "church in the wilderness," were restored to the world through the remnant movement under the symbol of the three angels' messages of Revelation 14. Praise God that the prophetic Word is sure and that the end of all things hastens on!

Table 7.1. Issues impacting foundational concepts about God in the end times and answers from the sanctuary or from those familiar with worship there.

Foundational concept	Defining issue	Prophetic reference	Specific Explanation	Answers from the sanctuary and the prophets
Mercy (Ps. 89:14)	Blasphemes God	Rev. 13:6	• Claims that priests can forgive sins	• Heb. 9:11, 15
			• Claims that Mary is involved in salvation	• Heb. 9:11, 15; 1 Tim. 2:5
			• Claims that Christ is present in the sacrifice of Mass	• Heb. 8:1, 2; 9:11, 12
			• Claims that the Holy Spirit is not a person	• Heb. 3:7–11; cf. John 14:26; 16:13
	Blasphemes God's name	Rev. 13:6	• Claims that God has an infallible human representative	• Isa. 45:21
			• Claims that God created through the evolutionary process	• Rev. 14:7; cf. Ps. 96:4, 5

Chapter 7. Christ Will Build His Temple 113

Foundational concept	Defining issue	Prophetic reference	Specific Explanation	Answers from the sanctuary and the prophets
Mercy (Ps. 89:14)	Blasphemes God's temple	• Rev. 13:6	• Claims that all prophecies were fulfilled in the first century BC or early first century AD	• Dan. 7:21–27; 8:26; Rev. 11:1, 2, 19; cf. Rev. 12:6, 14
		• Rev. 14:6; 18:4	• Everlasting gospel misunderstood, and the role of faith, justification, and sanctification confused	• Gospel includes: Faith: Heb. 3:16–4:2 Justification: Exod. 34:7; Isa. 43:25 Holiness: Exod. 19:6; Deut. 7:6; Isa. 57:15
Justice (Ps. 89:14)	Blasphemes God	Rev. 13:6; Dan. 7:25	• Claims that the Decalogue was changed by a human decree	Rev. 11:19; cf. Rev. 12:17; 14:12
	Doubts the Prophets	Rev. 12:17	• Rejects the immutability of God's Word	Exod. 20:1; 32:15, 16; 34:28; cf. Matt. 4:4; Rev. 19:10
	Blasphemes those in heaven	Rev. 13:6	• Declares immortal souls to be in heaven	Lev. 4:7, 34; cf. Gen. 3:19; Eccles. 3:19, 20

Characteristics Displayed by God's Last Church. The genuine believers who are part of God's faithful "remnant church" display certain specific characteristics. First, they depend on Christ. He is the center of the gospel, which is the center of the message proclaimed by the first angel (Rev. 14:6, 7). Not a vestige of self is found either in the message given or in the worship that the members offer to God. The essential place of faith in the Christian experience is proclaimed in all three messages given by the angels (see Rev. 14:12). The saints, that is, those who respond to these messages, are described as "virgins" and as being "without fault" (Rev. 14:4, 5). This condition is only possible through faith in Jesus' shed blood (Heb. 11:6).

The faith that justifies is also the faith that sanctifies. Our justification is retained only as day by day we live by faith in Jesus' merits (Ezek. 18:24; 1 John 3:4–6). Christ desires that we overcome even as He overcame—by faith (Rev. 3:21). The key response of the faithful to God is awe (Rev. 14:7). Whether people hold God in awe is demonstrated in a practical sense by their love response toward God (Deut. 10:12; cf. 1 John 5:1–5). Love for God can be seen in the obedience of His followers in the face of economic boycott and even threats against their lives, which the Scriptures declare will be part of the world order just before the Savior returns (Rev. 13:15, 17). Genuine love for God is evidenced by His saints when they obey, through faith, all of the commandments, including the fourth (John 14:15, James 2:10; Rev. 14:12; 22:14; cf. Isa. 58:12, 13).

The mighty angel of Revelation 14:7 declares: "The hour of His judgment has come." Christ, our Mediator, is in the heavenly sanctuary now undertaking the special work of investigating the life records of all His followers in response to Satan's accusations (Dan. 7:9, 10; Heb. 9:11–15). Thus, it is of the utmost importance that all give sincere attention to the ministry of Christ there. Christ wishes to cleanse sin from the lives of believers. This can be achieved only as they give themselves without reservation to Christ so that His love can transform them. The transforming experience is revealed in unselfish love expressed toward others. Such an exhibit of love is the most powerful manifestation to the world that God is love and that Satan's accusations are false (John 13:35). Members of the remnant internalize the truths of the three angels and share them with those with whom they come in contact. This constitutes the final demonstration of God's character to the world, which is also His final welcoming call to repentance. Christ will then finish His sanctuary ministry and return to earth.

For those who stand with Christ victorious, endurance—or perseverance—represents a vital quality (2 Peter 1:5–7). The faith of the saints will not fail, as it is based on a thorough understanding of Scripture and is backed by practical experience. Like their Master, "who endured such hostility of sinners against Himself" (Heb. 12:3, MEV), the saints display persistence, or patient endurance (Rev. 14:12). Such persistence is essential for the successful completion of the Christian walk of faith (Matt. 24:13). Those who endure unto the end will have developed by faith through the course of their lives character traits that are Christ-like (Rom. 15:5, 19).

Agencies Encouraging Faithfulness. God has placed special agencies in His last-day church to encourage faithfulness. The most important of these is the gift of prophecy (Eph. 4:11–13; Rev. 12:17; 19:10). This gift was promised to the church, and the Scriptures indicate that this gift will be evident in God's last church in the last remnants of time before Christ comes. It is most fitting that the Lord should provide encouragement (1 Cor. 14:3) to those who will meet the final ire of the dragon. Seventh-day Adventists believe that the gift of prophecy has been revealed in relatively recent history in the life and ministry of Ellen G. White.

Secondly, the prophecy of Revelation informs us that, before the coming of Christ in glory, a final call will be given by Spirit-filled men and women for people to respond to God's last offer of salvation. Borrowing from the calls for repentance by God's fiery messenger Elijah, this last-day call has been termed the "Elijah message" (Mal. 4:5, 6; Joel 2:28–31). We note that the messages delivered by John the Baptist, who came in the "spirit and power of Elijah," were also messages of rebuke and warning of judgment on the verge of execution.[100] The people of that day who responded constituted God's faithful "remnant." So, too, would we expect that God's last warning messages of rebuke, judgment, and hope would have its own "community faithful to God's call."[101] Indeed, there will be an end-time remnant group especially tasked by God to give His last call of mercy.

The Elijah Message

In this section, I will

- *contrast the message of rebuke that God delivered through the prophet Elijah anciently to His people with the rebuke given to God's last-day church;*

- *outline God's remedy to overcome lukewarmness in religious experience.*

Elijah was a prophet who operated in Old Testament times. He came with a message of rebuke to a people who had lost sight of God's ideals and had taken on pagan ideas and practices. Before the Messiah appeared, John the Baptist came bearing the Elijah message to prepare for the coming of the Messiah (Matt. 11:13, 14). Similarly, messengers were prophesied to come before "the great and dreadful day of the LORD"—the dramatic second coming of Christ—to give rebuke and advice to end-time believers (Mal. 4:5). Let us now look at Elijah's original message and the corresponding message of the end-time church.

Elijah's Message to Ancient Israel. The component elements of Elijah's rebuke were several (see Table 7.2). First, his message contained a call to repentance and to obedience to the covenant relationship. Elijah challenged, "If the Lord is God, follow Him" (1 Kings 18:21, NIV; cf. 1 Kings 18:37; 19:10). The people in ancient Israel wandered away from God because they had been seduced by the practices of other nations, their gods, and their methods of worship. They were ashamed of their distinctiveness. Elijah challenged the people to exercise their will to follow the promptings of the Holy Spirit and repent. In referring to the broken covenant relationship, the prophet was turning the people's minds back to the Ten Commandments, for the covenant agreement was made concerning these principles.

The message also challenged hearers to exercise faith in God. Elijah wished the people to sincerely declare, "You *are* the LORD God," and focus their minds on His ways (1 Kings 18:37). Elijah reminded his hearers of the patient endurance demonstrated by Abraham, Isaac, and Israel (1 Kings 18:36), and, by implication, he called them to experience the transforming power of God in their lives. The Israelites would not have wandered from God if their faith had been strong. Elijah appealed to them to re-establish a faith relationship with God so that obedience would be a continuing feature of their living. They had tried in their own strength to succeed. Since they did not exercise faith, the gospel they received did not profit them (Heb. 4:2). Elijah, by referring the mind of his hearers to Abraham, Isaac, and Israel, commended the enduring faith of these spiritual fathers to his audience. This faith was nourished through prayer by claiming the promises of God, by implicitly obeying God's instructions and rising above disappointments, and by asking God for daily help.

Elijah urged them, in response to these appeals, to offer acceptable worship at the altar of the Lord (1 Kings 18:30, 36, 37). The worship that the Israelites practiced was based on pagan ideas. It was egocentric—"hear us," they cried. The senses of hearing, seeing, and feeling were assaulted. It was then that Satan could more effectively work (1 Kings 18:26, 28). By contrast, God's worship is Christ-centered. Elijah appealed to the people first to identify with him, the representative of God. Then, by building an altar at the time of the evening sacrifice, he reminded them of God's instructions. Their attention thus was finally focused on the sacrifice on the altar (1 Kings 18:36, 37). It pointed to Christ.

The Elijah Message to Laodicea. The last-day church identified in the book of Revelation is Laodicea. It is pictured as having fallen well below God's ideal. The Elijah message to this church contains a call to repentance, which is linked to a call to respond to the Holy Spirit's prompting (see Table 7.2). "Eye salve" is needed desperately (Rev. 3:18). As end-time Christians, we have the profound knowledge of God's ways and of the Scriptures. Never before has the world been bathed in such knowledge. However, the prevailing sentiments of the society around us have been seeping into the church. For example, a dominant concept in today's Postmodern world, which has led people away from God and into the occultic New Age, is that there are no absolute standards of right and wrong. Leading practices that might be sought after are those designed to stimulate creativity, increase self-esteem and personal power, and satisfy the demands of desire.[102] We notice, unfortunately, that some of these sentiments are portrayed as being possessed by church members in the end-times, for followers declare, "I am rich and increased with goods" (Rev. 3:17, KJV). In expressing, "I feel comfortable, I feel good about my experience, I have great self-esteem," the emphasis is on relative values and on self. God pleads with His people to listen to the Reprover of sin, the Holy Spirit (John 16:7–11).

It is most apparent that there is a deficiency of understanding with regards to faith in the period of earth's history in which we live. This deficiency is so severe that repentance and reformation are the only remedies (Rev. 3:18, 19). Hearers are advised to put on the white raiment of Christ's righteousness by faith (Rev. 3:18; cf. Matt. 22:11, 12; Gal. 3:27). Such faith also shows corresponding works because believers are channels of God's love (Rev. 14:12; cf. Gal. 5:6; James 2:5). This outcome is described as gold tried in the fire (Rev. 3:18).

The Elijah message contains a call to acceptable worship. The focus of many believers has been on self-worship (cf. "I am rich").

Their worship needs to become Christ-centered (Rev. 3:17, 20). In the first angel's call to the world, the emphasis is on Christ (Rev. 14:6, 7). The people who have heeded and responded to the Elijah message to Laodicea are empowered to deliver this message. Their worship will spring from the principle of "fear," which in this context means awe and reverence. Such worship is a product of faith. Feelings of joy and of blessing are given by God in answer to such faith. This contrasts with worship that has crept into the apostate churches of Babylon as they have imbibed the rudiments of the world (Rev. 14:8, 9). God's warning to not follow the beast power is instruction for the faithful remnant to avoid following false methods of worship based on the applause and praise of men, on self-satisfaction, on entertainment, on excitement, on activities that are pagan in origin. Feelings drive such worship rather than faith. The senses of hearing, seeing, and feeling are assaulted in such worship so that the "spirits of demons" can effectively work; the babble of gibberish is heard; practitioners pray to the god within who resides in the silent place. Miracles are worked (Rev. 16:13, 14). And all of this is done, ostensibly, in praise of the one true God.[103]

The Lord God especially draws the attention of all to the meaning of the Sabbath as a symbol of Creation and worship on His blessed day. It is also a symbol of sanctification, a relationship possible only through faith (Rev. 14:7, 12; cf. Exod. 31:13). Christ desires to deliver worshipers both from the penalty of sin, which is justification, and also to give victory over sin, which is sanctification. In this antitypical day of atonement, it is the responsibility of believers to examine their relationship with God. The remnant people respond to this call, for they are described as "virgins" and as being "without fault" (Rev. 14:4, 5). The transformation of character they have accomplished through the strength that Christ has given them in response to the prayer of faith. Their love for God leads them to obey all of His revealed will (Isa. 1:18, 19) and it is evidenced in their love for humanity in witnessing and in deeds of kindness. Those who respond to God's call are among the redeemed.

The Elijah message contains a call to patient endurance. Jesus notices those who are obedient to Him and encourages them in the words, "he that shall endure unto the end, the same shall be saved" (Matt. 24:13, KJV). In Revelation 3:21, the same thought is again expressed. The reward is only for those who endure to the end. The people who are best prepared to endure patiently are those who have a sense of the times in which they live. They believe in the imminence of Christ's return and live with the fires of love, faith, and hope burning brightly.

Church of the Firstborn. At Christ's second coming, the genuine members of God's church become members of the "Church of the Firstborn" in heaven (Heb. 12:22, 23; Rev. 7:4; 14:1–5). The apostle Paul pictures the true believers of all ages around the throne of God. They constitute the Church of Christ, the Firstborn (Col. 1:15). He is the Rock on which the true church in every age has been built (1 Cor. 10:4; cf. Ps. 28:1). He is the "chief cornerstone" (Acts 4:10, 11; Eph. 2:20; 1 Peter 2:6). The apostle Peter had no doubt as to who the foundation of the church was (cf. Matt. 16:16–18; 1 Peter 2:7, 8), unlike some who named the name of Christ and proclaimed Peter the first pope. He would recoil in horror at such a thought. Let us make Christ the center of all our worship here so that we may be among the number who worship Him on the sea of glass!

Table 7.2. Comparison of the two Elijah messages recorded in Scripture relative to worship.

Elijah's Times (1 Kings 18)	The Remnant Church and Its Times (Mal. 4:5, 6)
Acceptable relationships outlined in the days of Elijah	**Acceptable relationships outlined by John the Revelator**
• Worship was centered on God; His revealed will is emphasized; note the key words: "follow Him," "altar of the LORD," "LORD God of Abraham," "God in Israel," "at Your word" (1 Kings 18:21, 30, 36).	• Worship is Christ-centered— "give glory to Him," meaning the Creator (Rev. 14:7).
• God is love—"Come near to me" (1 Kings 18:30).	• God is love—salvation "to every nation"; a message involving family relationships (Rev. 14:6; cf. Mal. 4:5, 6).

• Reasoned appeals—"How long" and "Come near" (1 Kings 18:21, 30). Encouraged the people to look at the history of God's dealings with Israel and the patriarchs (verses 31, 36).	• A reasoned approach to worship—"for the hour of His judgment has come"; "calculate the number of the beast" (Rev. 14:7; 13:18). The implied encouragement is to trust in the authority of God's prophetic word.
• Calmness—"Hear me, O LORD, hear me"; God speaks in a still small voice (1 Kings 18:37; 19:12). This behavior is in marked contrast with the worship offered by the priests of Baal (verses 26–28).	• Calm, purposeful mission carried out with "patience," "to preach," and to come "if anyone hears" God's "voice" (Rev. 14:12, 6; 3:20). This behavior is in marked contrast with the blasphemous activities of those who oppose God (Rev. 13:4–6).
• Visual senses quietly involved to awaken conscience (1 Kings 18:31–35).	• "Visions" and prophesying promised (Joel 2:28).
• Emotions involved, calmness and awe predominated; at Elijah's cry, "Hear me, O LORD," the people "fell on their faces" (1 Kings 18:37, 39).	• Emotions involved—zeal, awe, and reverence in response to the call for repentance—"Fear God" (Rev. 3:19; 14:7).
Lessons Taught	**Lessons Taught**
• Faith was central to the appeal; reminded of Abraham, Isaac, Israel (1 Kings 18:36).	• Faith is central in appeals (Rev. 3:18; 14:12; cf. 1 Pet. 1:7).
• Challenged to obey God's word (1 Kings 18:21, 37).	• Obedience to the Decalogue a hallmark of the message (Rev. 14:7, 12).
• Repentance urged (1 Kings 18:21, 37).	• Repentance urged (Rev. 3:19, 20).
• Promoted steadfast endurance by example (1 Kings 18:1).	• Call to endurance and sanctification (Rev. 3:21); consider the challenge to develop Christian character (2 Peter 1:2–11; cf. Rev. 22:11).

The Nature of Humanity

Chapter 8.
The Life Is in the Blood

Chapter Emphasis: *Sin brings eternal death. The loss of animal life symbolized by the shed blood of the sacrifice in the ancient worship activities and highlighted in the Bible point to Christ's sacrifice. These activities taught the reality of human mortality. Immortality belongs to God alone, but it will be given to the righteous at Christ's return.*

Spiritual Link: *Deceptive activities inspired by Satan and his agents center on the concept of the possession of an immortal soul and the supposed ability to communicate with the dead.*

The most valued gift in our world is life. We read of heroic efforts of those who dare to risk their lives to save the lives of others under perilous conditions. The question that all ultimately must ask is: What comes after death? This is a question that has intrigued all civilizations from the beginning of the world. In fact, we find that in Eden the fallen angel Satan tantalized the first woman, Eve, with the belief that there were other dimensions of existence than that which she was then experiencing. This special knowledge, this wonderful experience, would be hers if only she followed the principles of Satan's government. He promised her that, if she followed his teachings, she would not die. He was telling her that obedience to God and access to the tree of life were not essential for immortality.

In this chapter, I will examine the idea of life after death, the concept of reincarnation, and related issues. Of paramount significance, I wish to establish what the Bible has taught from the beginning regarding belief in the immortality of the soul and the possibility of holding communion with those who have passed to "the other side." It is also my plan to outline the instructions that God gave to His people on this subject through the sanctuary services.

Death, the Wages of Sin

In this section, I will

- *emphasize that death entered this world on account of sin;*

- *remind readers that animal sacrifices were introduced by God in order to indicate the consequences of sin and also to point to the coming Savior.*

God adequately warned the parents of the human race that the ultimate consequence of disobedience would be death (Gen. 2:17; cf. Rom. 6:23). God no doubt explained the basic nature of death to Adam and Eve and told them that it would bring eternal separation from the holy beings who were their companions. Since Adam and Eve had no practical experience with death, it is evident that God's statement, recorded in Genesis, had to be accepted by faith. Individual obedience could spring only from trust and love for their Maker.

The reality of death was soon apparent to the disobedient pair. Animals were first slain by God to provide them with clothing (Gen. 3:21). It is important to note that before Adam and Eve were expelled from the Garden of Eden, God gave them the promise that Christ would come and suffer on their behalf (Gen. 3:15). It appears evident that animal sacrifices would have been introduced to them at this early date and that they had some understanding that the covering of animal skins that was provided for them foreshadowed Christ's covering of righteousness (cf. Gen. 4:1). No doubt they taught their children the meaning of the sacrificial ceremony.

We are first made aware of the institution of animal sacrifices in the account of the murder of Abel by his brother Cain (Gen. 4:4–8). Abel offered a perfect lamb to the Lord in obedience to the instructions that he had received; Cain was rebellious and offered fruit. God accepted Abel's offering but not Cain's. Cain in his anger argued with his brother and slew him. This shedding of blood was abhorrent to God.

The practice of animal sacrifice was fully developed during the Exodus experience (Lev. 17:11). Releasing the animal's blood by humanely cutting the throat caused it to die. Hence, the blood represented life (Gen. 9:5; Lev. 17:14; Deut. 12:23). The slaying of the animal victims impressed on the suppliant the dreadful consequences of sin. The shed blood pointed forward to the life of the Son of God that would be forfeited in the future. His death would enable the sinner to live, for the Scriptures clearly affirm, "Without shedding of blood there is no remission" (Heb. 9:22). In requiring the life of a perfect substitute for sin that the people had committed, God was illustrating that their sin would cause the shedding of the blood of the holy Son of God at some time in the future (Heb. 9:28, 12; 1 John 1:7; Rev. 5:9).

In the worship service of the sanctuary and temple, the blood of the animal victim was caught and the majority poured out at the bottom of the altar in the courtyard. On reaching the earth, it returned to dust (Lev. 4:7, 18, 25, 30, 34; cf. Gen. 3:19). Hence, the spilling of the blood, which represented the life, conveyed the idea that sin led to eternal oblivion. The same truth was taught on the Day of Atonement when the goat for Azazel was led into the wilderness and perished there, presumably from natural causes (Lev. 16:21, 22). It too returned to dust.

The Scriptures declare a solemn truth about both human beings and beasts when they die. Both return to dust again (Gen. 3:19; Eccles. 3:19, 20). The latter texts clearly and unequivocally declare that human beings will return to the dust out of which they were made. Solomon, the builder of the magnificent temple in Jerusalem, indicated that both men and beasts go to the same place—they all return to dust. The question remains, do human beings have any advantage or pre-eminence over the beasts in death? On this point, Solomon is emphatic—they do not. Both man and beast possess the same life force, or "spirit."

This is in complete agreement with Job's account in which he uses the terms "breath" [Heb. *neshamah*] and "spirit" [Heb. *ruach*] interchangeably (Job 27:3, KJV). The question of whether this life force ascended at death, in the case of humans, and descended, in the case of the beasts, is one concept that Solomon raised but did not answer in the early section of his discourse (Eccles. 3:21). This, no doubt, was a question that arose from the pagan beliefs of his time. The Egyptians, for instance, believed in a blissful resting place in the heavens. The soul and the body were regarded as separate entities, and the soul was considered capable of independent movement from the body.[104] In Ecclesiastes 12:7, Solomon answered the question about the destination of the life breath: the "spirit," or breath of life (*ruach*), returns to God. Nowhere in the Bible does the Hebrew word *ruach* convey the idea of a conscious entity winging its flight to the heavens.[105]

Abominations of the Occult

In this section, I will

- *emphasize that from the time of the creation of humanity, Satan has sought to contradict God's statement that disobedience to His instruction would bring death;*

- *indicate how the idea of life after death is strengthened.*

Satan sought to divert the attention of Eve from the plain statements of God concerning sin and its consequences by introducing the idea that there was knowledge that God was hiding from her and that she would benefit from acquiring it. One of the supposed benefits of such knowledge was the concept of the immortality of the soul. He declared, "You will not surely die" (Gen. 3:4).

God, on the contrary, had emphatically said that, on the day that humans sinned, death would come (Gen. 2:17). The enemy of souls sought to contradict this by declaring that, in sinning, the person would not die but would, rather, attain a higher level of knowledge (Gen. 3:5). No doubt the serpent, through which Satan acted, ate a portion of the forbidden fruit to demonstrate that death did not immediately come.[106] This would have appeared to be conclusive proof to Eve of the claim being made. God's sentence, however, was sure. Death did not occur at the time of eating, but the sentence of death was passed then, and human vitality began to decline. The Hebrew of Genesis 2:17 literally says, "dying thou shalt die."[107] Instead of possessing immortality conditional on obedience, now humans were given "unconditional mortality."

The term "immortality of the soul," as used today, is explained in the following quotation. Immortality "implies that the being which survives shall preserve its personal identity and be connected by conscious memory with the previous life." And again, "By the human mind, or soul, is meant the ultimate principle within me by which I feel, think, and will, and by which my body is animated."[108]

Both anciently and in today's world the idea of a conscious state in death is fostered through the teaching of many Christian churches, but also by witches, wizards, familiar spirits or mediums, necromancers, spiritists, and the like (cf. Deut. 18:9–13; 2 Kings 21:6; 2 Chron. 33:6). Necromancers and those who consulted with familiar spirits were simply consulters of the dead. Witches and wizards were men and women who practiced sorcery, or the magic arts. The Jews regarded such individuals as being involved in evil activities. Characteristic of all workers of the magic arts was the thought that the magician could make contact with and "command the services of spiritual powers—demons, gods, and ghosts—malignant in their disposition and willing to do mischief."[109]

Today, the occult is popularized in movies, TV programs, computer games, magazines, and music. Psychics and clairvoyants openly advertise their services. The occult is attractive in our age to increasing numbers of people who are seeking exciting and novel experiences. These experiences can lead some to display bizarre behavior, to suffer mental breakdown, and to experiment with drugs and crime.[110] The fascination with Eastern religions and their emphasis on reincarnation leads devotees into the occult or makes them more susceptible to its influence.

Occultic powers may be able to make educated guesses about the future (1 Sam. 28:15, 19; cf. 1 Sam. 31:2, 4, 5). Under the circumstances of King Saul's communication with the witch of Endor, it was no great achievement for her to predict his death. He was downcast and discouraged and about to go into battle. The Lord had departed from him, and he was now directly disobeying God by attempting to communicate with the dead (1 Sam. 28:16). In our time, we might mention the predictions of the self-styled prophet Aladino Felix who correctly predicted the death of a Russian cosmonaut in 1966 as well as the forthcoming assassinations of Martin Luther King and Senator Robert Kennedy. He also predicted violence in his home country Brazil, which duly took place. In attempting to assess whether Felix was led by God, we note that he was caught leading a group of bank robbers in São Paulo who also planned to assassinate top government officials.[111] It is clear that it was not God but Satan who was behind these activities.

The apostle Paul speaks powerfully about principalities and powers of darkness operating in this world (Eph. 6:12). The news media continually give evidence that Satan and his associates are active. This is no different than it was in Jesus' day. These agencies were involved in influencing the rulers and people to call for the crucifixion of our Lord (Rev. 11:8; cf. Isa. 19:3). It is evident that those controlled by Satan were responsible for the scenes associated with His arrest, trials, and crucifixion. The same agencies will be involved in the climactic events of the great controversy on this earth (Rev. 16:13, 14).

Even though individuals might be caught up in such soul-destroying activities (Gal. 5:19–21), the witness of Scripture is that the Lord is ever willing to accept genuine repentance from such people and to count them as children of His kingdom. For example, Simon the sorcerer was baptized by the apostle Philip (Acts 8:9–13). His subsequent behavior was not exemplary (verses 14–24), and history is not kind to his memory. However, he was accepted as a potential candidate of God's kingdom, though his later poor choices sealed his destiny.

Unseen Agencies in Our World

In this section, I will

- *establish that both good and evil angels seek to influence the actions of human beings.*

The Bible contains the story of a conflict between the forces of good and evil. The controversy arose in heaven and spread to this earth (Rev. 12:7–9). The conflict is over the principles of love that regulate all of God's activities. Satan maintained that his own principles were superior to God's and has since sought to convince all intelligent beings of the correctness of his assertions. The Scriptures give us a preview of the future and show the controversy ending in triumph for the principles of love (Rev. 20:10; 21:1–5). It should not surprise readers that a basically similar controversy scenario was acted out each religious year in association with the ancient earthly sanctuary. (We will study this in greater detail in Chapter 11.)

Satan was not alone in his rebellion. Other angels joined him, and they, like him, are created beings (Ps. 8:5; Ezek. 28:13–15; Rev. 12:9, 3, 4). All were cast to the earth at the same time as Satan, who was the cherub occupying a position of honor next to Christ. These angels were created pure but, through belief in Satan's lie, they were banished forever and will perish with Satan in the lake of fire that will cleanse this earth after the return of the New Jerusalem (1 Cor. 6:3; 2 Peter 2:4; Rev. 20:10, 15).

The comforting aspect of the controversy is that God has unseen agencies present in the world to aid those who sincerely desire to please Him. The promise is: "The angel of the LORD encamps all around those who fear Him" (Ps. 34:7; cf. 2 Kings 6:15–17; Matt. 18:10). The involvement of angels in the ministry of salvation was taught through the sanctuary on earth. Two golden angels reverently bowed their heads over the mercy seat in the Most Holy Place (Exod. 25:18). History records that the veils of the sanctuary had three-dimensional angels woven into them to emphasize the angels' ministry.[112] The holy angels are based in heaven. They act as God's agents in protecting His children and leading the honest in mind to a knowledge of God (Gen. 28:12; Ps. 34:7; John 1:51).

Unconscious State in Death

In this section, I will

- *clearly establish from Scripture that there is no conscious state in death.*

In contemporary Christian thought, the idea is that, at death, the soul departs the body. The soul is thought to be an entity that feels, thinks, wills, and animates the body. The Scriptures do not give any credibility to this concept or to the doctrine of reincarnation (Rom. 5:12; Heb. 9:27). There are some powerful texts that declare unequivocally that in death a person is not able to think, feel, or participate in anything on earth or in heaven (Job 14:12, 21; Ps. 115:17; 146:4; Eccles. 9:5, 6, 10).

The Concept of the Soul. Confusion in some minds comes about with the use of the term "soul" in Scripture. The meaning of this term in the Bible is quite different from our usage of it today. First, we notice that Adam became a "living soul," or "living *being*," when God breathed "the breath of life" into the clay model that He had formed (Gen. 2:7). This text emphatically states that a body plus the "breath of life" are the components of a "living soul," that is, of a "living being." The Hebrew word in this verse for "soul" (KJV), or "being" (NKJV), is *nephesh*, which most commonly means "breath," "life," or "living being."

Secondly and most significantly, when an individual dies, the soul dies (Ezek. 18:4, 20). The Hebrew word used by the prophet Ezekiel for "soul" is also *nephesh*, or "living being." This means that when the breath of life no longer exists in the body, the person is dead, and there is therefore no longer such a conscious entity as a soul. In Ecclesiastes, we are informed that the life principle, or "spirit," returns to God and the dust of the body returns to the earth (Eccles. 12:7; cf. Job 27:3). This verse points out that, when a person dies, the process is the reverse of that indicated in Genesis when life was given. In support of this, we note that the Hebrew word (*ruach*) used in Ecclesiastes for "spirit" also means "wind."[113] In conclusion, if a soul can die, then it cannot be immortal. Indeed, Scripture consistently refers to humans as mortal (Job 4:17; Rom. 5:12; 1 Cor. 15:53).

This is precisely the position taken by Christ. He did not support the notion of a conscious state in death. This was evident when Lazarus died. He likened the occurrence to "sleep" in which conscious thought had ceased (John 11:11). Jesus rebuked the Pharisees for their traditions (Matt. 15:1, 6, 9). The Pharisees gave the oral law of their traditions a place in their beliefs equal to the written Torah, which is the Mosaic law formed by the first five books of the Bible. They believed in the immortality of the soul. This doctrine was not taught in the Torah. The Sadducees, by contrast, believed in the death of the soul.[114] In the texts recorded in Matthew, Jesus rebuked the Pharisees for their scripturally unfounded traditions. He did not include the Sadducees in this particular rebuke.

Some have sought support for the immortality of the soul in Jesus' comments to the thief on the cross. Jesus indeed indicated to the thief that he would be with Him in Paradise, but He did not say that this would be at the moment of death (Luke 23:43). This becomes evident with a little thought. Upon His own testimony, Christ did not go to His Father until after Sunday morning (John 20:11, 16–18), hence He was not in Paradise on the day that He spoke to the thief, which was Friday evening. We also must remember that there was no punctuation in the Greek. "In its early history the text of the NT appeared only in *scriptio continua*, so that punctuating the text was a matter of interpreting the meaning of an unbroken stream of Greek letters."[115] Hence, where one chooses to place the comma in Luke 23:43 will make a vast difference to the meaning of the verse. Notice the difference it makes: With the comma *before* "today," immortality of the soul can be inferred—"Assuredly, I say to you, today you will be with Me in Paradise." With the comma *after* "today," mortality of the soul can be inferred—"Assuredly, I say to you today, you will be with Me in Paradise."[116]

As a last resort in upholding the idea of immortality in Christian circles, many invoke the story of the Rich Man and Lazarus. This is actually a pagan story that was adapted by Hellenistic Jews, and it contains elements that Jesus Himself did not support by His teachings (Luke 16:19-31; cf. Matt. 25:31-46). The historian Josephus related this story in a discourse to the Greeks. The account asserted that, as souls descended into Hades after death, the just were guided to the right hand, that is, to the Bosom of Abraham, and the unjust were dragged to the neighborhood of Hell.[117] The story had its origins in the Egyptian folktale concerning the journey of Si-Osiris to the underworld.[118] Investigation of the Scriptures reveals that Jesus taught that the separation of the just and the unjust occurs at His coming at the end of the world (Matt. 25:31-33). His use of this popular account was principally to show that our destiny is determined before death and that God's judgments are irrevocable.[119] Abraham is, indeed, still in his grave, as the apostle Paul distinctly informs us (Heb. 11:8, 13-16, 39, 40). An additional evidence is the fact that the equivalent term for the Greek *hades* in the passage is the Hebrew *sheol*, which is usually translated "grave." It does not represent a hot, burning place, but a place of darkness and silence (Job 17:13; Ps. 31:17).

Immortality Promised. Jesus did indeed promise His followers that they would be given immortality when He came again to reward true believers (John 14:2, 3). The visible appearance of Jesus in the clouds of glory with great noise and the accompanying hosts of heaven is the glorious event associated with the raising of the dead and the putting on of immortality (1 Thess. 4:15-17; 1 Cor. 15:20, 23, 51-55).

As long as the second coming of Christ was considered imminent, it did not matter to the believers that they might be sleeping or waiting until the resurrection. (This view prevailed until as late as the fifth century). When this blessed event receded into the distant future, people did not wish "to postpone indefinitely the reward of the saved and the punishment of the damned," so they invented "the doctrine of the immediate judgment of each soul at death."[120] Similarly, the companion idea of purgatory was manufactured. Clement of Alexandria (who died before AD 245) and Origen (who died in AD 253/254) contributed to this idea taken in part from Greek religious tradition. Yet, the true father of the concept was Augustine (AD 354-430) of the Western Roman Church. The doctrine was officially defined by the Council of Florence in 1439.[121] It was a "powerful political weapon" used to induce obedience to the Latin Church.[122] It must be acknowledged: "Catholic philosophers ... have generally claimed to establish the validity of the belief apart from revelation." Evidence for the belief is even adduced from spiritualism.[123]

The concept of purgatory and hell are obnoxious ideas that make people anxious and fearful and that damage them psychologically. It can be an effective device to lead them into atheism.[124] These concepts have no foundation in the literature of the Bible, and they are not in accord with the idea of a loving God. In the context of our discussion, we must remember that the central idea conveyed through the sanctuary system was God's love for humanity and the need for an out-flowing response of love from believers toward others (Deut. 10:12, 15, 18, 19). Decisions for Christ are made every day, but there are limits to human probation (Lev. 23:29, 30; Ps. 95:7–11). This means that the sanctuary doctrine is implacably opposed to the idea of eternal punishment.

Startling Reminder of Mortality. The great Christian church of medieval times still exerts tremendous power. John the Revelator indicates something of its continuing influence in the thirteenth chapter of Revelation. He is careful to indicate that this power is promulgating blasphemous ideas against God, His name and tabernacle, and those in heaven (Rev. 13:6). In fact, any idea or action that misrepresents God's character and teachings is in the category of blasphemy (James 2:6, 7). One such blasphemous idea is the conscious state of the soul following death. This becomes evident when the truths relating to the "hour of His judgment" (Rev. 14:7) are considered.

If the souls of men and women are assigned to purgatory, heaven, or hell at death, the need for a judgment is negated. The apostle Peter, the supposed rock on which Christ's Church is built, has put the record straight. "The Lord knoweth how to deliver the godly out of temptations, and to reserve the unjust unto the day of judgment to be punished" (2 Peter 2:9, KJV). The end-time reminder from the sanctuary is that humans are mortal and that, after the judgment, the just are given immortality. To contend that judgment occurs at death is blasphemous in that humans have schemed to lay aside the teachings of the Bible and have replaced it with ideas of their own making or of extra-biblical sources.

Chapter 8. The Life Is in the Blood

The Gift of Immortality

In this section, I will

- identify the time when immortality will be given to the righteous.

Many in the Christian churches teach that men and women go either to heaven or hell at death as the reward of the deeds of their life. This unfortunate picture is not taught in the Scriptures. Only God has immortality (1 Tim. 6:15, 16); there is no such thing as an immortal soul departing the body at death.

Immortality a Gift. There is a clear stream of thought throughout the Bible on the resurrection of the whole body and the gift of immortality. There was early indication that immortality was God's gift to His faithful ones in that Enoch and Elijah were given immortality rather than dying (Gen. 5:24; 2 Kings 2:1–12). Abraham, a patriarch the Israelites all knew about and revered, understood that if Isaac had been slain by him, then God could have raised him up from the dead to fulfill the promises made (Heb. 11:17–19). This is not surprising since resurrection is as dependent on the creative activity of God as was the framing of the worlds (Heb. 11:3). As a startling reminder of God's ability, the ark of the covenant contained Aaron's rod that budded and fruited. Originally, this was a dry almond stick, but under divine influence it budded, flowered, and fruited in contrast to those of the rival princes who coveted Aaron's position (Num. 17:1–13).

Elsewhere in the Bible, the Creation is irrevocably connected with the idea of entering "rest" with God, of which the Sabbath is the memorial (Heb. 4:3–10). The Most Holy apartment of the earthly sanctuary contained the permanent stone document expressing this very thought (Exod. 25:21; 31:18). Indeed, the Sabbath was commemorated in the sanctuary system of ceremonies as its most prominent memorial and convocation (Lev. 23:1–3). It represents a call to recognize God's creative works, His transforming activities in the individual, and His promise to give the gift of immortality to the saints.

Deliverance Foreshadowed. The Feast of Tabernacles was the last of the obligatory gatherings at Jerusalem, which also included Passover and Unleavened Bread and the Feast of Weeks, or Pentecost (Deut. 16:16). The feast is described in Leviticus 23:33–43 and was a commemoration of the escape of the Exodus, which represented deliverance from slavery and death as vividly tangible in the Red Sea experience and the sojourn in tents, or "tabernacles" (Exod. 14:5–

31; cf. Exod. 15:2, 13, 17). The wilderness experience represented a rebirth as graphically explained by the apostle Paul (1 Cor. 10:1–4). Indeed, salvation was a dominant theme in the Hallel of Psalms 113–118, one of which was chanted every day during this major religious festival. The Feast of Tabernacles looked forward to Israel's entrance into permanent housing in the Promised Land. In its ultimate application, the feast looked forward to the experience of rejoicing following eternal deliverance at Christ's coming and the fulfillment in the new earth of the promised inheritance of God's eternal covenant (cf. Heb. 11:13–16, 39, 40). This joyous end-point was the dominant emphasis of the sanctuary and temple ceremonies, for they focused on the forgiveness of sin and the perfecting of the believer. Scholars have identified twelve elements in the feast that parallel events described in the book of Revelation as occurring during the period after Christ returns the second time.[125] (See Table 8.1.) This tells us that, from God's viewpoint, the sanctuary doctrine has not lost its significance.

Jesus will give rewards to the righteous and wicked at the same time, that is, at the end of this world's history and after the investigative aspects of the judgment are complete (Rev. 22:11, 12). At that time, the righteous are "caught up" and "meet the Lord in the air" (Matt. 13:37–43; 1 Thess. 4:16, 17). The Bible portrays the saints waiting in their graves until the call of Christ brings them forth at His second coming. This was Daniel's understanding (Dan. 12:2, 3, 13). Other Bible writers have confirmed the same (e.g., Job 19:25–27; Isa. 26:19).[126] When Christ returns, He will bring His reward with Him (Matt. 16:27; Rev. 22:12). It is at that time that God will give the greatest gift—the gift of immortality (1 Cor. 15:51–54; 1 John 3:2).

Associated with the last great climactic events occurring on earth before Jesus comes, the Scriptures reveal that the world will be deceived by signs and miracles carried out by evil agencies operating through religious organizations that are not true to God's Word (Rev. 16:13, 14). Such deceptions will be eagerly grasped by those who believe in communication with the dead. The Lord Himself, through the writings of the apostle John, said that those who will be counted as blessed in His kingdom are those "who are awaiting me, who keep their robes in readiness" (Rev. 16:15, TLB). The garments of our mind need to be fortified with the truths of God's Word, or we will not be able to stand in that awesome time.

Chapter 8. The Life Is in the Blood

Table 8.1. Highlights from the Feast of Tabernacles, or Ingathering, and the eschatological equivalent described by John in the book of Revelation.

Feast highlights	Old Testament reference	Imagery parallels in Revelation
Gathering	Lev. 23:35–37, 39; Num. 29:12	Rev. 7:9–17; 14:1–5
Rest	Lev. 23:35, 39	Rev. 16:17, 20; cf. Isa. 66:22, 23
Harvest	Exod. 23:39; Deut. 16:13	Rev. 7:9, 13, 14; 14:14–16
Rejoicing	Lev. 23:40; Deut. 16:13–15	Rev. 7:9, 10; 14:2, 3; 21:3, 4
Remembrance	Lev. 23:43; Deut. 16:17	Rev. 15:3, 4; 21:4, 5
Shelter	Lev. 23:42, 43	Rev. 7:15–17; 21:3, 4
Newness	Lev. 23:16	Rev. 21:5
Water	Zech. 14:16–19	Rev. 7:16, 17; 22:1
Fruit	Lev. 23:40	Rev. 22:2; cf. 14:4
Palm branches, boughs of leafy trees	Lev. 23:40	Rev. 7:9, 10; cf. Rev. 22:2
Gratitude	Lev. 23:36–38; Num. 29:12–39; Deut. 16:17	Rev. 7:9–12; 15:3, 4; 19:1–8
Light	Ps. 118:27	Rev. 21:11, 23
Salvation	Ps. 113–118; cf. John 7:37	Rev. 7:10; 12:10

Salvation, Atonement, and Reconciliation

Chapter 9.
The Way of Salvation in the Sanctuary

Chapter Emphasis: *The dynamics of salvation from Eden to the present remain the same. Christ's saving merits are available constantly and are accessed through confession of sin and the claiming of His merits through faith. In this way, the sinner is justified.*

Spiritual Link: *Living a life of commitment and service in sanctification is also a faith experience and rightly follows justification as the fruit of that experience.*

The Psalmist has well said: "Your way, O God, *is* in the sanctuary" (Ps. 77:13). The sanctuary services portray the way of God and, particularly, the way of salvation. They constituted the means of giving the gospel—or "good news"—to humanity for a period of time. However, the apostle Paul warned that even in his day a different or perverted gospel was being preached (Gal. 1:6, 7). There are several ideas prevalent in our world today regarding the exact nature of this good news. Is the good news that Jesus is coming again soon and will give all those who have not responded to His offer of salvation in this present life a second chance? Or, is the good news that we are actually gods who will someday become what the supreme God is now, the creator of our own world? Should we proclaim, as some presently do, that the gospel was taken from the earth for long centuries after Christ's death and that it has only relatively recently been restored? Is it true that salvation is dependent on our own efforts? These and other questions are abroad in the religious world today.

Soon after they had made the wrong choice in following the way suggested by Satan, Adam and Eve would learn about the gospel. At first, they hid from God in their frightened state. Yet, He sought them out. In the conversation that followed, God informed them of the results of their choice. However, the hope that came when God announced that He had a rescue plan must have made their hearts beat faster. It was apparently not long after sin had entered the world that God more fully unfolded His rescue plan to the sinful pair, for we notice that their sons were instructed regarding the need for sacrificing animals, which prefigured the coming Redeemer. As succeeding generations came upon the scene of action and the voices of Adam and Eve were no longer heard, it then became necessary to outline the details of the way of life more fully.

God chose to outline His plan of salvation in a tangible, structured way through the services performed in the sanctuary. The sanctuary continually drew the attention of the suppliant to the God of love and presented the necessity of a deep and abiding faith in the merits of the Savior who would one day appear on this earth. Christ, during His time on earth, gave a deep meaning to the services and symbols of the sanctuary, for they were fulfilled in Him. Although the earthly sanctuary system of worship came to an end at Christ's death, there remains in the Christian church today reminders of it, and the services point us to Christ's work in the heavenly sanctuary. The sanctuary services and the rituals surrounding them continue to teach us important lessons about God's master plan for the final eradication of sin and the ushering in of a new earth in which righteousness will dwell forever.

By looking at the sanctuary services, it is possible to answer questions and contend with misinformation widely circulating in the Christian world today. In this chapter, I will contrast the main features of the gospel taught in the Old Testament as understood and taught by our Lord and as identified in Scripture as appropriate for our day.

The Gospel Taught in the Sanctuary

In this section, I will

- *emphasize that the gospel was made known to the human race at the Fall and emphatically illustrated in the earthly sanctuary;*

- *emphasize that God loves the unlovable—no sinner has done anything to deserve His love;*

- *remind readers that salvation is made possible through Jesus Christ and Him alone;*

- *observe that our love response to God through faith is made evident in obedience.*

The gospel centers on Jesus Christ who is indeed the central figure throughout both the Old and New Testaments. The Scriptures talk of only one gospel through which God offers sinful people eternal life. Let us briefly examine the ideas of salvation presented in the Old Testament and, more particularly, in the sanctuary.

The Scriptures appear to indicate that on the evening of the very day in which our first parents sinned, God gave them hope by announcing His plan to rescue them from eternal destruction (Gen. 3:11, 15). In studying verse 15, we understand from the context that God is addressing Satan. "I will put enmity between you [Satan] and the woman [the church—2 Cor. 11:2], and between your seed [those who do the evil deeds of the devil—John 8:44; 1 John 3:10] and her seed [Christ—Gal. 3:16]; He [Christ] will bruise your head [Satan will be eternally destroyed—Rev. 20:10] and you [Satan] will bruise His heel [Christ was smitten for our sakes—Isa. 53:5]." Adam and Eve understood this promise, as is indicated by Genesis 4:1. On the birth of her first son, Eve said, "I have gotten a man, from the Lord" (literal Hebrew reading). She apparently considered that this child might be the son of promise. What disappointment awaited her! Instead of being a redeemer, Cain became the world's first murderer (Gen. 4:8).

The good news conveyed by Genesis 3:15 is that judgment is promised against the devil—his head is to be bruised. Elsewhere the Scriptures elaborate on this point by commenting that Satan will be destroyed in the lake of fire (Rev. 20:10). These texts establish the gospel as a message of complete restoration and reconciliation.

From the time of Adam and Eve, through the period of the patriarchs, the gospel was understood. This is evident when we trace the history of God's covenant with humanity (Gen. 3:15; 12:1–3; cf. Gal. 3:6–9). Clear knowledge of the plan of salvation was conveyed to the Israelites during their wilderness wanderings. Lessons of faith and dependence were given by the Lord who spoke from the vicinity of the sanctuary (Num. 14:10, 11; cf. Heb. 4:2). A short history of Israel's unfaithfulness to God under the leadership of Moses is recorded in Hebrews 3. God's invitation to enter into the "rest" of salvation was rejected by the great majority of the multitude who came out of Egypt. The gospel preached in the Old Testament was not meant for the Jews alone but also included the Gentiles (Isa. 49:9–12; Rom. 15:8–12).[127]

Features of the Gospel. Animal sacrifice was instituted to impress the sinfulness of sin upon the sinner and the need of a Savior as the only way of salvation. The lamb, and particularly a male lamb, was commonly used as the animal prescribed for regular sacrifices, but other animals and more mature ones were offered too (Num. 28). The symbol of the lamb is used almost uniformly in the Scriptures to refer to Christ, and the slain lamb pointed to the sacrifice that Christ would one day undertake to rescue the human race from eternal destruction (Rev. 13:8). As an example, this lesson was indelibly impressed on the people of the Exodus by the ceremony involving the Passover lamb. The ceremony was associated with God's imminent deliverance of the children of promise from Egypt, the land of bondage. The sprinkled blood of the animal on the doorposts ensured that those who exercised faith would be kept safe from harm while the angel of judgment did his work (Exod. 12:3, 11–14).

The life of each repentant sinner before the cross was assured on account of a substitute, symbolically paying the penalty of death for sin. The animal varied—it was often an ox, a lamb, or a goat (Lev. 17:3). God assured the Old Testament believers and all who read the Scriptures that the shed blood of the animal made "atonement for your souls" (Lev. 17:11). This was solely on account of the promised sacrifice of Christ through whom we have "been justified by His blood" (Rom. 5:9; cf. Heb. 9:8–15). In order to emphasize the constant availability of the gift of the Lamb of God, an unblemished lamb was offered in the sanctuary every morning and evening (Exod. 29:39; cf. Isa. 53:7). Once again, the lamb represented Christ

Chapter 9. The Way of Salvation in the Sanctuary

(John 1:29, 36). The offering ensured that the person who committed sin was not "condemned immediately, before they had an opportunity to bring their individual sacrifices in order to receive forgiveness."[128] When people understood that they had sinned, it was then necessary for them to bring a sacrifice for that sin, otherwise, they would not be forgiven (Lev. 5:1–13).

The provision of salvation was available to all sinners. This is evident in such statements as: "If a person sins unintentionally" and "If a person commits a trespass, and sins unintentionally in regard to the holy things of the LORD" (Lev. 4:2; 5:15). These statements conveyed the significant lesson that God loves sinful human beings who can do nothing to earn salvation. Salvation is a gift (Isa. 53:5, 6; Rom. 5:8; 6:23; Eph. 2:8).

Confession of Sin Needed. Irrespective of Christ's promised sacrifice, as represented in the continual burnt offering that signified that atonement was available, the sinner personally needed not only to recognize an individual sin but also to confess it. Confession was signified by the individual bringing a sacrifice, laying his hands on the head of the sin offering, and then slaying the victim (Lev. 4:4, 5, 29–31). Thus, the sinfulness of sin was impressed upon the consciousness of the sinner. The believer learned afresh that an innocent life was to be sacrificed on account of his or her transgression of the law. The necessity of confessing and forsaking sin was well recognized in the Old Testament, as expressed in Proverbs 28:13, "He who covers his sins will not prosper, but whoever confesses and forsakes *them* will have mercy." In bringing a sacrifice and slaying the innocent victim, the sinner acknowledged the place of the human will—the place of human choice—in God's plan of salvation (Josh. 24:15, 22).

The suppliant was never in the position of thinking that it was possible to live without committing an unwholesome act or entertaining a sinful thought. The Israelites were aware of two significant categories of sin—intentional and unintentional (Lev. 4, 5). When the sinner was convicted of unintentional sin through the activities of the Holy Spirit, it was then time to acknowledge the deficiency and seek forgiveness. Thus, the children of Israel were taught to depend wholly and continually on the merits of Christ and not to be smug in their own supposed righteousness.

The Faith Journey. Through the act of confession and the acknowledgment that a substitute had become responsible for the individual's sin, the sinner asked for and received forgiveness. In other words, justification, or deliverance from the guilt of sin, followed the expression of faith in the righteousness of the substitute that represented Christ (Lev. 4:20; cf. 1 Sam. 15:22; Heb. 11:6). The Lord desired that His people should conduct their lives in such a way that they would be delivered from the power of sin in sanctification. The Scriptures have expressed the idea of sanctification in the words, "by putting off the body of the sins of the flesh" (Col. 2:11; cf. Lev. 19:2; Deut. 10:16). This is a faith experience, the fruit of which is obedience.

The children of Israel, like all Christians, needed to exercise faith. God's testimony against Israel through Moses was that they were a people "in whom *is* no faith" (Deut. 32:20; cf. Rom. 9:31, 32; Heb. 4:2). The majority did not fear God (Deut. 32:15–17), which is simply another way of saying that they were deficient in maintaining the right relationship with Him. Such a relationship is impossible without faith (Heb. 11:6). The Israelites feebly recognized the necessity of a faith relationship and began to develop this quality, but development was minimal among the great majority (Heb. 11:29; 4:2).

Until the first coming of Christ, faithful followers not only needed to believe in His coming, but also to believe that He would triumph over Satan. In looking forward to the cross, believers were asked to place great faith in the evidences of God's presence in the universe. To the Israelites, the evidence was made abundantly clear. Not only was the manna given for forty years, but the visible presence of God's glory was evident over the sanctuary. Besides these daily miracles, other remarkable revelations of God were given to the multitude. The primacy of faith is illustrated especially by two examples during the experience of the Israelites. The first relates to the brazen serpent placed on a pole by Moses. When those who were bitten by poisonous serpents looked with faith to God's promised symbol of life, they were healed (Num. 21:8, 9). The uplifted serpent pointed to the coming Messiah who was to become sin for the whole world (John 3:14; 2 Cor. 5:21).

The second example relates to the experience of the ten spies in Canaan. Only those who demonstrated faith in God's promises entered the Promised Land (Num. 13:30, 31; 14:29, 30; Deut. 1:36, 37). The apostle Paul recognized the centrality of faith in the Old Testament when he quoted the prophet Habakkuk, declaring: " '*The just shall live by faith*' " (Rom. 1:17; Hab. 2:4).

Outcome of the Faith Journey. The compassion and mercy demonstrated by Christ in His sacrifice for the human race accounts for the

Chapter 9. The Way of Salvation in the Sanctuary 145

great drawing power of Christianity. As hearers respond, they experience the ever-present realities of freedom from guilt and daily victory over sin through faith. These concepts are well expressed by David in Psalm 51:9, 10: "Hide your face from my sins, and blot out all my iniquities. Create in me a clean heart, O God, and renew a steadfast spirit within me." David recognized that God's help was essential in order to live acceptably before Him. Notice his comment in verse 11, "And do not take Your Holy Spirit from me." The symbolism of the activities associated with the altar of incense taught the people about access to continual help in daily living. It was the rituals in the courtyard, portraying forgiveness, reconciliation, and justification, that enabled the worshiper to claim the "provisions which sanctify the character, as symbolized in the ministry in the holy place."[129]

God's almost unbelievable act toward sinful men and women has always been that He loves them in spite of their rebellion and that He offered to die in their stead. The only appropriate response to this great love is to love and serve God and our fellow man (Deut. 10:12, 15, 19, 20). This principle was reinforced by Jesus' famous exchange with a lawyer about the essence of God's requirements and the truehearted response to God's love (Matt. 22:36–40). Acceptance of God's offer of salvation brings rewards in this life and in the life to come. Freedom from guilt and knowledge of our worth before God, on account of His sacrifice, brings peace of mind. As we follow the principles of health, physical well-being improves (Deut. 7:12, 15). The gospel thus promises spiritual as well as physical restoration.

Administration of Justice. The second remarkable aspect of Christian belief is that justice is held to be compatible with mercy. To assert that God is love yet does not have a moral standard and will not administer justice is a proposition without credibility (Rom. 3:31; 7:21–25). Christ died in defense of the proposition that mercy and justice were the foundation of His throne (Ps. 85:10; 89:14). Those who accept His mercy will be vindicated when justice is applied to every intelligent being at the conclusion of the great controversy. This is indeed good news!

As indicated in the Old Testament sanctuary ceremonies, a day of judgment was scheduled near the end of the religious year (Lev. 23:26–32). Justice was about to be proclaimed and the saints to be vindicated. The ceremonies conducted on this day prefigured the events that would occur in the heavenly sanctuary. From a historic perspective, the message of the pre-advent judgment in heaven was not understood by Bible scholars until the early 1800s. It was then that a worldwide movement—the Millerite movement—commenced and proclaimed with great clarity the opening of Christ's judgment ministry in 1844. At no previous time in the history of the Christian church was such a proclamation made. The announcement of the judgment is an assurance that the coming of the Lord is at hand and that sin's reign is about to cease. The good news of salvation, when properly understood, proclaims deliverance (Isa. 61:1, 2) from the penalty (Rom. 6:23), the power (Gal. 5:16), and, finally, the presence of sin (1 John 3:2).[130] It also declares that the originator of sin and those who persecuted the saints will be justly rewarded (Gen. 3:15; Ezek. 28:18; Dan. 7:26; Rev. 20:9, 10).

The concept of the judgment has a deeper significance for the believer. In the typical day of judgment spoken of in Old Testament times (Lev. 16), God intended that a work of purifying the motives and reforming the life—that is, sanctification through faith in the power which God alone can give—should be the focus of attention in the period preceding and during the event (Lev. 23:23–25; cf. Isa. 58:6, 7; 2 Cor. 7:1). So, in the days when the pre-advent judgment is in progress in heaven, it is God's purpose that the people of this earth focus on preparing to meet their God. A sense of urgency is given to the proclamation of the gospel because time is about to be swallowed in eternity (Rev. 14:6, 7, 14–16; 18:2–4).

The Way of Faith

In this section, I will

- *provide assurance from the Scriptures that our sins are forgiven when we ask in faith;*

- *emphasize that the sanctuary service emphasized the constant accessibility of forgiveness and divine help;*

- *encourage believers in the thought that God offers daily help for living above sin in response to our prayers of faith.*

Heathen religions are distinguished from Christianity in that they appeal to salvation by works. Salvation by faith alone in Christ our substitute is the doctrine that characterizes genuine Christianity. It was this faith too that characterized the God-ordained belief system described in the Bible before the formal launching of Christianity.

Abraham, the patriarch of old, is well known as the father of the faithful. Those who demonstrate faith in the sacrifice of Christ as their Savior are His children (Matt. 8:11; Rom. 4:13, 16; Gal. 3:29). Abraham gave an example of unwavering faith when he was prepared to offer his only son as a sacrifice at God's command. God provided a substitute so that the son's death was not necessary. Today, God calls on us to show a similar steadfast faith as did Abraham. Clearly, both the Old and the New Testaments declare: "The just shall live by faith" (Hab. 2:4; Rom. 1:17; Gal. 3:11; Heb. 10:38). Praise God that the gospel in all ages has been the same (Heb. 4:2)! This is why it is called "the everlasting gospel" (Rev. 14:6). In this universe, there is only one person who has earned the right to save us—that is the Lord Jesus Christ (Heb. 2:9, 10).

Christ's Cleansing Work. On account of His sacrifice and victory over Satan, Jesus is able to cleanse "us from all unrighteousness" through His blood (1 John 1:9; cf. Col. 1:14; Eph. 1:7). Knowledge of the forgiveness of our sins before God through the merits of Jesus Christ brings great peace, and it gives hope and assurance (Rom. 5:1, 2; 8:1). This is justification. The continual burnt offering in the earthly sanctuary "assured the penitent Israelite of the constant accessibility of forgiveness. If he was sick, away from Jerusalem, or for some reason couldn't get to the sanctuary, he could still reach out in faith to the promise symbolized by these sacrifices, which burned on the altar 24 hours a day, every day—even on the Day of Atonement."[131] Today, we have this assurance of constant accessibility to forgiveness as Christ ministers in the heavenly sanctuary (Heb. 7:25). Our confessed sins are safe in His care.

When Christ is accepted by faith, we think and live differently than we did before. This is the essence of the new birth experience. The apostle Paul expressed it thus: "... all things have become new" (2 Cor. 5:17). The secret of the Christian life is that moment-by-moment the believer grasps hold of Christ by faith. Thus may it be said that Christ lives in us (Gal. 2:20). Maintaining a continuous dependent relationship with Christ is the secret of victory (1 John 3:6; Heb. 8:11). The same faith that justifies also sanctifies, or makes an individual holy (1 Cor. 6:11). The Holy Spirit accomplishes this work of transformation in believers so that the converted individual begins to develop a Christ-like character (Rom. 12:2). Believers have the assurance of salvation as their walk of faith continues with Christ through the guidance of the Spirit (John 5:24; 6:40; 1 John 5:11–13).

According to 1 John 5:4, 5, our faith in Christ's victory and His provision for us is the victory that overcomes the world. The idea conveyed by these verses is that victory over sin may be continuous so long as we rely on the provision that heaven has made. James outlines the secret of success: If we submit ourselves daily to God and choose to ask for help at the moment of temptation, victory is assured (James 4:7). In the earthly sanctuary, "perpetual incense" was offered morning and evening on the golden altar before the Lord (Exod. 30:7, 8). This represented the continual availability of divine help to the believer through intercessory prayer (2 Chron. 30:27; Heb. 4:16; James 5:16). This same assurance of divine help is given us today in response to the prayer of faith (John 16:23; Rev. 8:3, 4). We are strengthened in our Christian walk as we rely on the means that God has provided. Prayer is a vital part of successful Christian living. Like our Lord, we need to spend time in prayer (Mark 1:35). Jesus' instructions to His disciples apply equally to us today: "Watch and pray, lest you enter into temptation" (Matt. 26:41). Jesus also set us an example regarding the study of God's Word. He relied on the Word of God in the hour of temptation (Luke 4:4, 8, 12). Let us by God's grace determine to call on Him continually so that we may rejoice at His coming.

Chapter 10.
The Law and the Gospel

Chapter Emphasis: *The moral law of the Ten Commandments reflects God's character. The law is based on the principle of divine love, or agapē, and forms the basis of God's government. Since God also is love, this means that His law is not subject to change. The law is entirely consistent with the concept of the gospel invitation, for it points the believer to the place that amazing love can be experienced best—the foot of the cross of Christ. Here divine help may be found to keep all of God's instructions.*

Spiritual Link: *The law becomes a liberating document when its relationship to grace is understood correctly.*

In Chapter 9, I examined the gospel as it is taught in the Old and New Testaments. Here I wish to build on this knowledge and examine the relationship between the law and the gospel. There are various versions of the gospel in the world today, but as a result of our investigations of the Scriptures, many of these uncertainties have disappeared. Similar uncertainties also surround the law.

The moral framework of many societies is woven around the principles of the Ten Commandments. It has been frequently asked whether these moral principles originated with God or with humanity. Many believe that the moral framework of society is the result of evolutionary processes. The human race is the product of evolution, it is claimed, and the race is now in the position of controlling the evolutionary process. Others hold that the fourth commandment, though still binding, is changed within the Christian era. Their argument is that *the time element* mentioned in this commandment is merely ceremonial, making it unnecessary after Jesus' death on the cross. Still others hold that the fourth commandment does not hold a legitimate place in the moral law since it does not have to do with morality. Such seem to forget that it was God who included it among the other moral laws. Certainly "God is not *the author* of confusion" (1 Cor. 14:33). There is indeed a glorious unity in the Scriptures that sweep away uncertainties. In this chapter, we will observe the unity between the law and the gospel.

The Law and Sin

In this section, I will

- *outline the origin and nature of sin;*
- *highlight the principles of God's government;*
- *indicate the everlasting nature of God's law.*

All of the higher orders of beings created by God were made with the power of choice. In heaven, the most prominent angel, or "anointed cherub," was none other than Lucifer (Ezek. 28:14; cf. Isa. 14:12). He was a mighty angel who was honored above all other created beings (Ezek. 28:13, 14). Pride arose in Lucifer's mind, and he determined to challenge the principles of God's government in an attempt to gain greater responsibility and power (Isa. 14:13, 14). In Revelation 12:9, we are reminded that Lucifer, or Satan (as he was called in his fallen state), and his angels were cast out of heaven on account of their disloyalty. They had challenged God because they were against the principles of God's government, which are based on mercy and justice (Ps. 89:14).

Uncontrolled by Law. To sin is to act as one who does not recognize the existence or requirements of law (Ps. 119:172; 1 John 3:4; 5:17). The term "lawless" means "disobedient to, uncontrolled by, law."[132] Lucifer wished to live in heaven under a set of principles of his own devising, uncontrolled by God's principles. "Satan has been persevering and untiring in his efforts to prosecute the work he began in heaven, to change the law of God. He has succeeded in making the world believe the theory he presented in heaven before his fall, that the law of God was faulty and needed revising."[133]

Other illuminating texts that help us understand sin indicate that it encompasses failure to do good, failure to exercise faith, or actions showing disregard for the revealed will of God (see Matt. 12:30; John 16:8, 9; Rom. 14:23; James 4:17). Sin essentially indicates a broken relationship (1 John 3:6, 9).

The principle that Lucifer challenged in heaven was that God was the foremost individual in the universe. In reality, he wished to "be like" God (Isa. 14:14). Isaiah, chapter 14, is a proverb—that is, a concise statement—made by God against the king of Babylon who was controlled by Satan. Here Satan is revealed as originally being a glorious individual. He coveted and wished to seize God's power, glory, and honor. We note in the passage that Satan works through human agents to do his bidding. An illustration of this in the New Testament was when Satan used the apostle Peter, on one occasion, to tempt the Lord Jesus. Peter suggested that Jesus cease to entertain ideas of suffering and dying for sinful people. Jesus immediately turned to Peter and said, "Get behind Me, Satan! You are an offense to Me, for you are not mindful of the things of God, but the things of men" (Matt. 16:23).

The function of God's moral law is to point all people to the standard of behavior designed to bring sinners back to Him so that harmony will be re-established. This set of principles brings "the knowledge of sin" (Rom. 3:20; cf. Rom. 7:7). The moral law condemns the sinner and drives the penitent individual to the foot of the cross for pardon and power to do what the law demands. The Scriptures assure us that God is like a loving earthly father, earnestly awaiting the return of His wayward children (Luke 15:20–24).

Love Underpins the Law. God is love (1 John 4:8, 16), which is why all pronouncements and acts associated with Him are based on this principle. Jesus made it abundantly clear that the Decalogue is based on *agapē* love to God and to our fellow earth travelers (Matt. 22:36–40; John 15:10–14).

The first four commandments express our love to God. Giving a love response to God on account of His offer of salvation is a principle consistently emphasized in the Old Testament (Deut. 6:5; 10:12; 30:6). The last six commandments express our duty to be channels of love to our fellow travelers in order to share the good news of salvation (Lev. 19:17, 18). The principle of love is, indeed, the basis of the Ten Commandments (Exod. 20:6). The apostle Paul summarized this great truth in Romans 13:10 in these words: "Love does no harm to a neighbor, therefore love *is* the fulfillment of the law." It becomes evident that, since God is love (1 John 4:8), the principles underlying the law of God are eternal as God is eternal.

Agapē love embraces a number of crucial elements, which are not frequently acknowledged.[134] First, this type of love comes from God alone, for He is *agapē* (1 John 4:7, 8). This type of love also seeks the sinner and comes down from heaven; it is given freely (John 3:16). It is not a greedy type of love that seeks its own (1 Cor. 13:5). God's love, expressed most magnificently in the death of Christ on the cross, gives value to human beings. God's love does not consider the individual human's worth in assessing whether it acts (Matt. 10:32; Rev. 22:17). Since *agapē* originates with God and not with us, we humans can only serve as channels of that love to others (Matt. 5:16; 2 Cor. 5:20).[135]

Law before Sinai. The principles of the Ten Commandments were understood before their formal proclamation on Mount Sinai (Table 10.1). The principles found in it express the will of God for humanity. More precisely they express what God is like. They were not simply for the Jews but for the entire human race. They represent the goal of the believer's relationship with God. (See Table 1.1 in Chapter 1.)

When God gave the Ten Commandments, He wrote them on tables of stone with His own finger (Exod. 31:18). To think that these moral principles were of such significance that God wrote them Himself! Moses broke the first set of stone tablets, signifying his displeasure at the wanton disregard by the Israelites of God's righteous requirements (Exod. 32:19). God promised, however, to replace the written record of His requirements. Moses was commanded to fashion a second set of stone tablets, in contrast to God providing the first, but God still wrote the Commandments on the second set with His finger (Exod. 34:1, 28). It is significant to notice that the giver of the moral law was Jesus Christ Himself (see Mal. 3:1; Acts 7:38; 1 Cor. 10:4). Therefore, any change in the law could only come from Him. Moreover, to change the commandments, Jesus would have to change His character, and that is impossible.

Christ made it abundantly clear that it is not possible to change God's law this side of the destruction of heaven and earth (Matt. 5:18).

Chapter 10. The Law and the Gospel

The earth has not yet passed away, which means God's moral law is still ours to honor. Even when the earth does pass away, the principles of the law will continue, for the law is as changeless as God Himself. The Scriptures declare, "For I *am* the LORD, I do not change" (Mal. 3:6). The law of God is the basis of His "covenant," "testament," or "will" (see Exod. 25:16; Heb. 9:4, 15; Rev. 11:19).[136] The covenant is about salvation. To argue that either God has changed His will as expressed in the Decalogue or that it is the prerogative of human beings to change it is really issuing a passport to death.

Table 10.1. Textual evidence that the principles enshrined in the Decalogue were understood before the formal giving of the law on Sinai.

Moral Standard	Reference
1. God is the only authentic Creator God.	Gen. 15:7; 35:1–4; Exod. 3:14, 15
2. Images are not to be made or worshiped.	Gen. 35:1–4
3. God's name is to be honored and not profaned.	Gen. 25:32, 33; cf. Exod. 15:1–18; Heb. 12:16
4. The Sabbath, the seventh day of the week and the memorial of Creation, is holy.	Gen. 2:1–3; Exod. 16:22–28
5. Honor is due to our parents.	Gen. 9:21–25; 28:6–9
6. Murder does not represent God's way.	Gen. 4:8–11; 9:5, 6
7. Adultery and relationships outside of marriage are not the way of genuine love.	Gen. 12:18; 34:2, 27, 31; 39:7–9
8. Stealing is an unloving act.	Gen. 31:30, 31
9. Falsehoods misrepresent God's ways.	Gen. 12:12–20; 20:5–7, 9; 27:11–13
10. Covetousness is the root of much evil.	Gen. 3:5, 6; 6:1–3, 5, 6; 27:27–29, 32–35

Despite uninformed statements to the contrary, all the Ten Commandments are upheld in the New Testament. It is generally agreed that nine are mentioned specifically after the crucifixion (Rom. 2:22; 7:7; 13:9; James 2:11; cf. Gal. 5:19–21; 1 Cor. 8:6; Eph. 6:2; 1 Tim. 6:1; and 1 John 5:21), though only the last six are actually quoted.[137] Because of the blindness that has resulted from the long tradition of Sunday worship, most Christians fail to see the perpetuity of the fourth commandment. However, the apostle John makes it astoundingly clear that God's will is not only preserved in the "ark of His covenant" in heaven (Rev. 11:19; cf. Rev. 12:17; 14:12), but he also makes it just as clear that God sends a special message to earth's inhabitants requiring the honoring of the fourth commandment in the time of the end until the end of time (Rev. 14:7, cf. Exod. 20:11). No wonder there are moves afoot to produce a Bible without the book of Revelation incorporated in it.[138]

The Law and God's Character

In this section, I will

- *emphasize that the law of God tells us what God is like.*

We have noticed already that the essence of the Decalogue is *agapē* love, which is also the central aspect of God's character and of the gospel. It has been said that the law of God is a "transcript," or a recorded copy, of the nature of God's character.[139] (The accuracy of this statement is illustrated in Table 10.2.) Jesus perfectly fulfilled the law while on earth because it was in His character to do so.

The law of God is built on two inseparable motivations—love to God and love to humanity (Matt. 22:36–40). It becomes evident that the law of God is the standard by which the life of all is measured, for it expresses the perfection and fullness of God Himself. The law reveals to sinners the defects in their character and points them to God for salvation. This salvation can be accepted only through faith. The Christian is enabled to keep God's law—God's will—day by day only through the exercise of faith in Christ.

The Law and the Sanctuary

In this section, I will

- *remind again that the Ten Commandments are the basis of God's covenant, or agreement, with humanity;*

- *emphasize that justice, represented by the law, cannot be separated from mercy.*

Table 10.2. Characteristics of God and the Decalogue compared and contrasted.

Feature	Reference to God	Reference to the Law
Repository of the Truth	John 14:6	Ps. 119:142
Righteous	1 Cor. 1:30	Ps. 119:172
Holy	Isa. 6:3	Rom. 7:12
Love	1 John 4:8	Matt. 22:37–40
Perfect	Matt. 5:48	Ps. 19:7
Good	Luke 18:19	Rom. 7:12
Just	Deut. 32:4	Rom. 7:12
Pure	1 John 3:3	Ps. 19:8
Unchangeable	James 1:17	Matt. 5:18
Stands forever	Isa. 9:6; Dan. 7:14	Ps. 111:7, 8

The location of the Decalogue and the care with which it was treated tell us something about its sacredness.

Location in the Sanctuary. As soon as the Decalogue was given at Sinai, it was placed in the ark of the covenant, or the ark of the testimony (Exod. 25:16; 40:20; Heb. 9:4), which was in the Most Holy Place. This item of furniture and its location in the sanctuary expressed to all the most sacred nature of its contents. The law could not be viewed, as such, or approached except through the blood of a perfect sacrifice. The animal sacrifices pointed to Christ's perfect atoning sacrifice and to the truth that the law could not be kept except through faith in Christ's merits and enabling power.

The placement of the Decalogue in the ark was in contrast to the law of Moses, the code written by Moses containing the ceremonial law, which was placed in "the side of the ark" (Deut. 31:26, KJV). The Ten Commandments were the basis of the covenant agreement that God made with the Israelites (Exod. 34:26; Deut. 4:13; 1 Kings 8:9). It is significant to note that the ark of the testament, containing the tables of the "testimony," or the Ten Commandments, was seen in vision by John the Revelator in heaven during the last decade of the first century (Rev. 11:19). This means that whatever men may say, God's great principles stand intact in heaven. This is utterly reasonable, for the Commandments express the will of God for the human race (Micah 6:8; Matt. 22:36–40). God's wish for humanity is that they so appreciate His moral principles that they internalize them and, by the strength He provides, keep them (Heb. 8:10; 10:16; Rom. 7:22, 25; 8:7; James 1:25; 1 Cor. 7:19; Rev. 22:14).[140] The reality is that the Commandments can be written with all fidelity to the original language: "I promise you, you will not ...."[141] This expresses God's ideal for those who have the right relationship with Him.

God measures the character of the individual by their deeds, for these show the genuineness of their faith journey (James 2:10–26). The character of God, which is expressed in the Decalogue, is the basis for the assessment of the lives of men and women in the judgment. In other words, the fundamental question in the judgment will be: What have you done with Christ? When we realize how much Christ has done for us, our allegiance will be entire and complete. The fruits of this relationship with Christ will be evident to all; the believer can rest assured in Christ. This thought was expressed in the sanctuary in that the mercy seat was positioned above the Decalogue.

These features of placement and ceremony in the earthly sanctuary conveyed—and still convey—to all committed believers the comforting thought that Christ pleads the merits of His blood before the Father for the sins of the penitent and for those who have sinned ignorantly. In other words, Jesus intercedes for those who maintain a genuine relationship with Him through faith. He enables the believer to live in harmony with the law. In the judgment, Jesus' merits are seen and the sinner is vindicated. Justice and mercy are satisfied, and, at the same time, the principles of God's government are shown to be above reproach. Praise God for providing such a Savior!

Grace and the Law

In this section, I will

- *emphasize that the function of the moral law is to point believers to Christ;*
- *establish firmly the unchangeable nature of the law.*

Grace and law do not represent incompatible concepts. In reality, these form the foundation of God's throne (Ps. 85:10; 89:14).

Grace Gives Liberty. The question of utmost significance to us today is whether the law was done away at the cross with "the coming of grace." The apostle Paul was adamant that faith actually placed the law in the correct perspective—faith establishes the law (Rom. 3:31). He explained that, by doing the deeds required by the law, no one can be justified. The function of the law is to point to sin (Rom. 3:20). Through our knowledge of sin, we are driven to the foot of the cross to seek our Savior (Rom. 5:20). There, by faith, we are justified and enabled to "walk in newness of life" (Rom. 6:4) in sanctification, following repentance and the confession of sin. We are no longer slaves of sin, but rather slaves of righteousness (Rom. 6:1–6, 18). It is God's purpose that we be brought into more perfect obedience to divine law through daily association with Him by faith. In fact, obedience flows from a day-by-day saving relationship with Christ (1 John 3:6).

God's law becomes a vehicle of liberty (James 1:25), for it points the transgressor to Jesus Christ who can forgive our sins. Through faith Christ also can give us victory over, or liberty from, sin (Titus 3:4–7). In this relationship with God, we have great assurance of salvation. David expressed these same truths after Nathan the prophet challenged him concerning his transgression of the law (Ps. 51:7–14). One writer has expressed it thus: "The law of Jehovah is the tree; the gospel is the fragrant blossoms and fruit which it bears."[142]

It is worth noting, in the context of the question of doing away with the Decalogue at the cross, that the covenant—or agreement—of grace was first made in Eden (Gen. 3:15), and renewed for "all nations of the earth" through Abraham (Gen. 22:18). God said of him: "Abraham obeyed My voice and kept My charge, My commandments, My statutes, and My laws" (Gen. 26:5). The covenant of grace, which Abraham knew, was ratified by the blood of Christ. To do away with the moral law would actually mean dispensing with the need of a Savior.

Belief Involves Obedience. The person "who believes and is baptized will be saved" (Mark 16:16). Belief must be understood in the context of God's will, for even the devils believe and tremble. Genuine belief involves wholehearted confession of sin and dependence on God for victory. These are signified in James 4:8 by the commands, "cleanse your hands, you sinners" and "purify *your* hearts" (see also James 2:14–19, 26). It will result in commitment to obey all of God's requirements as they become known (James 1:22). Reformation and fruit bearing will be seen in the life in which genuine faith is present (Matt. 3:8–10). Harmony with God's law is what God requires now, as He originally required in Paradise. This means obedience will be seen in the life as a love response to God's great gift (1 John 5:1–5). Obedience is the fruit of a meaningful and continuing relationship with God.

God is declaring through His agents in the period of time immediately before He returns that the precepts contained in the Decalogue are changeless (Rev. 14:12). The commandments referred to are clearly identified in the words of Revelation 14:7: "… worship Him who made heaven and earth, the sea and springs of water." One will likely notice that this phrase corresponds to the wording of Exodus 20:11. Significantly, this verse gives the basis for the fourth commandment, which, of all the ten, is the one especially disputed and which is central to the Decalogue, linking the first section of the law to the second.

The fourth commandment is a bulwark against the theory of evolution, which has swept the world into unbelief regarding the adequacy of the biblical record. In Revelation 14, God is pointing us back to Eden, to our Creator, and to our Redeemer Jesus Christ. A Redeemer who is not also the Creator would be incapable of giving the new birth and new life experience that the Bible describes. God has set aside the seventh day as a reminder of His ability not only to create but to recreate (Exod. 20:10, 11; 31:13). This commandment also asserts the equality of all humanity in that all people, without distinction, are invited to worship God on this holy day (cf. Isa. 56:6, 7). It is a sign that God is able to sanctify those who believe in Him. The fourth commandment establishes the basis for worshipping the Creator as well as the reason the first three commandments should be kept. Thus, the moral nature of this commandment is established as it forms a bridge between the commandments that relate to God and those that relate to our fellow human beings.

The psalmist David challenges all believers to relate to God and His revealed will: "Give me understanding, and I shall keep Your law; indeed, I shall observe it with *my* whole heart. Make me walk in the path of Your commandments, for I delight in it. Incline my heart to Your testimonies, and not to covetousness" (Ps. 119:34–36).

The Temple in Heaven and the Eternal Law. The perpetuity of the Ten Commandments as the basis of a just and harmonious society is indicated by the fact that the temple of God in heaven contains

Chapter 10. The Law and the Gospel

the "ark of His Covenant" (Rev. 11:19). Significantly, the ark is here revealed in the time period when the rewards of the saints and of the wicked are to be made known (Rev. 11:18). Through this imagery, God in His mercy is directing our attention to the sanctuary in heaven, to His holy law, and to the pathway of salvation. God's great original moral law is in heaven from where our salvation comes!

Nailed to the Cross. The apostle Paul reminds readers, in Ephesians 2:15, that something disappeared following Christ's death. It was due to the nailing of the ceremonial law to the cross, signified by the parallel phrases, "commandments *contained* in ordinances" (Eph. 2:15) and "handwriting of requirements" (Col. 2:14). These two phrases were never used to refer to the Decalogue. The context of Paul's address refers to the Gentiles who were not commonly considered to have gospel privileges. This was a common Jewish attitude and not God's. At the cross, the special status of the nation of Israel ceased, and the ceremonial laws met their fulfillment. This is why the veil of the temple was torn from the top to the bottom. The Gentiles were now on an equal footing with the Jews. All were sons and daughters of Abraham (Gal. 3:29).

The Christian church was not to be encumbered with unnecessary ritualism borrowed from the Jewish economy (Acts 15:24–29).[143] Nonetheless, neither Paul nor the early church advocated the discontinuance of the Sabbath; indeed, Paul claimed, among other things, that he was blameless in all his behavior (Acts 28:17), and this would include Sabbath-keeping (Acts 13:14, 27, 42, 44; 16:13; 17:2; 18:4).[144] Paul enjoyed a vibrant relationship with Christ and understood that Christ's character was reflected in the law, which is why it cannot be changed.

Chapter 11.
The Veil of the Temple Was Torn

Chapter Emphasis: *The rending of the veil of the earthly temple from top to bottom signaled that the Person to whom the services pointed had fulfilled His mission as the Lamb of God, providing sacrificial atonement. Henceforth, Christ had an extensive reconciliation ministry to undertake in heaven before the reign of Satan could be brought to an end and the universe returned to a state of harmony—at-one-ment. The sequence of festivals and religious ceremonies associated with the earthly sanctuary give a broad outline of the highlights believers can anticipate experiencing along salvation's pathway to completion. This sequence parallels the one highlighted in the great controversy worldview.*

Spiritual Links: *The atonement ministry undertaken by Christ was not limited to His sacrifice on the cross.*

An appreciation of prophecy will always be incomplete without an understanding of the fundamental place of the struggle between good and evil. There is a cosmic battle between good and evil taking place in our world. This concept saturates the pages of the Bible. The hero of the drama is Christ who triumphs over the forces of evil. The text, "Surely the Lord God does nothing, unless He reveals His secret to

His servants the prophets" (Amos 3:7), emphasizes the central place of Christ's communication with His servants to encourage them concerning His righteous principles (cf. John 5:39). The great controversy theme has embedded in it the concept of the remnant. This concept carries with it a note of certainty that God will be victorious and people will be saved who value His friendship and the principles of His kingdom. Throughout the history of the controversy, God has always had a remnant group to preserve His name and righteous principles.

In this chapter, I wish to explain from Scripture the principal features of the earthly sanctuary services and show how they essentially illustrate the great controversy worldview. Such an outlook allows us to place the revelations of the writers of the Bible into a coherent system of understanding.

Christ's Activities Changed

In this section, I will

- *introduce the reader to the fulfillment of the earthly sanctuary types at the cross;*

- *indicate that Christ's ministry continues in heaven today.*

The record given by Matthew indicates that "the veil of the temple" was torn when Jesus died (Matt. 27:51). This was none other than the veil separating the Holy Place from the Most Holy Place (Exod. 26:31–33). It did not reach to the ceiling, allowing glimpses of the glory of God to reach into the Holy Place and allowing the smoke of the incense burned in the Holy Place to pass over into the Most Holy Place.

Sanctuary Typologies Focused on Christ's Sacrifice. At Christ's death on the cross, the veil of the earthly temple was torn from the top to the bottom (Matt. 27:51). The veil represented Christ's flesh (Heb. 10:20), and so it was fitting that this event happened just when He died (Matt. 27:50). Hence, the sacrifice of Christ represented the fulfillment of the typologies to which the sanctuary sacrifices pointed. Consider the following illuminating description of the response to the torn veil: "The most holy place of the earthly sanctuary is no longer sacred. All is terror and confusion. The priest is about to slay the victim; but the knife drops from his nerveless hand, and the lamb escapes. Type has met antitype in the death of God's Son. The way into the holiest is laid open. A new and living way is prepared for all."[145]

The supernatural act of exposing the Most Holy Place to the view of the common priests signaled that the earthly sanctuary sacrifices had served their purpose and that Christ's activities in the heavenly sanctuary were about to begin (Heb. 9:12–15). The earthly sanctuary services pointed to Christ's suffering and death for humanity. The lambs slain morning and evening represented Christ (Num. 28:3, 4) who was without blemish. He "knew no sin," although He was "in all *points* tempted as *we are*" (2 Cor. 5:21; Heb. 4:15).

The Scriptures also declare that the "blood of Jesus Christ His Son cleanses us from all sin" (1 John 1:7). We are redeemed through His blood (Rev. 5:9). The drink offering reinforced this idea and was poured out in association with the morning and evening animal sacrifice (Num. 15:10, 11; cf. Deut. 32:14). Fittingly, this represented the pouring out of the life of Christ for the salvation of all people at the cross (Matt. 26:27, 28).

The apostle Paul clearly indicates that Christ became high priest in the heavenly sanctuary following His resurrection and ascension. I have indicated previously that the literal translation of Hebrews 9:12 should be rendered "neither through blood of goats and calves, but through his own blood, did enter in once into the holy places, age-during redemption having obtained" (*Young's Literal Translation*; cf. Scrivener's Greek Interlinear). The prophet Daniel also spoke of another phase of the reconciliation process (Dan. 7:9, 10) about which I will comment later.

It is evident that Christ's sacrifice was effective for all, for He rose triumphant and poured out the Holy Spirit at Pentecost. No further sacrifice was needed; "the atonement for a lost world was to be full, abundant, and complete. Christ's offering was exceedingly abundant to reach every soul that God had created.... There must be enough and to spare."[146] Even though Christ's sacrifice caused the Father to say: "The atonement is complete," it is evident that in the sanctuary system there were other phases of ministry to complete before harmonious relationships—at-one-ment—in the universe could be realized.[147] Christ's death on behalf of humanity occurred at the time of the Passover (Mark 14:1). This proclaimed loudly that, before Satan could be destroyed, the activities prefigured by the services on the day commemorating the Feast of Weeks, (fulfilled in the power of Pentecost in the early and last-day churches), the memorial of blowing of Trumpets, the Day of Atonement, and the Feast of Tabernacles (fulfilled in events after the Second Coming of Christ), must occur. The pattern of events outlined in the earthly sanctuary was provided for the purpose of giving hope to the citizens of this earth. God has long advertised His plan, and He intends to follow it.

The Typologies Indicated That Satan Will Be Cast Out. The cessation of the earthly sanctuary services also had cosmic significance. Jesus declared that Satan was to be cast out at the cross (John 12:31). What is the significance of this declaration? "Satan saw that his disguise was torn away. His administration was laid open before the unfallen angels and before the heavenly universe. He had revealed himself as a murderer. By shedding the blood of the Son of God, he had uprooted himself from the sympathies of the heavenly beings. *Henceforth his work was restricted.* Whatever attitude he might assume, he could no longer await the angels as they came from the heavenly courts, and before them accuse Christ's brethren of being clothed with the garments of blackness and the defilement of sin. *The last link of sympathy between Satan and the heavenly world was broken.*"[148]

Satan was destined to experience three expulsions before his existence ends. Already he has experienced two of them. First, he was expelled from heaven on account of his rebellion there (Rev. 12:9). Then he was expelled from the sympathies of the heavenly world at the cross, as Jesus indicated (John 12:31). His third and final expulsion is yet future (Rev. 20:10).

The Great Controversy

In this section, I will

- *introduce the reader to some biblical evidence for the great controversy worldview;*
- *indicate that the principal ideas contained in this worldview were taught in the ceremonies associated with the earthly sanctuary.*

The scriptural record continually reinforces the idea that God has a plan for reconciling this world to Himself. The pivotal events in this schema are outlined in the Bible in order to give hope and encouragement to believers.

Outline of the Controversy Theme. Revelation, chapter 12, gives a clear indication that the great controversy commenced in heaven. Satan is identified as the one who accused God of lying and of hiding useful information from Adam and Eve (Gen. 3:4, 5). The apostle

Jude even featured him as disputing with Michael (or Christ) over the body of Moses (Jude 1:9). He no doubt intended to prevent him from being raised by Christ. His more mundane and typical work is to try to discourage the would-be followers of Christ (Rev. 12:10). This work is illustrated by the prophet Zechariah, who described the high priest Joshua as standing before God with filthy garments, unworthy, and without merit. In the depiction, God gladly took away Zechariah's sins and gave him the righteous covering, which comes from Christ. However, Satan contested the ground and sought, making discouraging suggestions to regain the one who had exercised faith in God's provisions (Zech. 3:2–5).

We might well ask: How did the disagreement with God commence? It happened this way: Satan, who was originally the covering cherub Lucifer, developed pride and had aspirations to be like God (Isa. 14:12–14; Ezek. 28:12–17). He was dissatisfied with his position in heaven, which was at the head of the angelic hosts. In his pride for his beauty and intelligence, he wished to have a higher place in heaven; in fact, he wished to be like God. He resented the fact that God would not exalt Him further, though no injustice had been done him as a created being. There is no excuse for the sin that arose in his heart.

God reasoned with Satan to no avail, for Satan persisted in His rebellion. Yet, God did not eliminate him immediately. When it was apparent that he could not be rescued from the path of rebellion, he was removed from heaven (Rev. 12:9). Though, for a time, he was allowed to come to the outer parts of heaven, his main place of activity was on earth (Gen. 3:4, 5; Job 1:6, 7; 2:1, 2). It was necessary to allow the principles of his kingdom to be revealed over time so that all intelligent beings in heaven and earth might be convinced of the superiority of God's principles. This alone would ensure that sin could not arise again.

Satan works through agents, and these may be either humans or the creatures of the animate world. We read of him operating through the serpent in the Garden of Eden. The startling spectacle of a talking snake would have made an amazing impression on Eve and would have emphasized the reality of Satan's claims that new abilities would be given to the human race if his principles were followed rather than God's. The prophet Ezekiel pictured Lucifer in a lamentation for the king of Tyre (Ezek. 28:12). Actually, Ezekiel is speaking of Satan, who is the power behind the wicked king of Tyre just as he was the power behind the king of Babylon in Isaiah, chapter 14. This interpretation is strengthened by the message given Daniel by the angel Gabriel (Dan. 10:20, 21). In these verses, Gabriel and Christ (or Michael, Israel's "prince") are shown contending with the forces of evil who operated through the king of Persia. Christ's object was to ensure that God's plan for the nations reached a satisfactory conclusion.

Leading Strategies Adopted. Satan has directed his most vigorous efforts against the fundamental principles underpinning God's government. When we remember that his rebellion is based on philosophical arguments, then we might anticipate vigorous initiatives in the areas of existence, knowing, and acting. The first prong of Satan's attack in Eden was in the area of *knowing*. How does one know that God statements are true? Satan asserted that God was untruthful and that he had superior knowledge to God's and that it was more reliable (Gen. 3:3, 4). Daniel the prophet outlined further initiatives in this arena that Satan would take during the course of history (Dan. 8:11, 12). Satan would work marvelously through the "little horn" power (verse 9), which is none other than the papacy.

This power has questioned aspects of God's mercy (cf. Ps. 89:14) and, by implication, has questioned how we know that God's assurances are real. The quaint terminology used in Daniel 8:11, requires an explanation. The emphasis in the passage is on the word often rendered "daily *sacrifices*." (Notice that "sacrifices" has been supplied.) The Hebrew word used here is *tamid*. The correct translation of this is simply "continual." The *Lexham English Bible* renders the verse: "Even against the prince of the hosts it acted arrogantly and took away from him the regular burnt offering, and the place of his sanctuary was overthrown." Like the *New King James Version*, *Young's Literal Translation* points out the supplied nature of "sacrifice": "And unto the prince of the host it exerteth itself, and by it taken away hath been the continual [sacrifice], and thrown down the base of his sanctuary."

The prophet is telling readers that views would be promoted in the Christian church contrary to those taught in the sanctuary. This is indeed what transpired. The view held in a great section of the Christian community today is that repentant sinners require priests and the ministry of the Virgin Mary rather than their approaching Christ directly. This is a fundamental violation of the typology of the Old Testament, which portrays Christ as both the sacrifice and the priest. The Catholic Church holds that the priest has power to forgive sins.[149] Distinguished professor of history and religious studies at Pennsylvania State University Philip Jenkins noted: "There is now talk that the Virgin [Mary] might be proclaimed a mediator and co-Savior figure, comparable to Jesus himself, even a fourth member of the Trinity."[150] Many years before Jenkins made this observation, Pope Pius XII had proclaimed Mary the "Mediatrix of peace," "taking an active part in the work of salvation" by interceding with Christ for Catholic believers so that He cannot refuse.[151] In other words, they are saying that prayer to God and faith in His Word are insufficient for the forgiveness of sins and the assurance of salvation. The Bible contradicts these assertions and assures us that Christ is ever ready to help. Therefore, there is no need for another intermediary between God and humankind (Heb. 7:25).

Jesus continually emphasized that He was the only source of salvation. One of the clearest statements He made is, "I am the light of the world" (John 8:12; 9:5). The affirmation given by the apostle Peter before the Sanhedrin was: "... there is no other name under heaven given among men by which we must be saved" (Acts 4:12). And the apostle Paul added that there is only "one Mediator between God and men, *the* Man Christ Jesus" (1 Tim. 2:5). Most importantly, the centrality of faith was continually emphasized in Jesus' miracles (see, for example, Mark 2:5; 5:34; 10:52). If any has remained in doubt about the need for faith, the apostle Paul's statement extinguishes all doubt—"The just shall live by faith" (Rom. 1:17). Moreover, the apostle James showed how faith gives rise to good deeds, thereby providing evidence that the Christian possesses the genuine article of faith (James 2:14–22).

Those opposed to God's Word promote themselves as having superior knowledge or, in some instances, of being God's representatives on earth. Daniel spoke about the papal power promoting itself in opposition to the Prince of princes (Dan. 7:25; 8:25). There are a number of areas in which this has happened. For example, the pope is declared confidently to be more than a "mere man" but the "vicar of God" and hence able to "modify, declare, or interpret even divine laws."[152] One way in which the pope has done this is in his authoritative statements about the origins of the creation and life. Pope John Paul II considered "the doctrine of 'evolutionism' a serious hypothesis, worthy of investigation and in-depth study equal to the opposing hypothesis." Arguing in favor of evolution, he made it clear that, in any comprehensive concept of human evolution, the Catholic view would have God intervening to give individuals a spiritual soul.[153] By supporting those who claim that human reason is superior to revealed truth, this power has allied itself against God in that it provisionally claims that God created through the evolutionary process.[154] Many other Christian churches have followed this same line of thinking.

John the Revelator carefully elaborated on some of these developments. He informed readers that the special emphasis of the first angel, who was designated to give the world God's last warning message, is centered about the Creator, His work, His memorial—the Sabbath—and His offer of salvation (Rev. 14:6, 7). Accepting the theory of evolution is, in reality, a denial of the role of Christ in the creation of humanity and His essential re-creative role in the lives of men and women. The memorial of Creation, the seventh-day Sabbath, naturally slips into obscurity as a result of such beliefs.

Satan is interested particularly in opposing God's moral law (Dan. 7:25), which guards the arena of moral behavior. The foundation of God's throne is both mercy and justice (Ps. 89:14). It stands to reason that an intelligent commander would direct his best efforts against these. This is exactly what Satan's agents on earth have done. They have attacked the moral law. John, the writer of Revelation, confirms that Satan's efforts will be against the Ten Commandments, downplaying the role of faith in the Christian journey (Rev. 12:17; 14:12). Christ was emphatic in His teaching about the moral law: "For truly I tell you, until heaven and earth disappear, not the smallest letter, not the least stroke of a pen, will by any means disappear from the Law until everything is accomplished" (Matt. 5:18, NIV).

It is a sobering thought that, around the time that Daniel wrote his book of prophecies, a number of philosophies arose that have impacted the world in a highly significant way. These include Confucianism, Taoism, Buddhism, and Zoroastrianism with its derivative Mithraism. All these rest on foundations differing from that on which Judeo-Christian thought is based. Some have made major departures from God's moral standards.

The Battle for Minds. The apostle Paul gives a vivid description of the struggle for the minds of men and women. He wrote, "We are fighting against forces and authorities and against rulers of darkness and powers in the spiritual world" (Eph. 6:12, CEV). In this statement, the apostle gives the clearest indication that the Christian is involved in a spiritual battle in which the forces of darkness leave no means untried in capturing the minds of humanity. Elsewhere Christ called the devil the "prince of this world" (John 12:31, KJV). The tussle for the minds of believers is intense, which is why the apostle Paul declares that only the Lord's strength can save. We need to use every advantage that God has offered in this spiritual struggle (Eph. 6:10, 11).

The war of ideas will end when Christ returns and Satan is destroyed eternally some time later (Rev. 19:11–15; 20:7–10). When Christ has finished His ministry of judicial reconciliation, probation will close. Those who have not availed themselves of Christ's offer of salvation will be eliminated by the brightness of His coming, and Satan will be banished for 1,000 years to solitude with nobody to tempt (Isa. 66:15, 16; Rev. 20:1–3). At the end of this period, the unsaved dead will be raised back to life. Satan will rally them in one last grand effort to defeat God. Then fire will come down from heaven, bringing an end to the sad reign of Satan (Rev. 20:7–10). The destruction of sin and sinners will be final and complete; there is no suggestion that the wicked will suffer forever. The words in the passage indicate complete destruction that will last forever (Mal. 4:1).

Reconciliation and Atonement

In this section, I will

- *introduce the reader to the biblical evidence that there are phases to the reconciliation of God and human beings in the atonement process.*

The word "atonement" means being "at one" with God. The oneness of humanity with God was destroyed in the Garden of Eden through transgression of God's instructions. The just consequence of doubting God and going against His instructions, which He had given to Adam and Eve in love, was eternal death. This result was unavoidable unless a perfect substitute could be found to suffer the penalty instead of fallen humanity. Jesus came willingly to earth as our sin-bearer to pay the penalty for breaking God's moral law. In this way, Christ not only covered, or atoned for, our sins with His blood, but He also provided strength for the sinner to live obediently through faith. His act of sacrifice on Calvary provided the means by which the estate that was lost in Eden might be reclaimed. Nevertheless, the final reconciliation of humanity to God still awaits realization. "Christ is our atonement with God. Any work He performs in our behalf to aid

Chapter 11. The Veil of the Temple Was Torn

in accomplishing atonement is a part of His atonement for us. That includes His sacrifice and all phases of His ministry."[155]

Table 11.1 below shows that certain great controversy events were well represented in activities within the sanctuary in the Jewish religious year. These activities also show a broad correspondence with the phases of the reconciliation and atonement undertaken by God. The atonement represents God's work to re-establish the Edenic state for humanity. As theologian Fernando Canale has pointed out: "… the Sanctuary Doctrine provide[s] the inner theological framework for the theological interpretation of Salvation History as the Great Controversy."[156] Table 11.1 is a demonstration of the relationships between the two.

Sacrificial Atonement. God has made known from the creation of the human race that the consequences of disobedience to His instructions would be eternal death (Gen. 3:1–3). This seems harsh to some, but we must understand that the choice to disobey God was actually a vote to accept a different philosophical and operational system for the world. This meant that malfunctioning of the biological machinery would occur and death would result. The only remedy possible was for a substitute to step into the breach to pay the just penalty for sin and re-establish harmony. Atonement for sins could not be made without the loss of life and the shedding of blood of a perfect substitute. This concept was conveyed in the earthly sanctuary service by a perfect animal forfeiting its life in place of the sinner (e.g., Lev. 9:3; 17:11; Heb. 9:22). The symbol pointed forward to Christ's death on this earth for humanity (Isa. 53:4, 5).

When the sanctuary system of worship was initiated, the offerings were made in the courtyard of the sanctuary, signifying that Christ would suffer and die on this earth (Isa. 53:4, 5). Without question, Christ's sacrificial atonement was all-sufficient (Heb. 10:11, 12). On Mount Calvary, He cried, "It is finished" (John 19:30). "Christ's words on the mountainside were the announcement that His sacrifice on behalf of man was full and complete. The conditions of the atonement had been fulfilled; the work for which He came to this world had been accomplished."[157] This means that when we come to Him in faith, we will be released from the guilt of sin and be regarded as if we had never sinned; we are justified (Rom. 5:1; 1 John 1:9). To receive this benefit, all must come with repentance and confession believing that God is faithful.

Table 11.1. Comparison of the highlights of the religious year activities of the Israelites, the great controversy between Christ and Satan, and the corresponding steps toward reconciliation planned by God.

Israelite religious year highlights/ festivals	Great controversy highlights	Highlights of reconciliation program
NA	Lucifer rebels (Isa. 14:13, 14).	God proactive—plan of salvation already existed (1 Peter 1:18–20)
NA	Satan and his followers expelled from heaven (Rev. 12:7–9)	
The subtext to the ceremonies—the fallen condition of humanity acknowledged (Lev. 4)	The Creation and the Fall (Gen. 1:27; 3:6, 7)	First gospel proclamation (Gen. 3:15). Sacrificial system of types introduced (e.g., Gen. 3:21; 4:4).
The seventh-day Sabbath memorial continually acknowledged as an invitation to enter intimate rest with God (Lev. 23:3; cf. Heb. 4:4–7)	The seventh-day Sabbath, established at the Creation, becomes the focus of Satan's attack (Dan. 7:25)	The completion of the reconciliation is acknowledged in heaven by use of the seventh-day Sabbath (Isa. 66:22, 23)
The Passover (Lev. 23:5)	Incarnation and the Cross (Luke 18:31–33)	Sacrificial atonement made; type pointed to the "Lamb" of God (Matt. 27:50, 51; John 1:29). Justification is the beginning of the faith journey.

Chapter 11. The Veil of the Temple Was Torn

Israelite religious year highlights/ festivals	Great controversy highlights	Highlights of reconciliation program
Unleavened bread (Lev. 23:6–8)		Christ the Bread of life (John 6:35) can transform the life (Rom. 12:2). Sanctification represents the continuation of the faith journey under the mediatorial work of Christ.
Wave sheaf of first fruits (Feast of Firstfruits) (Lev. 23:10–14)	Firstfruits—Christ and His trophies of salvation raised from the dead (Matt. 27:52, 53; 1 Cor. 15:20, 23)	Promises made to believers before the cross are honored on account of Christ's victory (Heb. 11:39, 40)
Feast of Weeks, or Pentecost (Lev. 23:15–22)	High priestly ministry of Christ commences in heaven (Acts 2:1–4)	Commencement of mediatorial ministry in heaven (1 Tim. 2:5; Heb. 5:5–10)
The memorial of the blowing of Trumpets (Lev. 23:23–25; Rev. 14:6, 7)	Announcement of the imminence of judicial ministry (Matt. 24:29)	
The regular ceremonies* on the Day of Atonement or Judgment (Lev. 23:27–32)	Judicial reconciliation commences (Dan. 7:9, 10)	Mediatorial and Judicial ministries (John 5:22; Heb. 7:24–28)
High priest changed robes (Lev. 16:23) Feast of Tabernacles (Lev. 23:34–44)	Probation closes and Christ comes (Matt. 24:30, 31; 25:6–13; Rev. 22:11, 12)	Mediatorial work finished and the judicial outcomes are finalized (Dan. 12:1, 2; 2 Cor. 5:10; Rev. 19:14–16; 22:11, 12)

Israelite religious year highlights/ festivals	Great controversy highlights	Highlights of reconciliation program
Azazel sent to the wilderness (Lev. 16:22)	Satan separated from his human followers (Rev. 20:1–3)	Review process conducted by the saints. Fairness demonstrated (Rev. 20:4, 6)
—	Resurrection of the wicked and the final assault of Satan on God (Rev. 20:5 first part; 7–9)	—
Azazel perishes (assumed)	Satan eliminated as the controversy has ended (Rev. 20:10, 13–15)	Eradicatory ministry re-establishes harmony (Rev. 19:20, 21; 20:10, 14, 15; 21:3–5)

* The mediatorial activity of the morning and evening sacrifice was continued on the Day of Atonement—Num. 28:3–8, 10, 15, 24, 31; 29:6, 11, 16.

Mediatorial Atonement. Christ's sacrifice for humanity fulfilled the just demands of the law. However, the drama of the ages had not been brought to a conclusion, for eternal harmony was yet to be restored. To progress toward this objective following Christ's resurrection, He immediately engaged in a different aspect of ministry. The Scriptures record that Christ went to heaven "to appear in the presence of God for us" (Heb. 9:24; cf. 1 Tim. 2:5). There He now accepts the confessions and prayers of those who wish to avail themselves of His sacrifice.

This ministry was foreshadowed in the sanctuary services. Following the sacrifice of the animal victim by the penitent believer, the priest performed a work of mediation on behalf of the believer. The Scriptures clearly state that the priest, who represented Christ, would "make atonement" (Lev. 4:20, 26, 31, 35; 5:6, 10, 13, 18; 6:7; 7:7). Since the priest did not slay the victim, we must conclude that the priest's work was additional to the sacrificial atonement. This mediatorial phase of the atonement was essential and took place in the first apartment of the earthly sanctuary. It consisted of sprinkling the blood (Lev. 4:5–7, 16, 17). Sometimes the priest did not sprinkle blood in the

Holy Place; rather he ate a portion of the flesh of the sacrifice to make atonement—Lev. 6:26; 10:17. Both types of activity signified that the priest was mediating on the sinner's behalf. The priest became a sin-bearer in type, representing Jesus.

These services represented Christ's future work in the heavenly sanctuary. He is represented as having a work of mediation in the first apartment of the heavenly sanctuary subsequent to His death on the cross (Acts 2:33, 34; Heb. 9:24; 1 John 2:1). Indeed, we notice the statement: "Jesus is our great High Priest in heaven. And what is He doing? He is making intercession and atonement for his people who believe in him. Through his imputed righteousness, they are accepted of God, as those who are manifesting to the world that they acknowledge allegiance to God, keeping all His commandments."[158] Christ has promised to give us help in time of need as we plead with Him (Heb. 4:14–16). The sanctifying influence of the Spirit of God in the life will transform us and make us like Christ in character (Acts 26:18; Rom. 12:2). The righteousness of Christ is thus imparted to us.

The vital information about Christ's sanctification ministry was taught by the incense, unleavened bread, and the lamps that continually burned in the Holy Place. In response to the prayers of faith represented by the incense, which the Holy Spirit presents to God, the worshiper pleads for strength to do the will of God as daily the bread of life—the Bible—is assimilated and the quickening power of the Holy Spirit is requested.

Both elements represented in the sanctuary constitute the gift of righteousness by faith. Note one expression of this thought: "Righteousness within is testified to by righteousness without. He who is righteous within is not hard-hearted and unsympathetic, but day by day he grows into the image of Christ, going on from strength to strength. He who is being sanctified by the truth will be self-controlled, and will follow in the footsteps of Christ until grace is lost in glory. The righteousness by which we are justified is imputed; the righteousness by which we are sanctified is imparted. The first is our title to heaven, the second is our fitness for heaven."[159] (*Imputed* means "ascribed to someone by virtue of a similar quality in another." *Imparted* means "given, granted, or communicated.")

Judicial Atonement. A significant ceremony in the reconciliation process took place near the end of the Jewish religious year on the Day of Atonement (Lev. 16:16, 30). The work of atonement occurred in the second apartment of the earthly sanctuary on that day. It is evident from chapter 16 of Leviticus that the work on this special day was a work of judgment (verses 29, 30). The Jewish sages saw it as a day in which "atonement is promised even to the completely wicked who repent."[160] The destinies of the people were settled (Lev. 23:28–30). This represented the closing aspect of making matters right in the atonement. This was a time when the high priest made final intercession for all those who by their actions and attitudes signified that they wished to be identified with God's people. The ignorant sins of the people were also represented before the Lord on this day (Heb. 9:7).[161] The work involved sprinkling the blood of the Lord's goat on and before the mercy seat (Lev. 16:15). By this symbolic act was signified that the just demands of the law were satisfied through the shedding of the blood of the goat representing Christ.

In the heavenly sanctuary, Christ entered into this final phase of ministry in 1844—the antitypical day of atonement, or judgment.[162] (This is a subject that we will take up in Chapter 19.) Christ did not cease His intercession on humanity's behalf during this phase of ministry (Heb. 7:25; cf. Rev. 3:5), a feature illustrated in the earthly sanctuary through offering the continual burnt sacrifice even on judgment day (Num. 29:7, 11).

Eradicatory Atonement. The final phase in the reconciliation of the universe to God involves cleansing the world of the root cause of sin and removing the effects of its reign. This can be described as an "eradicatory atonement." The responsibility for causing suffering, death, and temptation finally is placed to Satan's account. He bears this record into the lake of fire (Ps. 7:16; Rev. 20:10, 14).[163] Those who have chosen to follow his philosophy are likewise removed (Rev. 20:15). The earth will be cleansed by fire and a new one created (2 Peter 3:10; Rev. 21:1). In the new earth, God will dwell with humanity again in a place that does not know sorrow or suffering (Rev. 21:3, 4).

The universe will then be returned to a state of unity and perfect harmony, which is the completion of at-one-ment. This phase of atonement was represented in the Old Testament sanctuary service when the high priest symbolically placed the record of confessed sins on Azazel's goat (the alternate to the "Lord's goat," meaning Satan), and a "fit man" then led this goat into the land of oblivion in separation from the congregation (Lev. 16:9, 10, 21, 22).[164]

Chapter 12.
Examine Your Relationship with God

> ***Chapter Emphasis:*** *In preparation for Christ's soon return, believers are called to examine their life, motives, and ministry. Those that respond make a whole-hearted commitment to God. They uphold the truths of Scripture and commit themselves to living a life of obedience to Jesus' instructions through the exercise of faith in His enabling power.*
>
> ***Spiritual Link:*** *Survival through end times will be dependent on understanding the marked difference between the seal of God and the mark of the beast.*

In preparation for the Day of Atonement, which occurred once a year in the Jewish economy, the people were called upon by God to thoroughly examine their standing with Him. The ceremonies were meant to focus the worshipers' mind on the necessity of a vibrant and continuing relationship with Him. The actual day was a high day spiritually with no interfering interests intruding. Each person was to enter into a time of fasting and reflection and to seek a special blessing from God. These ideas are expressed in the following contemporary explanation: "The day is observed by fasting and prayer and by rededication to a religious life.... Yom Kippur marks the culmination of the Ten Penitential Days, which begin on Rosh Hashanah, or New Year's Day. Although Yom Kippur is solemn and regarded as a day of judgment, it is not mournful in character, since it is also a period of grace and offers an opportunity to seek forgiveness for sins committed against God; in the case of sins committed against one's fellow man, one must first ask forgiveness from the one who has been wronged."[165]

In Chapter 1, we discovered that the Jewish round of ceremonies conducted year by year not only conveyed important lessons about the dynamics of salvation but also gave insights into God's salvation timetable and the great events that would precede His coming in glory. We will discover in Chapter 19 that the antitypical day of atonement commenced in 1844 according to prophecy.

The question that faces us today, as it confronted God's people of old, is whether we are ready to meet our God in peace. What sort of people would God have us be in these closing days of earth's history? This is the question that I will seek to address in the present chapter.

Examine Your Life

In this section, I will

- *focus on the attitudes and behavior of true worshipers on the Day of Atonement anciently;*

- *outline the nature of the genuine religious experience that God calls for in His people today during the antitypical day of atonement.*

The services on the Day of Atonement were full of meaning. Those who did not humble themselves before God on this day were "cut off." They were expelled from the camp and forfeited their standing as Hebrews. Those who participated fully in the ceremony were entitled to celebrate the Feast of Tabernacles some five days later, which was a feast of victory and deliverance (Lev. 23:40, 43). This latter feast symbolized deliverance from the presence of sin, and it pointed forward to the second coming of Christ. It represented a continuation of the relationship previously established.

Ancient Practices on the Day. The activities in the ten days leading up to the Day of Atonement culminated in the activities of that day (Lev. 23:24, 25). This solemn day is known in Hebrew literature as "a

Chapter 12. Examine Your Relationship with God

day of 'afflicting the soul.' "[166] Anciently the people were to examine all aspects of their relationship with God and with their fellow believers (Lev. 16:31). The terminology used here carries a solemn message. The word expressed as "afflict" can also be rendered as "humble" or "mortify." The idea is thus conveyed that this was a time to examine the life, the motives, and the conduct. It was a day on which self-denial was to be practiced and the focus of attention was to be the pursuit of the things of God and relationships. The great issue to be grappled with was: Am I serving the living God, and am I fully surrendered to Him? Are His interests central in my life?

The only obligatory fast in the Jewish calendar, as stipulated by the Torah, was on the Day of Atonement (Lev. 16:29–31; 23:27–32; Num. 29:7; Acts 27:9).[167] The prophet Isaiah suggested that perverted activities were being carried out on this special day—celebration, exploitation, debate, strife, and the pursuit of selfish ends (Isa. 58:3, 4). Fasting had come to be practiced as a means to earn God's approval. Such forms of artificial godliness may even be practiced today. We must be careful that form does not take the place of genuine religious experience (2 Tim. 3:5).

An Antitypical Day. Today, we find ourselves in the antitypical day of atonement. Presently we are to meet with Christ by faith in the heavenly sanctuary and form a deep relationship with Him. We are to follow His ministry and His intercession there. We are to contemplate His life here on earth and the ideal for His children. In this time, we are to focus on Christ our Substitute who indeed was offered for the sins of the world (John 1:29; 2 Cor. 5:21; Gal. 1:4). As our Substitute, He justifies us and gives us assurance. Even more, God wishes to deliver us from the overwhelming power of sin in our daily life. In other words, He wishes to sanctify us (Ezek. 36:26, 27). He gives us an incredible assurance in the promise that no temptation can overthrow those who continue to hold on to Him in faith (1 Cor. 10:13). Truly, we are invited to enter the rest of salvation symbolized by the Sabbath (Heb. 4:7, 3, 4) and become serious about our relationship to God and our duties to Him.

In contrast to the behavior shown by Israel, Isaiah was clear about acceptable behavior. We might extend the advice to include the period of earth's history just before the second coming. The dramatic and urgent call given to the inhabitants of this world just before Christ returns is to come back to God, to sever the ties that bind them to the false forms of worship and religious experience commonly found in this world (Rev. 18:1–4, cf. Isa. 58:6–11). We should ever be ready and anxious to work for the salvation of others. Jesus' commission in Matthew 28:19 contains the compelling words, "Go therefore." As we share with others our concern about their salvation and express our love for them in practical ways, minds will be influenced to consider eternal things. God is calling men and women everywhere back to the principles of the Bible.

The theme in Isaiah 58:12 is that a great work of restoration, reformation, and revival will take place as we appeal to God's Word and ask for the outpouring of His Spirit. Truths long hidden under the cloak of human tradition will be restored. For example, the Sabbath is emphasized in verses 13 and 14; conscientiousness in health reform is brought to the fore in the very idea of fasting on the Day of Atonement. In addition, since we are in the antitypical day of judgment, we are admonished to wear ornaments of humility rather than decorative ornaments (Exod. 33:5, 1 Peter 3:3, 4). This is the work that God desires to take place on this earth among those who hear His call.

God wishes to form a deep relationship with believers (Jer. 9:23, 24). We must not be side-tracked by peripheral issues. "The character we cultivate, the attitude we assume today, is fixing our future destiny."[168] God desires that we settle "into the truth, both intellectually and spiritually."[169]

Holiness to the Lord

In this section, I will

- *emphasize that a close relationship with Christ is the secret of a successful Christian experience;*
- *inquire into the meaning and relevance of the "last generation."*

The Bible speaks a great deal about holiness and, in particular, about the character of the "last generation." Jesus declares of them: "He who is holy, let him be holy still" (Rev. 22:11). What if we are among those who live in the time when the first part of this verse is proclaimed—"He who is unjust, let him be unjust still; he who is filthy, let him be filthy still" (Rev. 22:11)? Solemn preparation is required for the most momentous events of all the ages—the close of probation and the coming of Christ in glory.

Chapter 12. Examine Your Relationship with God

The apostle Paul described Christians who are counted worthy to inherit eternal life in the following words: "Now may the God of peace Himself sanctify you completely" (1 Thess. 5:23). Another way of saying this is: "Higher than the highest human thought can reach is God's ideal for His children. Godliness—godlikeness—is the goal to be reached."[170] God desires us to be complete in all respects through the power supplied in response to faith. All aspects of the life are to be brought under the influence of God's molding influence, be it lifestyle and health, speech, thought, or our every-day activities. If we place our trust in the Lord through faith, He is able to keep us from falling (Jude 1:24). A person who maintains such a relationship is safe in God's hands (1 John 3:9, 10, 14).

Christ used no divine power to save Himself. His prayer was, "nevertheless, not as I will, but as You *will*" (Matt. 26:39). He could have summoned a legion of angels to His aid, but He did not. The taunt on the cross was: "He saved others; Himself He cannot save" (Matt. 27:42). Satan could not tempt Christ to lose faith, to sin against God. Consequently, Christ died a victor. We are promised access to the same strength and, through faith, are promised victory over the power of sin (Rev. 3:21). Jesus proclaimed, "I in them, and You in Me; that they may be made perfect in one, and that the world may know that You have sent Me" (John 17:23). In saying this, He indicated that our relationship with Him is to be as His was with the Father. Our allegiance is to be entire and complete—victory over sin will then be ours.

Satan's failure to induce Christ to sin did not lead to a lessening of his warfare against the people of God (Rev. 12:17). He is upset particularly with those who have a dynamic faith experience that enables them to keep the commandments of God (Rev. 14:12; 1 John 5:4). At the close of time, Satan observes with disapproval a group of people who hold to the body of truths held by Jesus, including the observance of His Commandments. These people are overcomers through faith, and they reflect the character of Christ. They hold the law and the gospel in perfect harmony. Such a demonstration of obedience to God effectively destroys the argument that Satan has advanced continually—that is, that humanity cannot keep the law of God. It also destroys the claim that, since the cross, the law (or certain aspects of it) has been done away with.

Safe in God's Care

In this section, I will

- *explore the nature of the mark of approval placed on the forehead of those who are God's friends.*

In the Jewish ceremonies associated with the Day of Atonement, the idea was that during the process of judgment the names of individuals were sealed in the book of life and that the destiny of each was decided.[171] A similar thought is expressed in relation to the last generation of genuine followers of Christ on earth just before Christ's work in the heavenly sanctuary is finished. They are recorded as having their Father's name, or seal, written in their forehead (Rev. 7:3, 4; 14:1).

Nature of God's Seal. Some wild ideas have been expressed over the nature of the seal of God. The Scriptures do not leave us in doubt, however. It is not a visible mark. It represents a mark of redemption, a mark of sanctification (Ezek. 9:4; Rev. 14:1, 5, 12). Both the holy angels and the Holy Spirit are involved in this process (Eph. 1:13; Rev. 7:2, 3). In fact, all heaven is involved in the salvation of human beings.

The sealing is said to take place in the forehead (Rev. 7:3; 9:4). Linked with the sealing is the writing of the Father's name in the forehead (Rev. 14:1; 22:4), which is the location of the powers of reasoning and decision. The Greek word translated "seal" may also be rendered "accredited by," "*authenticate* a document *with a seal,*" "*certify* an object *after examination by attaching a seal,*" "*seal* an object to show that it is pledged," "*accredit* as an envoy," or "*set a seal of approval upon, confirm.*" Hence, the seal of God is God's certification of fitness for heaven on the basis of the life of faith lived by His children.[172] Those who have a mark in their forehead give conscious assent and commitment to its Giver (Rom. 7:25).

The special seal of Revelation applies to those who have chosen to serve God during a period of earth's history when all are asked to obey human law rather than the law of God (Rev. 13:15–17). The Sabbath has become the great point at issue. It has always been God's sign, or seal, of a loyal and transforming relationship (Exod. 31:12, 13; Isa. 8:16). Yet, in the closing stages of earth's history, the law of God and its most contested commandment, the fourth, have become the point of intense contention. God places His mark of approval upon

Chapter 12. Examine Your Relationship with God

those, who in the face of a death decree, obey Him in all things and reverence the Sabbath because they love Him and know from experience the joy of victorious living through faith in Christ (Rev. 13:15–17; cf. Rev. 14:12). Those who receive this seal have made it a habit of standing for revealed truth rather than of following the crowd. They have independence of mind and spirit and test all things by the Word of God (Isa. 8:20). They remain faithful under test and trial because they have the right attitude toward God and a saving relationship with Him.

Nature of Satan's Work and Mark. It is of profound interest to note that the great issue in the final struggle is whether believers have the seal of God or the mark of the beast, which is the mark of Satan (Rev. 7:3; 13:2, 16). Satan has, since his fall from heaven, been using his powers to oppose God. In Ezekiel 28, God made certain observations through the prophet about the king of Tyre and the evil power activating him, as it was Satan, the former covering cherub who was once closest to Christ (verses 12–14), who activated the king. In these verses, we are given insights into some of the details of Satan's thoughts and activities before he was expelled from heaven. Let us notice one detail in verse 12. The phrase often translated, "Thou sealest up the sum" (KJV), may also be legitimately translated, "Thou attachest the seal to the ordinance."[173] Satan can be regarded, then, as the angel who, in heaven before the Fall, attached God's seal of approval to ordinances transacted in the government of heaven. Satan's dissatisfaction with God's government meant that he lost his position there. In defiance, Satan is working particularly through various apostate religious agencies in our world today. He places his mark, or seal, of character on their philosophies and activities. He is able to work effectively through various agencies, but his most successful work is accomplished through the "little horn" power revealed in Daniel 7 and 8, or, as the Bible presents elsewhere, through "the [one] destitute of law" (2 Thess. 2:8).[174]

Contrasted with God's seal on the forehead (Rev. 13:16), Satan's mark is placed either in the *forehead* or on the *hand*. The hand is a symbol of work (Eccles. 9:10). A mark in the hand thus signifies that the person will work as directed by the power without giving particularly strong intellectual assent. The word "mark" may be translated "inscription," "endorsement," or "character."[175] Those with the mark of the beast have Satan's endorsement, which means that they display aspects of his character. Those who refuse the mark of the beast will be those who have independence of mind and spirit, those who refuse popularity and conformity and would rather "fight for the dignity and integrity of truth."[176]

Characteristics of the Sealed. Just as it was with Israel on the Day of Atonement anciently, so will it be on the antitypical day of atonement with those who desire to be counted among the potential candidates of heaven. They are "now afflicting their souls, confessing their sins, and earnestly pleading for pardon through Jesus their Advocate."[177] "Those that overcome the world, the flesh, and the devil, will be the favored ones who shall receive the seal of the living God.... Only those who, in their attitude before God, are filling the position of those who are repenting and confessing their sins in the great antitypical day of atonement, will be recognized and marked as worthy of God's protection."[178] In Malachi 3:3, God is pictured as "a refiner and a purifier" so that His followers may offer "an offering in righteousness." God allows trials to come to His servants so that their character may be developed.

Those who have the seal of God display certain characteristics. The first of these is that they have contended with and rejected false doctrine; they do not identify with the faith of apostates who are symbolized by an immoral woman (Rev. 17:1–6; cf. Rev. 12:1–5). Rather, they are called "virgins" because they have accepted biblical truth and are covered with Christ's righteousness; they have "washed their robes and made them white in the blood of the Lamb" (Rev. 7:14; cf. Rev. 14:4, 5). Having the seal of God also means that they have the experience of victory over sin and that they are committed to following God's covenant requirements through faith (1 John 5:4; Rev. 3:21; 7:13, 14; 14:5, 12).

Those who bear the mark of God are committed to the pursuit of righteousness, and they sorrow "over all the abominations that are done" in the name of religion (Ezek. 9:4). While their acquaintances speak of God's promises and of multiple applications of prophecies, they show patience at the apparent delay of Christ and display a prayerful attitude in the face of apostasy among their brethren (Rev. 14:12; cf. Ezek. 9:4).

Chapter 12. Examine Your Relationship with God

Issues under Sustained Attack. The "little horn" power, or papal Rome, has been particularly adept at placing its own interpretations on God's Word. We have already spoken about some of these trends. However, we emphasize again two areas of truth under threat by this power. The first truth challenged is the all-sufficiency of Christ—the "Prince of princes," or the "Prince of the host"—as the source of revealed truth (Dan. 8:11, 12, 25). The truth proclaimed by the Lord is: "The just shall live by his faith" (Hab. 2:4). The second is regarding God's law, for the "little horn" power "intends to change" the ancient practice of the times of worship and other requirements contained in the Decalogue (Dan. 7:25).

In these passages of Scripture, the Bible reveals that the issues will be concerned with law and faith. The all-sufficiency of Christ as our Savior and Mediator has been denied by paganism and obscured by the papacy. The "little horn" power has cast truths to the ground regarding Christ's revealed will in the Scriptures, His ministry, His priesthood, and the heavenly sanctuary (Dan. 8:12, 25; 2 Thess. 2:3–5). This power regards tradition as having an equal footing with divine revelation.[179] It has replaced the sinless divine High Priest with a sinning human priesthood on earth. Instead of focusing on Christ ministering in His holy temple in heaven, it directs people to services and forms of worship in magnificent structures here on earth. Hence, it is truly said: "… he sits as God in the temple of God" (2 Thess. 2:4).

We also observe that the Decalogue has been changed in the official catechisms. (See, for example, Table 12.1.) The second commandment has effectively disappeared, the fourth commandment has been greatly shortened, and the tenth commandment has been divided to make up for the deletion of the second. It is of interest to note that those who are accounted worthy to inherit the world made new are distinguished by victory over sin, through faith, and by their acceptance of and joyful obedience to all of God's commandments (Rev. 14:12; 3:21).

Table 12.1. Comparison of the Ten Commandments taken from a Catholic catechism and the New King James Bible.[180]

Roman Catholic Catechism ["He shall think himself able to change times and laws." Dan. 7:25, Douay-Rheims]	The Bible Exodus 20:3–17, NKJV
1. I am the Lord thy God; thou shalt not have strange gods before Me.	1. You shall have no other gods before Me.
2. Thou shalt not take the name of the Lord thy God in vain.	2. *You shall not make for yourself any carved image, or any likeness *of anything* that *is* in the heaven above, or that *is* in the earth beneath, or that *is* in the water under the earth; you shall not bow down to them nor serve them. For I, the LORD your God, *am* a jealous God, visiting the iniquity of the fathers on the children to the third and fourth *generations* of those that hate Me, but showing mercy to thousands, to those who love Me and keep My commandments.
3. Remember thou keep holy the Lord's day.	3. You shall not take the name of the LORD your God in vain, for the LORD will not hold him guiltless who takes His name in vain.

4. Honor thy father and thy mother.	4. Remember the Sabbath day, to keep it holy. Six days you shall labor and do all your work, but the seventh day *is* the Sabbath of the Lord your God. *In it* you shall do no work: you, nor your son, nor your daughter, nor your manservant, nor your maidservant, nor your cattle, nor your stranger who *is* within your gates. For *in* six days the Lord made the heavens and the earth, the sea, and all that *is* in them, and rested the seventh day. Therefore the Lord blessed the Sabbath day and hallowed it.
5. Thou shalt not kill.	5. Honor your father and your mother, that your days may be long upon the land which the Lord your God is giving you.
6. Thou shalt not commit adultery.	6. You shall not murder.
7. Thou shalt not steal.	7. You shall not commit adultery.
8. Thou shalt not bear false witness against thy neighbor.	8. You shall not steal.
9. Thou shalt not covet thy neighbor's wife.	9. You shall not bear false witness against your neighbor.

10. Thou shalt not covet thy neighbor's goods.	10. You shall not covet your neighbor's house; you shall not covet your neighbor's wife, nor his manservant, nor his maidservant, nor his ox, nor his donkey, nor anything that *is* your neighbor's.

* An official spokesperson for Roman Catholicism has noted: "Logically, therefore, the Protestant second commandment has no reason of being, and was born of the exigency of controversy to justify the early Reformers" (Bertrand Louis Conway, *The Question-Box Answers: Replies to Questions Received on Missions to Non-Catholics* [New York: Paulist Press, 1903], p. 551).

A Call to Faithfulness. James, the brother of Jesus, tells us plainly that true faith reveals itself in loving obedience to all of God's requirements (James 1:22–25; 2:10–12). In other words, true faith is revealed in works of obedience to God and of love for others. This can only spring from a close relationship with Jesus. It is frequently maintained in the Christian world today that only nine of the Ten Commandments originally given to Moses on Mount Sinai are applicable. It is contended that these nine are alone part of the moral code of the moral law. The fourth commandment, which is ostensibly neglected under this rationale, does, however, have profound moral content in that it proclaims the equality of all men (see Isa. 56:1–8) on account of Christ's sacrifice for all. It also enjoins "belief in creation" and the "subordination of nature to God."[181] Hence, the fourth commandment complements the first three commandments and highlights significant moral content.

It is also held by some that, since Christ was victorious over all the assaults of Satan, human beings need not be overly concerned about victorious living. It is true that Christ triumphed gloriously at the cross, but it is equally true that He wishes every believer to triumph gloriously through faith in Him (Rom. 13:11–14; 1 John 5:4; Rev. 3:21). In reality, the glories of heaven are only promised to the overcomer (Rev. 3:12). "The very image of God is to be reproduced in humanity. The honor of God, the honor of Christ, is involved in the perfection of the character of His people."[182]

The apostle closest to Jesus has revealed the secrets of a saving relationship with Jesus Christ in the end times. In fact, John carefully recorded the words of the Lord to avoid all question. The instructions are simple: "... buy from Me gold refined in the fire ... and white garments ... and anoint your eyes with eye salve" (Rev. 3:18). The gold refined in the fire is "faith working through love" (Gal. 5:6; cf. James 2:5).[183] Love is the basis of all Christian activity, as God is love (1 John 4:8, 16). The white robe, which all must wear who are privileged to enter the marriage feast of the Lamb, is the robe of Christ's righteousness (Matt. 22:11; Gal. 3:27). Our righteousness is as filthy rags. Christ covers us with His righteousness, as we come to Him for the forgiveness of sins and plead with Him for strength to resist temptation. The eye salve is the "spiritual discernment" that God gives to us through the operation of the Holy Spirit (John 16:8–11).[184] The Spirit convicts us of sin and leads us into all truth (John 16:13).

Focus on Christ

In this section, I will

- *indicate how the Christian may, in a practical way, daily focus on Christ.*

The story of the Bible is a glorious account of God's overcoming evil with good. The victory that Christ gained over Satan, God wishes us to gain through faith in Him. The secret of success is to focus on Jesus Christ. This is also the message that was understood by those who participated fully in the ceremonies on the Day of Atonement. They were entitled to celebrate the Feast of Tabernacles some five days later, which was a feast of victory and deliverance (Lev. 23:40, 43).

Assurances Given. Faith in Christ's merits and the subsequent reception of power, which He readily gives, are the avenues to success for the Christian (1 John 5:4). Notice:

> The trial of our faith should not cause despair or discouragement. We should not cast ourselves away, saying, "I am a sinner, and when I become good enough, I will come to Christ; then I can believe and pray." You will never be good enough of yourselves to merit the favor and help of God. You must come just as you are. Christ meets you as you draw nigh to Him. Place your hand in the hand of Jesus, and he will direct

you. Believe that he keeps you, and then it will be found that in the trial of your faith you will come off more than conqueror through him that loved you. We gain the victory through faith in Christ's power to save us. Then the trial of our faith will be found unto praise and honor and glory at the appearing of Christ. You will praise God that you have found in Christ a present help in every time of need.[185]

The Bible outlines attitudes and practices that, if encouraged, ensure a victorious relationship with Christ (1 Cor. 10:13; 1 John 3:6). The individual first must believe that victory through Christ is possible through exercising faith in Him (Heb. 11:6, 24, 25). Consider this encouragement: "We should not make self the center, and indulge anxiety and fear as to whether we shall be saved. All this turns the soul away from the Source of our strength. Commit the keeping of your soul to God, and trust in Him."[186] We then are encouraged to rejoice under trial and give thanks, knowing that God sees something worthwhile in our character to purify (1 Thess. 5:16–18).

Our faith can be strengthened as we make God's Word our study. The Scriptures express this idea as hiding the Word in the heart, or mind (Ps. 119:11). Prayer also is a powerful weapon in the armory of the Christian (Luke 18:1; 1 Thess. 5:17). This is simply following Jesus' example. Prayer was the secret of His life of victory, the secret of His powerful ministry. David understood the power of prayer. He proclaimed, "My voice You shall hear in the morning, O LORD; in the morning I will direct *it* to You, and I will look up" (Ps. 5:3). God will answer the prayer of faith. Let us focus on Christ through prayer and the study of the Word of God. Remember also that, when tempted, Christ appealed to the Scriptures for counsel (Matt. 4:4, 7, 10).

Promises to the Overcomer. The word translated "overcomes" in Revelation 3:12 means "to keep on winning." Here is pictured continual victory through faith in Christ. The rewards of a vigilant Christian life are without comparison, making heaven cheap at any cost. The apostle Paul expressed this thought in a powerful manner in Romans 8, declaring his personal conviction that nothing can separate us from the love of God. He wrote: "… in all these things we are more than conquerors through Him who loved us. For I am persuaded that neither death nor life, nor angels nor principalities nor powers, nor things present nor things to come, nor height nor depth, nor any other created thing, shall be able to separate us from the love of God which is in Christ Jesus our Lord." (Rom. 8:35–39). How amazing it is that this experience can be ours!

Perhaps the most glorious promise made to overcomers is that they will sit with Jesus on His throne (Rev. 3:21). This means that the privilege of eating from the tree of life will be restored and the second death will have no power over the individual (Rev. 2:7, 11). God has given the people who take God's Word seriously other glorious promises as well (Revelation, chapters 2 and 3).

Christian Life and Worship

Chapter 13.
The Creator Is in His Temple

Chapter Emphasis: The Sabbath institution was a special time of remembrance of God's creative ability each week. The creative ability of God was brought regularly to the attention of the Israelite believers by the cloud of light and the glory associated with the sanctuary and by the daily ceremonies associated with His re-creative acts of the forgiveness of sin and the transforming of the life. His creatorship was remembered too in that the ark of the covenant contained a pot of manna and Aaron's rod that budded.

Spiritual Link: Only the Creator can be the Redeemer of fallen human beings who were originally created in the image of God. The belief that God created an elementary form of life and then used the evolutionary process denies this vital connection.

God is presented in the Bible as the Creator of all things. The simple narrative recorded in the Scriptures presents God's creative acts, including the creation of our solar system, as spanning seven, twenty-four hour days. The sequence in the Creation story is logical and sound. We notice, for instance, that on the third day the chlorophyll-bearing plants were created and, on the following day, the sun. Any period much greater than a day between these two events introduces serious problems of a scientific nature. The Creation story and the events immediately thereafter inform us of the origin of the weekly cycle, of man and woman, of sin and suffering, and of the originator of evil. More significantly, the Savior is introduced. He is none other than Jesus Christ.

The secular scientific community has difficulty explaining such phenomena as the origin of the weekly cycle and the appearance of sexual differences in organisms. Those who believe that God initiated the evolutionary process have problems explaining the origin of sin when death was supposedly a general feature in the world (Rom. 5:12).[187] Without a clear concept of the origin of this world and of sin, the need for a Savior becomes increasingly difficult to accept. The reality of the transforming power and re-creative actions of the Holy Spirit and the acquisition of immortality in creating a new order of beings at Christ's coming also become difficult to believe.

God Is Above All Other Gods

In this section, I will

- *outline features of the earthly sanctuary that reminded of Christ the Creator;*
- *emphasize the extent and uniqueness of Christ's creative activities.*

The prophet Habakkuk considered that the presence of the Lord in His holy temple effectively declared to all in the world the futility of any other system of belief. He wrote: "But the LORD is in His holy temple. Let all the earth keep silent before Him" (Hab. 2:20). Habakkuk is thought to have written his prophecy around 630 BC and thus referred to Solomon's magnificent temple, which was still standing at the time of his writing.

A Personal God. The prophet Habakkuk made significant declarations about God's personal qualities as Judah was rebelling against Him, and Habakkuk recorded God's thoughts concerning the practice of making and worshipping graven images. In contrast to idols, he declared, God possesses greatly superior qualities. An idol or image teaches lies (Hab. 2:18); by contrast, the true God is the way, the truth, and the life (John 14:6). An idol is dumb (Hab. 2:18) and possesses no breath (verse 19). The true God, on the other hand, is the giver of life, for He breathed into Adam's nostrils the breath of life (Gen. 2:7).

Chapter 13. The Creator Is in His Temple

He is everlasting and intimately involved in human affairs, dispensing mercy and justice (Hab. 1:12; 3:2–16).

The appearance of God's glorious presence in the sanctuary and temple was a continual reminder that our God is personally interested in human beings and their lives (Exod. 40:34, 35; 1 Kings 8:9–11). The Shekinah glory—the glory of God's presence—was visible in the holy of holies over the mercy seat, and this glory could fill the sanctuary (Isa. 6:1). As the incense was offered by the priest, the cloud of "divine glory descended upon the mercy seat and filled the most holy place, and often so filled both apartments that the priest was obliged to retire to the door of the tabernacle."[188] (See, for example, 1 Kings 8:10, 11.)

The glory associated with the sanctuary and temple reminds us of the lost glory of the holy pair in Eden and of their exclusion from the Garden and from God's presence by glorious angels (Gen. 3:10, 24; cf. Gen. 1:27; Ps. 104:1, 2). The Garden can be looked upon as being represented in the Most Holy Place. The state of perfection of the Creation could be regained only through the ministrations centered on this apartment.[189]

Sanctuary and Creation. Other features in the sanctuary indicated the greatness of the Creator God we worship. The Lord instructed Moses from the cloud of glory and worked miraculous creative acts through him (e.g., Num. 20:6–8). Not to be forgotten is the presence in the ark of Aaron's rod that budded and the pot of manna preserved (Heb. 9:4). These elements were not visible, but there is no doubt but that the people understood their reality—especially since the miracle of the manna occurred for forty years (Exod. 16:35).

The symbol of Christ's presence in this world is light. Light shone forth out of darkness at the Creation (Ps. 104:1, 2) and was associated with Christ's presence in the sanctuary. Both the prophet Habakkuk and the apostle John understood that the light and glory of Christ's presence are symbols of His creative and re-creative power (Hab. 3:3, 4; John 8:12). We notice that the Lord spoke to Moses, from the cloud of glory, words of pardon, mercy, and salvation, which involved re-creative acts (Num. 14:17–19). We must never forget that the ceremonies and rituals of the sanctuary and temple were put in place expressly "to reverse the evil effects of sin and align creation with ... [God's] loving purposes."[190] They had to do with restoration and ultimately pointed to the work of Christ who would come as the "last Adam" to reverse the failure of the first Adam (1 Cor. 15:21, 22, 45).

The ark of the covenant stood in the Most Holy Place. At the heart of the principles expressed on the stone tablets, housed in the Most Holy Place, was the memorial of God's Creation—the Sabbath (Exod. 20:11). Hence, it is evident that the Decalogue points us to Christ who was its Giver and the Creator of this and all other worlds (James 4:12; John 1:1–3, 14). It is interesting to note that the traditional understanding places the giving of the Decalogue at Sinai on the day of Pentecost and also on the Sabbath.[191] We cannot easily escape the concept that central to the earthly sanctuary was the understanding that the Creator God is real. In fact, God's creative ability is essential to maintain any consistency in the Creation story. The LORD prophesied about the final triumph of the principles of His kingdom over the obstinacy of men in the following words: "... all the earth shall be filled with the glory of the LORD" (Num. 14:21). The creation of the new earth is encompassed in this promise.

Sanctuary and Covenant. After the children of Israel were delivered from Egyptian bondage, they came to Sinai. There the Decalogue, or the tables of the covenant, was given together with instructions concerning the construction of the sanctuary (Exod. 20:1–17; 25:8; 34:28). The principles of the law express love, mercy, and judgment (Deut. 5:9, 10). They illustrate how believers, in their faith journey, express love to God and to their fellow human beings through their attitudes and actions (Matt. 22:36–40). The services in the sanctuary dealt with forgiveness of sin and restoration to the high standards required by the law. In other words, the sanctuary dealt with the particulars of maintaining a vibrant relationship between God and Israel. The people needed to indicate their personal commitment to the relationship by entering whole-heartedly into the spirit and proper practices of the ceremonies. The type of commitment required is likened in Scripture to a marriage undertaking.[192]

The glory of the divine presence shrouded in the cloud on Mount Sinai was, in fact, the glory of God revealed through Christ (Exod. 16:10; 1 Cor. 10:4). This glory was subsequently revealed in the sanctuary and temple (Exod. 40:34). The sanctuary services had to do with God's redemption through grace, and the tables of the covenant had to do with the features of God's character relevant to the lives of the people. The rituals associated with the sanctuary were meant to convey to worshipers God's means for restoring broken relationships. Some have suggested that the Sabbath was the sign of the covenant relationship that was established at this time (Exod. 31:13, 17).[193]

Originally, the day was kept in recognition of God's "sovereignty over man," and it was a time to sincerely commit to their Maker.[194] At Sinai, the people were asked to recommit their lives to the spiritual rest that God offered (cf. Exod. 20:8–11; Heb. 4:3, 9).[195]

Christ the Creator

In this section, I will

- *emphasize that our Creator is also our Redeemer;*

- *remind readers that immortal existence in the new heavens and earth is dependent upon the future creative activities of Christ.*

All the members of the Godhead—the Father, the Son, and the Holy Spirit—were involved in the Creation, as we understand from Genesis 1:2, 26. The term "us" in verse 26 indicates that at least two persons were involved. In Hebrews 1:2, it is made clear that both the Father and the Son were involved in the Creation, and in Genesis 1:2 the Holy Spirit is likewise indicated as playing a role. However, creative ability is required in more than one sphere in order to bring this world back to fulfilling its original purpose.

Creation. The primary agent in creation and re-creation is identified in Scripture as the Word, or Christ, who became flesh (John 1:1–3, 14). The futility of the creature worshiping objects fashioned with human hands is a principle clearly stated in the Scriptures (Isa. 42:5–8). To God alone our allegiance is due, for He "made the heavens" (1 Chron. 16:25, 26; Ps. 96:5; Acts 14:15).

In our own day, many worship the intellect to the extent that a vast majority believes in the theory of evolution. This theory is built on the presuppositions of humanism, which deny God a place in human thinking despite the evidences of intelligent design in the natural world. Humanists assert that the future of humanity lies in human beings' taking full responsibility for the future rather than placing any responsibility on "the shoulders of mythical gods or metaphysical absolutes."[196] Humanists declare: "… it is clear that man is only at the beginning of his period of evolutionary dominance, and that vast and still undreamt-of possibilities of further advance still lie before him.… Man's most sacred duty, and at the same time his most glorious opportunity, is to promote the maximum fulfilment of the evolutionary process on this earth; and this includes the fullest realisation of his own inherent possibilities."[197] Humanists proclaim that there is no higher intellect than that possessed by humans, and, therefore, they seek to explore and develop other "mind faculties" such as telepathy and extrasensory activities. Humanists argue that, when we understand the cause of good and evil, we achieve freedom. One humanist wrote: "Humanity has been 'God fearing', but now we can confront God. The true role of science has been to liberate humanity from ignorance. The true role of religion has been to comfort humanity while the search went on."[198]

The atheist denies the idea of a Creator God and hence does not entertain a supernatural explanation even in regard to origins (though their view of origins is nonetheless miraculous). To such the evolutionary theory is satisfying. By contrast, some theists who accept a supernatural Creator God believe: "Nothing in the nature of evolution precludes the *possibility* of divine direction."[199] More and more, we find a growing accommodation between atheists and theistic evolutionists who have pooled intellectual resources to bring discredit on believers in special creation, and, in doing so, they have diminished God's importance as well. There is a certain inconsistency in this approach as pointed out by Richard Dawkins. This reduces God, in his view, to the point of being so lazy as to be useless. He regards the possibility of the coexistence between a theory of special creation or intelligent design and gradual evolution as "close to being irreconcilably different."[200] On this point, we can agree.

In the acceptance of evolutionary theory by Christians, two significant issues can be identified. The most important relates to the origin of evil, the origin of sin. If we cannot account for the origin of sin, questioning the need of a Savior inevitably results. Without special creation, the concept of the sanctity of marriage and the home—continual reminders of the Creator's gifts through procreation—which are so clearly portrayed in the Genesis account, also has no fundamental basis. Hence, we recognize that the two great institutions that began in Eden—the Sabbath and marriage—are placed in jeopardy. An additional problematic issue for many believers is when and how a soul (for those who believe in this unscriptural doctrine) was inserted into the evolving organisms that eventually became humans.

Re-creation. The Christian story holds that Christ can re-create a new life in the believer. Since the Creator of this world also bought us back by His sufferings (1 Cor. 6:20; Heb. 1:3; Rev. 5:9), He is pre-eminently qualified to re-create a new moral nature in us. Christ creates a new life in His followers by renewing their mind (Rom. 12:2). Paul also stated, in effect, that by "beholding we become changed" (cf. 2 Cor. 3:18).[201] This is the principle by which the renewing of the mind takes place. By prayer (Matt. 26:41) and by growing in grace and in the knowledge of Christ gained through study of God's Word (2 Peter 3:18; 2 Tim. 3:16), the attitudes, actions, and motives are changed. Christ's ability to re-create us spiritually is evident in the life through the good works of Jesus in our life (Eph. 2:10).

It is comforting to think that all the power revealed in the creation of the worlds is made available to believers through faith in Christ the Creator that believers might be overcomers (1 Cor. 10:13). It has been said: "The change from earth to heaven will not change men's character; the happiness of the redeemed in heaven results from the character formed in this life after the image of Christ. The saints in heaven will first have been saints on earth."[202] (Compare 1 John 3:2.)

The New Creation. A God who cannot create is surely not able to save the believer in an earth made new. Our mortal bodies are in desperate need of reconstruction. The Bible assures believers that the putting on of immortality will occur at the second coming of Christ. Then the dead "will be raised incorruptible;" and they will have been changed (1 Cor. 15:52). The Lord Jesus Christ will change our vile bodies to be like His glorious body (Phil. 3:20, 21). Something of the glory associated with Christ's glorified body was revealed to Peter, James, and John on the mount of Transfiguration. There, Jesus was shrouded in glory and was accompanied by Moses and Elijah (Luke 9:28–31). Overcoming believers are promised glorious, disease-free bodies (Rev. 21:4, 5).

The second coming of Christ is the event that people of all ages have looked and hoped for longingly. The raising of the righteous dead and the fashioning of incorruptible bodies, creating human beings anew, will return the redeemed to the bodily state that Adam and Eve enjoyed before the Fall (1 Cor. 15:51–53). Some have imagined that immortality is received almost immediately following death. However, the Scriptures nowhere portray a conscious state in death. The Word of God clearly states: "The dead know nothing" (Eccles. 9:5; see also verse 10). The popular story of the rich man and Lazarus, recorded in Scripture, is recognized to have come from pagan authors (Luke 16:19–31).[203] Jesus used this pagan story to illustrate the necessity of making our calling and election sure at the present time; God's judgments are irrevocable.

The new creation comes after cleansing fire sweeps away all vestiges of sin, sinners, and their activities. It is then that all things will be made new (2 Peter 3:10; Rev. 21:5). Christ's creative ability is central to our belief that He can deliver us from the guilt of sin, the power of sin, and, finally, the presence of sin. Only those who believe in a Creator God can fully grasp the reality of the promise of earth and heavens made new.

The Memorial of Creation

In this section, I will

- *indicate that the Sabbath was set aside as the memorial of Creation and that it continues to be a perpetual reminder of Christ's creative ability;*

- *emphasize that Christ, the light of the world, can function as our Redeemer because He is our Creator.*

Since the concept of creation is central to our understanding of God, we should not be surprised that God established an institution in Eden by which He purposed to remind His children of His claims upon their love and devotion. After the crowning act of Creation in making humankind, God rested on the seventh day and blessed and hallowed it, that is, He "sanctified" it or set it aside as holy (Gen. 2:2, 3; cf. Exod. 20:11).

The threefold prominence given to the seventh day in Eden—God's rest and His blessing and making the day holy—is also mentioned by Paul in Hebrews 4:4–11. He urges us to remember the significance of the institution of the Sabbath, as it is a symbol of salvation as well as of Creation. It is a day of joyful rest and communion with our Maker, a sanctuary in time, and a recognition that God is able to finish His work of salvation for the believer. This theme is taken up by John the Revelator, for he identifies a movement in the period before Christ's second coming that returns this memorial to prominence (Rev. 14:6, 7).

The Sabbath points to a number of God's creative acts. First, it points to the creation of the world in six twenty-four-hour days (Exod. 20:10, 11). Since the Fall, entering into Christ's salvation rest has been linked to the Sabbath memorial. The apostle Paul is emphatic about this idea being resident in the Sabbath concept (Heb. 4:4, 8–10). The new birth experience and the continuing faith journey provide believers with spiritual rest. Jesus promised, "I will give you rest" (Matt. 11:28). Finally, the creation of the new earth and heavens is connected to the Sabbath institution (Isa. 66:22, 23) and represents the promise of intimate communion with God as in Eden. It has been said that, if this memorial of God's creative ability had been remembered, "there would never have been an idolater, an atheist, or an infidel."[204] Indeed, those who now choose to deny the Sabbath do so by questioning the reliability of the Bible.

As a continual reminder of the Sabbath's significance during the wilderness wandering of the Israelites, God gave the miracle of the manna. This miracle, which included a double portion of manna on Friday and none on Sabbath, was a weekly experience for 40 years. God commenced providing this food a short time before the formal giving of the Ten Commandments on Sinai (Exod. 16:1, 4, 5; Ps. 78:24, 25). This experience indicates that knowledge of God's memorial of Creation was possessed by the Israelites before Sinai. In fact, all the Ten Commandments were understood before they were formally given.

The Creation Week

In this section, I will

- *establish that the creation days were 24 hours in length;*

- *observe that the weekly seven-day cycle commenced at Creation;*

- *emphasize that the revelation of Christ as both the Creator and Redeemer gives power to the presentation of the gospel.*

The weekly, seven-day cycle is a constant reminder of God's creation of this world. There are no natural cycles that can account for its genesis. Several attempts have been made by governments to change this cycle but without lasting success. The most notable attempt was during the French Revolution when a ten-day week was substituted for the seven-day week of the Creation to destroy the last reminder of Christianity. Notice: "The objects which the advocates of a new calendar had in view were to strike a blow at the clergy and to divorce all calculations of time from the Christian associations with which they were loaded, in short, to abolish the Christian year; and enthusiasts were already speaking of 'the first year of liberty' and 'the first year of the republic' when the national convention took up the matter in 1793."²⁰⁵ Currently, certain movements to reform the calendar allow for 364 days with the 365th day left essentially blank and uncounted.²⁰⁶ Such reforms, if instituted, would effectively eliminate continuity with the ancient weekly cycle and the day of the seventh-day Sabbath rest, which has existed since the Creation. Some Christians are relaxed about changing the calendar, claiming that the seventh-day Sabbath has no relevance for them. In the first instance, they have accepted Sunday as the day of worship, and, in the second, they have grasped theistic evolution as a satisfactory theory of origins.

A Day in Scripture. If we accept the Scriptures as they read, then when a definite number is associated with the word for day (*yom*) as an adjective, the period always means a twenty-four-hour day (e.g., Gen. 22:4; 31:22; 42:18). The Hebrew word for day, when not associated with a definite number, sometimes was used to describe periods of time of greater than twenty-four hours (e.g. Gen. 2:4), and was even applied in a generic sense to the time when an event would occur (e.g. Job 21:30; 38:23).

In order to place the Creation beyond doubt in such a short period of time, the record indicates that each day was what we regard today as twenty-four hours in length (Exod. 31:15–17). These verses in Exodus assure us that, since the world was made in six days, the seventh day—the Sabbath—was set aside as a memorial. If a day represented 1000 years or longer, as some argue, then Adam's 930 years of life (Gen. 5:5) could have been lived in the span of the sixth day. Clearly, the Bible record does not present us with such an absurdity.

The twenty-four-hour day was marked from "even to even" (Lev. 23:32). Thus, the day commenced at "the going down of the sun" (Deut. 16:6), or at sunset. The significance of this is that the Creation episode that began with darkness and finished with light was re-enacted each day (Gen. 1:3–5, 8, 14–19). The Hebrew mind saw each day in this same way. "Every morning, when darkness disappears before the light, the initial act of creation is renewed."²⁰⁷

Redemption and Creation, Inseparable. In our attempts to reach others for Christ, it is important to preach Christ the Creator, the Redeemer, the Lawgiver, Judge, the Upholder and Restorer of all things (Acts 14:15; 17:24, 28, 31; Rev. 14:6, 7).

The fact that Christ is the Creator is the basis of His claim to worship and reverence. The psalmist expressed it thus: "Oh come, let us worship and bow down; let us kneel before the LORD our Maker"

(Ps. 95:6). In order to keep this great principle before humans, God instituted the Sabbath in Eden. At the heart of the gospel message and in the message to be proclaimed in the last remnant of time before Christ comes as a glorious King is a call to worship and reverence the Creator on His memorial of creation, the Sabbath (Rev. 14:6, 7). This is so because the last phrase of verse 7 comes from the heart of the fourth Commandment (Exod. 20:11, first part).

Jesus is called "the light of men" (John 1:4), which means that He is the source of salvation for all people. Within this expression is advanced the idea that Jesus the Creator is also the Redeemer and the great hero of all the created worlds in the universe. He has rescued this one lost world from darkness and has secured all others from failure. He will create a glorious new earth, and, in it, the Lord God Almighty and Christ the Lamb will be the light of the city (Rev. 21:22, 23).

The "light," or knowledge, of God, the truth that is expounded in the Scriptures, comes to us as we read and diligently search God's Word with a prayerful mind, seeking to know the will of God (John 14:6; 17:17). Through the great principles thus revealed, we are "sanctified" as we submit to God's molding power. As the book *Education* declares: "The creative energy that called the worlds into existence is in the word of God. This word imparts power; it begets life. Every command is a promise; accepted by the will, received into the soul, it brings with it the life of the Infinite One. It transforms the nature and re-creates the soul in the image of God."[208]

Chapter 14.
Measure the Temple

Chapter Emphasis: When the temple in heaven is examined, or measured, the standard Christ uses in His closing ministry— the moral law—is revealed. At the same time, the Sabbath, the memorial of His saving power, is brought to view. Thus, the Sabbath is linked inseparably to the six literal days of Creation and to the gospel. We are urged to honor God by keeping the Sabbath through our forming a vibrant relationship with Christ and sharing the good news of God's salvation-rest with others.

Spiritual Links: Obscuring the Sabbath principle is a special focus of Satan's work. Restoring it forms part of the special messages to be given to the world by God's last-day people.

The sanctuary in the wilderness built under Moses' direction, Solomon's temple, and the second temple were all magnificent in their own right. All were distinctly different from each other but still adhered to the same basic pattern. They were all patterned after the model that Moses was shown on Mount Sinai, which was based on the temple in heaven. In the earthly structures, each item of furniture, their contents, the details in the layout, and the ceremonies conducted

Chapter 14. Measure the Temple

in them conveyed deep significance regarding God's plan of redemption.

In the book of Revelation, the prophet John is instructed to measure, that is, to evaluate, God's temple, the altar, and the worshipers (Rev. 11:1). The temple being referred to here is the heavenly temple, for no earthly Jewish temple then existed, and, indeed, none exists even today. The temple in Jerusalem was destroyed in AD 70, sometime before John wrote the book of Revelation. In instructing the prophet to measure the temple, the angel sought to direct the attention of inquirers to the details and symbols of the sanctuary services that their deep significance might be more clearly understood. Measurement requires careful and detailed attention to the item being evaluated. In the context in which John wrote, the measurement of the temple ultimately referred to a judicial examination in that the worshipers are involved in the assessment. Significantly, the Day of Atonement was the final day of assessing, or "measuring," God's people spiritually.[209] In this chapter, I wish to examine some of the important principles that were discovered when the sanctuary was studied by those who lived just after the end of the 1260 years of persecution spoken of in Revelation 11, which ended in 1798.[210]

The Temple in Heaven

In this section, I will

- *outline some aspects of the glorious heavenly sanctuary to set the scene;*

- *briefly review the types of ministry undertaken by Christ in the heavenly sanctuary.*

The reality of a sanctuary in heaven cannot be doubted (Exod. 25:8, 9; Heb. 8:1–5), although some have strenuously sought to do so.

Heavenly Temple Indescribable. Isaiah saw a vision of God seated on His throne in the heavenly sanctuary with God's glory filling it. At the voice of the Lord, the very posts holding the doors shook. The prophet also saw a seraph taking coals from an altar (Isa. 6:1–7). In comparison to the earthly sanctuary and temple, the heavenly sanctuary has an indescribable magnificence and grandeur. God's heavenly throne room is vast, as indicated also by the prophet Micaiah (1 Kings 22:19). Daniel, in his vision, saw the angel hosts who were present at the opening ceremonies of the commencement of God's judicial examination. All were gathered about the throne. The glory of the place was indescribable, for the Father, who is "the Ancient of Days," and the Son of Man graced the temple with their presence (Dan. 7:9, 10, 13).

John the Revelator saw God's throne in heaven and the associated splendor. Before the throne, he saw a sea of glass like crystal and twenty-four elders seated before the throne clothed in white robes with crowns on their heads. He observed seven lamps burning before the throne (Rev. 4:1–6). John later also was shown the altar of incense, a golden censer, and the ark of the testament (Rev. 8:3; 11:19).

These scenes conveyed by the Bible prophets indicate that there is a sanctuary in heaven in which God carries out significant functions. Its vastness and magnificence are indescribable to the human tongue or pen. The sanctuaries and temples that were constructed by Israel on this earth were "copies of the things in the heavens," or "copies of the true" (Heb. 9:23, 24). In saying this, the inference is that they conveyed significant lessons associated with the sanctuary in heaven. In His mercy and wisdom, God sought to teach humanity important lessons about salvation, His unchanging character, and important events on earth and in heaven connected with the great plan of salvation. He chose to teach these lessons, in part, through the earthly sanctuary services.

High Priestly Functions. The Bible does not reveal which functions the heavenly sanctuary fulfilled before Christ's death, but one might imagine that it was the nerve center of God's salvation initiative, for God's throne is featured in it. Christ, the Lawgiver, is today High Priest in heaven (James 4:12; Heb. 5:5, 6; 9:11). This means that, like Aaron and the other high priests after him, He could minister in both the Holy Place and the Most Holy Place (Num. 18:7).

The only way that Christ could become a high priest was by sacrifice (Heb. 8:3; cf. Lev. 8:22–24, 30). Hence, He could only begin the high priestly work after the cross. Now He pleads the merits of His blood (justification) before the Father, as well as the merits of His perfect life (sanctification), on behalf of all who exercise faith in Him. In other words, to the one who is justified He "imparts power to live a new life, and for him He obtains acceptance of that new life with God."[211] In the earthly sanctuary, the shed blood of the sin offering for unintentional or unpremeditated sin was ministered by the priest in the Holy Place (Lev. 4:3, 7, 13, 18). Today, Christ offers grace to all sinners by virtue of His shed blood (1 Peter 2:24). Thus, He has become "the Mediator of the new covenant" (Heb. 12:24; cf. Acts 5:29–31).

In the earthly sanctuary, there was a second phase of ministry undertaken by the high priest in the Most Holy Place. The counterpart to this ministry was also initiated in the heavenly sanctuary at the beginning of the antitypical day of atonement, the fulfillment of the type (Dan. 8:14). On this day, the sins of the people that had been confessed previously and transferred symbolically to the sanctuary were removed. It follows, then, that the work in the Holy Place was a necessary prerequisite to the activities carried out on the Day of Atonement. Christ alone was suited to serve during all aspects of ministry in the heavenly sanctuary.

Measure the Sanctuary

In this section, I will

- *examine the instruction given to the apostle John to measure the heavenly sanctuary, which first involves understanding the events occurring there;*

- *emphasize that an understanding of the heavenly sanctuary gives us an appreciation of God's character, His grace, and a knowledge of the divine help available.*

Since Christ has now ascended into the heavens, it is a matter of vital importance that we understand the nature of His work in the heavenly sanctuary and His plans for His followers on earth. It is also of vital importance that we determine when His parting promise to return will be fulfilled. The instruction to measure, or "evaluate," the temple also involves a work of assessment by heavenly agencies, since the text says the worshipers are to be measured (Rev. 11:1).[212]

End-time Understandings. Chapters 10 and 11 of Revelation are connected in that both deal with the experiences of God's people in the time leading up to His return. This is evident if we compare Revelation 10:6 and Revelation 11:15, which both speak of the time remaining after the end of the Bible's longest time prophecy. The angel is instructing the dwellers on earth to make a careful study of the sanctuary in Scripture so as to gain a clearer understanding of Christ's ministry in heaven.

Historically, when believers began to understand the temple in heaven in the mid-nineteenth century, they appreciated the centrality of the Scriptures and emphasized the importance of the words written by God's own hand in the "testimony," or Ten Commandments. These words were on tablets kept in the "ark of His testament" (Rev. 11:19, KJV), which is another name for the "ark of the covenant of the Lord" (see Rev. 11:19, NKJV; Num. 10:33). Anciently, the ark contained the tables of stone on which the commandments written by God were housed (Deut. 9:10, 11; 10:1, 2). The mercy seat was positioned above the tables of stone. The forgotten aspects of the Decalogue became the central focus following the measuring of the temple by believers. The Decalogue is preserved in heaven, and we cannot view it properly except in the light of God's grace. (*Hilastērion*, which is translated "propitiation" in Romans 3:25, is rendered "mercy seat" in Hebrews 9:5.) Consequently, as long as we argue that we are under grace, we must argue that the Ten Commandments are applicable.

The special work in the earthly sanctuary that focused on the ark of the covenant was the cleansing of the sanctuary, which occurred once a year on the Day of Atonement (Lev. 16:13, 15, 34). In fact, the Greek word that John used in Revelation to express the idea of measuring also legitimately refers to a judicial work.[213] The focus of attention in this period of earth's history was thus to be upon judgment, the standard to be used, the mercy of God, the merits of Christ, and the restoration of harmonious relationships. In the lead-up to the central parts of this ceremony, the high priest offered incense on the altar of incense and carried a golden censer into the Most Holy Place. This incense was to cover the mercy seat, which was above the "testimony," or Decalogue. The incense offered by Aaron the high priest represented the merits of Christ offered with the prayers of the penitent saints (Rev. 8:3, 4).

The Day of Atonement was a special day of rest, called "a sabbath of *solemn* rest," a day in which to examine relationships with God (Lev. 23:27–32). In order to examine the life, the individual needed to open the channels of the mind to the Holy Spirit, allowing His convicting power to try the person's motives and acts. Preparation for the day of judgment commenced ten days earlier at the memorial of blowing of Trumpets (Lev. 23:24, 25). Drawing near to God on judgment day was facilitated by resting from work and fasting. The prophet Isaiah informs us about the nature of the work that God desired to accomplish in His chosen people before judgment day. His intent was to change their thinking and actions so their response would be from a mind motivated by love (Isa. 58:6–12; cf. Ezek. 36:26–28).

Special Characteristics of the Day. On the day of the fast, the Day of Atonement, mentioned by the prophet Isaiah, earnest worshipers ideally were meant to be involved in special tasks. They were not only to keep God's will, but each was to be a leader in reclaiming lost truths—a "Repairer of the Breach"—to honor God's memorial of Creation and redemption, which is the Sabbath (Isa. 58:12, 13). Earnest believers in every age are eager to uphold God's revealed word, to break free from tradition, to repudiate misunderstandings, to rededicate themselves wholeheartedly to God, and to become ambassadors for Him. In the beginning of the antitypical day of atonement, when Advent believers studied the subject of the temple in heaven, they discovered the significance of the entire law and Christ's last investigative work in heaven. They found that God has an unchangeable law and that, until the end of all things, nothing in it will change (Matt. 5:18).[214]

The Significance of the Sabbath

In this section, I will

- *observe that the Sabbath command is at the center of the Decalogue;*

- *aid readers to discover that the Sabbath command carries a special significance for Christians living just before Christ's second coming.*

The law of God shows us in what areas we are failing to accomplish His will for us (Rom. 3:20; 7:7; 1 John 3:4). God's law is a transcript of God's character. This is the central idea transmitted by Jesus to the man who asked Him which was the greatest commandment. The law, He said, is summarized in the concept of love to God and to humanity (Matt. 22:36–40). By indicating that the principle of *agapē* love is contained in the Decalogue, Jesus did not abolish the particulars. He could not do this, for God is *agapē* love (1 John 4:8) and is unchangeable. The law of God summarizes all of God's instruction to humans (Eccles. 12:13). Most significantly, each element describes an aspect of God's character. How important it is to understand them all, including the fourth commandment! Failure to understand its significance means that our understanding of God's character is diminished.

The Creator Honored. God specifically sanctified—consecrated or set apart—the Sabbath day at Creation (Gen. 2:1–3). The central verses of the Decalogue—Exodus 20:8–11—illustrate again that "the

Sabbath was set apart to be kept in honor of God's holy name."[215] It is a time for mental and physical rest and a time for intimate, joyful communion with God. As Satan has placed the Sabbath in obscurity, He has opened the floodgates to humanistic ideas, such as the theory of evolution, a theory that has no place for a divine Creator. Associated with the idea of a Creator God is the concept that He is able to save those who have fallen into sin. Only the Creator can justify, sanctify, and finally deliver from the power of sin, and only a Creator is worthy of worship on this memorial day.

When the early Adventist believers began to understand the heavenly sanctuary, in the course of time, they discovered the beauty of the reference in the Decalogue to the seventh-day Sabbath. This truth could no longer be hidden, and it became an important element in testing the commitment of disciples down to the end of time.[216]

Redeemer Honored. After the Fall, God chose the Sabbath as a symbol of entering into the "rest" of salvation and sanctification (Exod. 31:12–17; Heb. 3:11, 18, 19; 4:3–11). The term "rest," used by the apostle Paul, represents abiding in an intimate spiritual relationship with God, which in practical terms involves cessation from human striving in order to gain salvation (Matt. 11:28). This experience is likened to that of Adam and Eve. On the first Sabbath, they rested with God and communed with Him; they were safe in His presence. Honoring the Sabbath is, therefore, symbolic of accepting God's offer of salvation and His promise to bring believers to an eternal rest with Him where sin will no longer reign. This represents a faith journey. Paul emphatically wrote: "For we who have believed do enter that rest" (Heb. 4:3). This means that the Sabbath is a sign to all people today that God is challenging us to accept His power and authority (Heb. 4:7, 9). We should note that keeping the Sabbath does not sanctify. However, it does remind us of God's sanctifying power and His promises.

The Bible process of sanctification commences with the new birth experience. Through the operation of the Holy Spirit, when we ask for God's help, God gives us "new motives, new tastes, new tendencies."[217] This experience leads to a refining of the life so that a living relationship with Christ is evident to all. Then the experience of David will be ours—"I delight to do Your will, O God, and Your law *is* within my heart" (Ps. 40:8). The apostle John further describes the Christian's experience, "Whoever has been born of God does not sin, for His seed remains in him; and he cannot sin, because he has been born of God" (1 John 3:9). The close relationship that this experience implies is available to all Christians (Rom. 12:2). The apostles' words tell us that our life will be progressively transformed as we continue to maintain a close relationship with God. This represents a continuous process until life ends (Phil. 3:14).

King of Kings Honored. The Sabbath is a promise that God will be victorious over the forces of evil in this world and that the saints will worship before the Lord in the "new heavens and the new earth" (Isa. 66:22, 23; cf. Rev. 21:1–3). These concepts are presented in firm confidence by the prophet Isaiah. The Sabbath is to remind us that Christ has triumphed gloriously at the cross, and, hence, the ultimate banishment and destruction of Satan are assured. In the earth made new, the original purpose of the Sabbath in Eden will be fulfilled. God will again commune with His people face to face.

Conflict over the Law

In this section, I will

- *emphasize that the conflict over God's law and the Sabbath, in particular, has spanned the centuries.*

Disputes over the Sabbath commenced early. There are fragmentary records even in the Old Testament Scriptures of disregard for its holiness (e.g., Num. 15:32; Neh. 13:15–18), however, we can also be sure that this rest day lay casualty at an earlier period in the centers of rebellious paganism such as the tower of Babel.

The "little horn" power that arose in the midst of the Christian church was foremost in developing a perverse attitude. The seventh chapter of Daniel uncovers a religio-political power that will "think himself able to change times and laws" (Dan. 7:25, Douay-Rheims). The prophet indicated that this power would arise out of the remnants of the pagan Roman Empire (Dan. 7:3–7; 8:20–24; cf. John 11:48). The power that emerged from the dying embers of the Western Roman Empire was none other than the papacy, a point to which history clearly attests. The collapse of the western section of the Empire, as the eastern section was administered from Constantinople, left the papacy to fill the power vacuum that was created by the overthrow of the Ostrogoths in the city of Rome. Historian Leonard Elliot-Binns wrote: "The end of the Western Empire did not mean, at any rate in theory, that the West was independent; Constantinople still ruled over it. In practice, however, that rule was often ignored and the Church developed with very little interference from the civil power, room was thus given for the development of Latin, as distinct from Greek or Eastern, Christianity."[218] Indeed, the *Encyclopedia Britannica* points out that, thereafter, there was a "continual increase of [the papacy power's] moral and political influence." In particular, the accession of Gregory 1 (AD 590–604) "marked the commencement of a new era."[219]

I have pointed out already the "times and law" this power sought to change. The second commandment that speaks about worship directed to graven images is commonly ignored today. The Sabbath commandment is retained but no statement is made about worship on the original seventh day. A perusal of a Roman Catholic catechism will illustrate the accuracy of the above statements (refer to Table 12.1). This power has declared: "The [Catholic] Church changed the observance of the Sabbath to Sunday by right of the divine, infallible authority given to her by her Founder, Jesus Christ. The Protestant, claiming the Bible to be the only guide of faith, has no warrant for observing Sunday. In this matter the Seventh Day Adventist is the only consistent Protestant."[220] And again, "Perhaps the boldest thing, the most revolutionary change the Church ever did, happened in the first century. The holy day, the Sabbath, was changed to Sunday. 'The day of the Lord' (*dies Dominica*) was chosen, not from any direction noted in the Scriptures, but from the [Catholic] Church's sense of its own power.... People who think that the Scriptures should be the sole authority, should logically become 7th Day Adventists, and keep Saturday holy."[221] The commandments, and the fourth commandment, in particular, are under attack from other avenues as the following quotation reveals: "So long as the story of the creation in Gn 1 and 2 and the account of the giving of the Law on Mt. Sinai were regarded as historical, the question had to be faced: How can a divine command, directly given to men, be abrogated? The answer for us is plain: No such commands were ever given, and the stories which record them are legends. The Sabbath was made for man; and, under the guidance of Providence, it was made by man. Sunday, in its turn, was made by man and for man. Man, therefore, is lord both of the Sabbath and of Sunday."[222] To claim the prerogative for humans of changing God's law is to usurp the authority of God. Human religious leaders thus parade themselves as God on earth, blaspheming God's name among non-Christians by such statements. The Scriptures promise all who continue in such blasphemies a reward among the wicked (Rev. 13:5–8).

While humans may mock, the reality is: "Sacrilegious minds and hearts have thought they were mighty enough to change the times and laws of Jehovah; but, safe in the archives of heaven, in the ark of God, are the original commandments, written upon the two tables of stone. No potentate of earth has power to draw forth those tables from their sacred hiding place beneath the mercy seat."[223]

The attack on the authority of the Word of God rests not only with the church but also with the secular powers that have gained boldness from the example of religious authorities.[224] The church, which now has paramount influence in the world, sincerely believed it had a right to exercise infallible authority.[225] It took this supposed right to such an extent that it did not hesitate to "persecute the saints of the Most High" (Dan. 7:25; see also Dan. 7:21; Rev. 13:7).[226] The Scriptures clearly indicate that God is not behind such movements to change His revealed Word or persecute His followers. The divine Judge will sit and will declare in favor of the persecuted saints. Moreover, God will ultimately destroy the power responsible for the persecution of the saints, and He will set up His own kingdom based on the eternal principles of love and populated by the obedient (Dan. 7:26, 27).

God's Loving Last Call

In this section, I will

- *focus on the great issue now facing the world's inhabitants—namely, understanding God's will and responding positively to the knowledge of it;*

- *reiterate that God is calling all to rejoice in the great moral principles revealed in His law.*

The Scriptures forewarn us that the great religious question debated just before probation closes is whether individuals will choose to believe and obey God's words or those of human origin. The beast power of Revelation 13 brought to view in verses 3 to 8 is the same beast as seen by Daniel, for they both reign with great power for 1260 years (Dan. 7:19–21, 25; Rev. 11:2, 3; 12:6, 14).

Those acclaimed by God at the end of the age will demonstrate patience and obedience through faith to all of the commandments of God (Rev. 14:12). In this way, the world will see that they have responded to God's last thrilling messages recorded in Revelation 14:6–12. These messages are so important that they are illustrated as being borne to the world by three mighty angels. The particular emphasis in verses 6 and 7 is that the good news of salvation can be understood most clearly when it is linked with the idea that God is the Creator. This brings into focus His neglected memorial, the Sabbath. Part of the phraseology contained in the first angel's message is taken from the fourth commandment (Rev. 14:7; cf. Exod. 20:11). Clearly, God is calling attention to this neglected aspect of the moral law. He is preparing a people for heaven. He wishes to sanctify them so that they can present the Sabbath—the divine symbol of sanctification—to the world. He is calling all back to the purity of His word, which reflects His character. Will you not respond today to God's last great appeal to this world, saying, "As for me and my house, we will serve the Lord" (Josh. 24:15, last part)? Your choice will make you a candidate for the seal of God that will be given freely to all those who serve God with all the heart, mind, and soul (Rev. 14:1–5, 12). You will be honored as a "Repairer of the Breach" and a "Restorer of Streets to Dwell In" (Isa. 58:12).

Chapter 15.
Worship

Chapter Emphasis: *Worship involves demonstrating respect for and proclaiming allegiance to a superior power. People of all ages have been tested on the subject of worship. Elijah is a key example of those upholding acceptable worship practices during the earthly sanctuary period. Today acceptable worship is again being called for; it involves whole-hearted commitment to Christ the Creator and Savior.*

Spiritual Link: *The worldwide struggle over worship near the close of human history will involve fidelity to God's Word in contrast to acknowledging human traditions and instruction.*

The subject of worship is fundamental to all religions. Worship involves respecting the true God or any other god or role model that is supreme in the life of the worshiper. The Bible has considerable advice to offer, not only concerning the nature of the true Creator God but also on acceptable worship attitudes and forms. The Bible speaks of the worship begun here on the earth as being extended to the new earth. At that time, all the redeemed of the earth and the unfallen angels of heaven will willingly worship their God and Savior. What a glorious privilege it will be to stand on the sea of glass in the

New Jerusalem and sing heartfelt praises to God for His goodness and mercy!

A careful examination of the Scripture record shows that the parents of our race were led astray by giving their allegiance to Satan. Basic to any worship is the concept of allegiance. We cannot truly worship any being to whom we are not prepared to offer full allegiance. Adam and Eve's sons also were tested on this point. Cain was not careful to follow the prescribed form of public worship, or liturgy, outlined by God. God was openly displeased with Cain's misguided allegiance and his subsequent act of killing his brother.

In the sanctuary services recorded in the Scriptures, we also learn valuable lessons about this important subject (e.g., 1 Chron. 15:27; 2 Chron. 5:13). Music was commonly used in the social life of the people portrayed in Scripture. A clear distinction was made, however, between the types of folk music used during times of popular rejoicing and sacred music associated with temple worship. As we understand the principles associated with temple worship, we are led to appreciate God's character and how we may give glory to Him. As we come to the closing scenes described in the prophetic book of Revelation, we discover that the last great issues to face the world before the Lord returns in glory are connected with worship. Truly, this is a most important subject, which is why it will be covered in the present chapter.

God Focuses Attention on Worship

In this section, I will

- *introduce the essential and striking elements of God's worship call to this world just before His return;*

- *emphasize that the inhabitants of the world will be tested closely to determine if they are loyal to God or to human ideas and institutions.*

Some of the most striking and sublime messages in the whole of the Bible are recorded in Revelation, chapter 14. The three messages recorded in this chapter are introduced by three angels. They are provocative in nature. Understanding them was vital to the development of the fledgling Adventist church and to its continuing mission.

The First Angel's Message. The first angel calls on men and women everywhere to accept the everlasting good news of salvation, to "fear

God and give glory to Him," and to "worship Him who created heaven and earth, the sea and springs of water" (Rev. 14:6, 7). Historically, students of the Word began to understand this passage of Scripture in the mid-nineteenth century. It was then that they began to appreciate the 2300-year prophecy and preach it to an ever-widening audience. Naturally, appreciating this prophecy involved a developing understanding of Christ's work in the heavenly sanctuary. It was also in this period of earth's history that the authority of the Scriptures was being seriously challenged by the adoption of the historical-critical method and that theories of origins, which ignored the activities of a personal Creator God, were being advanced in a growing manner by thinkers and scientists.[227]

Those who fear God and have the correct attitude toward Him demonstrate faith, love, and obedience (Gen. 22:12; Deut. 10:12, 13; 13:4; Eccles. 12:13, 14). They have reverence and respect for God whom they humbly worship. This means, in practical terms, that all aspects of our worship—music, behavior, dress, thoughts, and gifts—are done as to the Lord of Hosts. We can be reasonably sure how this approach might operate as we examine God's guidance of the prophet Malachi regarding the acceptability of worship acts in the context of the Israelite social system. He advised the worshipers to imagine offering their gifts, service, and worship to their governor and then to judge if he would be pleased with them (Mal. 1:6–8). God is much greater than any governor. Thus, He is entitled to greater gifts, service, and standards of worship.

Genuine worship of God springs from the person who worships "in spirit and truth" (John 4:23). It comes from a personal and practical understanding of the truths of the Bible and of God's greatness as revealed by the Holy Spirit. The angel of Revelation 14, verse 7 draws attention to the seventh-day Sabbath, using a phrase taken from Exodus 20, verse 11. True worship is possible only as we enter into the experience of living by faith in Jesus Christ, of which the Sabbath is a sign (Exod. 31:12–17). The truly sanctified will be obedient by faith to all of God's clearly revealed will as they come to know it. This essential experience takes place in the time of God's pre-advent judgment, to which the angel gives special emphasis (verse 7, last part).

The Second Angel's Message. The second angel declared in dramatic fashion: "Babylon is fallen, is fallen" (Rev. 14:8). It is not my intention to answer fully here who Babylon is in the modern world. The term "Babylon" is the Greek form of the term "Babel" (Gen.

10:10, Septuagint), which means "confusion" (Gen. 11:9, KJV, margin).[228] The name comes from the city that was built on the plain of Shinar in defiance of God's explicit promise that the waters of a flood would not destroy the whole earth again. God confused the language of the people building the city, hence upsetting their purpose (Gen. 11:1–9). Spiritual Babylon represents those religious movements and their leaders who are characterized by confused thinking regarding to God's Word and His requirements. They choose to exalt human wisdom in place of God's. They substitute their own institutions, plans, and methods of worship for those revealed in Scripture, and they do not earnestly seek to enjoy a personal experience with God.

Historically, the second angel commenced sounding when the churches began to expel those who believed that the fulfillment of the 2300-year time prophecy would terminate with Christ's coming. When this did not happen first in 1843 and later in 1844 and believers sought alternative explanations, church authorities acted on the ones they considered troublemakers, disfellowshipping them from church membership. Thus, their disappointment in Christ's failure to return was compounded by the stigma of rejection by their fellow Christians. They regrouped and reassessed their understandings of Scripture, and then went out to convince others of the unadulterated truths of the Bible they had learned.[229]

The announcement that followed the proclamation that Babylon is fallen is recorded a few chapters later in the book of Revelation. Another mighty angel said: "Come out of her"—come out of Babylon—for God will destroy her (Rev. 18:2–4). Many of those honest in thinking, whom God wishes to save, are still in Babylon. They will yet learn and obey scriptural truth unadulterated by human traditions. The call to come out carries with it a call to diligent study of the Scriptures, for unless this is done there would be no conviction to sever connections with Babylon. The test that will come to every person on this earth is: Will I obey God rather than men? (See Acts 5:29.)

The call of the angel of Revelation 18 is also a plea to follow the light that has been given. Truth established under the leading and guidance of God, as chronicled in Scripture and experienced in the great reform movements in direct fulfillment of prophecy, will not disappear. Christ Himself gave the warning, "If therefore the light that is in you is darkness, how great *is* that darkness!" (Matt. 6:23). The early Christian believers, as shown in the book of Acts, searched the Scriptures and acted on the information revealed. They rejected the forms of godliness that had no power, which may include humanly inspired forms of worship, and God rewarded them with the gift of the Holy Spirit (see Acts 2:4).

The Third Angel's Message. The third angel of Revelation 14:9–12 carries a specific warning against worship supporting apostate religious movements. The heart of the warning message is in verse 12. This verse directs the readers' mind to Christ's ministry in the Most Holy Place of the heavenly sanctuary, which points to God's will as revealed in the Decalogue and to God's mercy. Those who heed the warning have access to mercy through faith, which is justification. These same ones have the assurance of victory over sin, which is defined by the law, through continual, active reliance on Christ through faith. This victory is sanctification. The same angel counsels against receiving the mark of approval from apostate movements (verse 9). Again, it is not my intention to examine the precise identity of the beast power here brought to view. Suffice it to say that the power represented is against God's truth and His methods, and it challenges all to receive its mark of approval, and this rather than God's seal of approval (Rev. 13:15, 16; 14:1, 12). We have already mentioned that the term "mark" can also be rendered "character," or "endorsement." Those who have the name of God in their foreheads are said to have the "seal" of God (Rev. 7:2–4). The word "seal" means to "authenticate," or "set a seal of approval upon."[230] The phraseology does not imply that a physical seal or sign is affixed to the forehead. Just as Nebuchadnezzar erected an image in ancient Babylon and commanded all his subjects to worship it or suffer death, so will the spiritual forces of Babylon require all people to bow to their spiritual institutions or suffer disadvantage and death (Dan. 3:3–6; Rev. 13:14–17).

We may expect honest people to depart from Babylon during the last moments of the third angel's call. In fact, we are told: "Notwithstanding the agencies combined against the truth, a large number take their stand upon the Lord's side."[231] This thought reminds me of the legendary account related about the original tower of Babel. When the tower was erected and the leaders eventually installed images of gods, the people that were destined to become Armenians departed under the leadership of Haik. They did this with great personal sacrifice when they understood the real sentiments of the Shinar leadership—hardened rebellion against God. The Armenian history of subsequent loyalty to Christian ideals is legendary; they were prepared to die for their faith.[232]

Sequentially, the third angel's announcement comes last, and this is just what occurred historically. In the early nineteenth century, those who preached the first angel's message, which declares that the hour of God's judgment has come, also preached the good news of salvation within the time of the fulfillment of the 2300-year prophecy. Their study of Scripture led them to recognize the sanctuary in heaven and gain knowledge about Christ's activities there. When the period of time they expected Christ to return had passed (from March 21, 1843 to October 22, 1844) and the resistance of their former churches led to their being disfellowshipped, they recognized that the second angel had begun to deliver his message about the fall of Babylon. Shortly, some recognized from Scripture that, rather than coming in glory, Christ had begun the last phase of His atonement ministry in the heavenly sanctuary. Some of these believers became aware of the seventh-day Sabbath and the role of Rome in changing the day of worship to Sunday. Believers understood, with the help of the prophetic gift among them, that in the change of activities in the heavenly sanctuary, Christ had opened a door of understanding on the seventh-day Sabbath that would never be closed. With this realization, it became apparent that the third angel's message about the mark of the beast and the seal of God was a call to acknowledge God's unchanging Word and nature. Furthermore, it was their task to share these understandings with the world.[233] The messages of all three angels are interlinked and appear in all their forcefulness in the third angel's proclamations. Hence, all are relevant today.[234]

Not surprisingly, when the first angel advised individuals everywhere to consider their Creator, the minds of listeners were drawn to His provisions in the Garden of Eden. This introduced the importance of living intelligently so as to enjoy abundant health. Thus, health reform would come to be considered a part of the third angel's message.[235] More importantly, at the heart of the third angel's message they found the concept of justification by faith. "It is the third angel's message in verity."[236] Faith in Christ is the experience that will deliver the believer, not only from the penalty of sin through justification but also from its power through sanctification. Those who receive God's seal have developed strong faith. This is the great determining factor as to whether believers receive the seal of God or the mark of the beast. Those who have the faith of Jesus are obedient to His instructions, and they patiently wait for His promises to be fulfilled (1 John 5:4; Rev. 14:12). They are not sensationalists in either their preaching or their worship, for faith and sensationalism are incompatible (cf. 1 Kings 18:26–30).

The Battle of Armageddon

In this section, I will

- *review some of the decisive spiritual contests in Scripture in which worship was the central issue;*
- *indicate that the battle of Armageddon brings the end-time contest over worship to a close as God is vindicated and His people are delivered.*

Much has been written about "Armageddon" (Rev. 16:16) and the battle to be fought there. The term means *"hill of Megiddo."*[237] The name brings to mind two remarkable events outlined in Scripture. Megiddo was the place where ancient Israel, under God's direction and the leadership of Barak and Deborah the prophetess, gained a remarkable victory against vastly superior forces (Judges 4, 5). This event occurred after the entry of the Israelites into Canaan (Judges 2:10–16) but before the reign of the kings.[238] God instructed His people to gather on Mount Tabor, the small mountain across the valley from Megiddo, in order to draw Sisera's army toward them. This battle strategy set up their victory, as they demonstrated their faith and obedience in God's leading (Judges 4:6, 7, 14, 15).

Mount Carmel was also in the vicinity of ancient Megiddo. On this mountain, a most remarkable contest, in which worship was the central issue, took place about 50 years after Solomon's death.[239] The account of the prophet Elijah's lone challenge to the wicked Ahab, his priests, and his subjects regarding whom they would choose to worship is quite thrilling. The great issues of the day were concerning the honor and worship of God, and God was vindicated in a most remarkable manner (1 Kings 18).

In the final crisis that will soon engulf the world, God's faithful people will again be at the apparent mercy of the wicked with no hope of deliverance (Rev. 13). God will deliver His people, as they stand upon the principles declared in His Word. In essence, they take their stand on the hill of "faith and obedience" as did ancient Israel on Mount Tabor and Elijah on Mount Carmel. Thus, the battle of Armageddon takes place in an end-time setting wherever God's faithful are surrounded by the servants of Satan intent upon their destruction. This contest at Armageddon is a world-encompassing event in which the forces of Satan will be utterly destroyed as they continue to defy their Creator.

Lessons from Ancient Megiddo. The challenges that occurred anciently on the mount of Megiddo are recorded for our benefit. The first account relates to the victory of Israel over Sisera, the commander of King Jabin's army, as indicated above. Under this ruler, the people had been harshly treated for twenty years. Deborah, the prophetess and judge, convinced Barak to fight the enemy with God. The result was an outstanding defeat of Sisera, but Barak was not responsible for the most significant aspect of the discomfiting of the enemy (Judges 4:1–22). Israel was challenged to demonstrate their commitment to God (Judges 5:2, 31). The song of Deborah and Barak proclaims that God honored those who "willingly offered themselves" to His service (Judges 5:2).

In the second account, the contest between Elijah and the pagan priests is recorded. The onlookers were challenged to choose between God's word and the words of human devising. This was an issue of worship. Elijah challenged the people in the words, "How long will you falter between two opinions?" (1 Kings 18:21). God had been dishonored by the heathen practices that took place on Mount Carmel and throughout Israel. He was about to display His great power and vindicate His name. A fiery flame descended from heaven in answer to Elijah's prayer of faith. The prophets of Baal were shown to be worshiping a false god. They were then slain on account of their rebellion (1 Kings 18:38, 40). In this record, we observe that all of God's commands are associated with the means to accomplish them—"All His biddings are enablings."[240] So in the conflict at the end of time, God's ways will be vindicated and His people will be delivered, triumphant over the powers of evil.

Lessons from Ancient Babylon Applied in Modern Times. A conflict over worship also is recorded as having occurred in ancient Babylon in the time of King Nebuchadnezzar. All citizens were instructed to "fall down and worship the gold image" (Dan. 3:5). The conflict involved choosing between obeying God's Word and obeying the instructions of mere humanity. God vindicated His servants by delivering them from the rage of their enemies (Dan. 3:23–27).

A similar conflict over worship will occur just before the close of human probation. This is described graphically in Revelation, chapter

13. Earth's inhabitants will be required to choose between the worship practices nominated by the dominant religious thought leaders and those outlined by God (Rev. 13:3–8, 14–18). The religious power identified in the first part of chapter 13 is the great medieval religious system that held sway over the minds and bodies of men and women until the French Revolution changed the course of history. Today, this same religious entity is a world power, and its leader is a superstar.[241]

Under the encouragement of political muscle provided by the lamb-like beast, which represents the United States of America, a series of events described in Revelation will set the stage for the persecution of those who choose to follow God's Word rather than the traditions and proclamations of religious leaders (Rev. 13:11–18).

The Climax. As in the days of Elijah, there are only two opposing powers at the end of time. God leads the armies of the saints. Satan leads all those who are not on the Lord's side. Those who fail to choose openly for God are choosing Satan's side (Matt. 12:30). At the battle of Armageddon, we can expect great strife and commotion as the passions and fury of people everywhere are expressed. It will then be too late for repentance, for God has declared, "It is done!" (Rev. 16:17). God's enemies will fail in their rebellion and will be destroyed. The saints will be protected during the turmoil and will receive their eternal reward (Rev. 6:15–17; 15:1–4; 19:1–8). There will then be a great display of God's power in which the works of humans are destroyed by a massive earthquake and other destructive events. God will be vindicated and will rule righteously over the nations (Rev. 16:16–21).

God warns His faithful people to "keep their garments" spiritually or they walk naked as the time of the last great spiritual contest draws near (Rev. 16:15). The advice here is to follow closely after Jesus with ever increasing faith, for He alone can cover us with His righteousness (Isa. 61:10). He has promised to save us (Joel 2:32; Acts 2:21).

The Nature of Acceptable Worship

In this section, I will

- *identify the essential elements of acceptable worship.*

To appreciate the nature of the contest over worship that will take place at the end of time, we need to consider briefly the nature of divinely approved worship. Worship is an experience that flows from an attitude of the mind (John 4:23). In worship, we express our gratitude to God for all His goodness. Worship may be either private or corporate in nature.

Authentic worship focuses on the Lord, the Creator of heaven and earth and the source of our salvation (1 Chron. 16:23–29). David, in the psalm of thanksgiving recorded in Chronicles, various reasons why we should worship God. Creation and salvation are identified as the leading reasons. On account of His creative ability, God is able to re-create and save us. Worship based on any other foundation is misguided.

There are some significant components of worship identified in Scripture. First, worship involves adoration, respect, and affection (1 Chron. 16:23–26; Ps. 103:1–6). The Lord is to be praised for His goodness toward humanity as a whole and toward each of us individually. Our adoration of the Lord springs from His forgiveness and from His deliverance from the power of sin. It also has its roots in our sense of awe and wonder at the marvels of God's creation. The Lord is our only source of lasting hope.

Worship involves thanksgiving—God is to be praised with songs of thanksgiving and gifts (Ps. 96:1–9; 100:1–5). Our expressions of thankfulness may be made with song. Music and singing have always been associated with the expression of joy and rejoicing (2 Chron. 5:13, 14). Offerings willingly given are appropriate expressions of gratitude as well (2 Cor. 9:7), for the Lord has given us the power to obtain wealth (Deut. 8:18).

Finally, worship involves devotion, which is loyalty and love. It also involves renewal. In worship, the Lord gives assurance of forgiveness of sin. The suppliant responds by surrender and commitment (Isa. 6:6–8; Jer. 29:12, 13). When we seek the Lord with all the mind, He hears, forgives, and restores us. The response to this experience is commitment in service to God in order to glorify His name. One of the songs sung by the sons of Korah, who were temple musicians, is recorded in Psalm 84:1–12. Notice the commitment given in the song: "For a day in Your courts *is* better than a thousand. I would rather be a doorkeeper in the house of my God than dwell in the tents of wickedness" (verse 10).

Chapter 15. Worship

Practical Aspects of Acceptable Worship

In this section, I will

- *indicate what attitudes of mind are associated with acceptable worship;*

- *focus on what total commitment in worship means in practical terms.*

We learned in previous sections that, in the period of time prior to Jesus' second coming, God calls on all people everywhere to focus on true worship. We also considered that the last great spiritual contest to be waged on earth between good and evil will also involve aspects of worship and the honor of God.

The attitudes and behavior of worshipers separate the genuine from the uninformed and rebellious. Acceptable worship comes spontaneously when God creates a new attitude of mind in the repentant sinner (Ps. 51:10–12). The peace that follows the knowledge that God has forgiven our sins leads to joy (Ps. 40:16; Rom. 5:11; 15:9–13) and we develop new attitudes and motives through the work of the Holy Spirit (Rom. 12:2). The apostle John is adamant that acceptable worship must be in spirit and in truth (John 4:23). This use of the term "spirit" means worshipping with the whole heart (1 Cor. 7:34; cf. Ps. 138:1). We are to focus on Jesus, the Creator and Redeemer, and our relationship with Him. Those who have the right relationship with Jesus also relate positively to the truths of God's Word and are sanctified by them (John 17:17). We cannot honor God or render Him acceptable worship by following human traditions that clash with the requirements of God (Mark 7:9, 13) or if our feet are set in the paths of habitual sin (John 9:31).

Guidelines for Worship. The Scriptures highlight some aspects of worship for our special consideration. (See Table 15.1.) First, there are attitudes and practices to avoid. King Solomon advised all readers to avoid the "sacrifice of fools" (Eccles. 5:1). This means we are to be deliberate, honest, and devoted in our response to God's promptings. He warned about making hasty decisions without a genuine desire to serve God. Such an approach is an unacceptable basis for worship.

Frivolity and the trivialization of worship have no place in the life of the true Christian. God will judge those who trivialize worship with eternal death, as He did Nadab and Abihu (Lev. 10:1, 2). God is a holy and great King (Zech. 14:16). As such, He is entitled to reverence and godly fear, or awe (Heb. 12:28). The veil was drawn aside for Isaiah, revealing the seraphim in heaven worshipping God. Isaiah saw them covering their faces in reverence as they cried, "Holy, holy, holy" (Isa. 6:3). Isaiah's personal reaction to God's holiness was, "Woe is me, for I am undone!" (Isa. 6:5). Our adoration should likewise respond to the greatness of God.

Pretentious display to draw the praise of others is always unacceptable to God. He will adversely reward such worship (Matt. 6:5, 6; cf. Amos 5:21–26). That our motivation in worship is very important is shown by the story that Jesus told concerning the worship of the Pharisee and the publican (Luke 18:10–14). The man who was small in his own eyes and who looked with faith to God for forgiveness was accepted. The Pharisee who specialized in comparing himself with others went away condemned. In worship, our music should not be a performance, our prayers should not be cold and formal, and our words should come from our experience. We are worshipping God, not bringing attention to ourselves. Our adoration and devotion must be genuine.

Music is a powerful tool to lead people down a pathway to acceptable or unacceptable worship. Satan has thought to pervert thankfulness by urging the unconsecrated and uncommitted to lead out or participate in unsanctified music (Amos 5:21–26; Luke 18:11–14). The Hebrew root word *toph* in Ezekiel 28:13, translated "timbrels" (NKJV) or "tabrets" (KJV), generally means a "small drum," a suggestion that Satan led the angelic choir in heaven in his unfallen state. Hence, we can expect music to be one of Satan's special devices to pervert God's chosen ways to praise Him.

Fortunately, the Scriptures are not filled with negatives about worship. There are many positives about worship that are encouraged. We can always praise God for His goodness and for His salvation. The consistent advice of the Scriptures is encapsulated in the apostle Paul's advice—"Rejoice in the Lord always" (Phil. 4:4; cf. Ps. 138:1, 2). When Jesus was born in the manger in Bethlehem, the angel choir praised God (Luke 2:13, 14). When the great controversy with Satan is ended, the redeemed and the angelic hosts will praise God for the justice and truth revealed in His mighty acts (Rev. 15:3, 4; 19:6, 7). Indeed, God Himself will rejoice! (Isa. 65:19; Zeph. 3:17). Thus, the apostle Paul rightly urges us to be thankful in this world for

Chapter 15. Worship

the abundant salvation offered us and for Christ's ever-present help (2 Thess. 2:13; Heb. 4:15, 16).

Praise in the first temple is a matter of record (1 Chron. 23:5; 25:7). The psalmist proclaimed that God is better pleased with praise than the sacrifice of animals (Ps. 69:30, 31). In the second temple, music played a more prominent role, with there being a number of temple musicians. They generally used two-stringed instruments like the psaltery and harp for the main body of the temple orchestra. They also used percussion and wind instruments. Instrumental music was the main form of accompaniment; in fact, the Hebrews knew little of music in the absence of song.[242]

Worship can involve the expression of intense feeling, as when Hannah "poured out" her soul before God, and He heard and answered her prayer (1 Sam. 1:15, 20). Human emotions find a place in genuine worship and God does not condemn them (Luke 18:13, 14). However, God rejects ecstatic emotionalism. The worship format that the heathen priests used on Mount Carmel was under Satan's control. In contrast to the excitement found in their worship forms, God's prophet Elijah showed earnestness, calmness, and a quiet dignity (1 Kings 18:26–30, 36, 37). God chose to speak to Elijah soon after this episode in "a still small voice" (1 Kings 19:12). Our God, who changes not, still speaks to us in like manner today (James 1:17; refer to Table 15.1).

In many heathen and "Christian" cultures today, an altered mental state is produced by rhythm in music, bodily movements, by repetition of set phrases, and other activities. Many of the churches that constitute spiritual Babylon lay great weight on spiritual exercises that emphasize feelings, emotions, and searching for closeness to God in the silent place within. Though our religious experience should not be based on feeling, they should lead to feelings of gladness and joy, which we can express. Our relationship with Jesus is the important commodity (2 Cor. 5:7). "Faith is ours to exercise, but joyful feeling and the blessing are God's to give."[243] The issues revealed on Mount Carmel of old are the same issues that will confront Christ's followers in the closing scenes of earth's history. Let us study God's Word that our worship may be acceptable to Him. Above all, when our worship is Christ-centered, it will spring from a genuine relationship with our Redeemer and will "give glory to God."

Table 15.1. The Elijah message, a comparison of the Elijah message recorded in Scripture as it relates to worship.

Elijah (1 Kings 18)	John the Baptist (Matt. 17:9–13)	Remnant Church (Mal. 4:5, 6)
Unacceptable worship outlined in the days of Elijah	**Unacceptable worship outlined in the days of John the Baptist**	**Unacceptable worship outlined by John the Revelator**
Self-centered: "Hear us" (1 Kings 18:26)	Centered on self—ancestry significant (Matt. 3:9)	Self-centered: "I am rich … and have need of nothing" (Rev. 3:17); worship the beast to preserve life (Rev. 13:15)
Appeals to the dramatic, to emotions; loud appeals made to their god; high emotions (1 Kings 18:26–28)	Deeds and personal bearing made to appeal to the senses (Matt. 23:5; Mark 12:38–44)	Spectacular appeals to emotions; visual senses engaged (Rev. 13:13, 26–28)
Rejected God as the supreme being. Manifestations: • God's word ignored (1 Kings 16:31; cf. Josh. 23:11–13) • Reinterpreted history to deny God's providences (1 Kings 13:20–31) • Cut-off the prophets of God (1 Kings 18:4) • Worshipped and served other gods (1 Kings 12:26–33; 16:32, 33).	Behaved as a generation of "vipers" (Matt. 3:7). Manifestations: • Loved praise (Luke 18:10–14) • Used ostentatious religious titles (Matt. 23:5–7) • Did not follow God's word (Mark 7:9) • Destroyed faith in God's messengers (Luke 11:47, 48) • Practiced discrimination (Luke 18:10–14; John 7:14–16)	Issue great boasts and blasphemies (Rev. 13:5). Manifestations: • Disrespect God's name; doubt His word (Rev. 13:6, 15, 16) • Belittle Christ's tabernacle ministry (Rev. 13:6; Dan. 8:11) • Misrepresent heaven's inhabitants; teach the immortality of the soul; promote earthly mediators (Rev. 13:6; 16:13)

Chapter 15. Worship

Elijah (1 Kings 18)	John the Baptist (Matt. 17:9–13)	Remnant Church (Mal. 4:5, 6)
Acceptable worship outlined in the days of Elijah	Acceptable worship outlined in the days of John the Baptist	Acceptable worship outlined by John the Revelator
Worship was centered on God; His revealed will is emphasized; note the key words: "follow Him" "altar of the LORD" "LORD God of Abraham," "God in Israel," "at Your word" (1 Kings 18:21, 30, 36)	Christ "must increase" (John 3:30)	Worship is Christ-centered—"give glory to Him," meaning the Creator (Rev. 14:7)
People serving—"Come near to me" (1 Kings 18:30)	People serving (Matt. 3:5; Mark 1:5)	People serving—"to every nation"; a message involving family relationships (Rev. 14:6; cf. Mal. 4:6)
Reasoned appeals—"How long" and "Come near" (1 Kings 18:21, 30)	Reasoned concerning religious experience (Matt. 3:7–12; Luke 3:7-15)	A reasoned approach to worship—"for the hour of His judgment has come" and "calculate the number of the beast" (Rev. 14:7; 13:18)
Calmness—"Hear me, O LORD, hear me;" God speaks in a still small voice (1 Kings 18:37; 19:12)	Calm, purposeful cry "prepare the way of the LORD" (Isa. 40:3; cf. Mark 1:3)	Calm, purposeful mission carried out with "patience," "to preach," and to come "if anyone hears" God's "voice" (Rev. 3:20; 14:6, 12)

Elijah (1 Kings 18)	John the Baptist (Matt. 17:9–13)	Remnant Church (Mal. 4:5, 6)
Visual senses quietly involved to awaken conscience (1 Kings 18:31–33)	Visual senses involved, John "baptized," "heaven was opened," and "the Holy Spirit descended" (Mark 1:9; Luke 3:21, 22)	"Visions" and prophesying promised (Joel 2:28)
Emotions involved, calmness and awe predominated; at Elijah's cry, "Hear me, O LORD," the people "fell on their faces" (1 Kings 18:37, 39)	Emotions involved—repentance seen (Mark 1:4)	Emotions involved—zeal, awe, and reverence in response to the call for repentance—"Fear God" (Rev. 3:19; 14:7)
Lessons taught	**Lessons taught**	**Lessons taught**
Faith was central to the appeal; reminded of Abraham, Isaac, Israel (1 Kings 18:36)	Faith in the coming Messiah (Matt. 11:10; Luke 1:17)	Faith is central in appeals (Rev. 3:18; 14:12; cf. 1 Pet. 1:7)
Challenged to obey God's word (1 Kings 18:21, 37)	Restore "all things" and focus on the Messenger of the covenant—the Lawgiver (Matt. 17:11; Mal. 3:1)	Obedience to the Decalogue a hallmark of the message (Rev. 14:7, 9, 12)
Repentance urged (1 Kings 18:21, 37)	Repentance urged (Matt. 3:2; Mark 1:4; John 1:29)	Repentance urged (Rev. 3:19, 20)
Promoted steadfast endurance by example (1 Kings 18:1)	Call to endurance—John the Baptist's example approved by Christ (Matt. 11:2–9)	Call to endurance and sanctification (Rev. 3:21); consider the challenge to develop Christian character—2 Peter 1:5–11; cf. Rev. 22:11)

Chapter 16.
Cleansed by Water and the Blood

Chapter Emphasis: *The symbols of blood and water in the worship exercises of the earthly sanctuary have equivalents in the Christian church today. Baptism by water immersion, symbolizing burial with Christ, and the Communion service, involving the taking of unleavened bread and unfermented grape juice, more faithfully illustrate the sacrifice and ministry of Christ than the adoption of alternate practices.*

Spiritual Link: *The ritual of foot-washing associated with Christ's institution of the first Communion service represents a commitment to unity and service.*

In the Scriptures, God frequently teaches important concepts through symbolism. When sin entered the world, death passed upon all (Rom. 5:12). Almost immediately after this event, God introduced His plan to save men and women from eternal destruction. His plan was based on an outstanding demonstration of love that meant that the Son, the second member of the Godhead, was to come to earth and suffer the penalty of death for the sins of the entire human race. This plan was realized in Jesus' life, death, and resurrection. As a result of the successful execution of the plan, salvation was assured to all who believed and formed a faith relationship with God. In order to deeply impress the significance of this plan on the minds of believers, God instituted animal sacrifice, first in Eden and then in the earthly sanctuary. The sacrifices themselves were not able to take away sin. Believers, as they exercised faith in God's provisions, were declared righteous before God. The sacrifices functioned to remind all about the enormity of sin and to encourage them to realize that although their sin would cost the life of the Seed to come, He would save them by His death. In this chapter, I wish to expand on the symbolism of the shed blood.

The concept of cleansing by water is also significant in the biblical account. Water is the universal solvent, and it has been used as a cleansing agent since time immemorial. In the Scriptures, cleansing by water is given a deep spiritual meaning. It is my purpose to study this symbolism and discover its application to our lives today.

The Shedding of Blood

In this section, I will

- *remind readers that God first sacrificed animals to provide clothes for sinful humans;*

- *establish that the shedding of animal blood pointed to the Great Substitute giving His life for the sinner.*

Soon after sin entered into the world, animals forfeited their lives to clothe the sinful pair. Subsequent to this event, God gave instructions for the institution of animal sacrifices (Gen. 3:21; 4:4). There is no doubt but that the shedding of innocent lives of animals to furnish coats for the naked pair forcibly focused their attention on the promise of the coming Redeemer and His suffering for their sin. This plan had been introduced to the sinful pair a short time after they disobeyed (Gen. 3:15). God, by clothing the sinful pair with a covering provided by His own hand, showed them that they were dependent on Him to take away the penalty of their sins, represented by their nakedness. The act of covering themselves with fig leaves illustrated the futility of human effort to counteract the effects of sin. Hence, the Scriptures sometimes speak of being covered by Christ's righteousness in terms of being covered by His robe, or outer garment (Isa. 61:10; Zech. 3:4).

Chapter 16. Cleansed by Water and the Blood

After this initial example, regular animal sacrifices were instituted to point to the coming Deliverer (Heb. 9:12). Abel is the first person mentioned in Scripture as offering a sacrifice by faith in obedience to God's instructions (Heb. 11:4), although we understand that Adam participated in similar ceremonies as well.[244]

The shed blood represented forfeited life (Gen. 9:4; Lev. 17:11) as a consequence of sin entering the world (Gen. 2:17). The shedding of blood more precisely represented the substitution of the life of the sinner by Christ. The Scripture tells us: "Christ was offered once to bear the sins of many" (Heb. 9:28). Cain, in refusing to offer an animal sacrifice, declared, in effect, that he had no need of a Savior.

John the Baptist referred to Jesus as the Lamb of God who was to take away the sins of the whole world (John 1:29). Old Testament writers also spoke of the Savior as a Lamb (Isa. 53:5, 7). The forfeiture of the life of an animal in sacrifice every time a person sinned directed minds continually to the magnitude of sin and to God's provision of a way of salvation. The blood of the victim was a type. It pointed the sinner, by faith, to the blood of Christ, the antitype, which was to be shed on Calvary to make atonement (Lev. 17:11; Rom. 5:10). Atonement means to cover, to reconcile, or, quite literally, to make two separated parties "at one." As we accept God's forgiveness by faith, the blood of Jesus cleanses us from sin, and we are justified and counted as if we had never sinned (Rom. 5:9; 1 John 1:7, 9). We are also sanctified through His blood and made perfect in every good work (Phil. 1:9–11; Heb. 13:12, 20, 21). Atonement, therefore, has both sacrificial and intercessory components.

The animal sacrifices did not have any merit in themselves. In reality, the sacrifices that God requires "are a broken spirit, a broken and a contrite heart" (Ps. 51:17; cf. Ps. 40:6–8). With this thought in mind, it is apparent that the plan of salvation, as outlined in the Old Testament, pointed forward to the coming of the Messiah. The ceremonies had no connection whatsoever with the practices of the surrounding nations. It was only by exercising faith in Christ, the promised Gift, that the sinner could claim the promises. The Lord desired obedience and righteousness rather than sacrifice (1 Sam. 15:22).

Deliverance Through the Blood

In this section, I will

- *briefly review the Passover feast that reminded believers of God's offer to deliver them from physical and spiritual bondage;*

- *firmly establish that the substitute lamb sacrificed in the Passover ceremony pointed to Christ our Savior.*

All the blood sacrifices of the earthly sanctuary system draw attention to the love and compassion of God who is rich in mercy. In sweating blood on our behalf in the Garden and then in laying down His life, our Savior illustrated graphically the true meaning of the blood sacrifices.

Passover Symbolism. The Passover feast was the first of the annual feasts of the Jewish year pointing forward to the ministry of Christ. It is not my purpose to look at the details of this feast here, but rather to focus on the symbolism of the blood. In the first instance, when this ceremony was instituted, it is clearly evident that deliverance was through the blood of the Passover lamb (Exod. 12:3, 5–7). The sprinkling of blood on the doorposts of the house signified that deliverance was offered to those who by faith gathered therein (Exod. 12:12, 13). Those who chose not to follow God's instructions were destroyed by the angel of death who passed through the land of Egypt.

The ceremony centered upon a lamb without a blemish, symbolizing the sinless Lamb of God. On the tenth day of Abib, or Nisan, the first Passover lamb was selected. Four days later it was slain at about the ninth hour of the day (Exod. 12:2–8). So Christ was condemned by the Sanhedrin several days before He was crucified. Significantly, the death of Jesus took place on the fourteenth day of the month Abib at the evening hour (Matt. 27:45–50; Luke 14:12, 25–28).

The shed blood of the slain lamb was applied with hyssop to the doorposts and the lintel of the dwelling, the crosspiece between the posts (Exod. 12:7, 22). The shed blood is represented in today's Communion service by partaking of unfermented grape juice. This represents the idea that, as participants accept the merits of Christ's shed blood by faith, they are delivered from both sin's penalty and its power (Rom. 5:9; Heb. 13:12).

The other important provision made in this feast was that unleavened bread was prepared and eaten along with the roasted lamb (Exod. 12:8). Not only was unleavened bread connected with the feast, but no leaven was to be found in the house for the entire week after the ceremony—the Feast of Unleavened Bread. Any person contravening this instruction was counted unworthy and "cut off" (Exod. 12:15). Leaven in the Bible is used as a symbol of sin and corruption. Since the bread represented Christ, it was to be without corruption (1 Cor. 5:7, 8). The symbolism of eating bread without leavening indicates that a life entirely given over to Christ is a life of victory over sin.

Resisting Unto Blood. In Christ's agony associated with His struggle in the Garden of Gethsemane, He shed great drops of blood (Luke 22:44). The phenomenon of sweating blood, known as "hematohidrosis," can occur when people are in a distressed physical or mental state.[245] Christ was suffering the horror of separation from God in addition to intense physical stress, as He bore the burden of the sins of the world. He continued this struggle against the powers of darkness when, on the cross, He gave up His life for the salvation of humankind. The apostle Paul advises us to resist sin with all the firmness, resolve, and faith that Christ exercised, resisting unto "bloodshed, striving against sin." (Heb. 12:4). Prayerful study of the life of Christ will lead us to cherish similar times of prayer and Bible study as He did. Thus, we will be strengthened to contend with evil and overcome the devil "by the blood of the Lamb" (Rev. 12:11).

Cleansed by Water

In this section, I will

- *establish that God has consistently used the concept of the washing with water as a symbol of cleansing from sin;*

- *call attention to some of the references in Scripture concerning the symbol of cleansing by the washing of water.*

Earthly Sanctuary Usage. In setting the Levites apart for the services in the sanctuary, water was sprinkled upon them as an outward sign of inner "purification" (Num. 8:7). We notice that in this ceremony the Levites did not wash themselves. Moses, a type of Christ, was to perform the sprinkling—they could not do it for themselves. By this ceremony the Lord was teaching them the necessity of regeneration, or rebirth, through the work of the Holy Spirit (Titus 3:5). To be fit ministers of the sanctuary, their lives needed to be molded and transformed so that they could truly represent God's way to others in their sphere of influence.

Prominently located in the outer court of the earthly sanctuary was a laver where the priests were to wash their hands and feet (Exod. 30:18–21). The water in the original laver may very well have come from the stream flowing from "the rock" at Mount Sinai. The rock represented Christ (Exod. 17:3, 6; 1 Cor. 10:4). The priests were to wash before they offered a sacrifice on the altar of burnt offering or entered the sanctuary. This ceremonial cleansing from physical uncleanness carried a deeper spiritual meaning in that it pointed to the washing away of sins through faith in Christ (1 Cor. 6:11; Eph. 5:26; Heb. 10:22).

Covenant Washing. When God entered into covenant relationship with the children of Israel at Sinai, He did so with the symbolic acts of washing them with water and anointing them with oil (Ezek. 16:9). Washing with water and anointing with oil were also a part of the preparations necessary for marriage (see Ruth 3:3). In the covenant relationship established between the people and God at Mount Sinai, they pledged to love and obey Him (Exod. 19:5–8; 24:7).

Justification and Sanctification Highlighted. God not only wished to wash the ancient Israelite people with the water of regeneration, in justification, but to pour out the "oil" of His Spirit—the agent of sanctification—upon them abundantly. He wished to cover them with the beautiful garments and ornaments of righteousness (Isa. 61:10). To explain the act of grace that God performs, the psalmist wrote: "Wash me, and I shall be whiter than snow" (Ps. 51:7). Hence, the symbol of washing is commonly used in Scripture to signify cleansing from sin (Isa. 1:16; Jer. 4:14).

Today, God has established His covenant, not with a nation, but with all those who accept Christ by faith. The same washing from sin and covering with Christ's righteousness, which God desired to do for Israel, He seeks to do for you and me, His followers. When, by faith, we ask God to forgive specific sins, He forgives us and declares us clean. Justified in Christ, we stand before Him as though we had never sinned (1 John 1:9).

Yet, God wishes to do more for us than to take away the guilt of sin (John 3:5). He wishes to "sanctify and cleanse" us "with the washing of water by the word" and present us "holy and without blemish" (Eph. 5:26, 27). He has promised to impress the principles of the law on the mind (Jer. 31:33; Rom. 12:2). God desires to make all believers a holy people—to sanctify us—through faith in His merits. Indeed, as a consequence of claiming this promise, the redeemed are represented as being without fault before God (Rev. 14:5; cf. Rev. 21:27).

Symbols in the Christian Church

In this section, I will

- *indicate that the symbols of the shedding of blood and the washing with water still have relevance in the Christian church;*

- *establish that the Lord's Supper, instituted by Christ, took the place of the Passover service and reminds us continually of God's great sacrifice.*

Many of the ceremonies performed in Old Testament times met their fulfillment at the cross. The symbols of cleansing with blood and with water have passed over into the Christian dispensation, and the meaning of these symbols for us today has been clarified by the words of Christ and the apostles.

Baptism by Immersion. Christ endorsed water baptism in the Christian church as a fitting symbol of His death and resurrection (Matt. 3:13–16; Rom. 6:3–5). Baptism by immersion was known among the Essenes before the baptism of John. There is little doubt that the concepts underpinning baptism were viewed as consistent with the principles underlying ceremonial washings established in the sanctuary system. When John the Baptist came boldly proclaiming baptism unto repentance, there is no record that the religious leaders objected in principle to the concept. They, in fact, hoped that He was Moses or one of the notable prophets whom they believed would return (John 1:21, 25). The apostle Paul reminds us that Moses symbolically baptized the children of Israel in the Red Sea (1 Cor. 10:2). As they passed through the waters, they were protected from the Egyptians by a cloud. Their deliverance from Egypt was made sure by their act of going through the opened water in faith. In so doing, they pledged their loyalty to God.

The word "baptism" comes from the Greek word *baptizō*, which means "to wash or immerse." Baptism by immersion was practiced by John the Baptist and the apostles (John 3:23; Acts 8:36–39; 9:18; 10:47, 48; 16:15). It was the prevailing practice in the Catholic Church until the twelfth century. In some places, it was found even as late as the sixteenth century. The practice is still permitted in the Latin Church. The rite of immersion is said to be "more suitable as a symbol of participation in the death and resurrection of Christ" than is the pouring of water—infusion.[246]

Baptism loses its meaning when it is not by immersion since baptism is a symbol of the burial of the old life of sin (Col. 2:12). The burial takes place after the crucifixion of the "old man" and his old ways (Rom. 6:4-6). In order to bury the old ways, a person must repent and claim forgiveness by faith in Christ's merits (Acts 2:38). After immersion, the person is raised from the water "to walk in newness of life" through faith in Christ (Rom. 6:4, 11). Baptism, then, is a sign of our discipleship, a public acknowledgment of our relationship to Christ. Baptism is, in the Christian era, what circumcision was to Abraham's children (Rom. 2:28, 29; Gal. 5:6). It is a symbol of our covenant relationship with God, a symbol of our having become heirs to the promises (Gal. 3:27-29).

In the Old Testament, when the children of Israel entered into covenant relationship with God, He sprinkled them with water and anointed them with oil (Ezek. 16:8, 9). Oil is a symbol of the Holy Spirit (Zech. 4:2-6, 11, 12). In the Christian dispensation, the outpouring of the Holy Spirit is also promised to believers (Luke 3:16; Acts 1:5; 2:1-4). However, the Spirit does not come in His fullness upon just anyone. Those who receive the gift participate in deep searching of self, humbling of the mind before God, confessing of sins, and yearning after God's presence through faith. This was the experience of the disciples in the ten days before Pentecost (Acts 1). Through the reception of the Holy Spirit, the disciples were empowered to witness effectively for Christ (Acts 1:8).

The days of preparation were days of prayer, study of the Word, and remembrance of the teachings of Jesus (Acts 1:14, 20-26). The disciples put away all their differences and the desire for supremacy. The prayer that Christ uttered just before His betrayal that His disciples might be one as He was one with the Father (John 17:21) was being fulfilled. They were "with one accord" in their affections, desires, and wishes (Acts 1:14; 2:46; 4:24; 5:12; 15:25). The Holy Spirit was guiding them into unity through an understanding of truth (John 16:13). We notice that the early disciples "were brought together, with their different faults, all with inherited and cultivated tendencies to evil; but in and through Christ they were to dwell in the family of God, learning to become one in faith, in doctrine, in spirit. They would have their tests, their grievances, their differences of opinion; but while Christ was abiding in the heart, there could be no dissension. His love would lead to love for one another; the lessons of the Master would lead to the harmonizing of all differences, bringing the disciples into unity, till they would be of one mind and one judgment. Christ is the great center, and they would approach one another just in proportion as they approached the center."[247] Today, let us take careful note of the preconditions for the outpouring of God's Spirit (Acts 5:32), and let us earnestly seek and pray for such an experience so that the coming of the Lord will be hastened (Mal. 4:5, 6).

The Lord's Supper. Christ introduced another ceremony into the Christian church to symbolize His death. The Lord's Supper proclaims "the Lord's death till He comes" (1 Cor. 11:26; cf. Matt. 26:26–28). It took the place of the Passover. The Passover pointed forward to Christ's sacrifice; the Lord's Supper points back to His death and forward to His second coming. It also commemorates deliverance from sin and liberation from the sentence of death (John 6:54). Jesus instructed all believers to remember His spilled blood and broken body until His second coming (1 Cor. 11:23, 26). Unfermented grape juice was used in this ceremony since leaven is a symbol of corruption and Scripture establishes that the pure juice of the vine is an appropriate symbol of the blood of Christ's perfect sacrifice (Matt. 16:6; cf. Deut. 32:14). The unleavened bread similarly pointed to the sinless Christ as the "bread of life" (John 6:48; cf. verses 51, 58). In other words, we are to focus not only on the crucified Christ but on the living and coming Christ. In commemorating this Supper, we acknowledge that the words of Christ are our spiritual meat and drink. They are the source of sustaining power, which is realized for us through faith (John 6:63; cf. 1 Cor. 10:4).

Jesus washed the disciples' feet with water just before they partook of the Lord's Supper. Many Christian communities typically neglect the ordinance of foot washing before the Lord's Supper (John 13:4–8). However, the ordinance provides the opportunity for the establishment of unity and harmonious relationships among the believers by the putting away of all differences. It is an acknowledgment of what Christ must do for us in order to make us clean (John 13:10). The priests' washing of their hands and feet in the sanctuary service did not cleanse the life. Nor does it do so for us today. Rather, Christ washes us clean spiritually when we confess our sins and enter a faith relationship with Him. The spiritual washing is the removal of the guilt of sin and liberation from sin's power. The Holy Spirit daily strengthens and sanctifies the individual who exercises faith in Christ (1 Cor. 6:9-11; Eph. 5:26; Titus 3:3-5). Participation in the ceremony of foot washing is a public expression of our acceptance of Christ individually as our Savior. Christ desires for all to drink freely of the "water of life," which He alone can give (Rev. 22:17; cf. John 4:10).

The ceremony of foot washing also symbolizes commitment to service. Christ demonstrated by His acts of unselfish love how believers may "through love serve one another" (Gal. 5:13). The service also represents a renunciation of any desire to occupy the highest place. Properly understood, this ceremony signifies a commitment to seek unity of doctrine, spirit, and faith in accordance with the Lord's prayer on unity spoken after the Lord's Supper (John 17:20-23).

Chapter 17.
The Body Temple

Chapter Emphasis: *God's original purpose in associating with the human race in Eden was altered by the entrance of sin. Evidence of His presence among humanity was apparent, particularly, in the sanctuary, from Old Testament times until Jesus lived on earth. Now God dwells with humanity through the agency of the Holy Spirit who directs the controlling sentiments of the mind of those who are committed to God. This experience among other things convicts believers to preserve their bodies as fit places, or temples, for the Holy Spirit. In practical terms, this means keeping our body as healthy and fit by living according to the biblical principles of health.*

Spiritual Link: *The ministry of the Holy Spirit and conversion are inextricably linked.*

In the Garden of Eden, God signaled that He wished to associate regularly and intimately with humanity. Hence, He walked with the ancestors of the human race in the garden in the cool of the evening. Sin, unfortunately, separated our forebears from God and marred His image in them. God was not willing that humanity should be separated from Him throughout eternity. Therefore, He announced to the sinful pair in Eden the plan He had formulated before Creation—to send Christ to restore His image in the race.

The concept of restoration was taught through the earthly sanctuary and temples. They became holy places when God's presence dwelt in them (Exod. 29:38, 42, 43; 40:34; Ps. 11:4). The apostle Paul used this thought to suggest that, if individuals yielded their mind to the molding influence of the Holy Spirit, they would be cleansed from sin and become temples for God (1 Cor. 6:19, 20).[248] God's image would thus be restored in them. As a consequence, corrupting thoughts and actions would be replaced by the fruit of love, and the purpose of God for humanity would again be achieved.

The apostle goes further and suggests that it is our privilege and duty to present our body "a living sacrifice, holy and acceptable to God" (Rom. 12:1). This means that the individual becomes devoted to keeping the body and mind in the best condition possible, thus fulfilling the call to stand apart from the practices of the world in obedience to God's principles of health.[249]

When Christ returned to heaven to take the role of the High Priest in the heavenly sanctuary, He promised to send the Comforter to influence the thoughts of each believer. When refined and molded by the influence of the Spirit, God's followers will become His temple and will reflect the image of the living God. It is this aspect of the Christian experience that I wish to examine in this chapter.

The Body Temple

In this section, I will

- *introduce the concept that our bodies can become the temple of the Holy Spirit—in other words, that God still wishes to dwell with humanity;*
- *indicate how we may treat our body so as to be a fit dwelling place for the Holy Spirit and thus give glory to God.*

In both the Old Testament and New Testament Scriptures, the word "temple" is frequently applied to a building. However, in the New Testament, we encounter another usage of the term. There we find Jesus prophesying that He would rise from the dead on the third day after His crucifixion: "Destroy this temple [His body], and in three days I will raise it up" (John 2:19, 21). The apostle Paul makes a similar application to the human body, challenging believers: "Do you not know that your body is the temple of the Holy Spirit" (1 Cor. 6:19).

Before Jesus departed from the earth, He promised His disciples that He would send the Comforter, or Holy Spirit, to "abide with you forever" (John 14:16). He then went on to promise that the Spirit will dwell "with you" and "in you" (John 14:17). It is evident from Paul's statement that the Corinthian believers did not fully understand the significance of this principle and that they did not know how to treat their bodies as a fit dwelling place for the Holy Spirit. The Spirit directs the key sentiments of the mind, transforming the thinking of willing participants (Rom. 12:1, 2). This spiritual fact should not lead to the conclusion that God has made within us an "inner sanctuary of the soul, a holy place, a Divine Center" where we can communicate with Him.[250] To conclude such is to enter territory occupied by antichrist forces, intent on introducing mystical Eastern religious practices into Christianity.

Glorifying God. The revelation that our body can be the temple of God has profound consequences. We are duty bound to glorify God in our mind and body because Christ has bought us back from Satan by His sacrifice (1 Cor. 6:20). Springing from the mind are decisions that affect all the affairs of this life (Prov. 4:23). The mind is involved in the re-creation of the image of God in human beings—"A pure heart [mind] is the temple where God dwells."[251] The book *Christ Triumphant* declares: "We must be 'labourers together with God,' for we are 'God's husbandry,' we are 'God's building.' In view of this, we must see that the temple is not defiled with sin. We should be lively stones, not dead ones, but live ones that will reflect the image of Christ. We must be worshipers in spirit and in truth."[252]

For this reason, God will consider the very thoughts in His final assessment of the life of every person (Jer. 17:10). Jesus Himself taught this profound truth (Matt. 5:28; 15:19), pointing out the revolutionary nature of true conversion. The apostle Paul expressed the same thought in Romans, chapter 12, verse 2, and considered that the word "transformed," implying a metamorphosis, communicates the proper concept of the depth of change necessary in our life. Notice his words, "And do not be conformed to this world, but be transformed by the renewing of your mind" (Rom. 12:2). Individuals with a renewed mind will ever desire to bring glory to God in the way that they act.

The Scriptures give clear advice about caring for the health of the mind. We are to carefully fill the mind with things which are true, noble, just, pure, lovely, and of a good report (Phil. 4:8). This descriptive list outlines the principles that should guide all the activities relating to the culture of the mind. We are to meditate on the Word of God, for it will strengthen the mind and quicken the conscience. The avenues to the mind are to be guarded with "all diligence," for what we receive into the mind and what we think about regulates our actions and, ultimately, determines our destiny (Prov. 4:23). How careful, then, should we be in choosing what we see, hear, and read. The world around us is certainly filled with violence and, many seem intent on feeding their minds on that which is sensational, sensuous, and bizarre. In many popular movies and television programs, the Ten Commandments are violated through lying, adultery, killing, and covetousness.

The Bible has some serious words of advice to those who continually refuse to guard the avenues of the mind. It declares them spiritually dead, eternally damned—"children of wrath" (Eph. 2:2, 3, 8; cf. 1 Tim. 6:5). It is only through transforming the mind that we have any hope of being saved eternally. The apostle Paul implores us to recognize God's desire that we willingly offer our "bodies a living sacrifice, holy, acceptable to God" (Rom. 12:1, 2). Caring for the body holistically reflects an understanding of the "principles of true sanctification."[253] Anciently, in the sanctuary service, the sacrifices were offered "without blemish" (cf. Exod. 12:5; Lev. 4:3; Lev. 23:12). Today, God urges us to give ourselves unreservedly in service to Him. A mind that is emptied of worldly thoughts must, however, be filled with the things of God (Luke 11:24–26).

The image of God in humanity has been progressively marred by unwholesome practices. To reverse the trend with Divine help, the apostle Paul has some good advice. He commenced first with human relationships. God designed humans to enjoy intimate relationships inside a single-partner marriage and to avoid sexual perversions (see 1 Cor. 6:15–19).[254] The Scriptures' advice is clear: "Flee sexual immorality" (1 Cor. 6:18; cf. Rom. 1:26–29). Related to the moral care of the body is the choice of food and drink taken into it (1 Cor. 10:31).

Throughout Jesus' experience on earth, He established a close connection between His physical and spiritual health (e.g., John 5:8, 9, 14). Our eating and drinking, mind culture, and other activities, including health therapies for sickness, are to be carried out in the sure knowledge that our body is the vessel the Holy Spirit wishes to sanctify by His influence. Revelation 14:7, which calls for giving God glory, trains the mind upon the life principles established in the beginning as we prepare to meet the King in His glory. God wishes to bless us that we may be a blessing to the world through our witness (Exod. 15:26). When we obey His principles by faith, He will qualify us to be heirs in the world that He is planning.

Principles of Eating and Drinking. The Scriptures identify and applaud principles of right eating and drinking. The story of the Jewish captives in Babylon indicates that God will honor those who choose to accept a simple diet similar to that given in Eden (Dan. 1:5-8, 12, 18-20). The original diet consisted of nuts, fruits, grains, and vegetables (Gen.1:29; 2:16). Daniel and his friends could have eaten clean meats available to them if those meats had not been offered to idols (cf. Dan. 10:3). However, they chose a total vegetarian diet, recognizing that it was their duty to preserve their body and mind in the highest state of health. Realizing that there is a vital connection between physical health and spiritual health, they resisted the temptation to satisfy—or worship—the cravings of appetite (Exod. 20:3). For their obedience to the principles of health, God singularly honored Daniel and his friends. In the example presented in the book of Daniel, only those who passed the test on diet were able to pass the greater tests that followed.

The Bible record of the lifespans of the ancients who lived after the Flood stands in marked contrast to that of those who lived before it (compare Gen. 5 and 11). This decline in lifespan may be linked in part to the tendency to favor a meat diet rather than to adhere to God's great original plan. After the Flood, God permitted humans to consume the flesh of animals. However, the flesh they consumed was to contain no blood. Hence, meat was slaughtered and treated in a particular manner to achieve this goal. This instruction was continued in the Christian era (Acts 15:28, 29; cf. Gen. 9:3, 4, which predates the instruction on Sinai).

The distinction between clean and unclean animals was known before the Flood (Gen. 7:1, 2) and was outlined again to the Jewish nation (Lev. 11; Deut. 14). God has made some striking statements about those who choose to disregard the distinction between clean and unclean meats right down to the end of time (Isa. 65:3, 4; 66:15-17).

Christian behavior is characterized by carefulness in eating, drinking, and the social activities we engage in (1 Cor. 10:5-11). The Bible contains explicit advice to abstain from alcoholic beverages (Prov. 20:1; 31:4). The consumption of alcohol leads to unsocial and unchristian behavior. Alcohol and other drugs damage the brain and other organs of the body.[255] The Scriptures advise against engaging in any activity that lessens life expectancy (Exod. 20:13). Whichever practice that interferes with clarity of thought or that lessens the impact of God's Word is to be avoided (Phil. 4:8). Not the slightest advantage should be given to Satan.

Preparing for the Second Exodus

Analysis of the first five books of the Bible indicates that Moses presented the first version of the NEWSTART program during the exodus with an emphasis on reform. (NEWSTART is a health recovery program designed to prevent and reverse disease through the use of the eight principles of natural healing.) Today this program finds its modern inspiration in Ellen White's book, *The Ministry of Healing* (1905). The emphasis in this program is on trust in God and the use of natural remedies, including the proper use of a plant-based diet, regular exercise, pure water, sunlight, moderation, fresh air, and proper rest.

Moses delivered the first outstanding series of prophetic challenges regarding health found in Scripture (Deut. 7:15). A summary of God's principles as delivered by Moses is presented in Table 17.1. Careful readers will find that Moses introduced all the points in our modern health program, though there are other points that Ellen White also mentioned.[256]

Table 17.1. Principles of physical health derived from the books attributed to Moses.

Key Thought*	Derived Principle	Reference
1. Trust in God	Trusting and obeying God is fundamental to human well-being.	Gen. 3:2–11; Exod. 12:23–30
2. Nutrition	Food intake in accordance with the manufacturer's initial recommendations is the ideal. Recognizing these recommendations and preserving and processing food as did Israel benefits the health.	Gen. 1:29; 9:24; 41:47, 48; cf. Lev. 11

Chapter 17. The Body Temple

Key Thought*	Derived Principle	Reference
3. Water	Hydration using the universal solvent of water is designed to give trouble-free operation of the body.	Exod. 15:25; 17:6
4. Air	Fresh air, indoors and outdoors, is designed to maintain efficient and problem free respiratory function.	Gen. 2:7; Lev. 14:34–45
5. Sunlight	Exposure to natural light confers biological and psychological benefits	Gen. 1:16; 2:15; 3:17, 19; Lev. 15:6, 7, 10, 11 (implied)
6. Exercise	Physical and mental activity ensures maintenance of function.	Gen. 2:15, 19, 20; 3:19
7. Rest	Rest ensures the maintenance and restoration of mental and physical vigor.	Exod. 16:4, 23–25; 20:8–11
8. Temperance	Moderation in all phases of living contributes to body homeostasis.	Num. 11:32, 33
9. Cleanliness	Sanitation and cleanliness have direct relevance to health outcomes.	Lev. 15:3–13; Deut. 23:12–14
10. Genetic diversity	Maintaining genetic diversity predisposes to favorable life outcomes based on hereditary traits.	Gen. 20:5, 12, Lev. 18:6–14

* The first letter of the first eight key points can be rearranged to spell NEWSTART

While the modern emphasis on health differs from that promoted by Moses, the fundamental concepts are the same, as they are based on natural principles. The one concept given prominence by Moses that is not widely discussed in most circles today is genetic diversity.

In some societies, the incidence of close family intermarriage has led unnecessarily to widespread and unfortunate genetic disorders.[257] The previous principle of sanitation is widely practiced in many societies and has outstanding relevance in maintaining food safety and general health. It is the one principle that non-government organizations universally emphasize in developing countries. We should not forget that one of the greatest problems of the human race is separating itself from human and animal waste products.

Moses' advice can be assessed by the outcomes recorded for East London's crowded quarters at the turn of the nineteenth century. Health practitioners were fascinated to observe the lower rates of infant deaths from infectious and respiratory diseases among the Jewish population. This positive outcome has been explained by the careful attention they gave to the biblical instructions on quarantine and by their attention to diet, the sparse use of alcohol, and personal hygiene. Personal hygiene requirements included hand washing before and after meals and keeping the surroundings clean. Utensils used in food preparation were also kept clean, and milk and meat were not mixed, nor were the utensils used in handling these food items.[258]

Besides these explanations, the Jews' low incidence of other diseases, like cholera, during this period has been attributed to the kosher requirements for meat preparation, with a lower risk of consuming diseased food, the practice of boiling water and milk, and the use of clean cooking and eating utensils. The religious laws also improved personal hygiene over the general population in that they required that nails be trimmed once a week and that women take a ritual bath once per month after menstruating. The immigrant Jews in London also customarily bathed on account of their general attitude towards cleanliness.[259]

I urge those who plan to participate in the second exodus, which takes us out of spiritual Babylon, to consider these principles and apply them in their modern setting, for health is one of the great emphases of the third angel's message.[260] The angel asks the followers of Jesus to separate themselves from the unhealthful cravings and practices of modern Babylon and to become God's ambassadors. Clear thinking is required in the stewards of God's reconciliation ministry; the brain circuits need to be functioning optimally.[261] Such an outcome reflects advanced ideas about healthful living, for care of the creation starts with the steward. The apostle Paul concisely states that we are to bring glory to God in our eating, drinking, and doing (1 Cor. 10:31). The outworking of this instruction is most readily achieved by adopting vegetarianism, an approach that is patterned after the original diet (Gen. 1:29) and that has been found to promote health.[262]

Joined Unto the Lord

In this section, I will

- *introduce the idea that the Holy Spirit influences us to make morally correct decisions;*

- *expand on the concept that the new birth of the conversion experience follows the individual's continued response to the promptings of the Holy Spirit.*

The Holy Spirit pleads with every human being to accept Christ (John 1:9). The Spirit is given to lead to repentance and to a deeper and more complete knowledge of God's will. If we do not resist, we will be brought to confess all our sins and reach out in faith to Christ for help. We are all that stands in our own way. "Through the Spirit God works in His people 'to will and to do of His good pleasure.' Phil. 2:13. But many will not submit to this. They want to manage themselves. This is why they do not receive the heavenly gift. Only to those who wait humbly upon God, who watch for His guidance and grace, is the Spirit given."[263]

Conversion. If we give ourselves unreservedly to God, we will experience the new birth, for our life is "hidden with Christ in God" (John 3:3; Col. 3:3). In a sense, such an experience joins believers to the Lord spiritually (1 Cor. 6:17). The Scriptures use a variety of terms to describe the experience of conversion. Notice a number of these written by the apostle Paul: "*born* according to the Spirit" (Gal. 4:29), "put on the new man" (Eph. 4:24; Col. 3:10), a "life is hidden with Christ in God" (Col. 3:3), and a "new creation" (2 Cor. 5:17; Gal. 6:15). These terms convey the idea not only of a complete change in the life but also of a continuing experience. The Old Testament also describes this continuing experience as walking with God (Gen. 5:22, 24). To the people in the times before the coming of Christ, God offered to give them a "heart of flesh" as a replacement for the "stony" heart that they possessed (Ezek. 11:19; 36:26). God promised to write His laws in their hearts and minds (Jer. 31:33; Heb. 10:16); He promises to do this for us today too (Heb. 8:10; 10:16). This shows that the gospel has been preached since the entrance of sin.

Conversion involves a number of steps. The first step is repentance. When we yield to the Holy Spirit's influence and ask God to give us repentance, our conscience is quickened (Acts 3:19; cf. Matt. 6:12, 14). Conviction brings a growing sense of the righteousness of God in contrast to the sinner's miserable condition. The sinner longs to accept the love offered, to turn from sin, and to be in harmony with God again.

A sense of our unrighteousness and of our need for forgiveness leads us to seek the forgiveness of God. True repentance of sin always precedes confession (Ps. 32:5; 34:18). Such confession is always of a specific nature, acknowledging the very sins that have been committed. Furthermore, the sinner does not seek to excuse the unhealthy behavior (Lev. 5:5; 1 Sam. 12:19). Those who have wronged other people will make things right as far as possible before coming to God to seek forgiveness (Ezek. 33:15; Luke 19:8, 9). If we confess our sins under these circumstances, Jesus is "faithful and just to forgive us *our* sins and to cleanse us from all unrighteousness" (1 John 1:9).

When we come to God, we will desire to abandon anything that separates us from Him (Luke 14:33; 2 Cor. 10:5). We will commit ourselves fully to God, asking Him to lead us at all times, and we will place all the strength of our will on the side of Christ (Rom. 2:13; 6:13).

God invites us to exercise faith that He has accepted our sincere confession and that He will prompt us and give us strength to walk in His ways (Mark 11:24; 1 Cor. 10:13; Heb. 11:6). As we maintain our commitment to depend on Him, our faith will grow and our relationship will strengthen (Eph. 4:15; Col. 2:6). The fruit of this faith relationship will be seen in the life. Love will be manifest by what we do, and obedience will spring naturally from this living principle (Ps. 40:8; 1 John 4:11; 5:3).

Accepting Christ is a daily experience. The apostle Paul, under the inspiration of the Holy Spirit, admitted that he needed to "die daily" (1 Cor. 15:31; cf. Gal. 2:20). Paul was speaking of dying to self, of gaining daily victories through faith, of having a new experience daily. Properly understood, "genuine sanctification ... is nothing less than a daily dying to self and daily conformity to the will of God. Paul's sanctification was a daily conflict with self.... His will and his desires daily conflicted with duty and the will of God. In the plan of not following inclination, he did the will of God, however unpleasant and crucifying to his nature."[264] As we thus respond to the promptings of the Holy Spirit, we may be said to experience daily conversion.[265]

Chapter 17. The Body Temple

That We May Be One

In this section, I will

- *emphasize that acceptance of Christ day by day brings the spirit of unity into our fellowship as Christians.*

We remember from Chapter 7 that Christ is also building the temple of His church (Zech. 6:12, 13). This means that, if Christ is working in us individually through the Holy Spirit, a journey toward unity will occur (John 17:11, 21).

When the day of Pentecost arrived, we read that the disciples were "together" (Acts 2:1, RSV—Greek *homou*). This idea of togetherness expressed a broader concept than we would normally attach to the word. Adam Clarke commented that their *"minds, affections, desires, and wishes, were concentrated on one object, every man having the same end in view; and, having but one desire, they had but one prayer to God, and every heart uttered it. There was no person uninterested—none unconcerned—none lukewarm; all were in earnest; and the Spirit of God came down to meet their united faith and prayer."*[266] Though the word *homothumadon* does not occur in all Greek manuscripts of Acts 2:1 (but only in a few older ones); it does occur in several other places in Acts (1:14; 2:46; 4:24; 5:12; 15:25), suggesting a more inclusive idea of togetherness in the early church.

The pioneers of the Seventh-day Adventist church were burdened to bring about a similar condition among the believers in answer to Christ's prayer. They desired to be one as Christ and the Father are one (John 17:21; cf. 1 Cor. 1:13). One testimonial of their experience states: "We would come together burdened in soul, praying that we might be one in faith and doctrine; for we knew that Christ was not divided."[267] This same experience can be ours today if we approach God earnestly in prayer and Bible study as did the early disciples.

For unity to be achieved, each believer must grow continually in an experience with Christ. The Lord admonishes us to read the inspired Word, for this is His chosen avenue of revealing truth to us and of developing our faith and trust (Rom. 10:17). As we search the Scriptures, they reveal Jesus Christ to us. They also reveal the beauty of God's love and character (John 5:39; 14:6). The Holy Spirit uses our time in the Word to impress truth upon our hearts and minds, convicting us of sin and leading us into right paths of thinking (John 16:8, 13). We can only be united with one another as we are one with God through daily conversion and walking daily with Him.

Jesus assures us in the Scriptures that, "If anyone wants to do His will, he shall know concerning the doctrine, whether it is from God or *whether* I speak on My own *authority*" (John 7:17). Added to this promise is the declaration: *"There is* one body and one Spirit, just as you were called in one hope of your calling; one Lord, one faith, one baptism; one God and Father of all, who *is* above all, and through all, and in you all" (Eph. 4:4–6). Hence, it is manifestly impossible to be joined to the Lord and not be joined with our brethren by common beliefs on major Bible doctrines. Division and confusion in doctrine are indicative of the devil's activity. The Scriptures do not speak of unity in a diversity of beliefs; they speak of unity built on unwavering truths (Matt. 12:25; 1 Cor. 1:13; Eph. 4:13; 6:14). "Unity in diversity" is the catch-cry of the New Age movement. One writer has captured the deceptive unity of this movement in the following statement: "The New Age ideal seemed a beautiful concept: to have unity in diversity so as to reveal the fullness of God and produce a society of loving understanding and mutual interdependence. This would be the New Age of love, light, and joy—the kingdom of heaven on earth."[268]

If we walk as "prisoner[s] of the Lord," various qualities will be shown—humility, meekness, longsuffering, love, peace, faith, hope, and unity of belief (Eph. 4:1–6; 13, 14). All these qualities and all the gifts given to the Christian come as a consequence of the Spirit's taking possession of our thinking. When we yield ourselves thus to God, we will be transformed in mind (Rom. 6:16; 12:2). We will be obedient through faith to the principles of God's government and to the laws of health pertaining to mind and body. Thus, we will be enabled to bring glory to God.

Last Events

Chapter 18.
The Lord Will Come Suddenly to His Temple

Chapter Emphasis: *Various events occur on earth and in heaven before Christ's final activities in the heavenly sanctuary. On earth, the Holy Spirit will be poured out in great measure, and Christ's sincere followers will be sealed for eternity. There follow distinctive signs in the religious, political, and natural realms.*

Spiritual Link: *Obscured and misplaced truths will be recovered and presented to the world as faith-testing concepts.*

When Jesus came to this earth to live as a human, He presented the truth regarding God's character—the principles of His government—and He offered the plan of salvation to the people in all its simplicity. The "gospel age" commenced with the outpouring of the Holy Spirit at Pentecost. It will end with the great outpouring of the Holy Spirit just before the return of Christ in glory. How eagerly we should pray for this outpouring in our life so that we can fulfill God's purpose for us.

The Scriptures speak a great deal about the hope of Christ's return in glory. In fact, in Malachi, chapter 3, the prophet speaks of Christ coming "suddenly" to the heavenly temple to complete the final phase of His atonement ministry before returning to this earth. God has a timetable that He earnestly awaits to fulfill. The Scriptures indicate that there are necessary events that must occur and conditions that will prevail in the world and in the church before this event will come about. In God's timetable, He mentions the possibility of delay owing to the unready state among His disciples and the lack of an enthusiastic sense of mission. In this chapter, I wish to examine the idea of the imminence of Christ's return and the experience that true believers must have before the Lord can return. Is it possible for His believers to hasten this event?

The Messenger Comes to His Temple

In this section, I will

- *introduce the reader to the Bible description of the scene in heaven that depicts Christ as commencing His final work in the heavenly sanctuary;*

- *call attention to aspects of the religious awakening and preaching that occurs on earth at the commencement of Christ's final work in the heavenly sanctuary.*

Jesus is called "the Angel of God," or simply "the Lord" (Exod. 14:19, 24–26; Zech. 3:1–5). In the book of Malachi, He is described as "the Messenger of the covenant" (Mal. 3:1), and also as "the Angel of the Covenant."[269] This indicates that Jesus was the Lawgiver who appeared on Mount Sinai amid awful splendor (James 4:12).

There are two instances identified in Scripture in which Jesus came suddenly to His temple. The first was at the close of His triumphal entry into the city of Jerusalem. It was then that He drove out those who were desecrating the temple (Matt. 21:12). The second event was at the commencement of the work of the pre-advent judgment in heaven in 1844 when Jesus came to the Father, who is "the Ancient of Days" (Dan. 7:9, 10, 13).

Some of the prophecies recorded in Scripture have more than one application. However, we should exercise caution in proposing double applications for prophecies. The particular scripture itself must indicate that such an application was intended. An illustration of this principle can be seen by referring to Malachi 4:5, 6. Here the Scriptures speak of Elijah the prophet coming before "the great and dreadful day of the Lord" to prepare a people for that event (Mal. 4:5). Clearly, this prophecy focuses in a primary sense on the preparation in our time for Christ's glorious return (Zeph. 1:14–18). Nevertheless, Christ also made an application of the prophecy to the work of John the Baptist at His first coming (Matt. 17:10–13). The prophecy in Malachi 3:1 also has a double application. Christ came to earth to demonstrate the true principles of His kingdom and to declare judgment on the Jewish nation. In His role of High Priest in the heavenly courts, the principles of His kingdom, which are summarized in the three angels' messages, are to be brought to the attention of the world in a startling manner before the close of human probation, before judgment is declared on the unjust (Rev. 14:6–12).

Applying prophecy to more than one fulfillment when indicated by Scripture itself does not require accepting the apotelesmatic principle, which states that there are dual or even multiple fulfillments to all prophecies. Proponents of this approach hold that an application can be made even when a prophecy is only partly or approximately fulfilled. For these interpreters, the different models of prophetic interpretation—preterist, futurist, historicist, and idealist—are all correct.[270] This is a sloppy way of approaching prophecy, and it casts reproach on God.

Jesus' Work in the Temple. During the closing phase of the first advent experience, Christ performed a number of functions. He restored the truths and authority of God's Word to their rightful place (Matt. 21:4, 23). He brought conviction to professed followers who held His words in contempt (Matt. 21:12, 13, 31, 32, 41, 45). On the occasion of His triumphal entry into Jerusalem, Jesus allowed Himself to be declared the King of peace (Luke 19:38). He used the occasion to call attention to different aspects of His kingdom of grace and of glory (Matt. 21:5).

The last work done by Christ during His earthly ministry has clear application to the work that He seeks to do among people today. He cleansed the earthly temple by declaring judgment upon those who worked in the temple precincts and by re-establishing biblical revelation as the basis for truth (Luke 19:45, 46). The prophecy of Malachi 3:1 points also to a second fulfillment, which is the judgment described in Daniel 7. The "little horn" power and its associates have perverted the teachings of the Word of God. Revelation, chapter 14, indicates that the inhabitants of the earth will receive a glorious revelation of the truths of God's Word before Christ returns in glory. The most essential of these concern the sanctuary and God's creatorship. Christ's messengers will proclaim with clarity the glorious unembellished truths of the gospel of grace and the centrality of faith. The three-fold messages of Revelation, chapter 14, also declare that the kingdom of God's grace is soon to be replaced by the kingdom of His glory. Probation is soon to close, and judgment will be proclaimed. In preparation for this event, a great work of investigation is proceeding in heaven.

Behold He Is Coming

In this section, I will

- *emphasize the conditions that will prevail on earth prior to Christ's return;*

- *note that Christ Himself indicated that probationary time may be extended.*

The last act of Christ in the heavenly sanctuary will be followed by His coming in glory (Mal. 3:1). The period of earth's history when Christ will come will be marked by decay in society, in the family, and in the church. Jesus called attention to the days of Noah and of Lot as indicative of the societal issues that will occupy human minds as the world is coming to an end (Matt. 24:37–39; Luke 17:26–28).

First, the word of God and of His prophets will be held in derision (2 Peter 3:2–4). One way this has occurred is that higher criticism has rendered the idea of a literal interpretation of Scripture unbelievable. Thus, the words of Scripture are willfully ridiculed and their significance argued away (2 Peter 3:4–6). We might illustrate this by reference to the Church of England's 2002 survey on fundamental beliefs. Many bishops of the church indicated their disbelief in the resurrection and the virgin birth! Some even shared in the thoughts of one theologian who described the resurrection of Christ as a "conjuring trick with bones."[271] The atheist Richard Dawkins commented that, in his view, the last time an educated person could believe in miracles without embarrassment was in the nineteenth century.[272] His appraisal is sadly and quickly being realized within portions of the Christian church.

Second, the doctrine of the second coming of Christ will be attacked (2 Peter 3:4). Worldly pursuits will even fill the mind of Christians (Matt. 24:38). As in the times of Noah, every imagination of the mind will tend toward evil (cf. Gen. 6:5). As a consequence, the earth will be filled with violence and every type of lustful activity (Gen. 6:2, 11; 2 Peter 3:3). These facts are highlighted daily in the news media. The emphasis in today's society centers on satisfying the senses of hearing, seeing, feeling, and in giving free reign to the imagination. It seems as if there are no absolutes. Many hold the individual's opinion or the constantly-changing mores of society to be the standard in guiding moral behavior. The Scriptures, on the other hand, declare that all things should be tested according to God's infallible standard—"To the law and to the testimony: if they speak not according to this word, *it is* because *there is* no light in them" (Isa. 8:20, KJV).

No Second Chances. The sequence of events from the Day of Atonement to the memorial of the blowing of Trumpets indicates that God's call to salvation is today. Ample opportunity was given before the Day of Atonement for preparation and even on the very morning of the event (Lev. 23:23–32). Those who failed to respond to the opportunities given were unable to participate in the ceremonies thereafter. In fact, they were "cut off," which certainly was not a pleasant fate. There were just two classes of people recognized, those who responded to God's mercy and those who refused (Lev. 23:29). There is no indication in Scripture of the possibility of the extension of probationary time after Christ's second coming. Jesus warned that He "is coming at an hour when you do not expect *Him*" (Matt. 24:44) and that, when He comes, it will be with His reward (Matt. 16:27). In the story of the bridegroom coming to the wedding, those virgins who had not prepared for the event were not permitted subsequent entry (Matt. 25:1–13). The Bible speaks of the beginning of the time of the end (Dan. 12:4). A careful evaluation of Daniel's prophecies shows this time to have commenced in 1798. However, there are no time prophecies defining exactly when the end of time will be. Jesus indicated that His return to earth is conditional on the gospel being given to every nation, kindred, tongue, and people (Matt. 24:14). We should not consider God as being unreliable (James 1:17). Rather, we should accept by faith the truth of Peter's statement, "The Lord is not slack concerning *His* promise" (2 Peter 3:9, cf. Rev. 10:7).

God extends probationary time for the simple reason that He is "not willing that any should perish" (2 Peter 3:9). In mercy, God delays judgment that there might be sufficient opportunity for all to hear and respond to the last message of grace. He is also merciful to His servants whom He has commissioned to give the message. Like the Israelites of old, the sense of mission and urgency in finishing the task has grown dim. The members of the last church of Laodicea are not all fully aware of their deficiencies; they do not have the right relationship with God (Rev. 3:18).

Imminence of Christ's Return

In this section, I will

- *focus on the concept of the imminence, or soon coming, of Christ in glory;*

- *identify signs indicating the soon coming of Christ.*

The early disciples believed in the imminence of Christ's return (1 Thess. 4:17; 2 Peter 3:11–13). These and other Scriptures indicate that the apostles hoped that Christ would come in their day; "expectancy of the coming of the Lord ran high in those early churches!"[273] Many Christians continued to cherish a similar hope into the third century. Yet, as Christianity increased in popularity, the hope of Christ's early return began to dim. At the close of the 12th century and at various periods since then, the hope of the Second Advent has revived once more.[274] Today, the sense of expectation has grown with the increase of destructive and revolutionary events around the world.

Just because some of God's followers have held a certain viewpoint of Scripture at some point in time does not mean that their view represented God's ideal (e.g. Matt. 19:7, 8). There are several instances in Scripture that believers misunderstood the significance of the words spoken to them. A good example are the mistaken expectations of Christ's disciples concerning His earthly mission (Luke 24:21, 25–27) and His early return following the ascension (Matt. 24:34; James 5:8; 1 Thess. 4:15, 17; Rev. 3:11; 22:7, 12, 20).[275] We could also cite the fact that Daniel the prophet did not fully understand the meaning of his writings (Dan. 8:27; 9:21–23; 12:8, 9). It is not surprising, then, that believers in the period immediately before 1844 misunderstood the application of the cleansing of the sanctuary mentioned in the "little book" of Daniel (Dan. 8:14; cf. Rev. 10:8–11).

These nineteenth-century believers interpreted the prophecy to mean that Jesus would return to this earth sometime between 1843

Chapter 18. The Lord Will Come Suddenly to His Temple

and 1844. However, with the passing of the time and no visible sign of Christ's return, they were thrown into distress. It was then that they understood that the prophecy of Revelation, chapter 10, foreshadowed such a misunderstanding and encouraged them to renew their efforts to spread the gospel message. Restudying the parallels of the yearly festivals in conjunction with Daniel, chapter 8, verse 14, they understood that the fall festivals pointed to the commencement of the last phase of Jesus' ministry in heaven in 1844, as He would suddenly come to the second apartment of the heavenly sanctuary.

Notable Events Expected before Christ's Return. The Scriptures indicate that significant events will occur in the world and the church before Christ's return. A most riveting set of Bible prophecies focuses attention on a great religious power arising antagonistic to God. This power would arise early in the Christian era and continue until the end of time, for it will be destroyed "with the brightness" of Jesus' coming (2 Thess. 2:8). The prediction was that it would hold great temporal power for 1260 years, from AD 538 to 1798. During this period, the saints were to experience intense persecution (Dan. 7:25; 12:7; Matt. 24:29; Rev. 12:6). (We will look at these prophecies in greater detail in Chapter 19.)

The prophecy about the emergence of a great religious power met its fulfillment in AD 538 when the Emperor Justinian finally broke the power of the Arian Ostrogoths in Rome and made important concessions to the papal church. (These wars would continue in Italy until AD 555.) This event greatly increased the papacy's temporal power and led to restrictions on religious liberty. Several years after this event, Gregory the Great would pompously write, "I wonder whether being pope at this time is to be a spiritual head or a temporal king."[276] The 1260-year prophecy terminated in 1798 with the capture of the Pope under Napoleon's general Berthier. The papacy had reached its lowest ebb in modern times, as a consequence of this momentous event.[277] However, the Scriptures predicted a resurgence of papal power and the continuance of that power until the Lord's return (Rev. 13:3–8).

Daniel indicated that, leading up to the time of the end until the end of time, knowledge would increase remarkably (Dan. 12:4). One outcome of the increase of Bible and general knowledge was that Bible prophecy and, more specifically, the 2300-year prophecy would be understood (Dan. 7:26, 27; 8:14). Scripture indicates that great celestial signs would precede this period of awakening. These signs were to occur while the door of mercy was still open, for we are assured that even after they have occurred "whoever calls on the name of the LORD shall be saved" (Joel 2:32; Acts 2:21; Rom. 10:13; cf. Matt. 24:29).

In a primary sense, the increase in knowledge predicted by Daniel the prophet relates to the increase in understanding of the prophecies of his book. This increase of prophetic knowledge coincided broadly with the technological and scientific revolution. A period of technological development began in Great Britain about 1760 and spread to other significant industrial countries over the next century. The economic stimulus that came from the replacement of manual techniques by the machine led to further scientific discoveries and technological progress that changed the nature of society and how "people related to time and space."[278] Today, remarkable increases in archaeological and scientific knowledge continue. This, unfortunately, has not led to widespread acceptance of the Bible or the idea that a pre-advent judgment is in process. Matthew and Joel mentioned celestial signs as associated with the awakening interest in prophecy. (See Exhibit 18.1). These events were designed to bring the moral issues in the controversy between Christ and Satan to the attention of the inhabitants of the world and to invite them to accept God's final offer of salvation.

The final sign that Jesus highlighted was that the gospel would be preached to the world (Matt. 24:14). At the same time, He predicted that the quality of life on earth would be in decline as the inhabitants set about by policy and practice to "destroy the earth" (Rev. 11:18).

Thus, the only task that remains to be fulfilled is the preaching of the gospel to all the inhabitants of the world, and then Christ will return triumphant. Modern methods of communication make fulfillment of the gospel commission achievable within a relatively short time frame. The religious and political forces in the great controversy are being stirred with a resurgence of religious movements within Islam and Christianity that seek to regain dominion of this world. Meanwhile, the planet is under unprecedented pressure as its resources are exploited, population burgeons, and levels of pollution continue to rise. Care for God's creation and acknowledging that He is the Creator are issues far from the minds of many, including many within the Christian community. This arises from the rejection of the Bible truth that God created the world and its inhabitants in six, 24-hour days and from neglect of the seventh-day Sabbath memorial.

Work Schedule in Heaven. Christ has a work to do in heaven before He comes in glory (cf. Matt. 22:1–14). This work involves His ministry as High Priest in sanctifying His people and blotting out the confessed sins of the saints from the books of record (Heb. 5:5, 6; Dan. 8:14; cf. Lev. 16:18–21). Just when Christ's work will have been completed in the courts of heaven is not revealed in Scripture. The work is to a degree tied to the response of God's people to the urgent tasks at hand. The angel with the seal of God is pictured in Scripture as crying to the angels who are to release God's restraining influence over the powers of darkness to delay until God's designated task is completed (Rev. 7:1–3). It is not that God is procrastinating in fulfilling His promise of Jesus' return. It is that He is longsuffering and is mercifully taking into account the weaknesses and indecisions so characteristic of human nature when it comes to things of eternal value (2 Peter 3:9). Like the apostle Paul, let us show no lack of faith in the Lord's coming (2 Tim. 4:6–8).

The Latter Rain

In this section, I will

- *establish that the special work accomplished in and by God's people before Christ's return is made possible through the activities of the Holy Spirit.*

Before Christ comes the second time, the Holy Spirit will be engaged in a special work that is described as the coming of the latter rain (Joel 2:23, 28–31; cf. Hosea 6:3). In Palestine, the early rains of October and November fell after the sowing of the seed while the latter rain of March and April matured the grain. Both rains were essential for the harvest. Using this familiar agricultural metaphor, God's prophets described the work of the Holy Spirit. The outpouring of the Holy Spirit at Pentecost can be regarded as the former, or early, rain (Acts 1:8; 2:1–3). John the Revelator described the outpouring of the Holy Spirit in tremendous power to present God's final message during the period preceding the coming of Christ (Rev. 14:6–9, 18:2). This event is featured by the angels of Revelation 14 and 18, proclaiming their messages with a "loud voice" to a world on the verge of destruction.

In all ages, believers in God have been dependent on the ministration of the Holy Spirit to give effectiveness and power to the proclamation of their message. Associated with this call is the inference that acceptance of God's salvation brings with it a commitment to be obedient by faith. The experience strengthens believers to pass through the great time of Jacob's trouble (Dan. 12:1; cf. Gen. 32:6–8; 33:1–4).

The Scriptures indicate that those of us who live through this time of trouble will "need an experience which we do not now possess" (cf. Rev. 3:18).[279] The necessity of the outpouring of the Holy Spirit in the life of followers in preparation for this event is clearly portrayed in the parable of the ten virgins (Matt. 25:7–9). The foolish virgins still required in their lives the ministry of the Holy Spirit, which was represented by the oil (Zech. 4:12, 6). The outpouring of the latter rain does suddenly prepare the believer for the coming of Jesus. It is to those who daily have sought God through consecration and surrender to Him and who have gained victory over every known sin by prayer and the strong arm of faith who will receive this great blessing. They have habitually responded to the Holy Spirit and have been obedient to His call (Acts 5:32). The same work undertaken by the early disciples before Pentecost is the work that we must seek to accomplish today.

Destiny Determined

In this section, I will

- *indicate that prior to Christ's return a special work must be accomplished in the lives of God's people.*

Before the close of probation, the servants of the Lord are to be sealed, or declared safe from destruction (Ezek. 9:2–5; Rev. 7:2, 3). The Holy Spirit has accomplished this special work. Probation closes as Christ completes His work in the heavenly sanctuary (Dan. 12:1; cf. Dan. 7:9). The religious leaders of the Jewish nation understood that the Day of Atonement was the time of "the signing of the verdict" when the "fate of every man is sealed."[280] The prophet Ezekiel spoke of a similar work near the close of probationary time. He depicted the Lord's lingering at the threshold of the temple, waiting for the sealing to be completed (Ezek. 9:3). The sealing referenced here is accomplished when the servants of God have the principles of God's law written on their minds and when their will is dedicated wholly to God. The opposition and persecution foretold in Scripture as coming upon this world are unable to sway their resolve to obey all the commandments of God through faith (Rev. 7:14, 15; cf. Rev. 13:15–17). In this last-day application, "sealing" occurs when Jesus' disciples have settled "into the truth, both intellectually and spiritually, so they cannot be moved."[281] We must now focus on the truth of God's Word and the special truths for this time. We have been issued a challenge: "The truth and the glory of God are inseparable; it is impossible for us, with the Bible within our reach, to honor God by erroneous opinions."[282]

Those who would be counted among the potential candidates of heaven are "now afflicting their souls, confessing their sins, and earnestly pleading for pardon through Jesus their Advocate."[283] "Those that overcome the world, the flesh, and the devil, will be the favored ones who shall receive the seal of the living God.... Only those who, in their attitude before God, are filling the position of those who are repenting and confessing their sins in the great anti-typical day of atonement, will be recognized and marked as worthy of God's protection."[284] In Malachi 3:3, God is pictured as "a refiner and a purifier" so that His followers may offer "an offering in righteousness." God allows trials to come to us so that our character may be developed.

Exhibit 18.1. Signs in the heavens and the earth that mark the commencement of the closing of the work of God and the nearness of Christ's return to earth.

> For nearly three centuries, the church suffered intermittently at the hands of pagan Rome. Even more horrific persecution would come in AD 538, with the beginning of the 1260 years of papal supremacy (Dan. 7:24–26; Rev. 11, 12). Intense persecution did not continue right up to 1798, the end of this prophetic period, for Christ had indicated that this period of persecution would be shortened (Matt. 24:21, 22) and that spectacular celestial signs would follow. These included the sun being darkened, the moon not giving her light, and the stars falling from the heavens (verse 29). Associated with these specific signs would be the more general signs of conflict, famine, and earthquakes (verse 7). The fulfillment of these signs near the end of the 1260 years can be briefly noted as follows:
>
> *Earthquakes.* There have been many earthquakes and some of them were more severe than the one I am about to mention. In the period of enlightenment about Bible prophecy, one earthquake stands out. "Probably the most famous of all earthquakes is that which destroyed Lisbon on Nov. 1, 1755. There were three great

earthquakes (the first was the largest) at 9:40 a.m., 10 a.m. and at noon. The main shock lasted six to seven minutes, an unusually long duration. Within six minutes at least 30,000 people were killed, all large public buildings and 12,000 dwellings were demolished. It was a church day, and great loss of life occurred in the churches.... Alexander von Humboldt stated that the total area shaken was four times that of Europe.... The Lisbon earthquake was remarkable for its effects in water.... The tsunami at Lisbon consisted of three large waves 15 to 40 ft. high. At Cadiz, Spain, it was 60 ft. high. It took the tsunami 10 hr. to reach Martinique (3,740 mi.) where it was 12 ft. in height."[285] This event set men thinking about the great day of God. Voltaire, the French philosopher, was apparently "profoundly moved" by it. "It was the last judgment for that region," he wrote. "Nothing was wanting to it except the trumpet." His biographer, speaking of the general mood, wrote: "The earthquake had all men thoughtful. They mistrusted their love of the drama, and filled the churches instead."[286]

Signs in the sun and moon. The darkening of the sun and the unusual appearance of the moon occurred May 19, 1780, commencing at about 10 a.m. along the east coast of America. Harvard mathematician Samuel Williams reported in the *Memoirs of the American Academy of Arts and Sciences*: [The English spelling of some words has been modernized so as to make the quote more readily understandable] "The *extent* of this darkness was very remarkable. Our intelligence, in this respect, is not so particular as I could wish: but from the accounts that have been received, it seems to have extended all over the *New-England* states.... With regards to its *duration*, it continued in this place at least fourteen hours: but it is probable this was not exactly the same in different parts of the country. The *appearance* and *effects* were such as tended to make the prospect extremely dull and gloomy. Candles were lighted up in the houses;—the birds having sung their evening songs, disappeared, and became silent;—the fowls retired to roost;—the cocks were crowing all around, as at break of day;—objects could not be distinguished but at a very little distance; and everything bore the appearance and gloom of night."[287] It was widely held that "the day of judgment was at hand."[288]

Signs in the stars. On November 13, 1833, one of the most remarkable meteoric displays appeared (far grander than the more recent Leonid meteor shower of November 1966). Nearly the whole of North America, the West Indies, and Mexico observed the display. The heavens were described as: "Thick with streams of rolling fire; scarcely a space in the firmament that was not filled at every instant." "Almost infinite number of meteors; they fell like flakes of snow."[289] "This shower is estimated to have furnished 200,000 meteors for a given station between midnight and dawn, numbers of them brilliant, and many leaving trains." The remarkable fact about this display is that, though "Sir Edmund Halley had calculated a fireball path in 1719," "still scientist neglected meteors almost entirely, and we may truly say that meteoric astronomy was born on Nov. 13, 1833, when the great Leonid shower appeared over America."[290] This same encyclopedia article describes the terror of the masses who fully expected that "the end of the world was about to come." A British writer recorded the impression made on the public: "In many districts, the mass of the population were terror-struck, and the more enlightened were awed at contemplating so vivid a picture of the Apocalyptic image—that of the stars of heaven falling to the earth, even as a fig-tree casting her untimely figs, when she is shaken of a mighty wind."[291] Another writer declared: "Everybody felt that it was the Judgment, and that the end of the world had come." A similar but less spectacular display in Europe in 1866 again served to bring attention to the certainties of the prophetic Word.[292]

When the signs commenced at the time specified and in the order given, the days of persecution being cut short as Jesus had predicted (Matt. 24:22), the people were drawn to the Word of God and what it declared regarding the end of the world. Coincident with these signs in the natural world, a worldwide religious movement began among students of the Scriptures from many churches urging that the coming of the Lord was near at hand. The religious world was stirred by the preaching conducted by the educated, the uneducated, and even children. The preaching focused on the fulfillment of the Bible's greatest time prophecy in 1844.[293]

The signs must be viewed against the backdrop of other prophetic fulfillments clustering around the period before 1844 and in terms of their impact on the people of the times and not in

> terms of the occurrence of similar events before or since. The significance of these events to the people living then was remarkable, as it focused their attention on the God of heaven, the salvation that He offers, and the certainty of His promises. In the future, signs in the heavens and earth will herald the deliverance of God's people by the appearance of the Son of Man in the heavens (Rev. 16:17–21).[294]

Chapter 19.
The 2300-Day Prophecy

Chapter Emphasis: *The longest time prophecy in the book of Daniel establishes the date for the commencement of the pre-advent judgment of judicial atonement in the heavenly sanctuary and the work undertaken there by Christ.*

Spiritual Link: *The historical-grammatical approach to the interpretation of time prophecy is valid and essential to interpretation.*

The fascination of the Bible resides, in part, in the many prophecies that it contains. The question that must be asked of all prophecies is: Have they proven true? The Bible itself challenges us to test prophecies and their veracity. Notice the following divine warning: "When a prophet speaks in the name of the Lord, if the thing does not happen or come to pass, that *is* the thing which the Lord has not spoken; the prophet has spoken it presumptuously; you shall not be afraid of him" (Deut. 18:22). Jesus Himself appealed to the words of the prophets to show that the things that had recently happened to Him at His crucifixion and resurrection had been predicted many years before (Luke 24:13–27). Thus, He reinforced the credibility of the Bible. The apostle Peter considered that the specter of fulfilled prophecies gave such remarkable evidence of the truthfulness of the Bible that it rivaled his own experience with Jesus Christ while He was here on earth (2 Peter 1:19).

In this chapter, I wish to investigate the longest time prophecy in the Bible, which deals with the cleansing of the heavenly sanctuary in Daniel 8. Fortunately, this prophecy has the same starting point—457 BC—as the prophecy of Daniel 9, which deals with the time of Jesus' coming as Messiah and His subsequent death. The prophecy concerning the coming of the Messiah is so well supported by history that we can have absolute confidence that the date of the fulfillment of the Bible's longest time prophecy is also correct.

I will commence with some historical information that gives us the background for the prophet Daniel and his writings.

Historical Background

In this section, I will

- *review some history relevant to a better understanding of Daniel's vision in chapters 8 and 9;*

- *identify the nature of Daniel's misunderstanding of the longest time prophecy in Scripture, a prophecy that has to do with the cleansing of the sanctuary.*

Nebuchadnezzar II, king of Babylon (605–562 BC), moved his armies into Palestine in 605 BC and retired to Babylon with prisoners. Unrest continued and deportation of prisoners took place in stages from 605 to 586 BC. The final deportation was associated with the destruction of the temple. Prisoners whose intellect and appearance qualified them to serve in important office in the conquered lands were assigned to be trained in the specially designated schools of the day. Daniel was one of these prisoners and, subsequent to his training, performed important functions in the government. Just before the fall of the Babylonian Empire to Medo-Persia, he was made the third ruler in the kingdom (Dan. 5:29, 30).

Cyrus ended the Babylonian Empire in 539 BC and established the Medo-Persian Empire as a dominant power as predicted by God (Dan. 1:21; 8:20). The military commander of Cyrus' army was Darius, and he was made king of Babylon after the conquest of the city. Darius made Daniel one of the presidents and, indeed, planned to make him the chief administrator (Dan. 6:1–3).

Chapter 19. The 2300-Day Prophecy

Before the conquest of Babylon by Cyrus, during Belshazzar's first year as king (553 BC), Daniel had a vision, recorded in Daniel 7, in which he saw four great, successive empires. The fourth empire particularly attracted his attention (Dan. 7:19), for it gave rise to a "little horn" power, which set itself against the saints and even against God Himself (verses 7, 8, 20, 21, 25). The information that the angel gave to Daniel about the fourth, world-changing empire and the politico-religious power that would arise from it "greatly troubled" him (verse 28). Two years later (551 BC), Daniel had another vision in which he saw other beasts and a mysterious "little horn" power (Dan. 8:1, 9, 10). In the context of gross meddling with and opposition to God's institutions, Daniel heard one angel say to another, "How long will the vision be?" (Dan. 8:11–13). In other words, he was saying, how long will this dreadful state of affairs continue? The holy messenger's answer is in verse 14: "For two thousand three hundred days; then the sanctuary shall be cleansed." Daniel was exceedingly perplexed and upset by the vision of this "little horn" power, and so much so that he became ill (verse 27).

Chapters 7 and 8 of Daniel's book were written in the first and third years of king Belshazzar (c. 553, 551 BC).[295] Yet, more than a decade later, in the first year of the reign of Darius (539 BC), we find that Daniel was still concerned about the "little horn" power.[296] He was seeking to determine whether the prophecies of Jeremiah (25:11, 12), concerning the length of time the people would be in Babylonian captivity, could shed light on the problem. He well knew that the 70-year desolation of Jewish territories by foreign powers prophesied by Jeremiah, Daniel's contemporary, was almost over. The period commenced with Nebuchadnezzar in 605 BC, and now it was 538 BC. Thus, sixty-eight of the seventy years had elapsed. Was the prophecy of Jeremiah about to be fulfilled, or had God changed His timetable because of the people's response? Daniel engaged in a prayer of confession and appealed for mercy and guidance (Dan. 9:4–19).

While Daniel was praying, the angel Gabriel was sent to answer at least some of his queries (verse 21). The angel informed him that Jerusalem would be restored and the coming of the Messiah to this earth would be related to this event (verse 25). The decree relative to the event would be issued in 457 BC. As for the "little horn" power, Daniel was left to conclude that its activities were also yet future since the angel had already informed him that the events connected with it would take place in the distant future (Dan. 8:26). In addition, the angel informed Daniel that the 70-week—or 490-year—prophecy concerning the coming of the Messiah was "determined," or "cut off." It is logical to conclude that he meant that it was to be cut off from the longer period of 2300 prophetic days, or 2300 years, which was to elapse before the judgment of the "little horn" power would commence. (See Figure 19.1 below.) Now that many of his uncertainties of mind were removed, Daniel was at ease with God's mercy and His timetable.

Three decrees were associated with the return of the Jews from Babylon. The re-establishment of the Jewish state with its civil and religious privileges would be completed with the third decree. The Bible evidence for this can be seen in the following summary: "In its completest form it was issued by Artaxerxes; king of Persia, 457 BC. But in Ezra 6:14 the house of the Lord at Jerusalem is said to have been built 'according to the commandment ['decree,' margin] of Cyrus, and Darius, and Artaxerxes king of Persia.' These three kings, in originating, reaffirming, and completing the decree, brought it to the perfection required by the prophecy to mark the beginning of the 2300 years."[297]

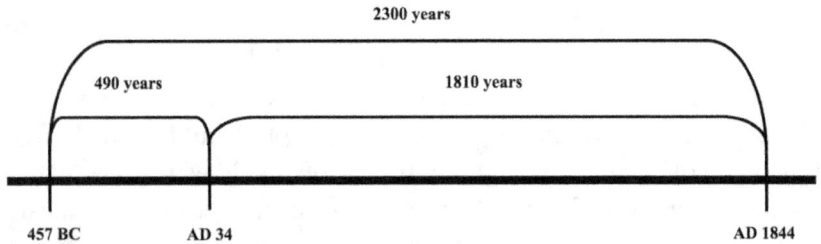

Figure 19.1. Schematic representation of the 70-week prophecy in relation to the 2300-year prophecy.

Temple reconstruction in Jerusalem began after Cyrus gave permission in 537 BC (Ezra 1:1–4). Sacred objects were returned at state expense and the exiles and their descendants were allowed to return. Daniel did not return with the exiles, for he would have been around 87 years of age at the time. The temple finally was rebuilt and dedicated in 515 BC under Darius I, who reigned from 522 to 486 BC (Ezra 6:1–15). The third decree occurred in the seventh year Artaxerxes I (Ezra 7:1–26), who reigned from 465–424 BC. Using the Jewish calendar, we calculate that his seventh year was 458/457 BC and Ezra arrived in Jerusalem in 457 BC.

With this background and having gone some distance in establishing a vital connection between the visions of chapters 8 and 9, let us take up the prophecy concerning the coming of the Messiah that gives us the commencement date for the 2300-year prophecy. That date is 457 BC. (See Figure 19.1 above and the discussion that follows.)

The Promise of the Messiah

In this section, I will

- *emphasize that Jesus Christ and the plan of salvation are the focus of prophetic utterances in the Scriptures;*

- *establish that an understanding of the prophecy dealing with the cleansing of the heavenly sanctuary is linked to the prophecy about the coming of the Messiah;*

- *seek to understand how literal time is calculated when symbolic Bible prophecy is involved.*

In Bible prophecy, we find that, when time is mentioned in a symbolic setting, the application of the time prophecy can be accurately calculated from historical events by using the rules that the Bible itself establishes. In symbolic prophecies, one day equals one year (see Num. 14:34; Ezek. 4:4–6; cf. Lev. 25:8).[298] The priestly calendar month contained 30 days, and the calendar year contained 360 days (Gen. 7:11; 8:3, 4). Hence, a month in prophecy would equal 30 literal years, and a prophetic year of time would equal 360 literal years.

Even though the Jews reckoned by 360-day years, they were fully aware that the natural year was slightly longer.[299] In actual practice, in applying biblical prophecy to world events, a prophetic year is counted as being equivalent to a literal year. How this works will become evident as we go along.

Messianic Time Prophecy. Arguably the greatest prophecy in the Bible relates to the anointing and sufferings of Christ and the probationary time allocated to the Jewish nation. Some have tried desperately to make the prophecy described in Daniel 9 say the time period allotted to the Jews and Jerusalem was "seven weeks of years" rather than seventy weeks (see Dan. 9:24, RSV), thus avoiding the principle contained in the prophecy that symbolic prophecies are understood by using the year-day principle. Within this 70-week period (490 literal years), the time from the decree to restore and rebuild Jerusalem

(Dan. 9:25) until the coming of the Messiah would be sixty-nine weeks (seven weeks plus sixty-two weeks), or 483 years (sixty-nine weeks times seven days). (See Fig. 19.2 below)

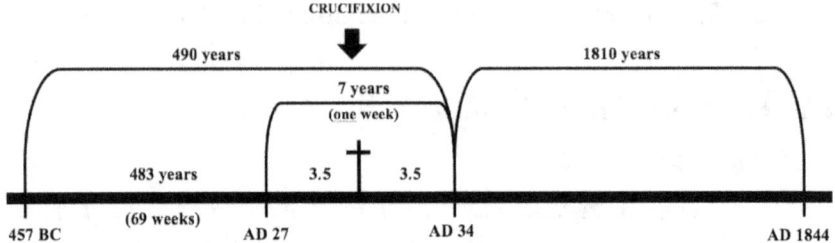

Figure 19.2. Schematic presentation of the details of the 70 weeks, or 490-year prophecy, and their relation to the 2300-year prophecy.

As mentioned already, there were several decrees, recorded in Scripture, that dealt with the return of the Jews and the restoration of Jerusalem. However, the decree of Artaxerxes in 457 BC was the first to give the Jews "signal spiritual, civil, and judicial privileges amounting to autonomy under the larger umbrella of the Persian Empire."[300] The seventh year of Artaxerxes ran from autumn 458 BC until autumn 457 BC. Considering that this decree did not go into effect until Ezra reached Jerusalem, the journey from Babylon to Jerusalem taking several months, the date 457 BC can be accepted with confidence (Ezra 7:7–9).[301]

"Messiah" is the Hebrew word for "anointed one." "Christ" is the Greek equivalent. Jesus was anointed with the Holy Ghost at His baptism and hence became the Christ (Acts 10:38). The 483-year period stretched from 457 BC to AD 27. (See Figure 19.2 above.) In our calculations, we must remember that in changing from BC to AD time, there is no year zero. So, we subtract 457 from 483 and get 26, though we must add one year to make up for the lack of a year zero, thus bringing us to AD 27. Indeed, this remarkable prophecy establishes that the method of prophetic reckoning outlined is accurate. More importantly, it indicates that the baby born in the manger of Bethlehem was the Son of God! John the Baptist recognized this fact, and his words of affirmation are recorded in Mark 1:3. He declared, "Prepare the way of the Lord." Jesus Himself said at this time regarding the prophecy, "The time is fulfilled" (Mark 1:15, cf. Luke 3:21, 22; John 1:32, 33, 35–37, 40, 41).

The date of Christ's baptism can also be established. John began to baptize in the fifteenth year of the reign of Tiberius Caesar (Luke 3:1–3). According to the non-accession year method of reckoning, Tiberius' fifteenth year would have begun on October 1, AD 27, which agrees with the math done above. Therefore, since the biblical and historical records harmonize, we can assume that AD 27 was the year of Jesus' baptism. At this time, Jesus was about thirty years of age (Luke 3:23). This text does not seek to establish His exact age, but simply remarks that He was at the age that the Jews considered a man to have arrived at full maturity and thus eligible to accept the duties of public life.

The prophecy provides other details that are highly significant. It says that Jesus was to be cut off in the middle of the last week (Dan. 9:26, 27, first part). The last week represents the last seven years of the prophecy. This period is divided into two equal parts, with Christ's ministry expected to last for three and a half years. His ministry does appear to have lasted for this period of time, for Jesus attended three Passover feasts and one unnamed feast (John 2:13, 5:1, 6:4, 12:1), which was probably also a Passover. As the lamb of God, Christ then died at the time of the Passover, AD 31 (Matt. 26:17–32; 1 Cor. 5:7). The remainder of the time period was "cut off," or set aside, for the Jewish people (Dan. 9:24). The end of this probationary period is considered to have been complete when Stephen was stoned (Acts 7:60), for the gospel then went to the Gentiles (Acts 8:1). The year would have been AD 34, which was also the possible year of Paul's conversion.[302]

There is no text that pinpoints the stoning of Stephen as the time when this prophecy ended. However, many scholars hold that the powerful ruling body in Israel rejected the covenant relationship with God by their response to Stephen (Acts 7:51–8:1). Saul's conversion experience began from this point and soon he became Paul, the apostle to the Gentiles. It is interesting to note that Paul's conversion occurred in AD 34, a date that can be calculated with reasonable accuracy. Paul reported that his first visit to Jerusalem as a Christian was three years after his conversion and that his second visit was 14 years later (Gal. 1:18; 2:1). Shortly after this, he visited Corinth and appeared before the proconsul Gallio under accusation of wrongdoing (Acts 18:12). Since Gallio functioned only in AD 51, according to historical evidence, Paul's conversion must have occurred in AD 34, that is, 51 minus 17 equals 34.[303]

Commencement of the 2300-Year Prophecy

In this section, I will

- *establish the starting point of the longest time prophecy recorded in Scripture for the cleansing of the heavenly sanctuary.*

As indicated in a section above, the angel Gabriel, in an effort to explain the timing and the meaning of the cleansing of the sanctuary to Daniel, gave the details of the coming of the Messiah. Understanding the meaning of the longest time prophecy depends on the interpretation of the words "are determined" in Daniel 9:24, a phrase that comes from the Aramaic word *chathak*.

"Cut off" Explained. The great majority of Hebrew lexicons render the primary meaning of the Aramaic word *chathak*, used in this instance, as "to cut," "dissect," "sever," "to cut off," or "divide." It should be noted that this is the only place in all Scripture that the word *chathak* is used. At the time of the writing of the book of Daniel in the sixth century BC, historical records indicate that its meaning was to "cut off." To convey the idea that the Messiah would be crucified, Daniel used the Hebrew word *karath* (Dan. 9:26). This word means to "cut down" or to "cut asunder." Daniel used another Hebrew word, *charatz*, to describe the destruction of the city of Jerusalem and the temple in Daniel 9:26, 27. It is translated "decreed" (NIV) or "determined" (NKJV). In using the word *chathak*, Daniel was trying to make it abundantly clear to the reader that the meaning of the word he chose to anchor the longest time prophecy was out of the ordinary. He wished to convey the idea that the shorter time period of seventy weeks, or 490 years, was *cut off* from the longer previously designated time period of 2300 years.[304]

Starting Point and Length. The simplest and most straightforward approach is to make the starting point of the longest time prophecy the same as that of the prophecy relating to the coming of the Messiah, that is, 457 BC (Dan. 9:24). The angel would have been less than informative if any other approach were taken. If the calculations of this time period are made so that the 2300-day prophecy ended at Calvary, the commencement date would have been 2272 BC. This early date has no historical significance. Calculations using other notable points identified by the Messianic prophecy similarly lead to non-significant dates.

Not surprisingly, debate has circulated concerning the prophetic time period mentioned. Is it 2300 prophetic days, or 2300 literal years? The words used in Daniel 8:14 concerning the 2300 year prophecy are correctly translated "unto 2300 evenings-mornings." This has led some to speculate that 1150 prophetic days are actually meant (e.g., the *Good News Translation*). Among those who take this line of argument are higher critics and those who seek to deny the message of the heavenly sanctuary (cf. Dan. 8:9–13). A simple yet sound answer to this problem is that the learned Jews who translated the Scriptures into Greek in the Septuagint version some centuries before Christ clearly understood the expression "evenings mornings" as referring to days. Other authorities agree with this.[305] The expression "evening morning" can be compared with the description of the days of the Creation described in Genesis, where the record states: "… the evening and the morning were the first day"—literally, "one day"—and so on for the remaining days of God's creating (Gen. 1:5, 8, 13, 19, 23, 31). The fact must also be noted that no historically significant event took place 1150 years (or even 1150 days) after 457 BC, the same cannot be said when the figure 2300 years is taken!

Some have advanced the idea that Daniel 8:14 and Daniel 9:24 refer to the same event, which turns out, upon examination, to be a proposition without credibility. Daniel 9 specifically focuses on "your people and … your holy city" (Dan. 9:24). Applying this to the whole human race (cf. Dan. 8:9) does not represent a coherent argument. The vision of Daniel 8 stretched historically from Medo-Persia through Greece to Rome and its derivatives, which is a period spanning from at least 539 to 168 BC. Furthermore, the vision relating to the "little horn" referred specifically to "the time of the end" (verse 17), not a postulated 1150 literal days (164.3 weeks) as popularly interpreted. An added issue is how a prophecy stretching over 490 weeks (see Daniel 9) can also fit one involving 164.3 weeks (Daniel 8).[306] The candid reader will realize that the proposition that Daniel 8:14 and Daniel 9:24 refer to the same event is a wild and unsupported concept generated to deny the reality of the statement, "Surely the Lord God does nothing, unless He reveals His secret to His servants the prophets" (Amos 3:7).

A concerted effort has also been made by some critics of the interpretation that is favored in this book to apply the prophecy of Daniel 8:14 to Antiochus Epiphanes.[307] Embarrassingly, the interpretation does not fit, though proponents press on without the least indication of discomfiture. Antiochus was a Seleucid king who reigned from 175 to 164 BC. His dominion included Syria, Israel, and part of Asia. He was a relatively weak and somewhat tragic king who reigned near the end of a line of Seleucid kings. Antiochus desecrated the Jewish sanctuary and interrupted the services for three years and ten days—1090 days (1 Mac. 1:54–59; 4:52–54; 2 Mac. 10:5, Apocrypha).[308] During this period, Antiochus erected an altar to the Greek god Zeus in the temple and sacrificed unclean animals upon it.[309] It can be readily observed that the time period required by the prophecy is not fulfilled by the 1090 days of the temple's desecration—even if we take the prophecy to refer to 1150 literal days rather than 2300.[310] Candid scholars uniformly reject the application of this prophecy to Antiochus. The less than candid have invented multiple applications of the prophecy in order to make it appear to nearly fit. However, *nearly* is not good enough when it comes to prophecy. This species of interpretation essentially represents a blaspheming of God's reputation.

It may be objected that the heavenly sanctuary cannot be "trampled under foot" (Dan. 8:13). Yet, careful reflection brings one to the conclusion that the heavenly sanctuary indeed can be trodden under foot in the same way that willful sinners can tread the Son of God under foot (Heb. 10:29). Such sinners have a casual regard for the message of salvation and the Savior. In the same manner, those who willfully reject the great issues brought to our understanding by the study of the heavenly sanctuary reject our High Priest, Jesus Christ, and tread His sanctuary down.

The Cleansing of the Sanctuary

In this section, I will

- *review the main features of the ceremonies carried out on the Day of Atonement in the cleansing of the earthly sanctuary;*

- *outline the nature of the activities in the heavenly sanctuary symbolized by the ceremonies carried out on the Day of Atonement.*

The cleansing of the sanctuary introduced in Daniel 8:14 is against the backdrop of the "little horn" power obscuring the truths of the sanctuary, treading them underfoot, and persecuting the saints (verses 9–13). The "little horn" power is one of the instrumentalities Satan has used to obscure the truth about God and His work in the heavenly sanctuary. It is also an instrumentality he has used to test the saints. God keeps records of the deeds, decisions, and devotion of the saints. Referenced in Daniel 7:10, these records are the basis for the proceedings that occur on the antitypical day of atonement. Both the little horn and the saints are involved in the work mentioned in Daniel 8:14 (cf. Dan. 7:9, 10, 22, 26, 27).[311] The little horn is condemned before a discerning jury for its perversion of biblical truths, its political alliances, and its lack of just dealings (Rev. 12–14). God's judgments against the "little horn" will be executed in the fullness of time (Rev. 18).

Meanings of the Word "Cleansed." The angel told Daniel that God would allow the interfering activities of the "little horn" power to continue for a prescribed period of time, and then God will put things right—or "cleanse"—the sanctuary (Dan. 8:14). Irrespective of what modern translators consider the text to mean, it is most instructive to understand how the Jews anciently regarded the verse. The Septuagint translation of the Bible, produced by Greek-speaking Jews centuries before the birth of Christ and in use in Jesus' day, rendered the word describing the work in the sanctuary at the end of the 2300 years as "cleansed." It is interesting to note that the Theodotian translation (the Greek translation by the Jew Theodotian) similarly rendered the word "cleansed." A number of translations from ancient to modern times, including the Douay-Rheims, the American Standard Version, the English Revised Version, the New King James Version, Knox's version, and Jerome's Vulgate, render it similarly.[312] The Jewish translation of the Holy Scriptures (*The Tanakh*) into English does the same.[313]

The Hebrew word used in Daniel 8:14, which has been translated as "cleansed" in the above examples, is *nisdaq*. It is derived from the verb *tsadaq*. The basic meaning of the native verb is "be just, righteous," and indicates conformity to a moral standard.[314] Translators commonly have rendered the word as "be put right," "be put in the right condition," "be righted," "be declared right," "be justified," "be vindicated," and "be cleansed." In order to confirm the appropriateness of the translation of Daniel 8:14 in the Scripture translations noted above, a short diversion is necessary.

The word *taher*, used in Leviticus 16 to explain cleansing of the earthly sanctuary, is used elsewhere in the Bible to convey parallel meanings of derivatives of the word *nisdaq* in Daniel 8:14. (See Table 19.1.) This principle can be illustrated by looking at examples of poetic parallelism found elsewhere in Scripture. Commonly, when this device is used, the first line is repeated in the second line, but different words are used to express the thought.

Table 19.1. Examples of the use of poetic parallelism showing that the actions described in Leviticus 16 and Daniel 8:14 are related.[315]

Text	Action described in prose	Hebrew word form used
Lev. 16:19, 30	cleanse, declare clean	*taher*
Dan. 8:14	to become, to be counted righteous, is justified	*Nisdaq*, derived from *tsadaq*
	Actions described in poetic parallelism	**Hebrew word form used**
Job 4:17; 17:9	• clean, pure, to be clean, cleansed • just, righteous, to be right	• *taher/təhor* • *tsadaq/tsaddiq*
Job 15:14; 25:4	• to be—or become—pure, clear, cleared • to be—or become—right, to be justified	• *zakah* • *tzadaq*
Ps. 19:9; Eccles. 9:2	• just, righteous, to be right • clean, pure	• *tsadaq/tsaddiq* • *tahor*

The use of these different meanings to express the basic idea behind the word "cleanse" should not bother us either. The word "cleansed" directs the mind of the reader to Leviticus, chapter 16, and indicates that, since 1844, the heavenly sanctuary is being cleansed and Christ our High Priest is completing His final work of judicial atonement in the heavenly sanctuary preparatory to the second coming. If translators have used the word "restored," it only directs the reader to the restoration of the purity of the Old Testament sanctuary on the Day of Atonement. In this anti-typical day of atonement since 1844, the truth of the sanctuary service has been restored with its focus on the ministry of Jesus Christ in the heavenly sanctuary. The word "vindicated" is preferred by some. It too directs us to the activities in the heavenly sanctuary since 1844. Through the events transpiring there, God is shown before the unfallen worlds to be just, fair, and righteous—He is vindicated.

The earthly sanctuary was considered ritually unclean owing to the confessed sins of the people being transferred to it (Lev. 16:16, 30). In the daily sanctuary service, the transfer of the record of confessed sins was symbolized by the act of applying some of the blood of the sacrifice to the altar of burnt offering and to the altar of incense in the Holy Place; this application was necessary before the priest was considered to have completed the initial phases of atonement (Lev. 1:5; 4:5–7, 20, cf. Lev. 10:17). On the Day of Atonement, the sanctuary was to be cleansed of sin and unrighteousness. We might remember that uncleanness is unrighteousness (Isa. 64:6; 1 John 1:9; 5:17). Furthermore, we notice that something that is without iniquity and sin is considered in the Bible to be just and right (Deut. 32:4; Rom. 3:23–26; 1 Peter 3:18). It follows, then, that when God, the just Judge, had removed the accumulated record of the confessed sins of the penitent believers, the sanctuary was declared to be just and righteous, or clean. The moral standard of the law was satisfied, and God was seen as being right in delivering His people. Those who falsely claimed to be God's followers were rewarded according to the record of their actions. They were cut off.

Because righteousness and justice occur in poetic parallelism with ideas of purity and cleanness (e.g., Job 4:17; 15:14; 17:9; Eccles. 9:2; see Table 19.1), the Jewish mind would naturally jump from Daniel 8:14 to Leviticus 16. A confirmation that judgment is intended here is the judgment parallels found in Daniel, chapters 7 and 8. (See Table 19.2, where the later chapter amplifies sections of the former.)

Table 19.2. Parallels between Daniel, chapters 7 and 8.[316]

Event/Feature	Daniel 7	Daniel 8
Sequence of worldly powers	• lion, first kingdom, representing Babylon (vss. 4, 17) • bear, second kingdom, representing Medo-Persia (vss. 5, 17) • leopard, third kingdom, representing Greece (vss. 6, 17) • dreadful beast, fourth kingdom (pagan Rome), vs. 7, 19, 23; then the "little horn" power (papal Rome) comes from the fourth beast (vss. 8, 24)	• [no symbol] • ram, representing Medo-Persia (vss. 3, 4, 20) • goat, representing Greece (vss. 5–8, 21) • fierce king (pagan and papal Roman power) arises (vss. 9, 23)
Status of saints in fourth kingdom	oppression (vss. 21, 25)	oppression (vss. 10, 24, 25)
Period of supremacy of "little horn" power	3½ times—or 1260 years—of supremacy (vs. 25; cf. Rev. 11:2, 3; 12:6, 14)	Time unspecified, but compare Dan. 8:24, 25 with Rev. 13:5–7 (42 months, or 1260 years); ends at "time appointed" (vs. 19)
The contest of "little horn" power is with heaven	• pompous words spoken against "Most High" (vs. 25) • persecute saints of "Most High" (vs. 25)	• exalts to the "host of heaven" (vs. 10) • exalts to the "Prince of the host" (vs. 11)

Event/Feature	Daniel 7	Daniel 8
The attitude of the "little horn" power toward Christ	• pompous attitude (vss. 8, 20, 25) • intends to change times and law—divine law (vs. 25)	• exalted itself against Christ (vss. 11, 25) • salvation, or the "daily" ministry of Christ obscured (vss. 11, 12; cf. Heb. 8, 9) • cast truth of God to the ground (vs. 12)
Sanctuary issues are the focus of the little horn's activities	• God's answer to the pompous words and destructive ways of the little horn is provided; warning given in the context of the judgment in the heavenly sanctuary and the giving of rewards (vss. 9, 10, 13, 14). The inference is that the little horn is willfully ignorant or opposed to these happenings, and God will destroy it (vss. 11, 26); this reminds the reader of the destructive fire that quelled a rebellion associated with the earthly sanctuary (Num. 11:1, 2)	• allusions to the sanctuary are made throughout the chapter; there are: sanctuary animals—a ram and a goat (vss. 3–5); "holy one[s]," which remind of the cherubim (vs. 13); four horns, which remind of altar imagery (vs. 8; cf. Exod. 27:2) • the sanctuary and the truths surrounding it are attacked (vss. 11, 12)

Event/Feature	Daniel 7	Daniel 8
View of Christ's activities in heaven (phase 1 of the judgment in the sanctuary)	• phase 1 of judgment activities highlighted (vss. 9, 10, 13, 14) • appears to vindicate the saints (vss. 18, 22)	• the cleansing and vindication of the sanctuary (vss. 13, 14) • "How long?" This question often refers to judgment and vindication of the saints (cf. Ps. 6; 13:1, 2; 35; 89; 94:3; Hab. 1:2–4; Zech. 1:12; Rev. 6:9–11) • the truth that is cast to the ground will be restored (vs. 14; cf. Rev. 14:6–12; 18:1)
Time after which amends is expected	• after the court is seated (vss. 25–27)	• not until after "two thousand three hundred days ["evenings-mornings"]" have transpired, (Dan. 8:14); these are *sanctuary* days (cf. Exod. 27:20, 21, which speaks of evenings and mornings) • "time of the end" (Dan. 8:17) • "many days *in the future*" (vs. 26)

Event/Feature	Daniel 7	Daniel 8
The nature of amends (phase 2 of the judgment)	• phase 2 of judgment: "little horn" power is destroyed (vss. 11, 26) • dominion of powers is taken away (vs. 12) • the saints possess the kingdom (vss. 18, 22)	• fierce king is broken (vs. 23, 25)
The nature of God's kingdom	Everlasting (vss. 14, 27)	not dependent upon human power (vs. 25)

Events in the Earthly Sanctuary and Temple. There are several prominent aspects of the ancient Day of Atonement that we should note. The services involved first the people, then the high priest, and finally the accumulated record of confessed sins.

The aspect of the service that involved the people was the regular morning service, which was offered continually (Exod. 29:38–42; Num. 28:3–10). This, in effect, meant that even on the morning of the Day of Atonement there was assurance of forgiveness of sins for any who might at this late stage be impressed concerning some unwholesome act not yet put right.

Another significant feature of the service involved the high priest who offered the sacrifice seeking atonement for himself and his household before presenting the offering for all the people (Lev. 16:6, 11–14). In both this and the succeeding ceremony, the high priest offered incense and sprinkled blood in the Most Holy Place (verses 12–15). In offering incense, some see prefigured the strong emotions expressed by Christ in Gethsemane (Luke 22:44; Heb. 5:7).

Finally, the high priest carried out a ceremony involving two goats. The Lord's goat was offered as a sin offering (Lev. 16:9). The blood of the Lord's goat satisfied the claims of the law with regard to the confessed sins of the people that had accumulated in the sanctuary throughout the year. Atonement was thus made for the sanctuary. In other words, it was declared free from sin. Although individuals had confessed their sins throughout the year and had been forgiven, the record of these sins still remained in the sanctuary. When this record was removed symbolically, reconciliation was complete (Lev. 16:20).

This ceremony took place in the Most Holy Place before the ark of the covenant, and it represented the high point of the day's services.

The final aspect of this ceremony involved Azazel's goat. (A more thorough exposition on this goat is found in Chapters 20 and 21.) The high priest, who represented Christ our Mediator, now left the Most Holy Place, bearing the confessed and forgiven sins and placing them on the head of the live goat, which represented the supernatural, antagonistic power arrayed against God (Lev. 16:21). This was the high priest's last act in the sanctuary. Satan was thus symbolized as bearing the ultimate penalty for the confessed sins of the righteous, for he is the agent who tempted them. The high priest represented Christ. The goat that received the accumulated sins from the hands of the high priest did not. It was taken away from the tabernacle to the wilderness, showing that it represented someone other than Christ. The blood of this goat was not shed, which reaffirms the conclusion that this goat was not connected with the forgiveness of sins (Lev. 17:11).

The central purpose of the ceremonies was to assure the worshipers that the blood of Christ completely covers the confessed sins of those who previously had availed themselves of the means of forgiveness. The worshipers were declared "clean from all [their] sins before the LORD" (Lev. 16:30). To the Jews, the Day of Atonement was a day when forgiveness was "granted to all who repent fully."[317] It was characterized by prayers of confession, a practice that has come from ancient times.[318] God, through these ceremonies, declared that the repentant sinner was safe in His love and forever protected from the accusations of Satan. The day was meant to be a time of assurance and quiet joy (Ps. 48:11). The Judge's intention was to justify, save, deliver, and vindicate.[319]

Events in Heaven. The services on the Day of Atonement were centered about the ark of the covenant (Lev. 16:13–15), as it symbolized matters of mercy and justice. The ark was absent from the second temple, which was built about 500 years before Christ according to historical records (2 Mac. 2:4–6, Apocrypha).[320] The temple was destroyed in AD 70. Therefore, Daniel's prophecy directs our attention to the heavenly sanctuary where the ark of His covenant is located (Rev. 11:18, 19). This is the only sanctuary that really counts, for it is the "true tabernacle" (Heb. 8:2). It is important to notice that Christ's ministry in the Most Holy Place of the heavenly sanctuary will finish before the execution of judgment, the distribution of rewards, and the destruction of the wicked takes place (Dan. 12:1–3; 1 Thess. 4:14–17; Rev. 20:7–9).

The Scriptures speak clearly regarding the purification of the sanctuary in heaven. The apostle Paul affirmed that it is necessary that the sanctuary in heaven "should be purified" with the blood of Christ, just as the individual believer needed cleansing (Heb. 9:23, 14).[321] Just as in the earthly sanctuary the confessed sins of the people were transferred to the sanctuary, so the confessed sins of God's professed people are transferred to the record books in the heavenly sanctuary. The records of the lives of all people are held in heaven (Dan. 7:10; Rev. 20:12). In case any should object that God's holy heaven cannot symbolically bear the stain of sin, we should remember that Christ became sin for us without destroying His holiness (2 Cor. 5:21; Heb. 9:28). Again, heaven is the place where the rebellion of Lucifer and his followers commenced (Rev. 12:7–9).

On the antitypical day of atonement that commenced in 1844, Christ our High Priest began the second phase of His ministry in the heavenly sanctuary. The apostle Paul makes it abundantly clear that the sanctuary and its services on earth have their counterparts in heaven (Heb. 9:21, 23, 24). During the year, mediatorial services took place in the Holy Place. At the end of the year, judicial services were conducted in the Most Holy Place. The activity in the two apartments and their sequential usage is also a feature of Christ's ministration in heaven.

For ease of conceptualization of the divine plan, some have pictured Christ as moving from one apartment to another and closing the door to the first apartment and then opening the one to the Most Holy Place to indicate the certainty of the change in the balance of Christ's activities.[322] Others dismiss this representation because they contend that there is no heavenly sanctuary with doors, disregarding the two-apartment symbolism of Old Testament sanctuary. Yet, using doors to conceptualize Christ's change in ministerial focus has a biblical foundation in Revelation 3:7, 8 (see also Rev. 4:1; 11:19). Here the apostle John saw Jesus with a key opening and shutting doors, which no earthly power or individual had the ability to interfere with. At the time of change in Christ's ministerial responsibilities in heaven when the Most Holy Place became the focus of attention, the ark of the covenant and the Sabbath truth were shown in all their brilliance.[323] At this same time, the meaning of the mark of the beast and the seal of God became clear. All this happened in the context of understanding the three angels' messages, which is a sanctuary-based concept.[324] The door to all these understandings was never to be closed!

Jesus did not cease His intercession ministry for people on earth in 1844. Just as in the earthly sanctuary on the Day of Atonement, provision was made for sinners to be justified by faith in the shed blood, so today Christ forgives sins. Also on that day, work was being done preparatory to the execution of decisions already made with the fulfillment of the event still future. Those who had not taken seriously the preceding ten days, holding God in contempt, had made their decision, and God accepted it. The ultimate villain, Satan, was identified on judgment day and held responsible in the ceremony represented by the Azazel goat (Lev. 16:21, 22; 23:29, 30).

Witness on Earth. A most remarkable religious revival occurred during the early part of the nineteenth century. Ministers and parishioners of many religious persuasions began preaching, based on their study, that some significant event was about to transpire on earth. We should remember that the remarkable phenomenon of the falling of the stars in 1833, which directed many people's attention to God, helped focus attention on God's Word. The cleansing of the sanctuary was the focus of their preaching, and it was generally believed that the year 1844 would be marked by the return of Christ to this earth, for it was generally believed that the sanctuary represented the earth. The message of Christ's soon return swept throughout many countries with preachers from all major denominations participating. Indeed, in the Scandinavian countries, child preachers, aged six to their teens, participated in this remarkable phenomenon in fulfillment of the prophecy of Joel 2. When asked the reason for their unusual activities, these children quoted Joel 2:28, 29 and Revelation 14:7. As the time anticipated drew near, the message that the hour of God's judgment had begun was brought before the people. With the passing of the time for Christ to have returned, a large number of people relinquished their faith or slipped into lukewarmness. Others, believing that the incredible events could not have been directed other than by God, restudied the subject of the sanctuary and realized that it referred to the cleansing of the sanctuary in heaven rather than the cleansing of the earth by fire. Christ was entering the final phase of His heavenly ministry before returning to this earth—the pre-advent judgment had begun![325]

Christ Stands Up. Just as in the earthly Day of Atonement the high priest made an end to reconciling or the making of atonement (Lev. 16:20), so in the heavenly sanctuary our Intercessor will one day stand up and declare that time is finished (Dan. 12:1). Then the door of probation will be closed forever. The rewards of all will have been decided. Jesus will then declare: "He who is unjust, let him be unjust still; he who is filthy, let him be filthy still; he who is righteous, let him be righteous still; he who is holy, let him be holy still" (Rev. 22:11). The only work that remains will be to place all confessed sins on the head of Satan, for he must accept the responsibility for placing temptation in the pathway of believers, and to send him into the "land of separation," which is eternal oblivion (Lev. 16:22, YLT; Rev. 20:10).

We note that the sin question in the world will be forever resolved before Christ finishes His ministry in the Most Holy Place of the heavenly sanctuary. Those who are righteous will be declared righteous for all eternity, and those who have rejected God's mercy and justice will be forever lost. For us, living on the borders of eternity, it is important to examine our relationship with God (Isa. 58) and to live by faith continually (Hab. 2:4). God will be sanctified in His people before the world (Rev. 14:12; cf. Ezek. 20:41; 28:25; 36:23; 39:27, 28). Let us each choose to allow God to do His marvelous work in us.

Chapter 20.
The Sanctuary and the Judgment

Chapter Emphasis: *The central theme of the pre-advent judgment is to give assurance of salvation to repentant sinners. Justification and judgment are not contradictory concepts. The judgment is part of the reconciliation process that functions to highlight the significance of the standard used, the Ten Commandments, and it represents a declaration of the ultimate triumph of good over evil. In saying this, the judgment is a declaration that the Creation and salvation were not mistakes. All the created intelligences of the universe are convinced by this process that God is both merciful and just.*

Spiritual Link: *The judgment functions to urge a close relationship between the Savior and His disciples.*

Though few of us have been involved in any aspect of the legal system, the idea of judgment immediately brings a number of things into sharp focus: the law—or standard—against which we are being assessed, the judge, and the options that are open to those who will deliver the sentence. Just as the standard accepted by society must be upheld in worldly courts, so must God's standard of heavenly justice and morality be upheld in the courts of heaven. In the drama transpiring on this earth, we are the agents who must one day give an account of how we have handled the privileges that have come our way of learning about God and sharing this knowledge with others. Those who have not responded positively to God's offer of salvation already have declared judgment on themselves. God will honor their choice.

As introduced in Chapter 19, the Day of Atonement was regarded by the Jewish people as a day of judgment, a day when all were to give careful attention to their standing before God.[326] The Bible speaks a great deal about the judgment, and this is the subject that I will investigate particularly here. Almost immediately following the solemn Day of Atonement anciently, the Feast of Tabernacles was commemorated as the last feast in the yearly round of religious services. This was a feast of rejoicing that all harvests had been gathered, that the yearly work had been completed, and that the worshipers were accepted by God. The feast pointed forward to the coming of the Lord of heaven to gather the harvest of the earth and then create a new earth. It pointed to the consummation of all things. Hence, it is evident that the commencement of the antitypical day of atonement in 1844 focuses our attention with riveting gaze on the most wonderful event of the ages—the coming of King Jesus in glory. Indeed, this event must soon come to pass.

Reconciliation

In this section, I will

- *identify the basic elements of God's ministry of reconciliation for the world—the sacrificial, mediatorial and judicial activities of Jesus Christ;*

- *remind readers that the central purpose of the earthly Day of Atonement ceremonies involved assurance of salvation to the repentant sinner and a declaration of the ultimate triumph of good over evil;*

- *impress upon the reader that "today" is the day of opportunity and decision.*

We already dealt with some aspects of Christ's end-time activities in Chapters 18 and 19. The word "reconciliation," or "at-onement," means "to bring (a person) back to, into peace, favor, etc.," "to restore," "to purify," or "to absolve or cleanse." In its broadest sense, "to reconcile" can mean "to reunite (persons or things) in harmony."[327] It is in this sense that the term is used here. "The atonement is descriptive of a work performed by Jesus Christ, first as a sacrificial victim on earth, then as High Priest in heaven, for the purpose of bringing the sinner into absolute harmony or one-ness with God."[328] When sin and sinners are finally destroyed, "one pulse of harmony and gladness" will beat "through the vast creation."[329]

During the preliminary service of the Day of Atonement, the high priest wore special garments including the "breastplate of judgment" (Exod. 28:15). In the Old Testament, it is clearly taught that the sanctuary was the place where judgment originated. Favorable judgments were made in the close vicinity of the tabernacle (Num. 11:16–30; 27:1–11) as well as unfavorable ones (Num. 16:50). The negative aspects of the judgment theme can be observed at several levels in the activities on this day. First, those refusing to claim the benefits offered were "cut off" from the camp (Lev. 23:29, 30). Second, Azazel's goat was sent into a "land cut off," or the wilderness (Lev. 16:21, 22, AMPC).

When the high priest finally came out of the earthly sanctuary, reconciliation was no longer possible (Lev. 16:20; cf. Lev. 23:29, 30). This impressed upon the Israelites the truth that "today" is the day of salvation (Heb. 3:13; 4:7) and that God will not always contend with the unrighteous (Gen. 6:3). He will make an utter end to sin and to sinners who persist in sin (Nah. 1:8, 9; Rev. 22:11).

Atonement Finished at the Cross? Christ's death on Calvary was all sufficient and effective "for the whole world" (1 John 2:2; cf. Rom. 5:18). No other sacrifice is necessary, for it was not only full and complete but also accepted by the Father (Heb. 10:10). Thus, repentant sinners, however vile, are justified as they come in genuine faith to the Redeemer (Rom. 3:26). *Sacrificial atonement* is the aspect of the atonement accomplished for us by Christ as the sacrificial victim. The Scriptures inform us that no atonement is possible without the shedding of blood (Lev. 17:11).

Christ's act of reconciliation becomes effective in us by accepting His offer—"whoever desires, let him take the water of life freely" (Rev. 22:17) and then by walking in the light (1 John 1:7). Until the Lord lays down His priestly ministry in the heavenly sanctuary, He reaches out to save men and women. Christ died on the cross and provided the means by which all could be saved. However, to be saved, individuals must repent and turn to God and walk daily by faith in the power that He is able to give, demonstrating that justification and sanctification are necessary. The benefits of the atoning sacrifice are thus appropriated to repentant individuals. Paul informs us: "Having been reconciled, we shall be saved by His life" (Rom. 5:10). Christ thus ministers the benefits of the blood of His sacrifice on behalf of the believer. The benefits are not ministered to all, but just to those who accept His salvation (John 5:40). This is the aspect of the atonement carried out in us through Christ's ministration as High Priest in heaven today. God wishes to deliver us from the guilt and from the power of sin so that the benefits of reconciliation can be ours. He is pleading His blood on behalf of sinners before the Father, *intercessory atonement* with *mediatorial* and *judicial* phases (Heb. 4:16; Rev. 3:5). The confessed sins of the saints finally are being blotted from the books of record. "As the priests in the earthly Sanctuary entered the Most Holy once a year to cleanse the Sanctuary, Jesus entered the Most Holy of the heavenly, at the end of the 2300 days of Dan. viii, in 1844, to make a final atonement for all who could be benefited by His mediation, and to cleanse the Sanctuary."[330]

At the second coming of the Lord, our bodies will be glorified, and we will "put on incorruption" (1 Cor. 15:53). The righteous will be delivered from the presence of sin. The next act will be to remove Satan and sinners, thereby establishing harmony in the universe.

Blotting Out of Sin and the Judgment

In this section, I will

- *focus on the judicial aspects of reconciliation brought to view by the Day of Atonement activities in the earthly sanctuary;*

- *emphasize that there is a counterpart to the blotting out of pardoned sins in the heavenly sanctuary and that the first phase of the judgment takes place before Christ's second coming;*

- *emphasize that, while we are in Christ, we are not under condemnation.*

On the Day of Atonement, the destinies of the people were determined (Lev. 23:28–30). This was the time in the year that the high priest made final intercession for those who had shown sorrow for their sins and identified themselves with the people of God. These earthly activities have a counterpart in the heavenly sanctuary. There the destiny of both the righteous and the wicked are irreversibly determined before the second coming of the Lord. The judgment follows the pattern of earthly courts where investigation precedes the issuing of sentence. Indeed, Christ clearly states that He will come with His reward (Rev. 22:12).

Assurance in Judgment. The services on the Day of Atonement gave assurance of salvation. The record of pardoned sins was transferred symbolically to the sanctuary on specified occasions. The priest either took the blood of the sacrificial victim and made an atonement by sprinkling the blood before the Lord, or he ate a portion of the meat, thereby signifying that he bore the sin in the place of the sinner (Lev. 4:6, 7, 17, 18; 6:30; 7:1–6; 10:17, 18). Nonetheless, the record of these pardoned sins remained in the sanctuary until the Day of Atonement, or Reconciliation (Lev. 16:21). This record was in reality a record of the instances the believer exercised faith in Christ's forgiveness and received pardon, with Christ's acceptance of the act of faith placed in their record (Rom. 3:24; 1 John 1:9). The judgment was when the records of confessed sins of the righteous were blotted out of existence symbolized by their removal from the sanctuary.[331] Thus, believers were assured of God's faithfulness, knowing that their confessed sins were safe in God's care (Exod. 34:6, 7).

Sins Blotted Out. The Bible speaks of names being blotted out from the book of life (Exod. 32:33; Rev. 22:19). The earthly sanctuary teaches us that pardoned sins are blotted out in the judgment (Lev. 16:16, 21) and the names of the faithful are retained in the book of life (Rev. 3:5). This is perhaps what the physician Luke had in mind when he wrote about conversion, the blotting out of sins, and the times of refreshing to come from the Lord before the Lord's return. Significantly, he placed the blotting out of sin chronologically in proximity to the latter rain and the coming of the Lord (Acts 3:19, 20).

The books of record are mentioned frequently in Scripture. These books contain the records of the deeds and attitudes of men and women. The books are opened for inspection by the heavenly authorities, which include the angels (Dan. 7:9, 10). Hence, the records represent more than the memory of God. The blotting out or the retention of names in the book of life is on the basis of the life record contained therein. The question asked is: What do you think of Christ? Have you sought Him for understanding and pardon and to obtain victory over every sin? (cf. Ezek. 18:24; Rev. 21:27). If the answer is in the affirma-

Chapter 20. The Sanctuary and the Judgment

tive, your name will be retained; if it is in the negative, your name will be removed (Rev. 21:27). Christ our High Priest represents the merits of His blood on behalf of repentant sinners. Either our pardoned sins will be blotted out in the judgment or our name will be expunged from the book of life (1 Tim. 5:24, 25; refer to the Exhibit 20.1). To summarize the cleansing of the heavenly sanctuary: "... the sins of all the truly penitent will be blotted from the books of heaven. Thus the sanctuary will be freed, or cleansed, from the record of sin. In the type, this great work of atonement, or blotting out of sins, was represented by the services of the Day of Atonement."[332]

The apostle Paul reasoned with Felix of "the judgment to come," that is, at some time in the future (Acts 24:25). Later, he indicated that this day would come after a period of fearful apostasy (2 Thess. 2:3). Thus, the time of its taking place would be in the distant future (Acts 3:19–21).

Professed Believers Examined. Those who have made a profession of faith in Christ have their names recorded in the book of life. It is not surprising then that judgment commences with those who profess to belong to God's church (1 Peter 4:17). The reality is that the pre-advent judgment considers the living and the dead whose names have been entered into the book of life (Phil. 4:3; Heb. 12:23). They have professed themselves God's children or have shown a willingness to be drawn in obedience to the light that has been given through the agency of the Holy Spirit (Rom. 2:13–15).[333]

The Bible indicates that the pardoned sins of the righteous are still on record, yet with the pardon of God written against them (Ps. 32:1, 2; Matt. 10:26; 1 John 1:9).[334] We are assured that our sins are forgiven, or "covered" (Ps. 32:1). One of the basic meanings of the Hebrew word used here that is translated "covered" is to "conceal." Confessed sin is covered sin (Ps. 85:2; Rom. 4:7). In other words, our confessed sins are concealed by the merits of Christ's blood (Col. 3:3).

The Scriptures clearly inform us that every work and thought will be considered in the judgment "whether *it is* good or whether *it is* evil" (Eccles. 12:14). This implies that a complete record is available. When the Scripture records that pardoned sins are to be remembered no more or that they are cast into the depths of the sea and removed as far as the east is from the west (Mic. 7:19; Ps. 103:12; Jer. 31:34), it does not imply that no record of pardoned sin is kept. These phrases are rather strong statements expressing the abundance of the pardon offered. Our sins are said also to be behind God's back (Isa. 38:17). We cannot logically hold that sins can be held behind God's back while, at the same time, being separated as far as the east is from the west. These are simply forms of expression that give us assurance that while we are in Christ we are not under condemnation (Rom. 8:1). Those who have chosen not to accept Jesus Christ are condemned already (John 3:18; Heb. 3:18–4:2).

At the second coming, Christ brings His rewards with Him, that is, the verdict of the pre-advent judgment is made evident. The saints will receive their reward (Matt. 16:27; 1 Thess. 4:13–17). However, the final execution of judgment upon Satan and his followers takes place after the millennium (Rev. 20:8–15).

Justification and Judgment not Contradictory. The work of the judgment does not contradict the concept of justification. The idea of a person living by faith without exhibiting the associated "good works" of Christ exceeds credibility (Eph. 2:10).[335] The apostle James clearly stated that faith without works is an indication that genuine faith does not exist (James 2:14–17). Paul declared that those saved by grace are "created in Christ Jesus for good works," as God had planned beforehand that they "should walk in them" (Eph. 2:8–10). Thus, it should not be surprising that people's faith will be judged by the deeds observed in their life (Gal. 6:7).

When we confess our sins, God's forgiveness is complete and our guilt is removed (Rom. 3:19–26; Heb. 10:22; 1 John 1:9). This truth has been clearly stated in the following words: "All who have truly repented of sin, and by faith claimed the blood of Christ as their atoning sacrifice, have had pardon entered against their names in the books of heaven; as they have become partakers of the righteousness of Christ, and their characters are found to be in harmony with the law of God, their sins will be blotted out, and they themselves will be accounted worthy of eternal life...."[336] If we subsequently reject the Savior, we then take full responsibility for our own sins (Ezek. 18:24–26; Matt. 18:32–34; Heb. 10:23).

The Heavenly Judgment Scene and the Standard Used in the Judgment

Chapter 20. The Sanctuary and the Judgment

In this section, I will

- *outline details of the pre-advent judgment revealed in Scripture;*

- *indicate that the standard used in the judgment is God's law—a transcript of His character, asking the most significant question: "What have you done with Christ?"*

Salvation is a heaven-inspired task that involves all of its inhabitants. The awesome account in Daniel, chapter 7, makes this clear.

Heaven Involved in Judgment. Jesus Christ, the Son of Man, is associated with the Father in the pre-advent judgment (Dan. 7:9, 10, 13; Rev. 3:5). In His high priestly role, Christ is our Mediator before the Father (1 Tim. 2:5; Heb. 7:25; 1 John 2:1). In other words, Christ makes final representation, or atonement, before God the Father on behalf of those who genuinely exercise faith in Him (Matt. 10:32). We read this apt summary: "The divine Intercessor presents the plea that all who have overcome through faith in His blood be forgiven their transgressions, that they be restored to their Eden home, and crowned as joint heirs with Himself to 'the first dominion.' Micah 4:8."[337]

The role of our divine Intercessor is presented powerfully in the story of Joshua and the Angel (Zech. 3:1–5).[338] The Angel represents Christ (Hosea 12:2–5; cf. Gen. 32:30; John 1:18). Christ our High Priest is our Mediator just as the high priest in the earthly sanctuary was the mediator (Heb. 8:6). Christ speaks out on behalf of Christians who abide in Him; He "confesses" them before the Father in heaven (Rev. 3:5). Those who deny Him, Christ cannot represent (Matt. 10:32, 33). We might say that Jesus, who is the *deciding* judge (John 5:22), pleads His blood on our behalf before the Father (Dan. 7:9, 10), who is the *presiding* judge.[339] This intercessory role continues until He puts off His priestly robes. This does not in the least imply that the Father is against the believer (John 16:26, 27). The Holy Spirit is involved in the judgment in that He expresses the heartfelt feelings of the individual to God (Rom. 8:26). All heaven is involved in our salvation. Justice is done and that justice is on display.

Standard Used in the Pre-advent Judgment. Since the judgment is focused on re-establishing harmony, it should not be surprising that the law of liberty is the standard used (Eccles. 12:13, 14; James 2:12). The law of God points us to the pathway of liberty, for it directs us to the Savior who gave the law. The main aspects of the services on the Day of Atonement anciently, which was a day of judgment, were carried out in the Most Holy Place before the ark of the covenant, which held the tablets of the law (Exod. 25:16; 31:18; Lev. 16:12–14). Obedience to God's revealed will is the criterion used in the judgment (John 14:15; Heb. 5:9). This is reasonable in that the "law of liberty" is a transcript of God's character. It shows clearly the imperfections in our character in just the same way that a mirror shows the true state of the person who looks into it (James 1:22–25).

The good news is that God has provided, in all ages, strength to enable victory over sin. The principles of His kingdom are just, for He provides the means by which these principles may be obeyed (Hab. 2:4; Rom. 4:13; 1 Cor. 10:13). Freed from sin's stranglehold through faith, the believer gains the highest liberty.

The Purpose of the Judgment

In this section, I will

- *emphasize that the pre-advent judgment in heaven coincides with God's last great call to the people of this earth to accept salvation;*

- *outline the functions of the pre-advent judgment for the inhabitants of this universe.*

The Scripture records, "The Lord knows those who are His" (2 Tim. 2:19). Hence, some have questioned whether there is a need for a judgment. God knows the secrets of the mind and understands the course that a person's life will take (Ps. 44:21; 94:11). As an example, we might cite His knowledge of Cyrus. One and a half centuries before Cyrus was born, the Bible spoke of his deeds (Isa. 44:28; 45:1–3). With such foreknowledge, it becomes evident that it is not God who needs the judgment to decide who are His servants (cf. 1 Peter 1:2). The judgment is for the benefit of God's intelligent created beings (1 Peter 1:12; 1 Cor. 4:9; Rev. 3:5). Nevertheless, the Bible speaks of a judgment of investigation near the close of earth's history. Indeed, we find that the Scriptures record that God investigates before passing sentence, even though He knows every detail of the case already (e.g., Gen. 3:8–19; 11:5; 18:21). This pattern was first established in Eden, and it is illustrated on a number of occasions in the Scriptures. An extensively documented example was the wickedness of Sodom and Gomorrah. This was well known to the Lord, yet he personally

Chapter 20. The Sanctuary and the Judgment

investigated and dialogued with Abraham about His intended dealings with the cities (Gen. 18:16–33). By God's investigation, Abraham understood that God's dealings were fair and just. This experience is recorded for our benefit, so that we may more fully appreciate the nature of the pre-advent judgment taking place today.

The judgment is associated with the worldwide proclamation of the everlasting gospel in its fullness (Rev. 14:6, 7). The "dominion," or "control," of the powers who are allied against God's people will be broken by the clear and certain truths of God's words in the period of God's judgment. The great, rousing call that is to echo throughout the earth is based on the definite teachings of Scripture. The cry is: "Come out of her [that is, out of Babylon], my people, lest you share in her sins, and lest you receive of her plagues" (Rev. 18:4).

The functions of the pre-advent judgment are several. Firstly, the announcement that the judgment has commenced is also an announcement that Christ is coming, and that those who would welcome Him in peace have a work to complete in God's vineyard (Rev. 14:7, 14–16). The parable of the ten virgins also instructs us that the work that the individual must accomplish before the bridegroom returns is to develop a close relationship with God (Matt. 25:1–10). In the parable of the marriage supper, an examination of the guests was held before the supper to determine who was fit to participate. Those wearing the robe (Matt. 22:1–13) of Christ's righteousness were accepted. Christ's "goal during this first phase of the judgment is to bring people into the unity, the one-ness, the at-one-ment, that Jesus prayed for on the way to the Cross."[340] (See John 17:20–22.) The necessity of this unity is apparent when we consider the trying experiences that those who live in the time of the judgment must go through (Rev. 7:13–15; 13:14–17). The work of purifying the life was taught in the earthly sanctuary (Lev. 16:30). A similar work is required today in the antitypical day of atonement.

Secondly, the judgment functions to give to the world and to the assembled universe the clearest demonstration that the commandments of God were not abolished at the cross and that the precepts of the law may be kept through faith (Rev. 14:12). At the cross, Satan was defeated and God was vindicated by the marvelous display of the inseparable nature of God's mercy and justice (John 12:31–33).[341] Satan now tempts people everywhere to believe that the law, or a portion of it, was abolished at the cross. However, when the end-time death decree is pronounced on those who believe fully in the merits of Christ, Jesus will be able to present to the world and to the universe a people who faithfully represent His character (Rev. 13:15–17; 14:4, 5, 12).[342]

God will be vindicated through His people in the same manner in which He was vindicated anciently through Elijah (1 Kings 18). Ezekiel actually records God's thoughts, which run along these lines: "And I will vindicate the holiness of my great name, which has been profaned among the nations, and which you have profaned among them; and the nations will know that I am the LORD, says the Lord GOD, when *through you I vindicate my holiness* before their eyes" (Ezek. 36:23, 24, RSV, emphasis added). The prophet then goes on to explain how this vindication would occur. "I will cleanse you. A new heart I will give you, and a new spirit I will put within you; and I will take out of your flesh the heart of stone and give you a heart of flesh. And I will put my spirit within you, and cause you to walk in my statutes and be careful to observe my ordinances" (Ezek. 36:25–27, RSV). Another way of saying this is: "God will have a clean people on earth who, because they have allowed God to cleanse them from their sin, bring honor and glory to Him. Simultaneously, God is also glorified in heaven when the sanctuary is cleansed of sin during the judgment."[343]

The judgment shows all the hosts of heaven that God is just. The question, "Shall not the Judge of all the earth do right?" (Gen. 18:25), is answered in the affirmative. The judgment has cosmic dimensions in that the events happening on earth are connected with those happening in heaven. The restoration, or cleansing, of the heavenly sanctuary is a reversal of the attacks of the "little horn" power of Daniel 8. The assembled intelligences of the other worlds are watching with intense interest the affairs of humanity (1 Cor. 4:9). God is showing the truthfulness of His ways to the universe (Rom. 3:4; Phil. 2:10, 11; Rev. 19:2, 11). The eternal security of the universe is dependent upon its inhabitants' recognizing that God is what He claims to be (Rev. 15:3, 4).[344] Indeed, "God's judgment ... restores the rule of right in the universe."[345]

Finally, the judgment is a statement of triumph and an announcement that Creation and redemption were not mistakes (Rev. 16:7). The judgment will deliver a sentence in favor of those who have sacrificed all for their Master, and it will deliver a sentence against the "little horn" power and those who supported it (Dan. 7:22, 26). The announcement that the judgment has come (Rev. 14:7) is a statement that the triumph of the saints is about to be realized.

Chapter 20. The Sanctuary and the Judgment   301

The judgment is good news for the believer who fully accepts Christ (Ps. 7:8–11; 26:1–7).

The Judgment: A Time to Rejoice

In this section, I will

- *emphasize that the pre-advent judgment in heaven is a time for the saints to rejoice in the salvation that God is urgently wishing to give to them.*

The judgment has positive implications for God's devoted followers. It is a time of salvation and triumph, for God assures the saints that He is favorable toward them (Dan. 7:22). At the same time, the Judge accepts the uncooperative attitude of those opposed to His rule and words. The inevitable result is acceptance of their own self-condemnation, which is against God's fervent desire for them (Ps. 102:20; 2 Peter 3:9).

The prophet Isaiah mentions both the joyful and condemnatory aspects of judgment. His encouraging words to God's friends are: "Say to those with fearful hearts, 'Be strong, do not fear; your God will come, he will come with vengeance; with divine retribution he will come to save you' " (Isa. 35:4, NIV). Such a message is repeated in Isaiah 61:1, 2. And it is significant that Christ's first sermon focused on elements from this passage (Luke 4:18, 19).

The Jewish people regarded the Day of Atonement as a time of awe as God was judging them. At the same time, they considered it an opportunity for the expression of joy in an atonement carried to completion by a merciful God.[346] Hence, we can begin to understand the psalmist's words: "Let the heavens rejoice, and let the earth be glad; ... for He is coming, for He is coming to judge the earth" (Ps. 96:11, 13). And again, "Oh, sing to the LORD a new song! ... For He is coming to judge the earth. With righteousness He shall judge the world, and the peoples with equity" (Ps. 98:1, 9).

Not all aspects of God's dealings with sin could be symbolized in the sanctuary service. We notice that no symbolic activity transpired in the earthly sanctuary to convey the idea that the confessed sins of former believers returned on their own heads. Neither was there any symbolism to represent how God dealt with sins that were confessed, but not forsaken. Yet, in both instances, the Scriptures elsewhere clearly indicate how God deals with such cases. We refer the reader to the following texts: Matthew 18:32–34, which says that confessed sins return to those who turn from God; 1 Samuel 15:22; Isaiah 1:11–15; Jeremiah 6:20; Micah 6:6–8; Matthew 5:24; and Luke 18:11–14, which say that the sacrifices of those who are not genuinely repentant are not forgiven; Hosea 8:13; Matthew 27:3–5; and Hebrews 12:16, 17, which say that confessed but unforsaken sins are not forgiven.

Exhibit 20.1. How God deals with sin.

The earthly sanctuary gives us a clear understanding concerning God's program of dealing with sin. The entrance of sin into the universe brought guilt (Gen. 3:8; Rom. 3:19, 20). God provided a means whereby men and women might be delivered from condemnation and the human race might be saved. Not only was salvation offered to the human race, but the entire universe was to be protected against sin arising a second time (Nah. 1:9). It is important to note at the outset that, in the Scriptures, the forgiveness of sin is not regarded as synonymous with the blotting out of sin (Neh. 4:5; Jer. 18:23). Let us follow the steps in God's plan.

1. *Condemnation is removed from the sinner at confession.* When the sinner laid his hand on the sacrificial victim in the old covenant dispensation, it signified that the weight of sin was transferred to the sin-bearer (Lev. 4), which, in turn, symbolized total dependence on Christ (Isa. 53:4, 5). By the act of confession, the sinner was covered, washed, cleansed, and justified. It is the same today. The penitent believer is freed from an evil conscience (Heb. 10:22). Assurance takes the place of guilt so that condemnation ceases (Matt. 11:28; Rom. 8:1).

2. *Transference of the record of confessed sins to the sanctuary.* In the earthly sanctuary, atonement for sin involved the priest's either taking the blood of the sacrificial victim and sprinkling it in the Holy Place or his eating a portion of the flesh in a holy place. By this faith transaction, the records of the penitent's confessed sins and the record of Christ's forgiving acts were left on the horns of the altar of incense before the veil (e.g., Lev. 4:6, 7, 18). Elsewhere the Scriptures speak of the deeds, thoughts, and words of all people being available

to God in the judgment (Eccles. 12:13, 14; Matt. 12:36, 37; Rom. 2:6; 1 Cor. 4:5; 2 Cor. 5:10). The confessed sins of the righteous are described as going beforehand to judgment (1 Tim. 5:24). In fact, nothing can be hidden (Luke 12:2), including the sins covered by Christ's merits (Ps. 32:1, 2; Matt. 10:26). Those who do not follow Christ to the end must bear the penalty of all their sins, for they have now denied the basis on which their sins were forgiven, that is, faith in Christ (Ezek. 18:21–24; Matt. 18:32–34).

3. *The Record of confessed sins removed from the sanctuary.* On the Day of Atonement, the sanctuary was cleansed and confessed sins were blotted out. The Lord's goat had no sin confessed over it; its blood was sprinkled in front of and upon the mercy seat in the Most Holy Place, signifying that the merits of Christ's sacrifice fully satisfied the law of God, the tables of which rested below the mercy seat (Lev. 16:15). Through this ceremony, final atonement was made for the confessed sins of the people and for sins that they had committed ignorantly (Lev. 16:16, 20, 33; Heb. 9:7). The record of confessed sins of those accepted by the Lord now ceased to exist, for mercy and justice were satisfied (Ps. 85:9, 10; in these verses the word "righteousness" may be translated "justice"). The cleansing of the heavenly sanctuary is referenced in Daniel 8:14. The physician Luke associated the final events occurring in this antitypical day of atonement, which include the blotting out of confessed sins, with the coming of the Lord (Acts 3:19, 20).

4. *Responsibility for sin placed upon Satan.* In the old covenant dispensation, on the Day of Atonement, the last act in the drama of salvation was to place the confessed sins of the people on the head of the Azazel goat, which represented Satan. The goat was led into the wilderness to perish there. The blood of this goat was not shed, therefore it did not serve as a savior (cf. Lev. 17:11). The symbolism of the sanctuary service represented the sins that Satan had led the people to commit being placed on his account, thereby re-establishing harmony between heaven and earth, or a state of being "at one" (Lev. 16:7–10). As the originator of sin and the tempter (John 8:44; 1 John 3:8), he has a responsibility to bear for

> his part in causing sin (Zech. 3:1–4; cf. Ps. 7:16). The Scriptures represent Satan as perishing at the end of the reign of sin (Ezek. 28:18; Rev. 20:10). This event has yet to take place. At no stage does Satan shed blood, hence he cannot atone, or act as a savior, for another (Lev. 17:11; Heb. 9:22; 1 John 1:7).

Chapter 21.
When Smoke Fills the Temple

Chapter Emphasis: The events in the heavenly sanctuary and temple will establish whether the claim of professed Christians is reflected in their lives. The close of Christ's ministry for humanity signals the close of human probation and ushers in a time of great strife on earth. After this, Christ will come to give His rewards. This occurs when He appears the second time and not at each individual's death. At the second coming, Satan will be banished to solitude for 1000 years while the righteous review God's judgments. When the period of Satan's solitude is finished, his followers are raised, and they will mount a final assault on God and the place of His dwelling, the New Jerusalem. God will rise and destroy them and cleanse the earth with fire. The destruction of the wicked will then be final and complete; they will not suffer for time without end.

Spiritual Link: Christ's coming will be evident to all; the saints will not be raptured away.

God's ways are indeed in His sanctuary. When the sacredness of the sanctuary here on earth was lost, the focus of attention shifted to the heavenly sanctuary. John, the Revelator, writing probably in the period AD 95 to 96, recorded a number of things about the heavenly sanctuary. Perhaps one of the most significant is contained in Revelation 15:6–8, a passage in which John recorded that the angels of God, at the close of this world's history, emerge from the heavenly temple bearing the seven last plagues. At this time, the temple is filled with smoke, and no person is able to enter it. Humanity's day of opportunity for salvation has passed. It is my intention to focus on these events.

In Chapter 19, we studied the services of the Day of Atonement, particularly as they related to the removal of the record of the confessed sins of the righteous from the sanctuary. We pointed out that the antitypical day of atonement commenced in 1844 and that it continues to this day, though the process will end someday soon. The Scriptures describe the pre-advent judgment in some detail and also give vital information about the close of human probation here on earth. When Christ comes, He comes with His reward. We will also look at events that will occur on earth and in heaven in the 1000-year period following the close of probation.

All Christians Judged Before Christ Returns

In this section, I will

- *emphasize that, when Christ comes the second time, all the inhabitants of the earth will be mentioned in the announcement regarding the results of the judgment;*

- *remind that there are only two classes of people recognized at Christ's return—the righteous and the wicked.*

The general theme of judgment occurs frequently throughout the Bible. In a sense, those who have not accepted Christ as their Savior, when given the opportunity, have already decided their destiny. The assessment of those who claim to be Christians is specifically described in Scripture as a pre-advent event.

Two Classes Recognized. From Genesis to Revelation, there are only two classes of people recognized by God: the righteous and the wicked, the wheat and the tares, the wheat and the chaff, the good and the bad, the saved and the unsaved, the sheep and the goats, those separated by Christ to the right and those separated to the left. The apostle John identifies these two classes of people in another manner (Rev. 14:9–12). The group of special note is represented by a virtuous woman, or even as virgins (Rev. 14:4; cf. 2 Cor. 11:2). This group is also likened to a woman clothed in white, which refers to a pure church (Ps. 51:7; Isa. 1:18; Rev. 3:4, 5, 18). The second group is associated with a woman dressed in scarlet. This group has committed spiritual adultery. Hence, it represents those who have aligned themselves with an apostate church or religion (Ps. 75:8; Rev. 17:4, 5).

The woman of Revelation 17, which represents a church, is wearing scarlet and purple and pictured as full of objectionable things (verse 4). This woman is called "Babylon the Great," and she has many daughters (verse 5). This same religious agglomeration of powers is considered in Revelation, chapter 14, verses 8 and 10, and judged to be fallen as a system, or beyond retrieval. As in Babylon of old, the sacred and the pagan are combined, thus calling down the judgment of God (Dan. 5:1–4, 25–28, 30). Those who, in the face of clear evidence, continue in the ways of human thinking rather than accepting the glorious truths of God's Word will be judged unworthy of eternal life (Rev. 18:4; 21:27). Jesus Himself contended with similar perversions of truth during His sojourn on earth, and He warned that God will judge those as unworthy who mix the traditions of men with their worship and moral philosophy of life, thus making the Word of God of none effect (Matt. 15:3, 6).

A Harvest of Two Types. Not surprisingly, two types of harvest are also mentioned in the book of Revelation. The first is the grain harvest. It represents the time of reward for the righteous (Rev. 14:15, 16). The second harvest is likened to the gathering of grapes. It represents the time of reward for those who have rejected God (Rev. 14:17–19). John's contemporaries understood the symbolism of the two harvests in Revelation, chapter 14. In Palestine, there were two main harvests, the harvest of grain in April and May and the harvest of grapes in late summer. In verses 15 and 16, the harvest of grain is clearly meant since the expression "is ripe" comes from a Greek word that means "to become dry or withered," a description applicable to cereal harvests. The grape harvest refers to the reward of the wicked. They are the recipients of God's wrath and are crushed as grapes in the harvest. A similar concept is taught in Jesus' parable of the wheat and the tares in which the angels of God bind the tares together to be burned before they gather the wheat to be kept as a valuable commodity (Matt. 13:30).

Class Involved in the Pre-advent Judgment. The pre-advent judgment is involved primarily with those who have claimed to be Christians. As stated already, those who have rejected God in a deliberate manner already have declared themselves unworthy (Rom. 2:12, 13). Those who have followed the general revelation of God in nature and have answered the call of conscience stand in a different class that will be dealt with favorably (Rom. 2:14–16). Of these it has been written:

> Those whom Christ commends in the judgment may have known little of theology, but they have cherished His principles. Through the influence of the divine Spirit they have been a blessing to those about them. Even among the heathen are those who have cherished the spirit of kindness; before the words of life had fallen upon their ears, they have befriended the missionaries, even ministering to them at the peril of their own lives. Among the heathen are those who worship God ignorantly, those to whom the light is never brought by human instrumentality, yet they will not perish. Though ignorant of the written law of God, they have heard His voice speaking to them in nature, and have done the things that the law required. Their works are evidence that the Holy Spirit has touched their hearts, and they are recognized as the children of God.[347]

For those who have enjoyed the full privileges of hearing the gospel, the following words are declared: "God will bring every work into judgment, including every secret thing whether *it is* good or whether *it is* evil" (Eccles. 12:14; cf. Matt. 12:36, 37). Those who have known the pure truths of God's Word and have turned aside from them will be judged adversely. Those who have exchanged their wicked ways for the ways of the Lord will be accepted (Ezek. 18:21–24, 30).

The pre-advent judgment commences "at the house of God" (1 Peter 4:17), that is, with those who make the highest profession of faith. The imagery used by Peter is similar to that spoken by the prophet Ezekiel who saw a man, clothed in linen, moving through Jerusalem, symbolic of God's church, with a device to place a mark in the foreheads of those who were loyal to God (Ezek. 9:3–5). The investigation seen by Ezekiel commenced with the elders, or religious leaders (verse 6). Their opportunity to know the truth and to withstand error has placed them in a most responsible position.

Chapter 21. When Smoke Fills the Temple

Today is the Day of Salvation

In this section, I will

- *appeal to the reader to decide for Christ today.*

There is a sentiment in parts of the Christian world that God is so kind and loving that He will not destroy the wicked without giving them a second chance to repent. Some see a golden age of opportunity to accept the gospel before the return of Christ. However, the Scriptures warn that it is not safe to leave the decision to follow God to a future time.

Decide for Eternity Today. The time to make decisions for God and for eternity is now (Ps. 95:7, 8; Heb. 3:7, 8, 12, 13, 15). God sought to teach this truth through the sanctuary service. On the Day of Atonement, which marked the end of the religious year, those who chose not to participate in soul searching and putting away sin were "cut off" (Lev. 23:27–30). Their day of opportunity, or probation, had passed.

The parable of the ten virgins clarifies the answer more persuasively. Those who did not make adequate preparation were surprised by the bridegroom's negative response (Matt. 25:12). It is important to recognize the setting for this parable. In Matthew, chapter 24, Jesus gave His great discourse on the signs of His coming and the end of the world. Then He introduced a number of parables to drive home the points that He wished to emphasize. The majority of these parables indicate that the opportunities for preparation given us must be grasped as they come to us. It is possible to put off our preparation too long. Notice a few of the points from these parables:

- Jesus revisited Noah's day and tells again the story of those who entered the ark of safety. The point of the story is in Matthew 24:38, 39: those who are lost were so busy with the affairs of life that they "did not know until the flood came and took them all away." That is how it will be for the lost at "the coming of the Son of Man." Human probation will have closed before Christ returns.

- Jesus told the parable of the coming of the thief to the household. The lesson drawn is that, if the householder had known the hour of the break-in, he would have had a guard ready to prevent it. But the fact is that he did not know when it would be. In like manner, "the Son of Man is coming at an hour when you do not expect *Him*"

(Matt. 24:44). In other words, if preparation is not made now, there will be no future with God.

- Jesus told the parable of the faithful and evil servants. The lesson He conveyed is that the servant who was found doing the master's will when he returned will be rewarded, while the servant who was unfaithful will be destroyed (Matt. 24:46–51).

- Jesus told the parable of the talents. In this account, the master of the servants went to a far country. When he returned, he asked what the servants had done with the means he had left them. The one who failed to improve the opportunities given him was cast "into the outer darkness" (Matt. 25:30). The parable does portray any second chances.

Immediately following these and other parables, the Lord taught the disciples the concept that, when He comes, He will do so with His reward (Matt. 25:31–46).

Not Raptured. Christ described His coming and the giving of rewards as a well-witnessed event. He will come in visible glory with the angels and with incredible sounds accompanying the event (Matt. 24:27, 31; 25:31). All nations will be aware of the spectacle and will then receive sentence (Matt. 24:30; 25:32–46). There will be no mistaking this event, nor will there be any danger of missing it. John the Revelator added his voice to Matthew's by giving further details. Unbelievable and spectacular signs will be seen in the heavens, the earth will shake and tsunamis will sweep the oceans. Those who have rejected God's call of mercy will pray for the earth to swallow them or fall on them rather than their facing the glorious returning Christ (Rev. 6:12–17).

Deceptions will precede the real event. Even today we have groups of Christians declaring that Christ has already come. This would mean that most of us have missed the event. Such a notion does not ring true to the biblical account. Jesus carefully warned His followers that, if any individual or organization claimed that He had come secretly, they were to immediately reject the thought (Matt. 24:23–26). The angels present at His ascension made it clear that Christ would come back as He was taken from them (Acts 1:11). At His second coming, Christ will not then walk about on the earth and plead with people to give their lives to Him. His coming will be accompanied by the raising of the righteous dead and their ascension to "meet the Lord in the air" (1 Thess. 4:17). Satan will anticipate the return of Christ and appear as an angel of light on earth (2 Cor. 11:13-15). His deceptive endeavors have been graphically portrayed:

> As the crowning act in the great drama of deception, Satan himself will personate Christ. The church has long professed to look to the Savior's advent as the consummation of her hopes. Now the great deceiver will make it appear that Christ has come. In different parts of the earth, Satan will manifest himself among men as a majestic being of dazzling brightness, resembling the description of the Son of God given by John in the Revelation. Revelation 1:13-15. The glory that surrounds him is unsurpassed by anything that mortal eyes have yet beheld. The shout of triumph rings out upon the air: "Christ has come! Christ has come!" The people prostrate themselves in adoration before him, while he lifts up his hands and pronounces a blessing upon them, as Christ blessed His disciples when He was upon the earth. His voice is soft and subdued, yet full of melody. In gentle, compassionate tones he presents some of the same gracious, heavenly truths which the Savior uttered; he heals the diseases of the people, and then, in his assumed character of Christ, he claims to have changed the Sabbath to Sunday, and commands all to hallow the day which he has blessed.[348]

Probation Closes

In this section, I will

- *indicate that a time will come when probation will close and God will no longer offer salvation to any person;*
- *outline the events that transpire on earth immediately following the close of probation and before Jesus returns the second time.*

The time of testing and the opportunity to make decisions for Christ will end one day soon. The deliberate rejection of light hardens a person in his or her course of action (Num. 15:29-31). Continued resistance to impressions made by the Holy Spirit eventually leads the individual to make deliberate and considered choices against God and His Word. This is what the Bible refers to as blasphemy against the Holy Spirit (Matt. 12:31, 32). The individual has by such actions refused to accept the evidence given, and the conscience becomes deadened. This means that such a person becomes unreachable. God appeals to us to respond promptly to His calls to obedience so that we do not remotely approach this sad situation.

Invitation to Repent Ceases. The Scriptures describe the close of probation in a number of ways. "Michael shall stand up" (Dan. 12:1) as smoke fills the temple (Rev. 15:8). Michael is none other than Christ. No one else has guarded His people so jealously. In Daniel 7, we find a solemn court scene described (verses 9, 10, and 13). We notice that all in the court are seated. It stands to reason that, when Christ stands up, His mediation for all humanity is at an end (cf. 1 John 2:1; Heb. 9:28). It is then that the court of the great judgment also rises.

The glory of the Lord then fills the temple and no intercession is available to any individual (Rev. 15:8). The imagery used in Revelation is similar to that used in Ezekiel, chapter 10, verses 3 and 4. In the ancient temple on earth, God's presence left the Most Holy Place, and He then paused over the threshold of the temple before departing entirely (Ezek. 11:21–24). There was no more intercession available for ancient Israel within the sanctuary at that time. In the book of Revelation, similar outcomes are pictured as taking place in heaven at the end of probationary time.

God will not always bear with rebellious humanity. A day will come, as in the time of Noah and Jeremiah, when God's forbearance will reach its limit. After Christ's intercession is finished in the sanctuary, a great time of trouble will descend on the earth (Dan. 12:1). The period of time elapsing between the close of probation and the pouring out of God's plagues has not been revealed in Scripture. When the last scenes on this earth come into play, there will be great strife and destruction, and the plagues will begin to be poured out (Rev. 15:1, 6–8; 16). The plagues are described as specific and widespread. The religious leaders who have participated in the deceptions of the people under their influence will be the targets of the fifth plague (Rev. 16:10, 11). Other plagues will apparently be more extensive in their impact (Rev. 16:4, 8).

After the plagues are poured out, God will declare, "It is done!" (Rev. 16:17). This announcement will signal the end of the deceptive and manipulative acts of the religious powers known as "great Babylon." The true nature and loyalties of these powers will have been revealed to the inhabitants of the world. This religio-political combination has sought to gather the "kings of the earth and of the whole world" against God's people (Rev. 16:14; cf. 16:13, 18, 19). It will be time for Christ to declare His sovereignty and put an utter end to the reign of evil under Satan the great deceiver. Finally, God will perform His strange act of destroying the wicked (Isa. 28:21; cf. Ezek. 18:32).

Rewards Announced

In this section, I will

- *outline the nature of the immediate rewards which Christ gives to the inhabitants of this world at the second coming;*

- *indicate the nature of Satan's immediate reward at the second coming and relate this to truths taught through the earthly sanctuary service on the Day of Atonement.*

The day of miracles has not ceased. Those who have declared that such happenings are not part of either the Christian record or experience will be shown to be deluded. When Christ appears in the clouds, the righteous dead will be raised, and the living righteous will be caught up together with them to meet Christ in the air (1 Thess. 4:16, 17). As all this is transpiring, the wicked will be slain at Christ's coming. The psalmist plainly declared, "A fire shall devour before Him" (Ps. 50:3; cf. 2 Thess. 1:7, 8; 2:8).

The righteous become immortal at Christ's coming and are gathered by the angels (1 Cor. 15:51–53; Matt. 24:31). These texts inform us that the righteous do not go to heaven at death, rather they wait in their graves for the second coming of Christ (Acts 1:11; John 14:3). There follow scenes of rejoicing in heaven (Rev. 7:9–17). The apostle John describes in majestic detail the adoration given to God for the wonder of His ways, His love and forbearance, and His deliverance.

Millennial Activities. The righteous are active in heaven during the 1000 years after Christ's return. The apostle Paul informs us that the saints judge the wicked—including the angels who have fallen (1 Cor. 6:2, 3). It must be remembered that God has already determined the fate of all inhabitants of this earth prior to the second coming. One could rightly ask what purpose this activity of the saints would serve. We are assured that the saints actually live and reign with Christ during this period (Rev. 20:4). It appears that they participate with Christ in determining the degree of punishment to be received by the lost. (Remember, only the record of the sins of those declared righteous were removed during the pre-advent judgment.) The saints, through this review process, will be forever convinced of God's mercy and justice. God will have demonstrated that He is completely trustworthy. Of the righteous during this period, we read: "In union with Christ they judge the wicked, comparing their acts with the statute book, the Bible, and deciding every case according to the deeds done in the body. Then the portion which the wicked must suffer is meted out, according to their works; and it is recorded against their names in the book of death."[349]

By contrast, Satan is chained in a "bottomless pit"—he is bound on this earth for 1000 years (Rev. 20:1–3). Scripture suggests that Satan is accompanied by his evil angels during this period of time (2 Peter 2:4; cf. Rev. 12:9). Satan is bound by a chain of circumstances with no humans alive for him to tempt. The Greek word *abussos*, which is often translated "bottomless pit," means a desolate place, a place "without form, and void," or one that is broken up and unpeopled (Jer. 4:23). This same term was used in the Septuagint to refer to the state of the world at Creation (Gen. 1:1, 2), which is translated into English as "unsightly and unfurnished" (Gen. 1:2, *Brenton's English Septuagint*).

Banishment of the Azazel Goat Symbolism Fulfilled. In the Old Testament sanctuary service on the Day of Atonement, the final part of the ceremony pointed to the banishment of Satan. This was when the sins of the truly repentant were symbolically taken from the sanctuary and placed on the head of Azazel's goat, which was then banished to a "place cut off."[350] In other words, the goat was sent into the desolate wilderness (Lev. 16:10, 20–22).

The term *Azazel*, which is often rendered "scapegoat," is used only in Leviticus 16 and it is applied to one who, by the context of the discussion, is against God (Lev. 16:8). A number of ideas have been expressed concerning the meaning of the word. "The parallelism of the phrases 'for Yahweh' and 'for Azazel' almost demands that the latter be a proper name, and it is preferable to see in Azazel a demon of some sort. This is the interpretation of the Syriac version of Lev, of the Targum, and of *1 Enoch*, which identifies Azazel as the prince of devils who was banished to the desert."[351] The Azazel goat was indeed sent away into an uninhabited or desolate place. The goat was not a savior, for its blood was not shed. The ultimate responsibility for all the confessed sins was symbolically placed on this goat as they will ultimately be placed upon Satan who will receive just retribution from God.

Sin and Satan Are No More

In this section, I will

- *indicate that Satan and sinners will not be punished forever, but will be destroyed forever by God;*

- *rejoice in the assurance that God's plan of salvation is so comprehensive that there is no possibility of sin arising in the universe again.*

Satan has yet to be destroyed. This will happen at the end of the 1000 years. However, before this transpires, a remarkable series of events will occur. The wicked dead will live again (Rev. 20:5, first part), and Satan will be "released from his prison" (Rev. 20:7), which means that he will be delivered from his desolating circumstances. Verse five has been a source of confusion for some. However, as presented in the New International Version of the Bible, the uncertainty disappears. The context shows that verses 4 and 5 are dealing with the righteous. Verses 4 (last part) and 5 read as follows: "They came to life and reigned with Christ a thousand years. (The rest of the dead did not come to life until the thousand years were ended.) This is the first resurrection." Notice that the translators enclosed in parentheses the details of events after the 1000 years to indicate that the sentence represents an interpolated thought. Understood thus, we recognize that the information about the wicked dead is extra detail placed at this point in the discourse and that the persons involved in the first resurrection are the righteous.

Final Assault on God's Kingdom. Zechariah 14:1 is the prophet's description of the "day of the Lord," when Christ will stand on the Mount of Olives in triumph (cf. Zech. 14:4, 9). The mountain will split in two, and a great plain will be formed to contain the New Jerusalem. "As the New Jerusalem, in its dazzling splendor, comes down out of heaven, it rests upon the place purified and made ready to receive it, and Christ, with His people and the angels, enters the Holy City."[352] The apostle John confirms the descent of the New Jerusalem from heaven to earth prior to the last rebellious activities of the wicked (Rev. 21:2).

After the New Jerusalem comes into place, the wicked, who are again alive upon the earth (Rev. 20:5), cooperate with Satan in attempting to overthrow the saints and the New Jerusalem (Rev. 20:8, 9, first part). Their plot is unsuccessful, and Satan and his followers witness the coronation of Christ as their judgment is pronounced (Rev. 20:11, 12). In that day, Christ will "be King over all the earth" (Zech. 14:9).

Death Has No More Victories. The Bible assures us that sin and sinners will one day cease to exist. After their final assault on God's kingdom, revealing unquestionable opposition to God, the rebellious will be destroyed by fire (2 Peter 3:7, 10, 11; Rev. 20:9, last part; 20:10, 14). This represents the second death from which there is no deliverance. This death is final and complete. Elsewhere the wicked are said to be reduced to stubble, to be ashes under foot, and to disappear in smoke (Ps. 37:10, 20; Mal. 4:1, 3). Concerning the devil, we are assured that he too will be reduced to ashes and will never be found anymore (Ezek. 28:17–19). The destroying fire should not be seen as something that torments for time without end, but rather as an unstoppable fire that completely destroys. The results are final and irrevocable.

In Christ's kingdom set up here on earth, there will be no further possibility of sin arising (1 Cor. 15:54, 55; cf. Isa. 25:8). Along the same lines, the prophet Nahum assures us: "Affliction will not rise up a second time" (Nah. 1:9). There are two reasons for this assurance. First, all the saved have first-hand experience of sin's hideous effects, and they have aligned themselves with Christ. Second, the human race will no longer be in the business of reproduction (Matt. 22:30), so there will be no new possibilities for sinners to arise.

Chapter 22.
God Is the Temple in the New Earth

Chapter Emphasis: *The relationship between Christ and the redeemed will be restored in the earth made new. In reality, this relationship will be a continuation of the one commenced on earth but will be at an elevated level of intimacy. Activities on the new earth will be challenging and rewarding and will include reminders and involve ceremonies linked to the worship practices described throughout the Bible. There will be continual reminders of the great sacrifice offered by Christ for the salvation of humanity.*

Spiritual Link: *Numerous reminders of sanctuary symbolism in the new earth will increase our understanding and appreciation of salvation.*

The story of redemption told in the Bible is really the story of God's love for fallen human beings. His plans to associate and communicate with His creatures, fashioned after His likeness, were thwarted by the deceptions of Satan. Sin brought a separation between humanity and

God. However, God in His great love determined to save sinners in a plan devised in heaven before sin entered. In order to convey more effectively to fallen humanity the nature of His plan, God initiated the sanctuary system of worship. Through its symbols and ceremonies, He taught important truths about the way of salvation. God also revealed, by means of the earthly sanctuary, important lessons about the ministry of Christ in the heavenly sanctuary, which will culminate in the rescue of humanity from the presence of sin and the destruction of Satan.

In the world made new, "there are glories that mortal lips cannot describe. The nearest we can come to a description of the reward that awaits the overcomer is to say that it is a far more exceeding and eternal weight of glory. It will be a blessed eternity of bliss, unfolding new glories throughout the ceaseless ages."[353] In this chapter, I will consider what the Scriptures tell us about the relationship between Christ and the redeemed in heaven and their anticipated experiences there. We also will discover in our search that there are many reminders of the earthly sanctuary.

The New Jerusalem

In this section, I will

- *remind readers that, in the earth made new, activities are focused in the capital where God dwells.*

The capital of the new earth, the New Jerusalem, will come to rest on the Mount of Olives, the place from which our Lord ascended (Zech. 14:4, 5, 9; Acts 1:9–11; Rev. 3:12; 21:1, 2). The New Jerusalem, which comes down from heaven, is a magnificent walled city of approximately 36,5000 square kilometers in area (Rev. 21:10–27). The prophecy of Zechariah is set for fulfillment on the day when "the LORD shall be King over all the earth" (Zech. 14:9). This happens immediately after the time of the descent of the New Jerusalem. On that day, the Mount of Olives, which was the scene of the Lord's sufferings on behalf of humanity (Luke 22:39–53), will be the scene of His eternal triumph. The Lord descends in the holy city with His saints. This will be His third coming to the earth.

The New Jerusalem is also termed the bride, the Lamb's wife. The saints represent the wedding guests (Rev. 19:7, 9; 21:2, 9, 10). The Lamb receives His kingdom, the New Jerusalem, after the close of

Chapter 22. God Is the Temple in the New Earth

His ministry as High Priest. He is made King before the assembled inhabitants of this earth. (Rev. 20:11, 12).

The Eternal Temple

In this section, I will

- *establish that, in the New Jerusalem, there is no temple for worship or for atonement because God will dwell there.*

One could anticipate some representation of a sanctuary or temple in the new earth, but the prophet John records, "I saw no temple in it" (Rev. 21:22). There is at this point in the history of the universe no need for a sanctuary, heavenly or earthly, because no one will ever sin again (Nah. 1:9; Heb. 9:28). The plan of salvation has ended. The earthly sanctuary's usefulness passed away when Christ completed His sacrifice. Type had met antitype. Then Christ commenced His ministry in the heavenly sanctuary. The work of investigation of the life records of the righteous represented the last phase of the High Priest's work in the heavenly sanctuary. This work will be completed before Christ comes.

God is the Temple. God takes the place of the temple in the New Jerusalem (Rev. 21:22). Sin no longer separates humanity from God. The communion that God planned in the beginning is restored (Gen. 3:8; cf. Exod. 25:8). Truly, God now dwells among humanity in the fullest sense. The experiences of Eden will again be those of the redeemed. God's desire to dwell with His people is one of the central thoughts taught by the sanctuary doctrine. The Scripture records, "He will dwell with" humanity, "and they shall be His people, and God Himself will be with them *and be* their God" (Rev. 21:3).

Reminders of the Sanctuary

In this section, I will

- *establish links between the sanctuary and some of the principal activities, associations, and features planned for the New Jerusalem.*

The term "temple," used in Revelation 7:15, refers to a place that the 144,000 visit, and it may be synonymous with the "glorious temple" outside the New Jerusalem on Mount Zion that Ellen White saw as the place that only the 144,000 can enter.[354] It may well contain many reminders of the work of redemption during the last scenes of earth's history. Even though there will be no physical temple in the new earth connected with worship, mediation, or associated activities, there will be many reminders of the significance of the sanctuary and temple in salvation history.

Outer Court Reminders. The outer court surrounded the earthly sanctuary. Here sacrifices for sin were made. The continual reminder in the new earth of the infinite sacrifice made by Christ on behalf of humanity will be the marks of the crucifixion that "the Lamb of God" will eternally bear (Rev. 21:23; John 20:27-29). It is a marvelous thought that Christ has identified Himself with humanity for eternity. Even in heaven, He is still referred to as "the Lamb." Throughout eternity, His glorified body will bear the scars of the cruel suffering of the crucifixion as a living memorial to the sacrifice that God made on behalf of humans. Oh, what wondrous love!

Holy Place Reminders. In the earthly sanctuary, the golden candlesticks were kept continuously burning. The light emanating from them represented Christ, the light of the world (John 8:12). John the Revelator pictured Jesus as standing among the seven lampstands as the "Son of Man" (Rev. 1:13). This symbolizes His guidance of the Christian church through the various periods of history till the end of time. Now Christ dwells among His people and is a constant source of light as the "Son of Man" (Rev. 14:14; 21:23).

In the earthly sanctuary, Christ was represented by bread, the source of life (Lev. 24:5-9; cf. John 6:47, 48). Bread was continually on display on the table of shewbread, or bread of the presence, in the Holy Place. The Scriptures quoted in the Gospel of John inform us that eternal life and Christ the "bread of life" are inseparably linked.

The Old Testament prophet Malachi calls Christ the "Sun of Righteousness" and assures us that the redeemed will "grow fat like stall-fed calves" (Mal. 4:2). Christ was also represented by the lamps, providing the light of wisdom and instruction in truth (Lev. 24:4; cf. John 8:12, 14). God is the source of wisdom and knowledge (Job 36:5). The saved will learn from the source of knowledge, Jesus Christ (Ps. 136:5). Their education will continue throughout eternity.

In the earthly sanctuary, the incense burned continually in the Holy Place and represented the sweet presence of Jesus Christ. In heaven, Christ associates with His people personally. Those who have emerged victorious from the final great time of trouble follow the

Lamb. They will enjoy a special relationship with Him, for they are in His presence continually to serve Him (Rev. 7:14, 15; 14:4).

Most Holy Place Reminders. Reminders of the final aspects of the ministry of Christ in the heavenly sanctuary abound. First, a great multitude of saints in heaven proclaims "salvation *belongs* to our God" (Rev. 7:9, 10). During Christ's ministry in the heavenly sanctuary, He made final representation for all who might be benefited for the "errors" (Heb. 9:7, *agno mat n*, or "sins of ignorance") that they committed.[355] The curse of sin and its originator have been forever banished (Rev. 20:10; 22:3). Those who have hidden themselves in Christ by faith are declared forever His children (Rev. 22:11, 14). The trophies of grace in heaven constitute powerful reminders of Christ's final ministry.

A symbol of creative and sustaining power found in the New Jerusalem also reminds us of the earthly sanctuary. This is none other than the tree of life (Rev. 22:2). In the earthly sanctuary, the ark of the covenant contained a pot of manna and Aaron's rod that budded (Heb. 9:4). These were symbols in their day of the creative and sustaining power of God. In the earth made new, the tree of life will be restored. Only one tree of life is mentioned in the Scriptures (Gen. 2:9), which indicates that this tree is the same as that present in the Garden of Eden. It is for "the healing [service, nurture, or care] of the nations" (Rev. 22:2). The tree of life itself points to Christ who is the source of eternal life, for God only has innate immortality. Yet, God gives immortality to the obedient at Christ's coming (1 Cor. 15:51–54). This state is maintained as they have the right to eat of the fruit of the tree of life freely (Rev. 22:14).

The great controversy that began in heaven between Christ and Satan, centers about God's law, which encapsulates the principles of His kingdom and reflects His character. Reminders of the everlasting nature of the Ten Commandments given at Sinai and kept in the earthly sanctuary are provided. First, love in action is the great principle by which the new earth is guided. God is love (1 John 4:8), and, since God will dwell with His people in the earth made new, all those who are there will demonstrate this principle. The principles of the law, which are embodied in the thought of love to God and to our fellow human beings, will be kept in heaven, for God does not change (Mal. 3:6). Second, the most disputed point in the Decalogue, the Sabbath, will be honored in the earth made new (Isa. 66:22, 23; Rev. 22:14).

Those who are privileged to enter through the gates of pearl into the city have been willingly obedient to God's commandments on earth. Those outside the walls have delighted in their own ways (Rev. 22:14, 15). The walls, in a sense, represent God's law, for obedience to it ensures liberty (James 1:25; 2:10–12). Entrance into the city is through faith in the Pearl of great price, Jesus Christ (John 10:7, 9; Matt. 13:45, 46).

Even the physical layout of the New Jerusalem reminds of the Most Holy Place on earth (1 Kings 6:20; Rev. 21:16). John wrote about a massive architectural structure in heaven with equal length and breadth. This is none other than holy city, the New Jerusalem. It is easy to agree with the suggestion made by some that the Most Holy Place on earth was symbolic of the New Jerusalem.[356] However, it is difficult to conceptualize the heavenly city. Some regard the Greek word *hupsos*, which is usually translated as "height," as capable of being rendered "the high part" or "the summit." This could simply mean that the perimeter of the top and the bottom of the wall are equal. Other interpretations have been proposed. Whatever the precise meaning, the plan of the magnificent city of the New Jerusalem is based on a square just as was the Most Holy Place.

The Most Holy Place in the earthly sanctuary was where God's presence appeared above the ark of the covenant. In the New Jerusalem, God is also present; no dividing wall now separates Him from the redeemed. The principles of the Decalogue are expressed in His character. Angels were embroidered on the hangings of the walls in the earthly sanctuary. The redeemed now walk the streets of gold in the holy city with the angels.

Other Reminders. Associated with the throne of God in heaven are four living creatures and twenty-four elders (Rev. 4:4, 6). The four living creatures in heaven are described as having the face of a lion, of a man, of an ox, and of an eagle (Ezek. 1:10). They appear to represent cherubim (Ezek. 10:14, 15, 20). The description of the four living creatures makes one think of the camp of the Israelites, which was arranged under the four standards of Judah, Reuben, Ephraim, and Dan at the four points of the compass (Num. 2:2, 3, 10, 18, 25). According to Jewish tradition, the four standards bore the images of the face of a lion, of a man, of an ox, and of an eagle.[357]

The twenty-four elders remind us of the twenty-four orders of priests set aside in Old Testament times to serve in the sanctuary (1 Chron. 24:4, 5; 2 Chron. 31:2). The elders in heaven appear to be individuals redeemed from the earth who have been given special functions there (Rev. 5:8–10). These special persons could be part of the host of trophies released from their graves when Jesus rose from the dead. They subsequently witnessed to His resurrection and were then taken to heaven (Matt. 27:51–53; Eph. 4:8). Moses, Elijah, and Enoch might conceivably be among their number (Matt. 17:3, 4). These and the other reminders of the earthly sanctuary found in heaven impress upon our finite mind the immense importance of the truths of the sanctuary to this present life.

Commemorative Services in the New Earth

In this section, I will

- *remind readers that some of the services that Christ instituted anciently in association with the earthly sanctuary and later in the Christian church will be continued, perhaps in modified form, in the new earth.*

Some commemorative services initiated on earth will be kept in heaven as a reminder of Christ's sacrifice. The Communion service initiated by Jesus just before His crucifixion will be kept, for He said, "I will not drink of the fruit of the vine until the kingdom of God comes" (Matt. 26:29, ESV; Luke 22:16, 18). This service points back to Christ's sacrifice made on Calvary. It also points forward to the enduring triumph of God. Consequently, it is a time for us to rejoice in His salvation.

The Scriptures assure us that all the redeemed will gather once a month to worship in a special manner (Isa. 66:23, first part). We might inquire whether there was an ancient practice performed once a month that casts light on the nature of the service in which the redeemed may expect to participate. In the Old Testament times, the Israelites held special festivities on the first day of each month. It was a day of gladness announced by two silver trumpets (Num. 10:10). The day was a day of festive meals, a time to visit God's appointed leaders (1 Sam. 20:5; 2 Kings 4:23), a day of refraining from ordinary labor (Amos 8:5), and a time of special worship (Num. 28:11–14).

The offerings made to the Lord on these festive days were sweet savor offerings. It is instructive to investigate the spiritual meaning of these offerings.

- The burnt offering symbolized the complete and unreserved consecration of the worshiper to God. This great truth was taught by the practice of burning the whole animal, thoroughly washed and eviscerated, on the altar. This principle also is suggested by the association of the offering with the consecration of Aaron and his sons and with the taking of the Nazarite vow (Exod. 29:15–18; Num. 6:13, 14). In its primary sense, the offering signified the perfect offering made by Christ. As the people offered the burnt offering and participated in this festival, they indicated their complete and unreserved acceptance, through faith, of the merits of Christ's promised death on Calvary. This unreserved commitment will continue in heaven.

- The peace offering "was a communion offering in which God, the priest, and the people participated. It was a communal meal, held in the precincts of the temple, in which joy and happiness prevailed, and the priest and the people held converse" (cf. Lev. 7:11–17).[358] Jewish literature declares: "Every peace offering culminated in a communal meal. Except for the portions burned on the altar or assigned to the priest, the sacrificial animal was given to the offerer. He used it as food for a communal meal for himself, his family, and also the levite in his community (Deut. 12:12, 18–19). This had to take place at the divinely appointed sanctuary...."[359] Communal rejoicing apparently will be a part of heavens regular celebrations.

In the new earth, the Sabbath will be kept as a reminder of the creation of this universe and its cleansing from sin (Isa. 66:23; Rev. 22:14). The verse in Isaiah expresses God's ideal; it will be realized in heaven when all the redeemed gladly honor all of God's commandments. The Sabbath kept in the new earth is a continuation of the Sabbath memorial given at Creation. As in the original Garden of Eden, so in Eden restored will God commune with His people face to face. All will rejoice in God's perfect creation and in the transformation, through the re-creative power of the Holy Spirit (cf. Rom. 12:2), of the vile characters that believers once possessed, enabling them to receive the reward of victors at Christ's second coming. Thus, the Sabbath will be a symbol of God's creative ability and of His re-creative power in the lives of men and women through eternity. The Sabbath in the new earth will be full of deep and abiding meaning for each of the redeemed.

The New Jerusalem, a Place of Eternal Joy

In this section, I will

- *indicate that the New Jerusalem will be inhabited by real people who were redeemed from the earth and who will continually rejoice as they fellowship with Jesus Christ their Redeemer.*

Some have pictured the new earth in cartoonish terms with people or spirits floating around on clouds playing on harps. However, the redeemed will be real people possessing glorious bodies performing useful activity (Phil. 3:20, 21; cf. Luke 24:36–43; Isa. 65:21, 22).

General Privileges. The Scriptures inform us that the redeemed will possess bodies like the glorious body of their Lord. Christ possessed flesh and bones and was capable of eating and functioning as a human being. Indeed, in the new earth the fruits of the tree of life are for the consumption of the righteous once a month (Rev. 22:2). Some have argued, using the statement "flesh and blood cannot inherit the kingdom of God" (1 Cor. 15:50), that those who inherit heaven will have spirit bodies. However, it must be remembered that this text was given in answer to the question posed in verse 35: "How are the dead raised up? And with what body do they come?" Verses 42 to 45 emphasize that the resurrection body is different from the mortal body that we now possess. "Flesh and blood," or the corrupt mortal bodies that we now possess, cannot exist in heaven. There we will possess incorruptible, immortal bodies (1 Cor. 15:50–53).

Jesus personally promised His true disciples that He would provide them with a mansion (John 14:2, 3). Jesus' disciples, who were often maligned and despised and rendered homeless here, will receive an incomparable reward in the earth made new. For this reason, the apostle Paul considered these present sufferings "not worthy *to be compared* with the glory which shall be revealed in us" (Rom. 8:18).

It is not possible for us to imagine fully the glories or the activities that God has prepared for those who love Him (1 Cor. 2:9). In the texts cited, the apostle Paul is drawing our attention to Isaiah 64:4, joining with the Old Testament writers in proclaiming that the rewards of the righteous are beyond the capacity of mortals to grasp fully. Surely, the Lord will give good gifts to His children both in this world and the world to come (Matt. 7:11). A wonderful account of what the new earth will be like declares:

> In the earth made new the redeemed will engage in the occupations and pleasures that brought happiness to Adam and Eve in the beginning. The Eden life will be lived, the life in garden and field. "They shall build houses, and inhabit them; and they shall plant vineyards, and eat the fruit of them. They shall not build, and another inhabit; they shall not plant, and another eat: for as the days of a tree are the days of My people, and Mine elect shall long enjoy the work of their hands."
>
> There every power will be developed, every capability increased. The grandest enterprises will be carried forward, the loftiest aspirations will be reached, the highest ambitions realized. And still there will arise new heights to surmount, new wonders to admire, new truths to comprehend, fresh objects to call forth the powers of body and mind and soul.[360]

Some of our present experiences will forever be things of the past, such as pain, sickness, sorrow, weeping, and death (Rev. 21:4). Isaiah, chapter 35, elaborates on this remarkable picture of the future glory of Zion when the "redeemed shall walk *there*" (verse 9). The saved will come with "singing, with everlasting joy on their heads. They shall obtain joy and gladness, and sorrow and sighing will flee away" (verse 10).

Special Privileges. Heaven is a place where all will be happy. Those who have passed through the time of trouble that bring this earth's history to a close will enjoy special privileges. The redeemed from this period are Christ's constant companions (Rev. 14:1, 4). The redeemed in this passage are those who have endured the final display of Satan's wrath. These are the 144,000 identified in Revelation 7. Let us plan to be among the redeemed, dressed in the white robes of Christ's righteousness. Whether we are among those who are called to pass through a time of great trouble or whether we are among those who have passed to their rest before this period, there will be blessed unity and contentment among the redeemed. The greatest privilege of all will be to meet with our Lord and Savior. All the hosts of heaven and the redeemed will sing one great anthem of praise and adoration that fills all heaven with joy (Rev. 15:3, 4; cf. Rev. 5:9–14).

> "Great and marvelous *are* Your works, Lord God Almighty!
> Just and true *are* Your ways, O King of the saints!
> Who shall not fear You, O Lord, and glorify Your name?
> For *You* alone *are* holy.
> For all nations shall come and worship before You,
> For Your judgments have been manifested." (Rev. 15:3, 4).

Lasting Assurances

Chapter 23.
Fiery Coals, Living Stones

Chapter Emphasis: *God is active in the heavenly sanctuary to bring the joy of salvation to as many people of all nations as possible. Christ, as well as the other members of the Godhead, and all the celestial beings are involved in this saving ministry. By accepting the magnificent offer of salvation and daily surrendering to Christ, the redeemed may become living stones in His temple. This gives great assurance.*

Spiritual Link: *The weakest believer is assured of victory through faith.*

The visions of God recorded in the Bible usually picture Him in a throne room or temple setting. The use of temple and sanctuary imagery throughout the Scriptures reinforces in our mind the value of understanding the basic concepts they convey. The temple in heaven is pictured as the communication and decision-making center of the universe. As this theme is explored, it becomes apparent that all the members of the Godhead are involved in ensuring the satisfactory completion of the reconciliation of this fallen world to God. The angels and other celestial beings also have their part to play. These same concepts were also conveyed through the symbols and ceremonies of the earthly sanctuary.

We have already indicated that anciently there was ample cause for the assurance of believers. This concept resided in representations of the continual nature of Christ's ministry in the earthly sanctuary. Readers will remember the continual burnt offering in the courtyard, and the continually burning lamps, the continually ascending incense, and the continually displayed "bread of the presence" in the Holy Place of the tabernacle.

I might refresh the memory specifically by referring to the continual burnt offering. This offering consisted of a lamb without blemish offered each morning and evening throughout the year and even on the Day of Atonement (Num. 28:1–8). This gave worshipers the assurance that, if they were at a distance from the sanctuary and had committed a sin, they would not be condemned. They had the opportunity to make an appropriate sacrifice for their sin and receive forgiveness when they returned to the vicinity of the sanctuary. In the Christian age, the same assurances apply. John the Revelator portrayed Christ moving among the perpetually burning candlesticks in the heavenly sanctuary (Rev. 1:12, 13), and later he saw an angel offering the incense with the prayers of the saints (Rev. 8:3, 4). In case any doubt should linger in our minds, the apostle Paul assures readers: "Therefore He is also able to save to the uttermost those who come to God through Him, since He ever lives to make intercession for them" (Heb. 7:25).

In this chapter, I wish to explore in particular the ministry of God the Father, the Holy Spirit and the angels. This will provide additional assurances to us that heaven is on our side.

Visions of God

In this section, I will

- *highlight the involvement of all celestial beings in the salvation of humanity.*

Isaiah's vision of God's throne was recorded in 740/739 BC, which was the year that king Uzziah died (Isa. 6:1). Uzziah had long resisted the marauding advances of Assyrian king Tiglath-pileser III. However, now that King Uzziah was dead, Isaiah was wondering what would happen to the kingdom of Judah.[361] Not only were there security threats from without, but also was there within the kingdom a lack

Chapter 23. Fiery Coals, Living Stones

of spiritual responsiveness (Isa. 6:9, 10; 7:1). Yet, God urged Isaiah to make another appeal to His chosen nation and assured him that a remnant would respond (Isa. 6:9, 13). Similarly, God gave the first vision of God's throne to the apostle John (Rev. 4:1-9) immediately after he received the discouraging appraisal of the Laodicean church, that is, the body of Christ functioning during the last period of earth's history (Rev. 3:14-17). This church is God's chosen instrument to give the three angels' messages of warning to a perishing world. Again, a faithful remnant is found (Rev. 14:12). In both instances, the beings seen around God's throne emphasized the holiness of God and the righteousness of His cause.

Feelings of Unworthiness Answered by Assurances. The prophet Isaiah expressed his own utter inadequacy following his vision of God and his attendants (Isa. 6:5). The apostle John also saw the holy beings around God's throne praising His righteousness (Rev. 4:4-9), and he noted that they "give glory and honor and thanks to Him who sits on the throne, who lives forever and ever" (verse 9). The information given Isaiah and the inferences conveyed to John were that reformation was needed and that the means for achieving spiritual regeneration were readily available (Isa. 6:7; Rev. 8:3). In the visions recorded by John, the Spirit of God is represented as a present and active partner by the seven lamps burning (Rev. 4:5; cf. Rev. 5:5, 6). In fact, all of heaven—all living creatures, seraphim, angels, elders, and members of the Godhead—are behind the salvation initiatives.

The incense from the altar of intercession figures in both Isaiah and John's visions. A seraph, which is a celestial being, took a live coal from the altar and placed it in Isaiah's mouth, with startling positive effect in his attitude (Isa. 6:6-8). John, on the other hand, saw the prayers of the saints continually arising with the incense offered on the altar (Rev. 8:4). No doubt these prayers were a call for forgiveness, guidance, deliverance, and strength. The intercessory ministry of Christ is indicated by the imagery. We are assured: "By the holy beings surrounding his throne, the Lord keeps up a constant communication with the inhabitants of earth."[362]

The magnificent and awe-inspiring scene observed by Isaiah was meant to give confidence and hope at a difficult time historically. Similarly, other prophets saw visions of God at critical times in national or salvation history (Exod. 24:10-12; 1 Kings 22:19).

Ministry of God the Father and the Holy Spirit

In this section, I will

- highlight the ministries of God the Father and God the Holy Spirit.

The prophet Isaiah makes a very significant statement in chapter 48. He pictures Christ, the eternal One and the Creator, speaking (verses 12, 13). In verse 16, all members of the Godhead are mentioned. The Father sent Christ at the appropriate time to come to this earth to fulfill His mission of sacrifice. It was then, too, that the Spirit rested upon Him to give knowledge, understanding, and wisdom to cooperate in the proclamation of liberty and judgment to the inhabitants of the earth (Isa. 11:2; 42:1; 61:1–3). This was the confession that Christ made in His first sermon, in which He proclaimed that the day of opportunity had come and the plan of redemption was to be revealed in its fullness (Luke 4:16–20). Later, He spoke about judgment (Matt. 10:11–15; 12:36; John 5:24–30). Other aspects of the ministry of the Godhead are revealed in Scripture, but much is left unsaid. I will briefly consider the aspects that are revealed.

Ministry of the Father. The story of Abraham being asked to sacrifice his son Isaac is an illustration of the involvement of the Father in the Son's sacrifice (Gen. 22:6–12; Matt. 27:46). Abraham was familiar with the promise of the Redeemer, for he understood the meaning of the animal sacrifices. He desired to see the fulfillment of the promise. In a sense, he did see it in the sacrifice asked of him. He understood something of Heaven's commitment to humanity as well as the anguish of the Father in carrying it out. "This terrible ordeal was imposed upon Abraham that he might see the day of Christ, and realize the great love of God for the world, so great that to raise it from its degradation, He gave His only-begotten Son to a most shameful death."[363]

"Abraham learned of God the greatest lesson ever given to mortal. His prayer that he might see Christ before he should die was answered. He saw Christ; he saw all that mortals can see, and live. By making an entire surrender, he was able to understand the vision of Christ, which had been given him. He was shown that in giving His only-begotten Son to save sinners from eternal ruin, God was making a greater and more wonderful sacrifice than ever man could make."[364]

The prophet Zechariah made it clear that Christ, the Branch, came to build the church of God on the earth and to sit and rule on

His Father's throne (Zech. 6:12, 13). That the Father is involved is conveyed clearly by the phrase "the counsel of peace shall be between them both" (verse 13). It has been said: "The love of the Father, no less than of the Son, is the fountain of salvation for the lost race.... God was 'in Christ, reconciling the world unto Himself.' 2 Corinthians 5:10.... 'God *so loved* the world, that He gave His only-begotten Son, that whoever believeth in Him should not perish, but have everlasting life.' John 3:16."[365] The apostle Paul emphasized this truth too: "But God [the Father] demonstrates His own love toward us, in that while we were still sinners, Christ died for us" (Rom. 5:8). This means: "God suffered with His Son. In the agony of Gethsemane, the death of Calvary, the heart of Infinite Love paid the price for our redemption."[366]

At the cleansing of the temple in Jerusalem, Jesus claimed that the temple was His Father's house as well as His own (Luke 19:46; John 2:16). At the first cleansing of the temple at Jerusalem at Passover time, Jesus fashioned a whip of cords and drove the traders and moneychangers from His Father's temple (John 2:14–16). At the second cleansing just prior to His crucifixion, He called the temple "My house" (Luke 19:46). In this play on words, the idea is forcefully conveyed that the Father was intimately involved in all aspects of the plan of salvation just as Christ was. This is heightened by the information supplied by Daniel the prophet, who informs us that the Father presides over the pre-advent judgment (Dan. 7:9, 10) while Christ presents the merits of His sacrifice on the repentant sinner's behalf. The assurance is given that judgment will be given in favor of the saints and against those who oppose God's will (Dan. 7:22, 26, 27). This is indeed good news!

Ministry of the Holy Spirit. The involvement of the Holy Spirit in the plan of salvation is substantial. The Spirit has been involved in urging men and women to accept God's offer of salvation from the beginning (Gen. 6:3). We notice that in the construction of the first temple, the Spirit gave wisdom and skill to the workmen, enabling them to complete the structure according to the heavenly pattern (Exod. 31:2–4). Then, through the gift of prophecy, the Spirit has influenced individuals to lead God's people to fulfill their mission (1 Sam. 10:10; 16:13; 2 Chron. 24:20; Ps. 51:11, 12).

All through the time that the earthly sanctuary was in existence, the role of the Holy Spirit was held uppermost in the minds of priests and worshipers through the oil used to keep the lamps continually burning in the Holy Place. The oil represented the Holy Spirit's work, as indicated by the prophet Zechariah (Zech. 4:3, 6). The sufferings and beatings of Christ were prefigured in the beating of the olives to gain the pure oil for use in the lamps. This would imply that the Spirit suffered with Christ.[367] Indeed, the apostle Paul informs us that Christ was offered "through the eternal Spirit" (Heb. 9:14).

Rebellion against the instruction and moral wisdom given by God is spoken about in the Bible as an act against the Holy Spirit. Anciently, the Israelites are said to have "rebelled and grieved His Holy Spirit" (Isa. 63:10; cf. verses 7–9). The delivery of the children of Israel from slavery in Egypt was an act of loving kindness, of redemption, and it indicates God's intentions toward both the past and present spiritual children of Israel. He led them on a miracle-studded journey from slavery through the Red Sea and wilderness to the Promised Land. He showed them His grandeur and moral principles at Sinai. He illustrated His plan of redemption through the sanctuary services that were instituted then. Yet, despite all this, most did not benefit from the evidences and help offered. The people generally did not accept the ministration of the Spirit, evident in the urgings of their conscience. Ezekiel spoke on these matters (Ezek. 36:27; 37:14) and indicated that God was prepared to do amazing things for Israel, and, by inference, for all those who are willing to give themselves unreservedly to Him. Today, we may grieve the Holy Spirit through similar actions that, sadly, may lead to the unpardonable sin, the sin that God cannot convict us to abandon (Matt. 12:31, cf. Matt. 12:24–30; Eph. 4:25–32). We notice incidentally but significantly that, since the Spirit can be grieved and suffer with Christ, that we are speaking of a real person—the third Person of the Godhead.

Christ promised that "the Spirit of truth," whom He called "another Helper," would have a special involvement in the lives of believers after His return to heaven (John 14:16, 17). Careful note of Christ's words to His disciples before the crucifixion impresses the reader with the thought that the Godhead is intimately and totally involved in the salvation of humanity. Christ said that He would ask the Father to send the Spirit of truth. "I will not leave you orphans," He said (verse 18). The Spirit will guide into all truth, convict of sin, righteousness, and judgment, and lead individuals to glorify God (John 16:7–14).

The nature of certain aspects of this work is indicated in Revelation 3:18. God pleads with those who are self-satisfied and comfortable in their knowledge of spiritual things. If they are willing, He will show them their deficiencies. The apostle John indicates that the work of the Holy Spirit in these individuals can be likened to the use of a powerful eye salve—it will restore their vision.

Ezekiel likened the energizing effect of the Spirit's activities to the reverse outcome of a horror movie (Ezek. 37:1–14). Rather than humans being turned into walking skeletons, he saw piles of bones being reassembled, with muscle and skin being placed on them, and the Spirit breathing life into the restored bodies so that they came alive as "an exceedingly great army" (verse 10). This vision might be imagined as having parallels with the experience of the disciples recorded in Acts 2. "It is not the human agent that is to inspire with life. The Lord God of Israel will do that part, quickening the lifeless spiritual nature into activity. The breath of the Lord of hosts must enter into the lifeless bodies."[368] The Spirit that was active at Creation (Gen. 1:2) has a vital part to play in the re-creation of the image of God in humanity.

Ministry of the Angels

In this section, I will

- *highlight the ministry of the angels.*

The Scriptures are full of references to angels interacting with humans. They may appear in human form or as beings of light. Abraham, on the one hand, entertained three regular travelers, or so he initially thought. At the end of his interchanges with them, he knew that two were angels (Gen. 18:1–33). Manoah's wife, on the other hand, was visited by what she considered a "very awesome" being (Judges 13:6). These examples might be substantiated by similar references to angels conveying information or making important announcements. The most memorable was the announcement of Jesus' birth by a host of angels (Luke 2:9–15) and the announcement of His resurrection by two mighty angels (John 20:12).

Each individual has a guardian angel (Matt. 18:10) whose task appears to involve protection from danger and to supply their physical needs in accordance with God's will (Ps. 34:7; 78:25; Dan. 6:22). They also protect from spiritual danger. While the former activity is related to the latter, I will focus more specifically on the role of God's angels in the outworking of the plan of salvation in human lives.

Agents of Mercy. God has given believers a reassuring promise of assistance from the angels of heaven: "Are they not all ministering spirits sent forth to minister for those who will inherit salvation?" (Heb. 1:14). Angels have been involved in the outworking of the plan of salvation since its announcement. We well remember that cherubim, which are an order of angels, are pictured with a "flaming sword" at the entrance to the Garden to prevent access to the tree of life so that a race of immortal sinners would not arise. However, there is another meaning that can be attributed to the key word in the task that the cherubim were entrusted to do—"to keep the way of the tree of life" (Gen. 3:24, KJV). The word *shamar*, translated "keep" in this verse, is also used in Genesis 2:15 to describe the work of the human pair in the Garden—they were to *keep* the Garden in proper condition. There was an element of judgment in the presence of the cherubim at the Garden entrance as well as an element of keeping the communication lines with heaven open, for it was at the entrance to the Garden that Adam and his sons came to worship and that the divine glory was revealed.[369] Scholar of the Old Testament sanctuary Leslie Hardinge wrote: "The Edenic cherubim, illuminating the path back to the tree of life with the sword of light, were symbols of all those whose characters and ministry help to keep Jesus, 'the way' of life, clear for all who choose to walk in it."[370]

God's mercy, justice, and divine glory were on display at the entrance to the Garden. These very features were again evident in the earthly sanctuary. Here cherubim reverently bowed over the mercy seat, thereby indicating the "reverence with which the heavenly host regard the law of God, and their interest in the plan of redemption."[371] Angel figures were also embroidered on the innermost veil (Exod. 26:31). We have noted that the veil represented Christ's flesh (Heb. 10:20). Emblems of cherubim on the veil indicated their involvement in the ministry of salvation.[372]

The angels of God are actively involved in communication between heaven and earth, as illustrated by Jacob's vision of the ladder (Gen. 28:11–16). Angels were very active in the time of the apostles. One directed Philip to explain the Scriptures concerning Christ to an Ethiopian official (Acts 8:26–39). Another directed Cornelius to send men to find Simon Peter at Joppa (Acts 10:3–8). Angels are symbolically represented as taking the last gospel call to the world (Rev. 14:6, 7). In practical terms, this conveys the important truth that angels cooperate with humans in the work of making known the gospel message.

The central idea conveyed by these examples is that the angels of heaven encourage and direct help to those seeking to understand God's ways as well as those who are working to encourage and instruct their fellow humans in darkness. Thus, the angels are actively participating in the salvation of humanity, for they recognize that the redeemed will be members of "the heavenly family, a companion through the eternal ages of God and Christ and the holy angels. Heaven will triumph, for the vacancies made by the fall of Satan and his host will be filled by the redeemed of the Lord."[373]

Agents of Rebuke. Sometimes angels act in what might seem uncharacteristic ways, shocking believers into a more consistent and faithful witness. I can think of two examples of this kind in the Bible. The first relates to Moses (Exod. 4:24–26). He was on his way to Egypt to deliver the children of Israel at God's command. However, he had disregarded explicit instructions given him by God to circumcise his youngest son. This called forth God's displeasure so that the angel "sought to kill" Moses (verse 24). Zipporah avoided tragedy by performing the rite herself, though initially persuading Moses to desist. Thus was impressed upon Moses the necessity of being a good example to the people he was about to lead and of not doing anything to "lessen the force of the divine precepts upon the people."[374]

The second example involved Balaam (Num. 22:16–35). Balaam has been held up as the Old Testament equivalent of Judas. He was well aware of duty but tried to serve two masters—God and Satan. His focus was on riches and honor and, by cherishing these ambitions; he neglected to follow the instructions of God faithfully delivered by angels and by other means. He let covetousness ruin his ministry as a prophet, and he died a traitor and lawbreaker.[375] His life stands as a warning against neglecting the call of conscience and the guidance of God in the events of life. Ultimately, God allows each person to choose to serve Him or Satan. However, we carefully note that the angels place stumbling blocks in the way of those pursuing unrighteous ways in an effort to turn them around. Balaam knew his duty, but he chose to disobey God's instructions. Despite this, an angel contended with him in the way to impress upon him the seriousness of his course of action (verse 22).

Agents of Destiny. God's prophetic Word assures us that the events of history are moving toward their climax as indicated in Scripture. This is no haphazard affair. Both Christ and the commanders of the angels are involved in convincing world leaders and decision makers about desirable directions to take in the tumultuous times in which they are operating (Dan. 10:13, 20, 21).

Living Stones

In this section, I will

- *emphasize that God's goal is to save even the weakest believer.*

The apostle Peter paints a reassuring picture of the role of believers in the Christian church. Christ is the cornerstone of the church, and believers are living stones in the spiritual house that God is raising up as a witness to the world (1 Peter 2:4, 5).

The apostle Peter was enthusiastic about the transformation that the gospel brought to hearers in the past and that it will bring to hearers in the future. The assurance of sins forgiven, of being "kept by the power of God," and of having "an inheritance ... reserved in heaven for you" caused Peter to rejoice exceedingly (1 Peter 1:3–6). He carefully explained to his audience that the focus of the mind is to be kept on the righteousness of Christ and His instruction to follow holiness (verses 13–16). In other words, a vital and continuing connection with Christ will ensure victory. Peter went on to assure readers that both the Father and the Holy Spirit are vitally interested and involved in the work of salvation and that the Word of God is to be reverently studied and treasured, as it is God's love letter and guide book for all God's human children (verses 17, 22–25).

The prophet Isaiah gave the encouraging insight about the Messiah: "He shall see the labor of His soul, *and* be satisfied" (Isa. 53:11). There is no question but that a vast number of people will be saved as a result of Christ's sacrifice. The apostle John saw a special group of people who had come victoriously through the last great scenes of strife on the earth before the return of Jesus; he also saw a multitude that "no one could number" (Rev. 7:9). This extraordinary scene of assembly takes place before the throne of God, and it is witnessed by all the celestial beings who do not fail to give praise to God (verses 9–12). After all, they have all been involved in the salvation of the individuals assembled. Christ is exceedingly joyful with the harvest of souls received (Heb. 12:2).

A magnificent assurance has been given to the weakest believer. God will "not allow you to be tempted beyond what you are able, but

Chapter 23. Fiery Coals, Living Stones

with the temptation will also make the way of escape" (1 Cor. 10:13). We have noted already that all heaven is involved in the salvation of individuals, and we might remind ourselves that God is "not willing that any should perish but that all should come to repentance" (2 Peter 3:9). With these assurances, all are encouraged to "Think of Jesus. He is in His holy place, not in a state of solitude, but surrounded by ten thousand times ten thousand of heavenly angels who wait to do His bidding. And He bids them go and work for the weakest saint who puts his trust in God. High and low, rich and poor, have the same help provided."[376]

In answer to the believer's cry for help, the assurance comes: "In times of sudden difficulty or peril the heart may send up its cry for help to One who has pledged Himself to come to the aid of His faithful, believing ones whenever they call upon Him. In every circumstance, under every condition, the soul weighed down with grief and care, or fiercely assailed by temptation, may find assurance, support, and succor in the unfailing love and power of a covenant-keeping God."[377] This is the message of the sanctuary.

Endnotes

1. Originally written in Letter 63 (March 17), 1893, to P. B. W. Wessels of Auckland, New Zealand, and published in the *Advent Review and Sabbath Herald*, vol. 70, no. 33 (August 15, 1893), p. 513, before publication in *Our High Calling*.
2. The term "antitypical" is a derivative of the word "type" (Greek *tupos*) which Hebrews 8:5 used to describe the Old Testament symbols of salvation realities. Thus, "antitypical" means fulfillment.
3. Sanctuary Review Committee, "Christ in the Heavenly Sanctuary (Consensus Document)," in *Doctrine of the Sanctuary: A Historical Survey (1845–1863)*, ed. Frank B. Holbrook (Silver Spring, MD: Biblical Research Institute, 1989), p. 227.
4. Fernando Canale, "From Vision to System: Finishing the Task of Adventist Theology: Part I: Historical Review," *Journal of the Adventist Theological Society*, vol. 15, no. 2 (Autumn 2004), p. 17.
5. Fernando Canale, "The Eclipse of Scripture and the Protestantization of the Adventist Mind: Part 2: From the Evangelical Gospel to Culture," *Journal of the Adventist Theological Society*, vol. 22, no. 1 (Spring 2011), p. 131.
6. Ellen G. White, *Christ in His Sanctuary* (Mountain View, CA: Pacific Press Publishing Association, 1969), p. 87; originally published in Ellen G. White, *The Spirit of Prophecy*, vol. 4 (Battle Creek, MI: Seventh-day Adventist Publishing Association, 1884), p. 258.
7. Available at http://1ref.us/gj (accessed 8/3/16).
8. Fernando Canale, "From Vision to System: Finishing the Task of Adventist Theology. Part III: Sanctuary and Hermeneutics," *Journal of the Adventist Theological Society*, vol. 17, no. 2 (Autumn 2006), pp. 56, 57.

9   In this book, I assume the Pauline authorship of the epistle to the Hebrews.

10 Implied by God's rest in Gen. 2:1–3, which the evidence throughout Genesis from the predominance of the number seven over other numbers (Gen. 21:28–30; 29:18, 20, 27, 30; 33:3; 41:2–7, 18–20, 22–24, 26, 27, 29, 30, 34, 36, 47, 48, 53, 54; 46:25), the grouping of seven days (Gen. 7:4, 10; 8:10, 12; Gen. 31:23; 50:10), and the concept of the week (Gen. 29:27, 28) indicate that the human race knew about. Additionally, could Adam and Eve have engaged in labor knowing that God was resting?

11 William J. Dumbrell, *Covenant and Creation* (Nashville, TN: Thomas Nelson Publishers, 1984), p. 35.

12 Ellen G. White, *The Adventist Home* (Nashville, TN: Southern Publishing Association, 1952), p. 541; originally published in *The Spirit of Prophecy*, vol. 4, p. 465.

13 Don Mackintosh, "Living a Faithful Life," *Adventist Review*, vol. 119, no. 19 (Sept. 24, 2014), pp. 10, 11.

14 The term *hupodeigma* used in Hebrews 9:23, translated "patterns" (KJV), can also be legitimately translated "copies" (NKJV, NIV), for it is both. The sanctuary on earth was constructed "after the pattern" shown to Moses (Exod. 25:9)—making it a copy—and the earthly sanctuary also formed "patterns" of things in the heavens that were yet to be realized (Heb. 9:23). Because the heavenly already existed before the one on earth was constructed, the earthly post-dates the sanctuary in heaven. Because the earthly symbolized salvation events that were to come, it pre-dates the sanctuary in heaven. Thus, it both post-dates and pre-dates the sanctuary in heaven—it is both "copies" and "patterns."

15 Elias Brasil de Souza, "Sanctuary: Cosmos, Covenant, and Creation," *Journal of the Adventist Theological Society*, vol. 24, no. 1 (Spring 2013), p. 32.

16 Notice that the seventh day is not linked to the Exodus but to the seventh day of Creation. It reminds of the Exodus only in the sense that Israel could not keep the Sabbath while they were in slavery. Deuteronomy 5 is Moses reminding Israel (Deut. 5:1) of what God declared from Sinai (Exodus 20:1), paraphrasing God's words with emphasis. In reminding that they were to keep the Sabbath, Moses emphasized the reason for keeping all of God's commandments—God brought them out of bondage (Deut. 5:15; cf. Deut. 5:6; Exod. 20:2). The two motivations endures for all people created by God whom He has freed from bondage.

17 Richard M. Davidson, "Typology in the Book of Hebrews," in *Issues in the Book of Hebrews*, ed. F. B. Holbrook (Silver Spring, MD: Biblical Research Institute, 1989), pp. 124, 133, 175, 182, 183; see also Alwyn P. Salom, "Sanctuary Theology," in *Issues in the Book of Hebrews*, pp. 205–209.

18 Marcie Lenk, "Rebuild the Temple? Not in Our Time," *The Algemeiner*, April 1, 2014; Cecil Roth, ed., *Encyclopaedia Judaica* (Jerusalem: Keter Publishing House, 1971-1972), vol. 15, cols. 990, 993, 994.

19 William Tyndale translated Luther's term *"der Gnadenstuhl"* into "the mercy seat." Brevard S. Childs, *The Book of Exodus: A Critical, Theological Commentary* (Louisville, KY: John Knox Press, 1974, 2004), p. 524.

20 Ellen G. White, *The Story of Patriarchs and Prophets* (Mountain View, CA: Pacific Press Publishing Association, 1958), p. 357.

21 The simplest evidence that Michael is Christ is found in whose voice it is that raises the dead. After the Lord Jesus Christ descends from heaven with a shout and the voice of the archangel, the dead in Christ will rise to life (1 Thess. 4:16). The archangel is Michael (Jude 9). Jesus declared that the voice that raises the dead is "the voice of the Son of God" (John 5:25). Thus, the "archangel" whose voice raises the dead is "the Son of God." Other evidences to be cited are the verbal link in the LORD and Michael choosing to rebuke Satan without a railing accusation (translated "evil speaking," Eph. 4:31) with the simple command, "The Lord rebuke thee" (Zech. 3:2; Jude 9); the Son of God being described in the Old Testament as God's "Angel," or "Messenger" (Gen. 48:16; Exod. 23:20–23; 32:34; Mal. 3:1); Jesus being portrayed in Revelation as the supreme commander of the angel hosts, riding His white horse across the skies to rescue His children (Rev. 19:11); and Jesus the King of kings (Rev. 19:16; 1 Tim 6:15), which links to His being the Prince of princes (Dan. 8:25).

22 An Egyptian cubit was approximately 20.6 inches, or 0.52 meters.

23 *Patriarchs and Prophets*, p. 352; Leslie Hardinge, *With Jesus in His Sanctuary: A Walk Through the Tabernacle Along His Way* (Harrisburg, PA: American Cassette Ministries, 1991), p. 136 [http://1ref.us/fy, p. 66].

24 *Encyclopaedia Judaica*, vol. 5, cols 1384–1386.

25 Frank B. Holbrook, Daniel and Revelation Committee, "Issues in the Book of Hebrews," *Ministry*, vol. 58, no. 4 (April 1985), pp. 12–16, 21.

26 Holbrook, p. 14; George E. Rice, "Hebrews 6:19: Analysis of Some Assumptions Concerning Katapetasma," *Issues in the Book of Hebrews*, p. 229.

27 More precisely, it is an adjective that functions as a noun, which is common in many languages.

28 Herbert Kiesler, "An Exegesis of Selected Passages," *Issues in the Book of Hebrews*, ed. F. B. Holbrook, (Silver Spring, MD: Biblical Research Institute, 1989), p. 77. See also A. P. Salom, "*Ta hagia* in the Epistle to the Hebrews," *Andrews University Studies*, vol. 5, issue 1 (January 1967), pp. 59–70; William G. Johnson, "Hebrews: An Overview," *Issues in the Book of Hebrews*, ed. F. B. Holbrook, pp. 14, 15.

29 *Babylonian Talmud*, tractate Yoma 5.

30 George Ricker Berry, *Interlinear Greek-English New Testament with a Greek-English Lexicon and New Testament Synonyms* (Grand Rapids, MI: Zondervan, 1958), pp. 570–573, 575, 583; Alfred Marshall, *The R.S.V. Interlinear Greek-English New Testament* (London: Samuel Bagster, 1975),

pp. 871, 873, 874, 876, 879, 892; Robert Young, *Young's Literal Translation of the Holy Bible*, revised edition (Grand Rapids, MI: Baker Book House, 1898).

31 Ministerial Association, *Seventh-day Adventists Believe: A Biblical Exposition of Fundamental Doctrines* (Washington, DC: General Conference of Seventh-day Adventists, 1988), p. 152.

32 Ellen G. White, *Education* (Mountain View, CA: Pacific Press Publishing Association, 1952), p. 29.

33 For "beguiled," see Gen. 3:13, KJV; for "deceived," see Gen. 3:13, NKJV; and for "charmed," see Ellen G. White, "The Test of Loyalty," *Signs of the Times*, vol. 22, no. 7 (Feb. 13, 1896), p. 102. Regarding Satan's hypnotic movements, see Letter 159 (July 30), 1903, in F. D. Nichol, R. F. Cottrell et al., eds., "Ellen G. White Comments," *The Seventh-day Adventist Bible Commentary* (Washington, DC: Review and Herald Publishing Association, 1956), vol. 5, p. 1081.

34 Rick Howard, *The Omega Rebellion* (USA: Rick Howard, 2010), pp. 50, 51, 115; Thomas R. Kelly, *A Testament of Devotion* (N. Y: Harper & Brothers, 1941), pp. 92–100; Robert Trabold, "Contemplative Prayer: the Discipline of Silence," *Quest*, vol. 96, no. 6 (November-December 2008), pp. 230, 231.

35 John Grinder and Richard Bandler, *Trance-formations: Neuro-linguistic Programming and the Structure of Hypnosis* (Moab, UT: Real People Press, 1981), p. 99; cf. J. Christopher Clarke and James Arthur Jackson, *Hypnosis and Behavior Therapy: The Treatment of Anxiety and Phobias* (New York: Springer Publishing Company, 1983), pp. 119–141.

36 J. D. Douglas, *The New Bible Dictionary* (London: Inter-Varsity Fellowship, 1962), p. 478.

37 Canale, "From Vision to System ... Part III," pp. 45–56.

38 Nichol, et al., *Seventh-day Adventist Bible Commentary*, vol. 1, p. 636.

39 Canale, "From Vision to System ... Part III," pp. 45–56.

40 God will reveal the ark in His own time and with astounding clarity.

41 Josephus mentions the Maccabees' restoring to the sanctuary the "vessels, the candlestick, the table [of shewbread], and the altar [of incense]," but not the ark of the covenant (Josephus, "The Antiquities of the Jews," book 12, chap. 7, par. 6, verse 318, *The Works of Josephus*, Complete and Unabridged [Peabody, MA: Hendrickson Publishers, 1987], William Whiston, trans., p. 328). He also stated: "In this there was nothing at all. It was inaccessible and inviolable, and not to be seen by any; and was called the Holy of Holies" (Josephus, "The Wars of the Jews," book 5, chap. 5, par. 5, verse 219, *The Works of Josephus*, p. 707).

42 *Encyclopaedia Judaica*, vol. 15, col. 1167.

43 "The Godhead was stirred with pity for the race, and the Father, the Son, and the Holy Spirit gave themselves to the working out of the plan of redemption. In order to fully carry out this plan, it was decided that Christ,

the only begotten Son of God, should give Himself an offering for sin. What line can measure the depth of this love?" (Ellen G. White, Letter 12, 1901, Jan. 21, 1901).

44 See also *Medical Ministry*, p. 92, par. 1: "Human beings cannot explain themselves, and how, then, dare they venture to explain the Omniscient One?" Letter 26 (Nov. 22), 1894, par. 12: "An all-powerful and omnipresent Providence is revealed in their entire history."

45 On the other hand, the angel of Revelation did not permit his being worshipped (Rev. 19:10; 22:9).

46 Hardinge, *With Jesus in His Sanctuary*, p. 509 [http://1ref.us/fy, p. 261].

47 Charles Beecher, *Redeemer and Redeemed* (Boston: Lee & Shepard, 1864), p. 65, best known through the adaptation of the thought gem in Ellen G. White, *The Desire of Ages* (Mountain View, CA: Pacific Press Publishing Association, 1940), p. 25.

48 Henry Melvill, *Sermons* (New York: Stanford & Swords, 1844), p. 47.

49 Melvill, p. 47; Tim Poirier, "Sources Clarify Ellen White's Christology," *Ministry*, vol. 62, no. 12 (Dec. 1989), p. 7.

50 White, *The Desire of Ages*, pp. 311, 312.

51 White, *Patriarchs and Prophets,* p. 184.

52 Hardinge, *With Jesus in His Sanctuary*, p. 210 [http://1ref.us/fy, p. 103].

53 Leslie Hardinge, *Shadows of His Sacrifice* (Maranatha Media, 2001), p. 30.

54 *Encyclopaedia Judaica*, vol. 3, col. 1002.

55 Hardinge, *Shadows of His Sacrifice*, p. 30.

56 See NASB Lexicon, available at http://1ref.us/fz, accessed 10/24/16.

57 Josephus, "The Antiquities of the Jews," bk. 3, chapter 6, par. 7, verse 144, *Life and Works of Flavius Josephus*, pp. 88.

58 Hardinge, *Shadows of His Sacrifice*, p. 20. Sukkah 5:3 says: "From the worn out pants of the priests and from their [worn out] belts they would tear [pieces], and they would [use them as wicks to] light with them."

59 Ellen G. White, *Spiritual Gifts*, vol. 1 (Battle Creek, MI: Seventh-day Adventist Publishing Association, 1858), p. 170.

60 Marvin R. Vincent, *Word Studies in the New Testament* (New York: Charles Scribner's Sons, 1900), vol. 4, p. 384.

61 Henry George Liddell and Robert Scott, *"kathiēmi,"* *A Greek-English Lexicon* (Oxford: Clarendon Press, 1968), p. 854.

62 J. D. Douglas, *The New Bible Dictionary* (London: The Inter-Varsity Fellowship, 1962), p. 503.

63 *"Dexios,"* Liddell and Scott, p. 379.

64 Kiesler, "An Exegesis of Selected Passages," *Issues in the Book of Hebrews*, pp. 56, 57.

65 Clifford Goldstein, *Between the Lion and the Lamb* (Boise, ID: Pacific Press Publishing Association, 1995), p. 65.

66 Robert Young, *Analytical Concordance to the Holy Bible* (Grand Rapids, MI: Wm. B. Eerdmans Publishing Company, 1983), p. 488.

67 Jay P. Green, *A Literal Translation of the Bible* (Peabody, MA: Hendrickson Publishers, 1987), p. 975.

68 "Statement on Desmond Ford Document," *Ministry*, vol. 53, no. 10 (Oct. 1980), p. 51, referencing Desmond Ford, "Daniel 8:14, the Investigative Judgment, and the Kingdom of God." p. 229.

69 Ellen G. White, *The Great Controversy* (Mountain View, CA: Pacific Press Publishing Association, 1911, 1950), pp. 428, 429.

70 White, *Spiritual Gifts*, vol. 1, p. 163.

71 Alexander Cruden, *Cruden's Complete Concordance to the Old and New Testaments* (London: Lutterworth Press, 1958), p. 517.

72 "*Prophēteia*," Liddell and Scott, pp. 1539, 1540.

73 Term "school of the prophets" used by Ellen G. White, *Education*, pp. 46, 47.

74 Charles H. Watson, *The Atoning Work of Christ, His Sacrifice and Priestly Ministry* (Washington, DC: Review and Herald Publishing Association, 1934), p. 101.

75 White, *The Desire of Ages*, p. 112.

76 Ellen G. White, Letter 22 (Jan. 18), 1889, in *Selected Messages* (Washington, DC: Review and Herald Publishing Association, 1958), vol. 1, p. 368.

77 White, *The Desire of Ages*, p. 756.

78 Ellen G. White, *Christ's Object Lessons* (Hagerstown, MD: Review and Herald Publishing Association, 1941), p. 120.

79 Ministerial Association, *Seventh-day Adventists Believe*, pp. 322, 323.

80 Richard M. Davidson, "Christ's Entry 'Within the Veil' in Hebrews 6:19-20: The Old Testament Background," *Andrews University Seminary Studies*, vol. 39, no. 2 (Autumn 2001), pp. 175–190.

81 William G. Johnsson, *Hebrews* (Atlanta, GA: John Knox Press, 1980), pp. 49–54.

82 Adam Clarke, *The Holy Bible, Containing the Old and New Testaments: with a Commentary and Critical Notes*, comments on John 1:14.

83 Ellen G. White, "Conditions for Obtaining Eternal Riches," *Advent Review and Sabbath Herald*, vol. 67, no. 23 (June 10, 1890), p. 353.

84 Ellen G. White, "The Peace of Christ," *Signs of the Times*, vol. 23, no. 46 (Nov. 25, 1897), pp. 4, 5.

85 Ellen G. White, "Words to the Young," *Youth's Instructor*, vol. 42, no. 48 (Dec. 6, 1894), p. 381.

86 Ellen G. White, "The Work of the Holy Spirit in Conversion," *Signs of the Times*, vol. 37, no. 10 (March 8, 1910), pp. 6, 7.

87 E. Y. Mullins, quoted by Josh McDowell, *Evidence that Demands a Verdict* (San Bernardino, CA: Here's Life Publishers, Inc., 1979), p. 328.

88 Ellen G. White, *The Acts of the Apostles* (Mountain View, CA: Pacific Press Publishing Association, 1911), p. 520.

89 White, *The Spirit of Prophecy*, vol. 4, p. 492; *The Great Controversy*, p. 678.

90 Ellen G. White, "Christ Glorified," *Signs of the Times*, vol. 25, no. 19 (May 10, 1899), pp. 1, 2.

91 *The Desire of Ages*, pp. 597, 598, originally published in *The Spirit of Prophecy*, vol. 3, pp. 33, 34.

92 *The Great Controversy*, p. 416.

93 The New Testament term "Pentecost" (Acts 2:1; 20:16; 1 Cor. 16:8) means "fiftieth day."

94 Beresford J. Kidd, *A History of the Church to A.D. 461* (Oxford: Clarendon Press, 1922), vol. 1, p. 60.

95 Kenneth Scott Latourette, *The History of the Expansion of Christianity* (Grand Rapids, MI: Zondervan Publishing House, 1976), vol. 1, pp. 251, 252.

96 Heidi Heiks, *AD 538 Source Book* (Ringgold, GA: Teach Services, Inc., 2010), pp. 267–269.

97 Michele Maccarrone, "Innocent III Did Not Claim Temporal Power," *Innocent III Vicar of Christ or Lord of the World?* James M. Powell, ed., second edition (Washington, DC: Catholic University of America Press, 1994), pp. 73–78. Maccarrone pointed out: "In addition, by giving an official approval to these words [the vicar of Christ] which designate the pope, he pointed out for theological speculation a new problem, that is to say, whether the pope received all the powers which Christ had while on earth and is His vicar. This problem had an immediate influence on political ideas because, given the then common doctrine that the "reign" of Christ was not only spiritual, but also temporal, it followed that the pope, as vicar of Christ, held by right not only the spiritual power but also the temporal . . ." See also Telesphore Cardinal Toppo, Luis Cardinal Aponte Martinez et al., "Cardinals' Letter Promoting Marian Doctrine," February 11, 2008, available at http://1ref.us/g0 (accessed 7/27/2016).

98 Carlyle Boynton Haynes, *From Sabbath to Sunday* (Washington, DC: Review and Herald Publishing Association, 1928, 2005), pp. 41–45; John Henry Newman, *An Essay on the Development of Christian Doctrine*, ed. J. M. Cameron (Harmondsworth, Middlesex: Penguin Books, 1845, 1974), available at http://1ref.us/g1 (accessed 8/20/16); Warren A. Shipton, *The Golden River That Flows through Time* (Tamarac, FL: Llumina Press, 2010), pp. 247–252, 269, 270.

99 Clifford Goldstein, *The Remnant* (Boise, ID: Pacific Press Publishing Association, 1994), p. 107.

100 White, *The Desire of Ages*, p. 135.

101 Fernando Canale, "On Being the Remnant," *Journal of the Adventist Theological Society*, vol. 24, no. 1 (Spring 2013), p. 131.

102 John Ankerberg and John Weldon, *Encyclopedia of New Age Beliefs* (Eugene, OR: Harvest House Publishers, 1996), pp. 246–249, 425, 426; Gene Edward Veith, *Postmodern Times* (Wheaton, IL: Crossway Books, 1994), pp. 194–198.

103 Rick Howard, *Meet It* (Coldwater, MI: Remnant Publications, 2014).

104 James Hastings, ed., *Encyclopaedia of Religion and Ethics* (Edinburgh: T. & T. Clark, 1971), vol. 12, p. 517.

105 Jesus Himself commended His "spirit" to God while informing Mary that, on the morning of the Resurrection, He had not ascended to His Father (Luke 23:46; John 20:17). Thus, no conscious part of Him entered heaven when He breathed out His last (Luke 23:46).

106 Ellen G. White, *The Spirit of Prophecy* (Battle Creek, MI: Steam Press of the SDA Publishing Association, 1870), vol. 1, p. 37. This demonstration is inferred by verse 6, which says that the woman "saw that the tree was good for food."

107 Adam Clarke, *The Holy Bible*, comments on Genesis 2:17; Francis D. Nichol, Raymond F. Cottrell et al., eds., *The Seventh-day Adventist Bible Commentary* (Washington, DC: Review and Herald Publishing Association, 1953), vol. 1, p. 225.

108 Charles George Herbermann, ed., *The Catholic Encyclopedia* (New York: The Encyclopedia Press, 1913), vol. 7, pp. 687, 689.

109 *Encyclopaedia of Religion and Ethics*, vol. 8, p. 301.

110 Mattia Harris-Bolton, *Lord of the Supernatural: Out of the Occult and Into the Arms of Jesus* (Bloomington, IN: AuthorHouse, 2012), p. 160.

111 George E. Vandeman, *Psychic Roulette* (Mountain View, CA: Pacific Press Publishing Association, 1973), p. 125.

112 Hardinge, *With Jesus in His Sanctuary*, p. 89 [http://1ref.us/fy, p. 43]; *Patriarchs and Prophets*, p. 347.

113 Young, *Analytical Concordance*, pp. 924, 925.

114 *Encyclopaedia Judaica*, vol. 14, col. 621; Josephus, "The Antiquities of the Jews," book 13, chap. 5, par. 9; book 18, chap. 1, par. 2.

115 John C. Poirier, " 'Day and Night' and the Punctuation of John 9:3," *New Testament Studies*, vol. 42 (Sheffield: T&T Clark, 1996), p. 288.

116 The Greek is even clearer, placing "with me" before "you will be"—"*Amen* [Truly] *soi* [to you] *legō* [I say] *sēmeron* [today] met' emou [with me] *esē* [you will be] *en tō paradeisō* [in the paradise]."

117 Josephus, "An Extract Out of Josephus' Discourse to the Greeks Concerning Hades," pars. 1–4, *Life and Works of Flavius Josephus*, p. 813.

118 Joachim Jeremias, *The Parables of Jesus*, revised third edition (London: S.C.M. Press, 1972), p. 183.

119 Also, Abraham's summary statement is that one should hear Moses and the prophets—meaning, the Scriptures. What they teach about death is that a person who dies, sleeps (Deut. 31:16; 2 Sam. 7:12).

120 Daniel Pickering Walker, *The Decline of Hell: Seventeenth-Century Discussions of Eternal Torment* (Chicago, IL: Chicago University Press, 1964), p. 35.

121 *The Companion to the Catechism of the Catholic Church: A Compendium of Texts Referred to in the Catechism of the Catholic Church* (San Francisco: Ignatius Press, 1994), p. 406.

122 Jacques Le Goff, *The Birth of Purgatory* (London: Scholar Press, 1984), trans. Arthur Goldhammer, pp. 52, 60.

123 Michael Maher, "Immortality," *The Catholic Encyclopedia*, vol. 7, pp. 689, 690.

124 Richard, *The God Delusion* (Boston; New York: Houghton Mifflin Co., 2008), pp. 357–360.

125 Edwin E. Reynolds, "The Feast of Tabernacles and the Book of Revelation," *Andrews University Seminary Studies*, vol. 38, no. 2 (2000), pp. 245–268.

126 Jon Paulien, "The Resurrection and the Old Testament," *Journal of the Adventist Theological Society*, vol. 24, no. 1 (Spring 2013), pp. 3–24.

127 For Romans, chapter 5, verse 9, Paul quoted 2 Sam. 22:50 or Ps. 18:49; for verse 10, he quoted Deut. 32:43; for verse 11, he quoted Ps. 117:1; and for verse 12, he quoted Isa. 11:1, 10.

128 Roy Gane, *Altar Call* (Berrien Springs, MI: Diadem, 1999), p. 142.

129 Hardinge, *With Jesus in His Sanctuary*, p. 140 [http://1ref.us/fy, p. 69].

130 *The Great Controversy*, pp. 355, 356.

131 Clifford Goldstein, "Investigating the Investigative Judgment," *Ministry*, vol. 65, no. 2 (February 1992), p. 7.

132 George William Turner, ed., *The Australian Concise Oxford Dictionary* (Oxford: Oxford University Press, 1987), p. 607.

133 Ellen G. White, Ms. 32, 1896, in *Christ Triumphant* (Hagerstown, MD: Review and Herald Publishing Association, 1999), p. 339.

134 Anders Nygren, *Agape and Eros* (Chicago, IL: University of Chicago Press, 1982), trans. P. S. Watson, pp. 75–81, 210.

135 *The Acts of the Apostles*, p. 601.

136 Turner, *Australian Concise Oxford Dictionary*, p. 1174.

137 It should not be forgotten that thirty years after the crucifixion, Luke included the women's resting on the Sabbath "according to the commandment" (Luke 23:56), suggesting that he assumed that Theophilus would know which commandment called for rest on the seventh day.

138 Wayne Jackson, "The Jesus Seminar—2," *Christian Courier*, available at http://1ref.us/g2 (accessed 7/27/2016).

139 White, *The Great Controversy*, p. 434.

140 The earliest Church Fathers to quote Revelation 22:14 render it: "do His commandments." These include Tertullian (AD 220), Cyprian (AD 258), and Tyconius (AD 380), as well as the Syriac Peshitta, Harclean, and Philoxenian versions. The first Church Father to quote Revelation 22:14 as "wash their robes" was Athanasius, Bishop of Alexandria (AD 326-373). The original reading, "*Makarioi* [blessed] *hoi poiountes* [the ones doing] *tas entolas* [the commandments] *autou* [of him]," was changed in later manuscripts to read: "*Makarioi* [Blessed] *hoi plunontes* [the ones washing] *tas stōlas* [the robes] *autōn* [of them]."

141 Richard M. Davidson, Andrews University, in a public lecture at Mt. Gravatt Church, Queensland.

142 Ellen G. White, "The Perfect Law," *Advent Review and Sabbath Herald*, vol. 75, no. 14 (April 5, 1898), p. 213.

143 The listing for Gentiles in Acts 15:20 comes from the requirements of the law of "Moses" (Acts 15:21) that apply to "strangers"—Lev. 17:12, 15; 18:26–30. According to Acts 15:29; 21:25, the phrase "pollutions of idols" means "things offered to idols."

144 With all the Jews' complaints against him, Scripture does not mention anyone ever accusing him of not keeping the Sabbath.

145 White, *The Desire of Ages*, p. 757.

146 White, *The Desire of Ages*, pp. 565, 566.

147 Ellen G. White, "Without Excuse," *Advent Review and Sabbath Herald*, vol. 78, no. 39 (September 24, 1901), p. 615.

148 White, *The Desire of Ages*, p. 761, emphasis added.

149 A. Boudinhon, "Priest," *The Catholic Encyclopedia* (New York: Robert Appleton Company, 1911), vol. 12.

150 Philip Jenkins, *The Next Christendom: The Coming of Global Christianity* (Oxford: Oxford University Press, 2002), p. 118.

151 Pope Pius XII, "*Ad Caeli Reginam*. Encyclical on Proclaiming the Queenship of Mary" (October 11, 1954), articles 51, 38, 42.

152 Lucius Ferraris, *Prompta Bibliotheca Canonica, Juridica, Moralis, Theologica, Ascetica, Polemica, Rubristica, Historica*, trans. from Latin (Petit-Montrouge, Paris: J. P. Migne, 1858), vol. 5, col. 1823, Latin.

153 John Paul II, "Message to the Pontifical Academy of Sciences," *The Quarterly Review of Biology*, vol. 72, no. 4 (December 1997), pp. 381–383.

154 Patrick Cusworth, "Pope Francis's Comments on the Big Bang Are Not Revolutionary. Catholic Teaching Has Long Professed the Likelihood of Human Evolution," *Catholic Herald*, Oct. 31, 2014.

155 T. H. Jemison, *Christian Beliefs* (Mountain View, CA: Pacific Press Publishing Association, 1959), pp. 202, 203.

156 Canale, "The Eclipse of Scripture ... Part 2," p. 131.

157 White, *The Desire of Ages*, p. 819.
158 Ellen G. White, "The Remnant Church Not Babylon," *Advent Review and Sabbath Herald*, vol. 7, no. 34 (Aug. 22, 1893), p. 531.
159 Ellen G. White, "Qualifications for the Worker," *Advent Review and Sabbath Herald*, vol. 72, no. 23 (June 4, 1895), p. 353.
160 *Encyclopaedia Judaica*, vol. 5, col. 1383.
161 Ellen G. White, *Early Writings* (Washington, DC: Review and Herald Publishing Association, 1882, 1945), p. 253; see also *The Great Controversy*, p. 480.
162 Ellen G. White, "Lessons from the Life of Solomon—No. 9, The Ark of the Covenant," *Advent Review and Sabbath Herald*, vol. 82, no. 45 (Nov. 9, 1905), p. 10.
163 Gane, pp. 249–254.
164 White, *Early Writings*, p. 178; *The Great Controversy*, pp. 422, 485, 658.
165 Louis Shores, ed., *Collier's Encyclopedia* (New York: Crowell-Collier Publishing Co., 1965), vol. 23, p. 702.
166 Herman Wouk, *This Is My God* (London: Jonathan Cape, 1960), p. 84.
167 *Encyclopaedia Judaica*, vol. 6, col. 1195.
168 Ellen G. White, "The Righteousness of Christ," *Advent Review and Sabbath Herald*, vol. 67, no. 32 (Aug. 19, 1890), p. 497, in *Reflecting Christ* (Warburton, Victoria: Signs Publishing Co., 1985), p. 303.
169 Ellen G. White, Ms. 173 (Sept. 15), 1902, in *Maranatha: The Lord is Coming* (Washington, DC: Review and Herald Publishing Association, 1976), p. 200.
170 White, *Education*, p. 18.
171 Hardinge, *With Jesus in His Sanctuary*, pp. 519, 520 [http://1ref.us/fy, p. 259].
172 "*Sphagízō*," Liddell and Scott, p. 1742.
173 Milian Lauritz Andreasen, "Fall 1999 Newsletter: The Final Generation," available at http://1ref.us/g3 (accessed 8/16/16).
174 Francis D. Nichol, ed., *Seventh-day Adventist Bible Commentary* (Washington, DC: Review and Herald Publishing Association, 1957), vol. 7, p. 273.
175 "*Charagma*," Liddell and Scott, p. 1976.
176 Leif Kr. Tobiassen, "Mark of a Man or Mark of the Beast," *Journal of True Education*, vol. 17, no. 3 (February 1955), p. 13.
177 Ellen G. White, *Testimonies for the Church* (Mountain View, CA: Pacific Press Publishing Association, 1948.), vol. 5, p. 472.
178 Ellen G. White, *Testimonies to Ministers and Gospel Workers* (Mountain View, CA: Pacific Press Publishing Association, 1923, 1962), p. 445.
179 *Catechism of the Catholic Church*, 2003, par. 82.

180 Francis J. Connell, *The New Confraternity Edition, Revised Baltimore Catechism and Mass, No.3* (New York: Benziger Bros, 1949), p. 115.

181 *Encyclopaedia Judaica*, vol. 5, col. 1447.

182 White, *The Desire of Ages*, p. 671.

183 White, *Christ's Object Lesson*, p. 158.

184 White, *Testimonies for the Church*, vol. 5, p. 233.

185 Ellen G. White, "The Enduring Treasure," *Advent Review and Sabbath Herald*, vol. 69, no. 10 (March 8, 1892), p. 145.

186 Ellen G. White, *Steps to Christ* (Mountain View, CA: Pacific Press Publishing Association, 1957), p. 72.

187 See Leonard Brand, "What Are the Limits of Death in Paradise?" *Journal of the Adventist Theological Society*, vol. 14, no. 1 (spring 2003), pp. 74–85.

188 White, *Patriarchs and Prophets*, p. 353.

189 de Souza, pp. 34, 35.

190 de Souza, p. 36.

191 Shipton, *The Golden River*, p. 63.

192 Gudmundur Olafsson, "God's Eternal Covenant and the Sabbath," *Journal of the Adventist Theological Society*, vol. 16, no. 1–2 (Spring-Autumn 2005), pp. 155–163.

193 Unlike *the rainbow* that was the "token" of the covenant in Gen. 9:12, 13, and *circumcision* that was the "token" of the covenant with Abram in Gen. 17:11, the Sabbath is not said to be the "token," or "sign" (same Hebrew word *'owth*), of the Sinai covenant. However, God did designate it to be a "sign" that He is the sanctifier of His people (Exod. 31:13) and that He rested on the seventh day in the Creation (Exod. 31:17). He also designated the Sabbath as a perpetual "covenant" with the people (Exod. 31:16).

194 Olafsson, fn. 10, p. 157.

195 The Syriac of Hebrews 4:4 expressly states: "According to what He said about the Sabbath, 'God rested on the seventh day from all of His works' " (Bauscher). Then it goes on to say, in verse 9: "So then it remains for the people of God to keep the Sabbath" (Bauscher). The lexical meaning of the Greek word *sabbatismos* is "Sabbath keeping," which is how it is used in all the early literature—Plutarch, *De Superstitione* 3.10; Justin Martyr, *Dialogue with Trypho* 23.3; Epiphanius, *Panarion Haereses* 30.2.2; *Martyrdom of Peter and Paul*, chapter 1; *Apostolic Constitutions* 2.36.2 (Kevin Morgan, "Sabbatismos in Hebrews," available at http://1ref.us/g4, accessed 8/31/16).

196 Julian Huxley, *Evolution: The Modern Synthesis*, third edition (London: Allen and Unwin, 1974), p. 578.

197 Julian Huxley, *Religion Without Revelation* (New York: The New American Library of World Literature, Inc, 1957), pp. 193, 194.

198 Jeremy Griffith, *Beyond the Human Condition* (Sydney: Foundation for Humanity's Adulthood, 1991), p. 47.

199 J. Peter Zetterberg, ed., *Evolution versus Creationism: The Public Education Controversy* (Phoenix, AZ: Oryx Press, 1983), p. 470.

200 Dawkins, *The God Delusion*, pp. 85, 144.

201 Ellen G. White, *Thoughts from the Mount of Blessing* (Mountain View, CA: Pacific Press Publishing Association, 1955), p. 85.

202 Ellen G. White, "Let the Trumpet Give a Certain Sound," *Advent Review and Sabbath Herald*, vol. 69, no. 49 (Dec. 13, 1892), p. 670.

203 Jeremias, *Parables of Jesus*, p. 183.

204 *The Great Controversy*, p. 438.

205 Arthur William Holland, "French Revolution," *Encyclopaedia Britannica* (New York, The Encyclopædia Britannica Company, 1910), Hugh Chisholm, ed., vol. 11, p. 170.

206 Paul Couderc, "Calendar" *Encyclopedia Americana*, International edition (Danbury, CT: Grolier Incorporated, 1995), David T. Holland, ed., vol. 5, p. 190; "COMPARE CALENDARS," available at http://1ref.us/g5 (accessed 7/27/2016).

207 *Encyclopaedia Judaica*, vol. 5, col. 1374.

208 White, *Education*, p. 126.

209 Kenneth A. Strand, "An overlooked Old-Testament Background to Revelation 11:1," *Andrews University Seminary Studies*, vol. 22, no. 3 (Autumn 1984), pp. 317–325.

210 There are seven references to the prophetic period of "one thousand two hundred and sixty days," using the alternate designations of forty-two months and "a time and times and half a time." These are Dan. 7:25; 12:7; Rev. 11:2, 3; 12:6, 14; 13:5.

211 Watson, *Atoning Work of Christ*, p. 95.

212 Ranko Stefanovic, *Revelation of Jesus Christ* (Berrien Springs, MI: Andrews University Press, 2002), p. 335.

213 Stefanovic, p. 335.

214 Ellen G. White, *Christ in His Sanctuary*, pp. 111, 112, originally published in *The Great Controversy* (Mountain View, CA: Pacific Press Publishing Association, 1888), pp. 434, 435.

215 White, *Early Writings*, p. 33.

216 Ellen G. White, Letter 5 (April 21), 1849, in Arthur L. White, *Ellen G. White: The Early Years* (Hagerstown, MD: Review and Herald Publishing Association, 1985), vol. 1, pp. 262, 263.

217 Ellen G. White, "Sanctification Through the Truth," *Advent Review and Sabbath Herald*, vol. 69, no. 15 (April 12, 1892), p. 225, in *Maranatha*, p. 237.

218 Leonard Elliot Elliott-Binns, *The History of the Decline and Fall of the Medieval Papacy* (Hamden, CT: Archon Books, 1967), p. 12.

219 J. Henry Middleton, "Rome," *Encyclopaedia Britannica*, ninth edition (New York: The Henry G. Allen Company, 1890), William Robertson Smith, ed., vol. 20, p. 783.

220 "The Question Box: By what authority did the Church change the observance of the Sabbath from Saturday to Sunday?" *Catholic Universe Bulletin*, August 14, 1942, p. 4.

221 "Pastor's Page," *Saint Catherine Catholic Church Sentinel* (Algonac, MI), vol. 50, no. 22 (May 21, 1995), p. 1.

222 *Encyclopaedia of Religion and Ethics*, vol. 12, p. 110.

223 Ellen G. White, "Never Yield the Sabbath," *Signs of the Times*, vol. 4, no. 9 (Feb. 28, 1878), par. 10 p. 65, in *Maranatha*, p. 286.

224 Sky News US Team, "Ten Commandments Monument Banned by Court," *Sky News*, August 8, 2014, available at http://1ref.us/g6 (accessed 7/27/2016); Irene F. Starkehaus, "Lech Walesa Contemplates New Secular Ten Commandments," *The Illinois Review*, October 23, 2013, available at http://1ref.us/g7 (accessed 7/27/2016).

225 Patrick Toner, "Infallibility," in *The Catholic Encyclopedia* (New York: Robert Appleton Company, 1910), available at http://1ref.us/g8 (accessed 7/27/2016).

226 John Paul II, "Homily of the Holy Father, 'Day of Pardon,'" March 12, 2000, available at http://1ref.us/g9 (accessed 7/27/2016). Yet, the pope only obliquely acknowledged the persecution. For John Paul II's acknowledgment of the work of the "mystery of iniquity" (Latin *mysterium iniquitatis*) in the persecution of Orthodox Christians, see "Pope Asks Forgiveness for Roman Catholic Sins of Persecution!" available at http://1ref.us/ga (accessed 8/16/16).

227 John Kendrew, ed., *Encyclopaedia of Molecular Biology* (Oxford: Blackwell Science, Ltd, 1994), pp. 250–253; Edgar Krentz, "Historical Method Set Free: 1890–1920," *The Historical-Critical Method* (Philadelphia, PA: Fortress Press, 1975), pp. 22–30.

228 Greek *Babulōn*, Gen. 10:10, Septuagint; Gen. 11:9, KJV, margin.

229 C. Mervyn Maxwell, *Tell It to the World*, revised edition (Boise, ID: Pacific Press Publishing Association, 1976, 1977), pp. 27, 85, 86.

230 "*Sphagízō*," Liddell and Scott, p. 1742.

231 *The Great Controversy*, p. 612.

232 Serpouhi Tavoukdjian, *Exiled: Exciting Story of Armenia* (Washington, DC: Review and Herald Publishing Association, 1933), pp. 5–15.

233 Maxwell, *Tell It to the World*, pp. 26, 27, 85–94.

234 Ellen G. White, Letter 209 (Dec. 19), 1899, in *The Voice in Speech and Song* (Boise, ID: Pacific Press Publishing Association, 1988), p. 329.

235 Ellen G. White, *Advent Review and Sabbath Herald*, vol. 57, no. 4 (Jan. 25, 1881), par. 15, in *Counsels on Diet and Foods* (Washington, DC: Review and Herald Publishing Association, 1938), p. 32.

236 Ellen G. White, "Repentance the Gift of God," *Advent Review and Sabbath Herald*, vol. 67, no. 13 (April 1, 1890), p. 193.

237 Young, *Analytical Concordance*, p. 50.

238 Francis D. Nichol, Raymond F. Cottrell et al., eds., *The Seventh-day Adventist Bible Commentary* (Washington, DC: Review and Herald Publishing Association, 1954), vol. 2, p. 302.

239 S. H. Horn, "Elijah," *Seventh-day Adventist Bible Dictionary* (Washington, DC: Review and Herald Publishing Association, 1960), p. 306.

240 White, *Christ's Object Lessons*, p. 333.

241 Jim Yardley, "Pope Francis, Superstar," *The Indian Express*, March 14, 2014, available at http://1ref.us/gb (accessed 7/27/2016).

242 Mircea Eliade, ed., *Encyclopedia of Religion* (New York: Macmillan Publishing Co., 1987), vol. 10, p. 183; *Encyclopaedia of Religion and Ethics*, vol. 9, pp. 39–43; *Encyclopaedia Judaica*, vol. 12, cols. 560, 566.

243 White, *Early Writings*, p. 72.

244 White, *Patriarchs and Prophets*, p. 68.

245 Hemangi R. Jerajani, Bhagyashri Jaju, Meghana M. Phiske and Ntin Lade, "Hematohidrosis—a Rare Clinical Phenomenon," *Indian Journal of Dermatology*, vol. 54, no. 3 (July-September 2009), pp. 290–292.

246 Charles George Herbermann, *The Catholic Encyclopedia*, vol. 11, pp. 259, 262; Jovian P. Lang, *Dictionary of the Liturgy* (New York, Catholic Book Publishing Co., 1989), p. 52.

247 White, *The Desire of Ages*, p. 296.

248 White, *The Desire of Ages*, p. 161.

249 White, *Education*, p. 201; Ellen G. White, *Testimonies for the Church* (Mountain View, CA: Pacific Press Publishing Association, 1881, 1902, 1948), vol. 3, p. 63; Rev. 18:2–5.

250 Thomas R. Kelly, *A Testament of Devotion* (New York: HarperCollins Publishers, Inc., 1996), p. 3.

251 Ellen G. White, Letter 117 (Jan. 26), 1897, in *My Life Today* (Hagerstown, MD: Review and Herald Publishing Association, 1980), p. 263.

252 Ellen G. White, Ms. 49, 1886, in *Christ Triumphant*, p. 155.

253 Ellen G. White, "Bible Temperance," *Good Health* [formerly *The Health Reformer*], vol. 17, no. 11 (Nov. 1, 1882), p. 337, in *The Sanctified Life* (Washington, DC: Review and Herald Publishing Association, 1937), pp. 27, 28.

254 White, *Patriarchs and Prophets*, pp. 101, 338.

255 Samuele Bacchiocchi, *Wine in the Bible* (Berrien Springs, MI: Biblical Perspectives, 1989), pp. 286–302; Harley Stanton, "Doctor, Is a Drink a Day Good for My Heart?" *Record*, vol. 102, no. 19 (May 17, 1997), pp. 8, 9.

256 White, *The Adventist Home*, p. 22; *Education*, p. 276.

257 A. S. Teebi, ed., *Genetic Disorders among Arab Populations*, second edition (Berlin: Springer-Verlag, 2010), pp. 3–36.

258 Lara Marks and Michael Worboys, eds., *Migrants, Minorities, and Health* (London: Routledge, 1997), pp. 179–209.

259 Marks and Worboys, pp. 194, 207.

260 Warren A. Shipton, *The Distant Sound of Wisdom: Biblical Perspectives on Health* (Ringgold, GA: Teach Services Inc., 2015). *Testimonies for the Church*, vol. 8, p. 168.

261 White, *Education*, p. 209.

262 See "Study busts meat-eating myths," updated June 4, 2012, available at http://1ref.us/gc (accessed 9/12/16).

263 White, *The Desire of Ages*, p. 672.

264 Ellen G. White, *This Day with God* (Washington, DC: Review and Herald Publishing Association, 1979), p. 251, from Letter 49a (Aug. 30), 1878.

265 See White, *Steps to Christ*, pp. 70, 89.

266 Clarke, *The Holy Bible*, comments on Acts 2:1.

267 Ellen G. White, "Search the Scriptures," *Advent Review and Sabbath and Herald*, vol. 69, no. 30 (July 26, 1892), p. 465.

268 Will Baron, *Deceived by the New Age* (Boise, ID: Pacific Press Publishing Association, 1990), p. 105.

269 White, *Patriarchs and Prophets*, p. 196.

270 Roberto Ouro, "The Apotelesmatic Principle: Origin and Application," *Journal of the Adventist Theological Society*, vol. 9, no. 1–2 (Spring–Autumn 1998), pp. 326–342.

271 Jonathan Petre, "One Third of Clergy Do Not Believe in the Resurrection," *The Telegraph*, July 31, 2002, available at http://1ref.us/gd (accessed 7/27/2016).

272 Dawkins, *God Delusion*, p. 187.

273 W. B. Quigley, "Imminence: Mainspring of Adventism—3," *Ministry*, vol. 53, no. 8 (August 1980), p. 18.

274 Bryan W. Ball, *The English Connection* (Cambridge: James Clarke & Co., 1981), pp. 179, 181, 182; Hastings, ed., "Second Adventism," *Encyclopaedia of Religion and Ethics*, vol. 11, pp. 284–286.

275 On the word "generation" used in Matt. 24:34, see J. R. Spangler, ed., "Christ and His High Priestly Ministry," *Ministry*, vol. 53, no. 10 (October 1980), p. 30. There are other legitimate alternatives including the word "race." See footnote in NIV translation.

276 St. Gregory the Great, *Epistolae*, bk. 1, ep. 25, in *Patrologia Latina*, vol. 77, p. 476, translated from the Latin in Fernand Mourret, *A History of the Catholic Church* (St. Louis, MO; London: B. Herder, 1946), Newton Thompson, trans., vol. 3, p. 47.

277 Laurent Cleenewerck, *His Broken Body* (Washington, DC: Euclid University Press, 2007), p. 237; Leon L. Bram, ed., *Funk & Wagnalls New Encyclopedia* (New York: Funk and Wagnalls, 1975), vol. 19, p. 163.
278 Christopher J. Murray, ed., *Encyclopedia of the Romantic Era, 1760–1850* (London: Taylor & Francis Books, Inc., 2004), p. 558.
279 *The Great Controversy*, p. 622.
280 *Encyclopaedia Judaica*, vol. 5, col. 1383; Hardinge, *With Jesus in His Sanctuary*, pp. 519, 520 [http://1ref.us/fy, p. 259]; Morris Jastrow, Jr., and Max L. Margolis, "Day of Atonement," *The Jewish Encyclopedia* (New York: Funk & Wagnalls, 1906), I. Singer, C. Adler et al., eds., vol. 2, pp. 284–289, available at http://1ref.us/ge (accessed 7/27/2016).
281 Ms. 173, 1902, in *Maranatha*, p. 200.
282 *The Great Controversy*, p. 597.
283 White, *Testimonies for the Church*, vol. 5, p. 472.
284 White, *Testimonies to Ministers and Gospel Workers*, p. 445.
285 Harry Scott Ashmore, ed., "Earthquakes," *Encyclopaedia Britannica*, fourteenth revised edition (Chicago, IL: Encyclopaedia Britannica, Inc., 1961), vol. 7, p. 848.
286 Stephen G. Tallentyre (pseudonym of Evelyn Beatrice Hall), *Life of Voltaire* (London: Smith, Elder & Co, 1903), p. 319, in William Ambrose Spicer, *Our Day in the Light of Prophecy and Providence* (Washington, DC: Review and Herald Publishing Association, 1918), pp. 80, 81.
287 Samuel Williams, "An Account of a Very Uncommon Darkness in the States of New-England, May 19, 1780." *Memoirs of the American Academy of Arts and Sciences*, vol. 1 (1783), p. 235.
288 Spicer, p. 90.
289 Hubert A. Newton, "Meteor," *Encyclopaedia Britannica*, ninth edition (Philadelphia: Maxwell Sommerville, 1894), Thomas Spencer Baynes and William Robertson Smith, eds., vol. 16, p. 115.
290 Charles P. Olivier "Meteor," *Encyclopedia Americana* (New York: Americana Corporation, 1961), Lavinia P. Dudley, ed., vol. 18, p. 713.
291 Thomas Milner, *The Gallery of Nature: a Pictorial and Descriptive Tour Through Creation* (London: Wm. S Orr & Co, 1846), p. 140, in Spicer, p. 99.
292 Spicer, p. 100.
293 C. Mervyn Maxwell, *God Cares* (Mountain View, CA: Pacific Press Publishing Association, 1985), vol. 2, pp. 353–364.
294 *The Great Controversy*, pp. 635–658.
295 Horn, "Belshazzar," *Seventh-day Adventist Bible Dictionary*, p. 128.
296 Daniel 9:21, 22. For the date 539 BC, see Horn, "Darius," *Seventh-day Adventist Bible Dictionary*, p. 254.
297 White, *The Great Controversy*, pp. 326, 327.

298 Desmond Ford, *Daniel* (Nashville, TN: Southern Publishing Association, 1978), pp. 300–305; Gerhard Pfandl, "In Defense of the Year-Day Principle," *Journal of the Adventist Theological Society*, vol. 23, no. 1 (Spring 2012), pp. 3–17; see Spangler, pp. 13, 18, 44, 45, for use of the texts.

299 *Encyclopaedia Judaica*, vol. 5, cols. 48–50; vol. 16, col. 725.

300 Arthur J. Ferch, "Commencement Date for the Seventy Week Prophecy," in *The Seventy Weeks, Leviticus, and the Nature of Prophecy*, ed. Frank B. Holbrook (Washington, DC: Biblical Research Institute, 1986), p. 74.

301 William D. Halsey, ed., *Collier's Encyclopedia* (New York: Macmillan Educational Corp., 1974), vol. 2, p. 706; Gerhard F. Hasel, "Interpretations of the Chronology of the Seventy Weeks," *The Seventy Weeks, Leviticus, and the Nature of Prophecy*, pp. 49, 50.

302 White, *The Great Controversy*, pp. 327, 328; William H. Shea, "The Prophecy of Daniel 9:24–27," *The Seventy Weeks, Leviticus, and the Nature of Prophecy*, pp. 103, 104.

303 William. H. Shea, *Daniel: A Reader's Guide* (Nampa, ID: Pacific Press Publishing Association, 2005).

304 Marcus Jastrow, *A Dictionary of the Targumim, the Talmud Babli, and Yerushalmi, and the Midrashic Literature* (New York: P. Shalom Publications Inc., 1967), vol. 1, p. 513. See also P. R. Newell, *Daniel: the Man Greatly Beloved and His Prophecies* (Chicago, IL: Moody Press, 1962), p. 139; Athal Tolhurst, "'Cut off' or 'Determined'?" *Australasian Record*, vol. 88, no. 41 (October 22, 1983), pp. 6, 7, 14.

305 C. Mervyn Maxwell, *God Cares* (Mountain View, CA: Pacific Press Publishing Association, 1981), vol. 1, pp. 179, 180.

306 See Pfandl, pp. 3–17; and Spangler, pp. 39–41.

307 Spangler, p. 32.

308 The Temple was desecrated on the 15th day of the Jewish month of Chislev in 168 BC (1 Maccabees 1:54) and was rededicated on the 25th day of Chislev in 165 BC (2 Maccabees 10:5).

309 John Bright, *A History of Israel* (London: SCM Press, 1960), pp. 401–412.

310 Gerhard F. Hasel, "Fulfilments of Prophecy," *The Seventy Weeks, Leviticus, and the Nature of Prophecy,* pp. 319–321.

311 George R. Knight, *The Apocalyptic Vision and the Neutering of Adventism* (Hagerstown, MD: Review and Herald Publishing Association, 2009), pp. 68, 69.

312 Maxwell, *God Cares*, vol. 1, p. 187; Clifford Goldstein, *1844 Made Simple* (Boise, ID: Pacific Press Publishing Association, 1988), pp. 65, 66.

313 *The Tanakh* (Jewish Publication Society, 1917), available at http://1ref.us/gf (accessed 7/27/2016).

314 R. Laird Harris, Gleason. L. Archer et al. eds., *Theological Wordbook of the Old Testament* (Chicago, IL: Moody Press, 1980), vol. 2, p. 752.

315 *Hebrew Interlinear Bible*, authorized version, available at http://1ref.us/gg (accessed 7/27/2016); Spangler, p. 35; W. E. Read, "Further Observations on Sadaq," *Andrews University Seminary Studies*, vol. 4, no. 1 (1966), pp. 29–36; Young, *Analytical Concordance*, pp. 171, 172, 785, 817, 818.

316 Desmond Ford, "Daniel 8—Its Relationship to the Kingdom of God," *Ministry*, vol. 33, no. 1 (January 1960), pp. 18–21; Desmond Ford, "The Linguistic Connection between Daniel 8:14 and 11:31," *Ministry*, vol. 38, no. 12 (December 1965), pp. 34–36; William H. Shea, "Unity of Daniel," *Symposium on Daniel*, pp. 165–255; Edwin Richard Thiele, *Outline Studies in Daniel* (Berrien Springs, MI: Emmanuel Missionary College, 1947), pp. 59–97.

317 Paraphrase of Jubilees 5:17, 18, "Day of Atonement," *Jewish Virtual Library*, available at http://1ref.us/gh (accessed 8/16/16).

318 *Encyclopaedia Judaica*, vol. 5, cols. 1379, 1380.

319 Jiří Moskala, "The Gospel According to God's Judgment: Judgment and Salvation," *Journal of the Adventist Theological Society*, vol. 22, no. 1 (Spring 2011), pp. 28–49.

320 Josephus, "The Antiquities of the Jews," book 12, chap. 7, par. 6, verse 318; "The Wars of the Jews," book 5, chap. 5, par. 5, verse 219, *Works of Josephus*, pp. 328, 707.

321 It is interesting to note that the Greek word for "purified" in Hebrews 9:23—*katharizō*—is the same as that used for "cleansed" in the Greek Septuagint translation of Daniel 8:14.

322 Arthur L. White, pp. 262, 263.

323 Arthur L. White, pp. 260–262.

324 Maxwell, *Tell It to the World*, pp. 88–93.

325 Maxwell, *God Cares*, vol. 2, pp. 353–371.

326 *Encyclopaedia Judaica*, vol. 5, col. 1383.

327 J. A. H. Murray, H. Bradley et al., eds., "Reconcile," *The Oxford English Dictionary*, second edition (Oxford: Clarendon Press, 1989), vol. 13, pp. 352, 353.

328 A. F. J. Kranz, *Christ's Complete Atonement* (Warburton, Victoria: Signs Publishing Co., 1937), p. 22.

329 *The Great Controversy*, p. 678.

330 White, *Spiritual Gifts*, vol. 1, p. 162.

331 Alberto R. Treiyer, "The Day of Atonement as Related to the Contamination and Purification of the Sanctuary," *The Seventy Weeks, Leviticus, and the Nature of Prophecy* (Washington, DC: Biblical Research Institute, General Conference of Seventh-day Adventists, 1986), pp. 228, 229.

332 White, *Patriarchs and Prophets*, p. 357.

333 White, *The Great Controversy* (1888), p. 480; *The Desire of Ages*, p. 638.

334 Ellen G. White, *The Youth's Instructor*, April 1, 1854, in *Lift Him Up* (Washington, DC: Review and Herald Publishing Association, 1988), p. 379.

335 Ivan T. Blazen, "Justification and Judgment," *The Seventy Weeks, Leviticus, and the Nature of Prophecy*, pp. 339–368.

336 White, *The Great Controversy*, p. 483.

337 White, *The Great Controversy*, p. 484.

338 White, *Testimonies for the Church*, vol. 5, pp. 472–474.

339 Hardinge, *With Jesus in His Sanctuary*, p. 542 [http://1ref.us/fy, p. 271].

340 Maxwell, *God Cares*, vol. 2, p. 352.

341 Ellen G. White, "Purifieth Himself," *Signs of the Times*, June 20, 1895, in *Faith and Works* (Nashville, TN: Southern Publishing Association, 1979), pp. 118, 119.

342 Ellen G. White, Ms. 48, 1893, in *That I May Know Him* (Washington, DC: Review and Herald Publishing Association, 1964), p. 292.

343 Clifford Goldstein, *False Balances* (Boise, ID: Pacific Press Publishing Association, 1992), p. 125.

344 *Testimonies to Ministers and Gospel Workers*, p. 433.

345 "Christ in the Heavenly Sanctuary," *Ministry*, vol. 53, no. 10 (October 1980), p. 19.

346 Moskala, "The Gospel According to God's Judgment," pp. 43, 44.

347 White, *The Desire of Ages*, p. 638.

348 White, *The Great Controversy*, p. 624.

349 White, *The Great Controversy*, p. 660.

350 Frederic Charles Cook, *The Holy Bible According to the Authorized Version (A.D. 1611)* (London: John Murray, 1871), vol. 1, part 2, Leviticus Deuteronomy, p. 9.

351 Raymond E. Brown, J. A. Fitzmyer et al., eds., *The New Jerome Biblical Commentary* (Englewood Cliffs, NJ: Prentice Hall, Inc., 1968), vol. 2, p. 733, art. 157. See also Robert Helm, "Azazel in Early Jewish Tradition," *Andrews University Seminary Studies*, vol. 32, no. 3 (Autumn 1994), pp. 217–226.

352 White, *The Great Controversy*, p. 663.

353 Ellen G. White, *Testimonies for the Church* (Mountain View, CA: Pacific Press Publishing Association, 1948), vol. 8, p. 131.

354 White, *Early Writings*, p. 19.

355 George R. Berry, *Interlinear Greek-English New Testament* (Grand Rapids, MI: Baker Book House, 1984), p. 572.

356 Hardinge, *Shadows of His Sacrifice*, p. 6.

357 Hardinge, *Shadows of His Sacrifice*, p. 5; Ron Wallace, "The Four Banners of Israel," available at http://1ref.us/gi (accessed 7/27/2016).

358 Milian Lauritz Andreasen, *The Sanctuary Service*, second revised edition (Washington, DC: Review and Herald Publishing Association, 1969), p. 123.

359 *Encyclopaedia Judaica*, vol. 14, col. 604.

360 *The Adventist Home*, p. 549, originally published in RH, vol. 92, no. 32 (July 1, 1915), p. 4.

361 F. D. Nichol, R. F. Cottrell et al., eds., *The Seventh-day Adventist Bible Commentary* (Washington, DC: Review and Herald Publishing Association, 1955), vol. 4, p. 127. Uzziah, or Azariah, was mentioned in the annals of Tiglath-pileser under the name "Azriau from Iauda" (*The Seventh-day Adventist Bible Commentary*, vol. 4, p. 127).

362 Ellen G. White, "Prepare to Meet Thy God," *Advent Review and Sabbath Herald*, vol. 74, no. 29 (July 20, 1897), p. 449.

363 White, *The Desire of Ages*, p. 468.

364 White, *The Desire of Ages*, p. 469.

365 White, *The Great Controversy*, pp. 416, 417.

366 White, *Steps to Christ*, p. 13, 14.

367 Hardinge, *With Jesus in His Sanctuary*, pp. 152, 153 [http://1ref.us/fy, p. 74].

368 Ellen G. White, "The Church Must Be Quickened," *Advent Review and Sabbath Herald*, vol. 70, no. 3 (Jan. 17, 1893), p. 33.

369 White, *Patriarchs and Prophets*, p. 62.

370 Hardinge, *With Jesus in His Sanctuary*, p. 204 [http://1ref.us/fy, p. 100].

371 White, *Patriarchs and Prophets*, pp. 348, 349.

372 Hardinge, *With Jesus in His Sanctuary*, p. 206 [http://1ref.us/fy, p. 101].

373 Ellen G. White, Ms. 21, 1900 (Feb. 16, 1900), par. 39, in *The Truth about Angels* (Nampa, ID: Pacific Press Publishing Association, 1996), p. 287.

374 White, *Patriarchs and Prophets*, p. 255.

375 White, *Patriarchs and Prophets*, p. 452.

376 Ellen G. White, *Advent Review and Sabbath Herald*, vol. 77, no. 22 (May 29, 1900), pp. 337, 338, in *The Faith I Live By*, p. 205.

377 Ellen G. White, *Conflict and Courage* (Washington, D.C.: Review and Herald Publishing Association, 1970), p. 262.

We invite you to view the complete
selection of titles we publish at:

www.TEACHServices.com

scan with your mobile
device to go directly
to our website

Please write or email us your praises, reactions, or
thoughts about this or any other book we publish at:

11 Quartermaster Circle
Fort Oglethorpe, GA 30742

Info@TEACHServices.com

TEACH Services, Inc., titles may be purchased in bulk for
educational, business, fund-raising, or sales promotional use.
For information, please e-mail:

BulkSales@TEACHServices.com

Finally if you are interested in seeing
your own book in print, please contact us at

publishing@TEACHServices.com

We would be happy to review your manuscript for free.

www.ingramcontent.com/pod-product-compliance
Lightning Source LLC
Chambersburg PA
CBHW070934230426
43666CB00011B/2431